Rural Hours

Rural Hours

SUSAN FENIMORE COOPER

Edited by Rochelle Johnson and Daniel Patterson

THE UNIVERSITY OF GEORGIA PRESS | ATHENS AND LONDON

© 1998 by the University of Georgia Press

Athens, Georgia 30602

All rights reserved

Designed by Kathi Morgan

Set in Berthold Baskerville by G& S Typesetters, Inc.

Printed and bound by Maple-Vail Book Manufacturing Group

This book is printed on recycled paper that meets the guidelines

for permanence and durability of the Committee on Production Guidelines

for Book Longevity of the Council on Library Resources

Printed in the United States of America

02 01 00 99 98 C 5 4 3 2 1

02 01 00 99 98 P 5 4 3 2 1

LIBRARY OF CONGRESS CATALOGING IN PUBLICATION DATA

Cooper, Susan Fenimore, 1813 – 1894.

Rural hours / Susan Fenimore Cooper ; edited by Rochelle Johnson

and Daniel Patterson.

p.   cm.

Originally published: New York : G. P. Putnam : London : Putnam's

American agency, 1850. With new introd.

Includes bibliographical references and index.

ISBN 0-8203-1974-0 (alk. paper).–ISBN 0-8203-2000-5 (pbk. : alk. paper)

1. Natural history – Outdoor books   2. Country life.   I. Johnson,

Rochelle.   II. Patterson, J. Daniel.   III. Title.

QH81.C793   1998

508 – dc21   98-2689

BRITISH LIBRARY CATALOGING IN PUBLICATION DATA AVAILABLE

Contents

Acknowledgments

FOR INSTITUTIONAL SUPPORT, the editors wish to acknowledge California State University, San Bernardino, and the Claremont Graduate University. For permission to publish from Cooper's letters in their holdings, we thank the following: the Manuscripts Department of the University of Virginia Library; the Beinecke Rare Book and Manuscript Library, Yale University; and the Historical Society of Pennsylvania, Philadelphia.

We also wish to thank the following friends and colleagues for various kinds of support: John Elder, for fostering this project and for his patience; Ed Cahill, for the gift of an old book; Jessie Ravage, our woman on the ground in Cooperstown; Hugh MacDougall, for making a place for Susan in the James Fenimore Cooper Society; Leslie Schilling, for early computer help; Bob Hudspeth, for steady encouragement and wise counsel; and for helping prepare readers for nature writing generally and Susan Fenimore Cooper specifically, we thank Mike Branch, Larry Buell, and Cheryl Glotfelty.

Finally, we thank Malcolm Call and his colleagues at the University of Georgia Press for seeing quickly the value of *Rural Hours*.

Introduction

WITH THE APPEARANCE OF *Rural Hours* in 1850, Susan Fenimore Cooper (1813–94) became the first American woman to publish a book of nature writing. *Rural Hours* is written in the form of a year's journal entries organized by the passage of the four seasons, beginning with spring. As Cooper herself wrote, her book presents "a record of our simple rural life," an account of the culture and atmosphere of her home village, Cooperstown, New York. Yet *Rural Hours* also offers readers insights into the environmental concerns of an educated mid-nineteenth-century woman and a broad yet detailed view of the natural history of the Otsego Lake region surrounding Cooperstown.

Cooper's journal entries range from brief mentions of a day's weather to discussions of the many types of birds found in her village, and from an account of a visit to a nearby farm to a lengthy critique of literary representations of autumn. While she describes her area's plant and animal life, as well as other aspects of her region – rivers, weather patterns, and even agricultural practices – Cooper also narrates the geologic and human history of her place. Through *Rural Hours,* Susan Cooper seeks to convey the fullness of both human and nonhuman life in her region, to expose the links between human and nonhuman history, and to suggest a more sustainable approach to the environment – not just that of Cooperstown in particular but also of her country in general.

Page by page, the larger purposes of Cooper's book emerge: she hopes to educate Americans about their natural world, to instill in them a pride of place based on this deeper knowledge, and finally to convince them of a moral obligation to preserve their environment. By means of the form of the natural history essay and through narratives and descriptions of Cooper's walks and excursions, *Rural Hours* presents what ultimately emerges as Cooper's argument for a sustainable balance between human culture and its natural surroundings. Her ideal society is a rural one, carefully poised between the receding wilderness and a looming industrialization.

IN THE EARLY 1840s, when the eldest child of America's most famous and successful author—James Fenimore Cooper—began to think of herself as a writer, she did not intend to base her career on nature writing. Beginning in the summer of 1826, when she was thirteen, Susan Cooper lived in France, Switzerland, Italy, and England. In Europe she enjoyed a formal education in literature and languages, in which she excelled, and occasionally she experienced the formal company of General Lafayette and lesser knowns of the French elite. Her family returned to the United States in November of 1833, when she was twenty. Although her life in Cooperstown seems to have been largely uneventful through the rest of the 1830s, in 1843 Susan Cooper asked her father to try to publish some stories she had written, and his letter of September 22 seems to be encouraging her in a decision to become a publishing writer: "I have got your manuscript, and shall sell all your tales together. This will be the best plan. I make no doubt of getting one or two hundred dollars for the whole. A name will sell the remainder, and a little habit will set you up" (Beard 4:411). There is no evidence that any of these "tales" ever appeared in print, but her publication of a sentimental romance, *Elinor Wyllys,* in early 1846 suggests that her interest in writing about nature was yet to emerge.

In Susan Cooper's mind, her passion for nature writing had its origins in a loving relationship with her maternal grandfather:

> Our Grandfather De Lancey must have been a charming companion— he was very amusing with his grandchildren, and told us many pleasant things, as he drove us about in his gig and farm-waggon. . . . And my dear Grandfather soon commenced my botanical education—being the eldest of the little troop, I often drove with him, in the gig, about his farms and into his woods, and it was my duty to jump out and open all the gates. In these drives he taught me to distinguish the different trees by their growth, and bark, and foliage—this was a beech, that an oak, here was an ash, yonder a tulip-tree. He would point out a tree and ask me to name it, going through a regular lesson in a very pleasant way. Such was the beginning of my *Rural Hours* ideas. ("Small Family Memories," 32–33)

Not until the spring of 1848, however, did she begin "the simple record of those little events which make up the course of the seasons in rural life"— and then only for her own "amusement" (*Rural Hours,* 3). As she continued making these written observations over the next twenty months or so, and as she apparently shared them with family and friends, the idea of making them into a coherent book grew. On December 10, 1849, her novelist-father received the completed manuscript and began immediately the task of finding a publisher for his daughter's new book (Beard 6:93). Four days later, he signed a contract granting George Putnam the right to publish the book for five years and allowing Susan a royalty of 12.5 percent after the first thousand copies were sold (Beard 6:94).

One of the most remarkable strengths of *Rural Hours* as natural history writing results from Susan Cooper's scholarly perseverance in Cooperstown. The book has typically been described as a literary diary or journal organized by the passage of the seasons, which in fact it is, but such a characterization tends to obscure the depth of research into contemporary natural history by which Cooper brought to her work a dynamic interplay of science and literary nature writing. Removed as she was from book dealers and libraries, she assiduously and patiently gathered, through a variety of methods, the natural history works she needed to give her volume a bioregional thoroughness that her own observations alone would not have achieved. Typically, Cooper charged her father, on his visits to Philadelphia or New York City, with finding and purchasing books she needed. As early as 1842, we hear him possibly even complaining a bit: "Tell Sue I will get some of her books for her—how many will depend on her order and my purse" (Beard 4:230–31). Later, just a few weeks after the publication of *Rural Hours* late in July of 1850, she wrote to a family friend in New York City, asking him to persuade a public library there to help the "country folk" in Cooperstown by allowing "its books to be carried into the country for several weeks at a time." The same letter reveals the frustration caused by her distance from bookstores and libraries: "it frequently happens now-a-days that my fingers are idle, and my patch-work labours at a stand, for the want of some volume to consult, which if it lay within reach would speedily remove the obstacle in my way, and set me at work again." Despite such delays, however, Cooper's work reflects a prodigious depth of research.

James Fenimore Cooper's evolving view of *Rural Hours*—as he read the pages and negotiated its publication with Putnam in New York City and Richard Bentley in London—helps us see the enigma that nature writing posed for many in the reading public. Even though the genre of nature writing had fully emerged by the late eighteenth century, it was new enough in 1850 to find readers still expecting that natural history and travel writing would keep to their respective genres and publishers' lists. Even in his first words of praise to his favorite child for *Rural Hours*, for instance, James revealed his own uncertainty about his daughter's work by mixing in a word of caution while, as he sensed, her hopes for success were building:

> My Dear Sue,
>
> I can not let the occasion pass without expressing to you the great satisfaction I have had in reading the sheets. So far from finding them disjointed and tame, they carry me along with the interest of a tale. The purity of mind, the simplicity, elegance and knowledge they manifest, must, I think produce a strong feeling in your favour with all the pure and good. I have now very little doubt of its ultimate success, though at first the American world will hesitate to decide. (Beard 6:149)

James expressed similar caution and a bit more reservation in a letter to his wife three days later, on March 3, 1850:

> I have written to Sue to say how much I am pleased with her book—It is not strong perhaps, but is so pure, and so elegant, so very feminine and charming that I do not doubt, now, of its eventual success—I say eventual, for, at first, the world will not know what to make of it. . . . We shall get something, I make no doubt. Let her be at ease—I shall do all I can for her. She has struggled nobly, and deserves success. At any rate, she has pleased us, and that is a great deal for so dear a child. (Beard 6:151)

That one of the country's leading men of letters thought of the book as "not strong perhaps" would suggest that other readers might also fail to see the strengths of *Rural Hours*. This suggestion gains ground when we consider that James had both personal and financial motives to find reasons to praise his daughter's work. At this point, however, a few weeks before publication, he was already preparing wife and daughter for the need to find consolation within the family if the book was a public failure. This family context, he knew, was very important to his daughter, who wrote to him on March 3 that "to satisfy yourself, and my dear Mother, has always been a chief object of my authorship, and hitherto I have met with little enough of encouragement from other quarters."

In James's March 14 letter seeking to persuade Richard Bentley to publish *Rural Hours* in London, his praise for his daughter's book is clear but moderate: "I give you an honest opinion, in saying that I think the 'Rural Hours' will succeed. . . . Its purity, truth, elegance and nature ought to give it a reputation, whatever may come of it. There is a great deal of information in it, besides" (Beard 6:156). A few weeks later, having spent more time reading and proofing the sheets as Putnam printed them, James's posture toward Bentley, who had taken *Rural Hours* on, was much more confident. He rather boldly advised Bentley on May 18: "You had better begin to print at once, as it is a work that should be got up handsomely." The same letter then reveals that both his greater familiarity with the text and the approaching publication by Putnam in New York had raised his confidence and deepened his understanding of his daughter's book: "You may think me extravagant in my opinions of this book, but to me it seems just the most pleasing work of its kind that I ever met with. It is full of quiet elegance, has a great deal of curious information, and, though sweetly poetical in parts, has not the slightest pretension. Do not be afraid of it" (Beard 6:176). Having overcome his own fears, he could now advise others.

Upon publication, sales were good and James's excitement was high. On September 19, he wrote to his wife, "Right and left, I hear of Rural Hours. I am stopped in the street, a dozen times a day to congratulate me. The price of the fine edition is $7, Putnam making from one to two dollars a set at retail, and from three to four at wholesale. It will be the presentation volume of the season. I can see that Putnam expects to sell some eight hundred or a thousand of them" (Beard 6:218–19). The rapid sales in New York continued, and on September 30, James wrote home about his daughter's real and potential profits:

> Putnam has just told me that he had put to press another 500 of the fine edition, the demand in that form being much greater than he expected. He cannot publish for several weeks. He will have to publish another plain edition 'ere long, also, making 3000 copies, in all. This will give Sue $300, besides the plates. She may count on about $100 a year, for the next five years; perhaps more; after that her receipts from the book will be materially increased. It is good for $100 a year for life, in my opinion. (Beard 6:225–26)

As a way of understanding these dollar amounts, one might consider that in a letter dated October 26, 1846, Susan Cooper proposed allowing a new live-in housekeeper free room and board plus a dollar a month. Thus the success of *Rural Hours* became substantial, and the book became part of the father's sense of his daughter's identity. In a letter to his longtime friend William Branford Shubrick in December 1850, he referred to his wife, daughter, and himself, respectively, as "The old lady, young rural hours,"

and "old rural hours" (Beard 6:243). Later in the same month, he boasted
to Shubrick, "What do you think of Sue! She has reached the honour of . . .
having her autograph desired, and some two or three professors have actually written to her letters full of learning, all about birds and flowers" (Beard
6:246).

Bentley's two-volume British edition, however, did not succeed. In June
of 1851, Bentley apologetically lamented to the renowned and profitable
James Fenimore Cooper, "'Rural Hours' has not paid its expenses" (Beard
6:274). The American success of the book had so impressed the author's
father, and his desire to protect his daughter was so great that, even amid
the ever-worsening illness that killed him on September 14, his quick response to Bentley was angry to the point of accusing the man of lying: "That
a book like Rural Hours of which edition after edition has been selling here
and which is so well spoken of in so many of your own publications should
not pay for itself excites so much surprise that nothing [short?] of an account of sales will enable me to satisfy my own sense of duty as regards my
daughter—" (Beard 6:276). On August 5, 1851, just five weeks before his
death, the century's chief American practitioner of the historical romance
was deeply concerned about a volume of nature writing; he wrote again to
Bentley:

> My astonishment continues as great as ever, for I tell you frankly that I
> consider Rural Hours is the best American book you have published in
> ten years. I think it admirably suited to your market, too, and that in-
> creases my surprise. I did not expect it would prove a very quick sell-
> ing book any where, but I did believe that a thousand copies would
> go off in the first twelvemonth. Sell it must, if I am the least judge of a
> book, and I know from their own mouths that Irving, Bryant, and most
> of our highest class writers speak of it with great admiration. Here it is
> considered as having placed its author in the foremost ranks of Ameri-
> can literature, and given her a claim to be mentioned with our very best
> writers. (Beard 6:282)

Even taking the father's parental bias into account, it is fair to say that Susan
Cooper's book was broadening the popular audience for nature writing. It
is also fair to conclude that Cooper's success with her first volume of nature
writing encouraged her to prepare and publish three subsequent large volumes of related material.

In 1853 she published both her annotated edition of John Leonard
Knapp's *Country Rambles in England; or, Journal of a Naturalist* and a collec-

tion of original nature essays entitled *Rural Rambles*. In 1855 she published the anthology of nature poetry that she dedicated to William Cullen Bryant, entitled *The Rhyme and Reason of Country Life; or, Selections from Fields Old and New*. In the same year, several excerpts from *Rural Hours* were included in John S. Hart's *The Female Prose Writers of America*, where Cooper is praised as a nature writer who avoids "extravagant embellishments" and "ecstacies": "Her work . . . contains an admirable portraiture of American out-door life, just as it is, with no colouring but that which every object necessarily receives in passing through a contemplative and cultivated mind" (413).

Within four and a half years of its first publication, *Rural Hours* appeared in six distinct editions. And even though sales were slowing by 1855, Richard Bentley went ahead that year with the seventh edition, this time changing the title to *Journal of a Naturalist in the United States* in order to echo Susan Cooper's work in the recent edition of John Leonard Knapp's *Country Rambles in England; or, Journal of a Naturalist*. Thereafter, only two new editions of the original text of *Rural Hours* appeared, both by Putnam, in 1868 and 1876. For the 1868 edition, the author added a new preface and a chapter titled "Later Hours." After these nine editions, Cooper persuaded Houghton Mifflin in Boston to publish a radically abridged version, for which she cut more than 40 percent from the original. And there the neglect of *Rural Hours* began. In this century, the abridged version was published once, in 1968. The present edition of the full text of the original 1850 *Rural Hours* makes Cooper's complete work available for the first time since 1876.

Susan Cooper published many other works in her lifetime. In addition to a number of fiction and nonfiction contributions to several magazines, she published patriotic pieces, often written with children in mind. A major literary project was the series of introductions she wrote for the Household Edition of her father's novels, which appeared between 1876 and 1884. All the while, she also funded, raised funds for, worked in, and directed an orphanage in Cooperstown (see Kurth).

Rural Hours WAS UNIFORMLY PRAISED in the nineteenth century for its accuracy, clarity, simplicity, and lack of pretension. These same qualities, however, have caused some later readers to undervalue the literary merit of the work and sometimes to miss altogether its concern for cultural issues. When the truncated 1887 version was reissued in 1968, its editor epitomized this more recent reading when he apologized that "*Rural Hours* is not, like *Walden*, a multi-level book" (Jones xxxvii). Until very recently, how-

ever, almost all good nature writing—with the exception of *Walden* and a few
other books—has been neglected or not fully understood and appreciated.
But as the human population has continued to grow and as various environmental crises have worsened, we have understandably become much
better readers of nature writing, and the subtleties of *Rural Hours,* not surprisingly, became apparent only after many readers had discovered the long-
hidden achievements of nature writers. Susan Cooper's father was more
correct than he knew when he rather casually prophesied that "at first, the
world will not know what to make of it" (Beard 6:151).

The book by the daughter of the famous novelist should first of all be seen
in the context of her pioneer grandfather's settlement of the Cooperstown
region. As the American Revolution came to its close, the myth of the new
American settler as the "second creator" came to imbue the settlers's ex-
pansionist work (Taylor 33). In 1810, Judge William Cooper's written account of the Otsego Lake region was published in the form of a pamphlet,
A Guide in the Wilderness, intended to explain how to go about settling an
American wilderness. Early in his narrative of how he brought agriculture
and villages to the regions west of Albany, he sets the following prophetic
and visionary scene:

> In 1785 I visited the rough and hilly country of Otsego, where there ex-
> isted not an inhabitant, nor any trace of a road; I was alone, three hun-
> dred miles from home, without bread, meat, or food of any kind; fire
> and fishing tackle were my only means of subsistence. I caught trout in
> the brook and roasted them on the ashes. My horse fed on the grass
> that grew by the edge of the waters. I laid me down to sleep in my
> watch coat, nothing but the melancholy Wilderness around me. In this
> way I explored the country, formed my plans of future settlement, and
> meditated upon the spot where a place of trade or a village should af-
> terwards be established. (8)

Writing in 1807, he boasted, "I have already settled more acres than any
man in America" and "forty thousand souls now [hold], directly or indi-
rectly, under me" (7). Judge Cooper achieved all this, as Alan Taylor ex-
plains, by making it financially possible for cash-poor settlers to move into
Otsego County, where they "felled the forest and created farms filled with
crops, livestock, barns, fences, and homes." They turned natural resources
into "marketable commodities" that "generated the profits to build substantial homes and found the public institutions of a civilized people" (Taylor 33). When Judge Cooper considered the meaning of this work, he cast

himself in the role of a second creator: "I am now descending into the vale of life, and I must acknowledge that I look back with self complacency upon what I have done, and am proud of having been an instrument in reclaiming such large and fruitful tracts from the waste of the creation" (7). It is clear that in this land developer's mind, he was, in Alan Taylor's words, completing "a divine task left undone by the Creator" (33).

Even though Susan Cooper (according to her letter of March 30, 1872) did not see her grandfather's pamphlet until long after writing *Rural Hours,* she was thoroughly familiar with this interpretation of the good and necessary work of Otsego County's pioneers. It imbued her father's life and work as well. She describes her father, in introductory remarks to *Wyandotté,* as "most thoroughly a pioneer in spirit":

> He delighted in the peculiarly American process of "clearing;" not in its ruder forms, of course, where the chief object of the colonist often appears to consist in felling a noble wood, and leaving the unsightly wreck—a lifeless array of half-charred stumps—to moulder slowly away, under the storm and sunshine of half a life-time. It was the work of improvement, in all its different stages, in which he took pleasure, from the first opening of the soil to the sunlight, through all the long course of removing the wood, burning the brush, the first tilling, and the first crop. About a mile and a half from the village, on the eastern bank of the lake, lay a small farm, belted on all sides by the forest, and which he had taken great pleasure in improving, from the first stages of clearing the ground by means of that ingenious Yankee contrivance, the stump-extractor, to the neat drain and finished stone wall. To this little farm, lying on the eastern mountain-side, he drove daily, to overlook his laborers and direct the work. (*Pages,* 409)

In his fiction, as well, James Fenimore Cooper depicted the clearing, settling, and cultivating of the wilderness as the heroic and progressive actions of moral men. In the first of his Leatherstocking novels, *The Pioneers; or, the Sources of the Susquehanna* (1823), this is a dominant concern, as it is in *Wyandotté; or, the Hutted Knoll* (1843), a novel set in a pioneer settlement that he composed in Cooperstown a few years before his daughter began to write the same landscape into her journal entries.

Susan Cooper thus enjoyed the landscape that was tamed and cultivated largely by the motive to wealth and the risky, if also apt, financial practices of her pioneering grandfather. (Alan Taylor's entire *William Cooper's Town* is essential to an understanding of this layer of Susan Cooper's background.)

She was also influenced by a father who celebrated the region's pioneer history. As the third authorial Cooper voice to write this region into the minds of readers, she also had a chance to eulogize those who had so altered the wilderness, but because of the excesses and losses that she saw in her generation, she also had other motives and found various ways to modify the myth of the second creator and to craft her book so as to help shape the kind of culture she thought Americans needed.

Her chief method for achieving this educational goal was to deepen her readers' knowledge of the land, composing natural history essays on the flora, fauna, and geologic history of the Otsego region and laying over all this the history of the successive stages of human habitation in the region. Her theory was that knowledge of place causes people to approach the land more humbly and gratefully and with less greed. Both through the form of the natural history essay, then, and through narratives and descriptions of her walks and excursions, Cooper presents what ultimately emerges as her argument for a sustainable balance between human culture and its natural surroundings. In her recurring discussions of the forests, for example, a central concern of *Rural Hours,* Cooper praises the speed with which the wild areas have been converted into cultivated farmland, creating a landscape in which a traveler "passes from farm to farm in unbroken succession" and in which "the aspect of the whole region is smiling and fruitful." Even the mountains, she writes, "are easily tilled—arable, many of them, to their very summits" (88–89). On the other hand, she criticizes practices she deems unsustainable, particularly the rapid destruction of ancient forests for fuel and lumber: "One would think that by this time, when the forest has fallen in all the valleys—when the hills are becoming more bare every day—when timber and fuel are rising in prices, and new uses are found for even indifferent woods—some forethought and care in this respect would be natural in people laying claim to common sense" (213–14). The type of culture that *Rural Hours* endorses is an idealized rural one in which, ideally, the means of maintaining an enlightened and moral human civilization would be sustainable, not destructive to the land.

It seems clear that sometime between the publication of *Elinor Wyllys* in 1846 and the composition of her journal entries in 1848 and 1849, Susan Cooper came to see nature writing as a means to cultural change. In addition to instilling in readers a greater sense of national identity and even pride, by means of her nature writing she saw that she might also contribute to the "moral and intellectual progress" of her young nation (334). In *Rural*

Hours she cites a shift toward greater accuracy in "descriptive writing, on natural objects" that has occurred in the preceding fifty years, and this she sees as a response to her culture's call from "the head for more truth" and from "the heart for more of life" (208). Cooper thus links accuracy in nature writing with the health of her culture, and the accuracy of her representations of nature in *Rural Hours* enables her to participate in the ongoing creation and maintenance of a morally and intellectually healthy culture. An important further implication of this theory of the cultural work of nature writing is that she, as author, suggests to her readers that they have a moral obligation to deepen their knowledge of the natural history of their respective places.

Susan Cooper's ideas about how humans should treat the land are framed by her belief in a cosmos in which a Christian God provides not only for humankind but also for all other life forms. In this cosmos, everything exists for a purpose determined by God, and while the Bible is the chief means of God's revelation, nature also signifies in this teleological worldview. Cooper offers the example of nature's ability to console the grieving human heart when the efforts of even the wisest of humans fail to do so: "It seems as though at such moments the witty become dull, the eloquent tedious, the wise insipid, so little are they enabled to effect" (45). The contemplation of nature, however, because of God's providential design of the universe, soothes the weary heart: "It was not merely to gratify the outer senses of man that these good gifts were bestowed on the earth; they were made for our hearts, the ever-present expression of love, and mercy, and power. When the spirit is harassed by the evils of life, it is then the works of God offer to us most fully the strengthening repose of a noble contemplation" (46). This providential design that Susan Cooper envisions, however, is nonetheless human-centered; that is, the natural environment from which God's power, love, and wisdom emanate is also intended to serve human needs. It is consistent with God's will, then, that humans convert the wilderness into a land that is shaped and cultivated. When Cooper treats the large predatory mammals that compete with humans, for example, she provides what is known of their natural history, but she does not once suggest that they have a right to coexist on the land or that their eradication is to be lamented. When a lone mountain lion appears in the area and is finally killed by hunters, Cooper expresses no sympathy for the individual animal and no pang of ecological conscience for the local extinction of a species; she is simply disappointed—even mortified—that the "panther" was killed along the Mohawk River and not in her own county (282). She comments also that it is fortunate how rare the wolverine has become, specifically because it steals bait from the traps of hunters (313).

Much more pervasive, however, is her reporting of the depletions and losses of numerous plant and animal species from the Otsego region. This reporting becomes a recurring refrain in *Rural Hours* and builds to a cumulative lament. Species of wildflowers that once were common are now rare; formerly vast flocks of migratory birds are now greatly diminished; the original forests are practically gone; various species of fish prized as food and incredibly abundant in former times are much reduced. In the past, "Moose, stags, deer, wolves must have all passed over the lake every winter," but "To-day the forests are quite deserted in winter, except where the wood-cutters are at work, or a few rabbits and squirrels are gliding over the snow" (310). This subtle lamentation might seem merely the effete ramblings of the privileged elite if not for Cooper's criticism of the capitalistic culture that is responsible for the unsustainable practices she opposes; for example, she clearly blames "cupidity, and the haste to grow rich" for much of the destruction of the forests (139). She finds no cause for restraint at all, however, in a report of 1,104 rattlesnakes having been killed in two days: "They are taken for their fat, which is sold at a good price" (54).

Prominent in *Rural Hours* is Cooper's desire to blend aesthetics with ecology in her writing about nature. Pleasing scenery, which she values highly, takes on a redeeming ecological depth. For example, when she considers the differing aesthetic effects of meadows and grain fields, she makes impossible the shallow view of any field as static and its beauty as simple:

> Grain, to appear to full advantage, should be seen at a little distance, where one may note the changes in its coloring with the advancing season, where one may enjoy the play of light when the summer clouds throw their shadows there, or the breezes chase one another over the waving lawn. It is like a piece of shaded silk which the salesman throws off a little, that you may better appreciate the effect. But a meadow is a delicate embroidery in colors, which you must examine closely to understand all its merits; the nearer you are, the better. One must bend over the grass to find the blue violet in May, the red strawberry in June; one should be close at hand to mark the first appearance of the simple field-blossoms, clover, red and white, buttercup and daisy, with the later lily, and primrose, and meadow-tuft; one should be nigh to breathe the sweet and fresh perfume, which increases daily until the mowers come with their scythes. (76)

Cooper contributes to the move that the genre of nature writing was making toward an emphasis on process and on the interconnectedness of things (that is, toward ecology) by means of her tendency to meditate not so much on static objects–the named and categorized flora, fauna, and minerals–as on the causes of phenomena and on natural processes occurring in time. The vision she expresses in *Rural Hours* brings an ecological awareness to what might have been a much shallower anthropocentric aesthetic presentation.

Susan Cooper, who referred to herself once as merely a "rustic bird-fancier" (72), saw her rural world diminishing and perhaps believed that an appeal to the moral and ethical duties of Americans would help to ensure the continuation of a rural America. In 1949, nearly one hundred years after the publication of *Rural Hours*, Aldo Leopold's *Sand County Almanac* was published. In his book, Leopold proposed his now well-known "land ethic." He wrote, "Perhaps the most serious obstacle impeding the evolution of a land ethic is the fact that our educational and economic system is headed away from, rather than toward, an intense consciousness of land" (261). Susan Cooper believed, long before the state of environmental crisis we face at the end of the twentieth century, that education was the key to preserving the natural environment. In *Rural Hours*, she undertook the work of educating a readership about the value and the necessity of a human culture that was sustainable in the natural world.

Works Cited

Beard, James Franklin, ed. *The Letters and Journals of James Fenimore Cooper*. 6 vols. Cambridge: Harvard University Press, 1960.

Cooper, James Fenimore. *The Pioneers; or, the Sources of the Susquehanna*. London: Murray, 1823.

——. *Wyandotté; or, the Hutted Knoll*. Philadelphia: Lea and Blanchard, 1843.

Cooper, Susan Fenimore [Amabel Penfeather, pseud.]. *Elinor Wyllys; or, the Young Folk of Longbridge: A Tale*, ed. J. Fenimore Cooper. 2 vols. Philadelphia: Carey and Hart, 1846.

——. *Rural Hours*. New York: Putnam, 1850.

——. *Rural Hours*. Abridged, Boston: Houghton Mifflin, 1887. Reprint, Syracuse: Syracuse University Press, 1968.

——. *Rural Rambles; or, Some Chapters on Flowers, Birds, and Insects*. Philadelphia: Hazard, 1853.

——. "Small Family Memories." In *Correspondence of James Fenimore Cooper*, ed. James Fenimore Cooper, 1:7–72. 2 vols. New Haven: Yale University Press, 1922.

——. Letter to W.W.C. 30 March 1872. MS. 6245-k, box no. 2. Manuscripts Department, University of Virginia Library.

——. Letter to James Fenimore Cooper. 3 March 1850. Beinecke Rare Book and Manuscript Library, Yale University.

——. Letter to Mr. Jay. 2 September 1850. MS. 6245-l, box no. 2. Manuscripts Department, University of Virginia Library.

——. Letter to Mrs. Ransom. 26 October 1846. The Historical Society of Pennsylvania. Philadelphia.

——, ed. *Country Rambles in England; or, Journal of a Naturalist.* By John Leonard Knapp. Buffalo: Phinney and Company, 1853.

——. *Pages and Pictures, from the Writings of James Fenimore Cooper, with Notes by Susan Fenimore Cooper.* New York: Townsend, 1861.

——. *The Rhyme and Reason of Country Life; or, Selections from Fields Old and New.* New York: Putnam, 1855.

Cooper, William. *A Guide in the Wilderness; or, the History of the First Settlements in the Western Counties of New York with Useful Instructions to Future Settlers.* Dublin: Gilbert and Hodges, 1810.

Hart, John S., ed. *The Female Prose Writers of America: With Portraits, Biographical Notices, and Specimens of Their Writings.* Philadelphia: Butler, 1855.

Jones, David. Introduction to *Rural Hours,* by Susan Fenimore Cooper, xi–xxxviii. 1887. Reprint, Syracuse: Syracuse University Press, 1968.

Kurth, Rosaly Torna. "Susan Fenimore Cooper: A Study of Her Life and Works." Ph.D. diss., Fordham University, 1974.

Leopold, Aldo. *A Sand County Almanac.* 1949. New York: Ballantine, 1991.

Taylor, Alan. *William Cooper's Town: Power and Persuasion on the Frontier of the Early American Republic.* New York: Vintage, 1995.

Editorial Principles

THIS EDITION OF Susan Fenimore Cooper's *Rural Hours* reproduces the full text of Putnam's 1850 first edition.

In making corrections and adjustments, we have operated on two assumptions: Cooper would have wanted errors corrected, and she would have wanted consistency in spelling and hyphenation. We have therefore corrected obvious errors and adjusted spelling and hyphenation to achieve consistency. Accordingly, we reproduce the first edition's use of asterisks to mark section breaks and to open several entries (the latter being a practice the 1850 text does not explain). This edition, however, does not reproduce the right-hand page headers, which briefly indicate the subjects treated on each page. Every editorial change is noted in the list of emendations; no silent changes in the text have been made.

We decided whether to hyphenate a compound noun or verb that is divided at the end of a line in the 1850 text on the basis of comparisons, first by checking for occurrences of the compound elsewhere in the text, and should there be no other occurrence, by checking the abridged 1887 edition, the only edition that in its typesetting varies from the original stereotyped text. If the question cannot be decided by either of these two methods, we hyphenate a compound if *The Oxford English Dictionary* lists it as hyphenated.

Because Cooper drew on journal entries from nearly two years in composing *Rural Hours,* there is one dating inconsistency that cannot be corrected. Hugh MacDougall has shown that the entries from March 4 through May 24 are from journal entries written during the year 1848, the entries from May 25 through August 9 are from journal entries written during 1849, and the entries from August 11 through February 28 are from journal entries written in the latter part of 1848 and early in 1849 (*James Fenimore Cooper Society Newsletter* 6, no. 3 [1995]: 2). Even taking this into account, the following sequence of dates remains inconsistent: Tuesday, May 29; Thursday, May 30; Friday, May 31; and Friday, June 1.

To help readers with words and allusions not identified in standard dictionaries, we have compiled a glossary. And for those interested in Cooper's readings in natural history and other subjects, we include a works cited that identifies many, though not all, of the authors and works she cites in *Rural Hours*. We have also compiled an index, which the 1850 text did not have.

RURAL HOURS.

BY

A LADY.

"And we will all the pleasures prove
That valleys, groves, or hills, or field,
Or woods, and steepy mountains yield."

MARLOW

NEW YORK:

GEORGE P. PUTNAM, 155 BROADWAY,

LONDON: PUTNAM'S AMERICAN AGENCY.

1850.

TO

THE AUTHOR OF "THE DEERSLAYER,"

THESE NOTES ARE

VERY RESPECTFULLY, GRATEFULLY,

AND MOST AFFECTIONATELY

Inscribed,

BY

THE WRITER.

Preface

The following notes contain, in a journal form, the simple record of those little events which make up the course of the seasons in rural life, and were commenced two years since, in the spring of 1848, for the writer's amusement. In wandering about the fields, during a long, unbroken residence in the country, one naturally gleans many trifling observations on rustic matters, which are afterward remembered with pleasure by the fireside, and gladly shared, perhaps, with one's friends. The following pages, therefore, are offered to the reader more from the interest of the subject, than from any merit of their own. They make no claim whatever to scientific knowledge, but it is hoped that they will be found free from great inaccuracies; and we may add, that they were written at least in perfect good faith, all the trifling incidents alluded to having occurred as they are recorded.

Should the volume give pleasure to any who, like the honored Hooker, love the country, "where we may see God's blessings spring out of the earth," some little reluctance with which it has been printed will be more than repaid to the writer.

March, 1850.

Spring

Saturday, March 4th.—Everything about us looks thoroughly wintry still, and fresh snow lies on the ground to the depth of a foot. One quite enjoys the sleighing, however, as there was very little last month. Drove several miles down the valley this morning in the teeth of a sharp wind, and flurries of snow, but after facing the cold bravely, one brings home a sort of virtuous glow which is not to be picked up by cowering over the fireside; it is with this as with more important matters, the effort brings its own reward.

Tuesday, 7th.—Milder; thawing. Walking near the river this afternoon, we saw a party of wild ducks flying northward; some few of these birds remain here all winter, but they are seldom observed except by the sportsman; these were the first we had seen for several months. In the spring and autumn, when so many of the different varieties are passing to and fro, they are common enough. Three large waterfowl also passed along in the same direction; we believed them to be loons; they were in sight only for a moment, owing to the trees above us, but we heard a loud howling cry as they flew past like that of those birds. It is early for loons, however, and we may have been deceived. They usually appear about the first of April, remaining with us through the summer and autumn, until late in December, when they go to the sea-shore; many winter about Long Island, many more in the Chesapeake. Not long since we saw one of these birds of unusual size, weighing nineteen pounds; it had been caught in Seneca Lake on the hook of what fishermen call a set-line, dropped to the depth of ninety-five feet, the bird having dived that distance to reach the bait. Several others have been caught in the same manner in Seneca Lake upon lines sunk from eighty to one hundred feet. It may be doubted if any other feathered thing goes so far beneath the water. There is however another, and a much smaller bird, the Dipper, or ousel, which is still more at home in the water than the loon, and that without being web-footed, but it is probably less of a diver. The Dipper must indeed be a very singular bird; instead of swimming on the surface of the water like ducks and geese, or beneath like the loons, or wading along the shores like many of the long-legged coast tribes, it actually runs or flies about at will over gravelly beds of mountain streams. Mr. Charles Bonaparte mentions having frequently watched them among the brooks of the Alps and Apennines, where they are found singly, or in pairs, haunting torrents and cataracts with perfect impunity, or running hither and thither along the stony bottom of more quiet streams. They cannot swim, however; and they drop suddenly into the water from above, or at times they walk leisurely in from the bank, flying as it were beneath the surface, moving with distended wings. Their nests are said to be usually built on some point projecting over a mountain stream, either in a tree, or upon a rock; and the young, when alarmed, instantly drop into the water below, for safety. They are not common birds even in their native haunts, but wild and solitary creatures, smaller than our robin, and of a dark, grave plumage. Until lately the Dipper was supposed to be unknown on this continent, but more recently it has been discovered at several different points in our part of the world, frequenting, as in Europe, wild lakes and rocky streams of limpid water. The American bird differs slightly in some of its markings, from those of the Eastern continent.

Wednesday, 8th.—Very pleasant day; quite spring-like. The snow is melting fast. Spring in the *air*, in the *light*, and in the *sky*, although the earth is yet unconscious of its approach. We have weather as mild as this in December, but there is something in the fulness and softness of the light beaming in the sky this morning which tells of spring,—the early dawn before the summer day. A little downy woodpecker and a blue-jay were running about the apple-trees hunting for insects; we watched them awhile with interest, for few birds are seen here during the winter. It is true neither the downy woodpecker nor the jay leaves this part of the country; both remain here during the cold weather, but they are inactive, seldom roving abroad.

Thursday, 9th.—Winter again; the woods are powdered with snow this morning, and every twig is cased in glittering frost-work. The pines in the churchyard are very beautiful—hung with heavy wreaths of snow; but it is thawing fast, and before night they will be quite green again. This effect of the snow lodging on the trees is much less frequent than one might suppose in our highland climate; it is seldom found to last more than a few hours at a time, soon vanishing before wind or sunshine; indeed it scarcely occurs half a dozen times in the course of a winter: and it is the same with the hoar-frost on the branches, which is by no means so common a spectacle as a Cockney might fancy. This morning both these specimens of winter's handiwork are united, and the effect is very fine, though it looks as if spring might yet be a hundred years off.

Friday, 10th.—A bunch of ten partridges brought to the house; they are occasionally offered singly, or a brace or two at a time, but ten are a much larger number than are often seen together. Last autumn we frequently came upon these birds in the woods—they were probably more numerous than usual. Several times they even found their way down into the village, which we have never known them to do before; once they were surprised in the churchyard, and twice they were found feeding among the refuse of our own garden.

When this valley was first peopled by the whites, quails were also found here in abundance, among the common game-birds of the region, but they have now abandoned us entirely; one never hears of them, and it is said that they soon disappeared after the country had been cleared. This is not according to their usual habits, for generally they are found to prefer the farm lands to the forest, feeding on different kinds of grain, building about fences, and rarely resorting to the woods. In some of the oldest parts of the country they are quite common, and so familiar, that in winter they will occasionally mingle with the poultry in the barn-yard. Instead of fearing the advance of civilization, they would delight in it, were it not for the sportsman's gun. It is true that in this county we approach the northern limits of the quail, for they are found from Honduras to Massachusetts only; our Partridge or Pheasant, or Ruffed Grouse, as we should rather call it, is a more hardy bird, partial to mountains and wooded countries, and found as far north as Hudson's Bay.

Saturday, 11th.—Very pleasant. Walking on the skirts of the village this afternoon, we came to a fence blown down by some winter storm, and stepping over it strolled about the fields awhile, the first time we had walked off the beaten track since November. We were obliged to cross several snow banks, but had the pleasure at least of treading the brown earth again, and remembering that in a few short weeks the sward will be fresh and green once more. A disappointment awaited us—several noble pines, old friends and favorites, had been felled unknown to us during the winter; unsightly stumps and piles of chips were all that remained where those fine trees had so long waved their evergreen arms. Their fall seemed to have quite changed the character of the neighboring fields; for it often lies within the power of a single group of trees to alter the whole aspect of acres of surrounding lands.

Wednesday, 15th.—Unusually cold for the season, the thermometer having fallen last night to six below zero. Half-cloudy day; wind from the north.

Thursday, 16th.—The cold still continues; ten degrees below zero last night! This would be thought very severe at midwinter.

Friday, 17th.—Severely cold night, thermometer seven below zero. Happily, it is now growing milder; the mercury above zero this evening.

Saturday, 18th.—Spring weather again, quite pleasant to-day. Thermometer forty-six, the mercury having risen some forty degrees within the last eighteen hours.

Long walk of several miles on the lake. We fancied the waters impatient to be free: there was a constant succession of dull, rumbling, and groaning sounds beneath our feet, as we passed over the ice, so much so as to disturb our four-footed companion not a little. Dogs are often uneasy on the ice, especially when they first set out; they do not like the noise from below; but there was no danger whatever this morning. The crust is still eight or ten inches thick, and must have been much strengthened by the last severe weather. A number of sleighs and cutters were gliding about, several of the last driven by children, and well loaded with little people making the most of the last snow.

It was thawing in the village, and the streets were muddy; but on the lake the snow scarcely yielded at all, the ice making a climate of its own. We enjoyed the walk very much; it is particularly pleasant to wander about at will over so broad a field, confined to no track, and without an obstacle to arrest one's progress, all which gives a freedom to these walks upon the lake, beyond what we are accustomed to on terra firma, where roads, and fences, and bridges must be consulted at every turn.

Monday, 20th.—Passing beneath some maples this afternoon, we observed several with small icicles hanging from their lower branches, although there was neither ice nor snow on the adjoining trees; we broke one off, and it proved to be congealed sap, which had exuded from the branch and frozen there during the night—natural sugar candy, as it were, growing on the tree. These little icicles were quite transparent and sweetish, like *eau sucrée*. At this season, the sap very frequently moistens the trunk and limbs of sugar maples very plentifully, in spots where there is some crevice through which it makes its way; one often sees it dropping from the branches, and probably the Indians first discovered its sweetness from this habit. One would think that the loss of so much sap would necessarily injure the trees; but it is not so; they remain perfectly healthy, after yielding every spring, gallons of the fluid.

Wednesday, 22d.–A thunder-shower last night, by way of keeping the equinox, and this morning, to the joy of the whole community, the arrival of the robins is proclaimed. It is one of the great events of the year, for us, the return of the robins; we have been on the watch for them these ten days, as they generally come between the fifteenth and twenty-first of the month, and now most persons you meet, old and young, great and small, have something to say about them. No sooner is one of these first-comers seen by some member of a family, than the fact is proclaimed through the house; children run in to tell their parents, "The robins have come!" Grandfathers and grandmothers put on their spectacles and step to the windows to look at the robins; and you hear neighbors gravely inquiring of each other: "Have you seen the robins?"–"Have you heard the robins?" There is no other bird whose return is so generally noticed, and for several days their movements are watched with no little interest, as they run about the ground, or perch on the leafless trees. It was last night just as the shutters were closed that they were heard about the doors, and we ran out to listen to their first greeting, but it was too dark to see them. This morning, however, they were found in their native apple-trees, and a hearty welcome we gave the honest creatures.

Thursday, 23d.–The snow is going at last; the country has the dappled look belonging properly to March in this part of the world; broad openings of brown earth are seen everywhere, in the fields and on the hill-sides. The roads are deep with mud; the stage-coaches are ten and eleven hours coming the twenty-two miles over the hills, from the railroad north of us.

The Phœbe-birds have arrived as well as the robins. In many parts of the country, their return is looked upon as the signal for beginning to make garden, but that would not do here; there is too much frost in the ground for the spade. They are making hot-beds, however, in spite of the snow banks still lying in many gardens; early lettuce and radishes are raised in this way, and both melons and tomatoes require to be helped forward by the same process to ripen their fruits thoroughly in this highland region. There is a sort of tradition in the village, that the climate has undergone a degree of change since the arrival of the first colonists; the springs are said to have become more uncertain, and the summers less warm; so say elderly people who knew the place forty years since. The same remark is frequently heard, also, in settlements of about the same date as this, on the St. Lawrence, and the Genesee. But there may be some self-deception in the case, for we are naturally more apt to feel the frost of to-day, than that of last year, and memory may very possibly have softened the climate to those who look back from age to youth. There seems, however, some positive foundation for the assertion, since it is a fact well known, that fruits which succeeded here formerly, are now seldom ripened. Water-melons were raised here without hot-beds forty years since, and a thriving little vineyard existed on the same spot where the grapes have been cut off by frost every season for the last ten years.

Friday, 24th.—The first plant that shows the influence of the changing season in this part of the country, is very little like the delicate snow-drop, or the fragrant violet of other lands. Long before the earliest trees are in bud, or the grass shows the faintest tinge of green, the dark spathe of the skunk-cabbage makes its way in the midst of snow and ice. It is singular that at a moment when the soil generally is frost-bound, any plant should find out that spring is at hand; but toward the close of February, or beginning of March, the skunk-cabbage makes a good guess at the time of the year, and comes up in marshy spots, on the banks of ponds and streams. With us it is almost a winter plant. The dark spathe or sheath is quite handsome, variegated, when young, with purple, light green, and yellow; within it grows the spadix, not unlike a miniature pine-apple in shape and color, and covered with little protuberances, from each of which opens a purple flower. Although a very common plant, many persons familiar with its broad glossy leaves in summer, have never seen the flower, and have no idea how early it blossoms. Its strong, offensive odor is better known; an American botanist has observed, that "it is exceedingly meritorious of the name it bears;" but this seems too severe, since a harsher thing could not well be said of a plant. In the neighborhood of the village, it has been up these three weeks, but the flowers open slowly.

Saturday, 25th.—High wind from the south this evening; our highest winds are generally from the southward. The withered leaves of last autumn are whirling, and flying over the blighted grass of the lawns, and about the roots of the naked trees—a dance of death, as it were, in honor of winter as he passes away.

Monday, 27th.—A flock of wild pigeons wheeling beautifully over the mountain this afternoon. We have had but few this spring; there is a great difference in the numbers which visit us from year to year; some seasons they are still very numerous, large flocks passing over the valley morning and evening as they go out from their general breeding-place in quest of food. Some few years ago they selected a wood on a hill, about twenty miles from us, for their spring encampment, making as usual great havoc among the trees and bushes about them; at that time they passed over the valley in its length, large unbroken flocks several miles in extent succeeding each other. There have not been so many here since that season. But the numbers we saw then were nothing to the throngs that visited the valley annually in its earliest history, actually darkening the air as they swept along. It seems their nature to fly rather low, but they have grown more wily now, and often take a high flight; frequently, however, they just graze the hill-tops, and the sportsmen, after observing their usual course of flight morning and evening, go out and station themselves on some hill, shooting the birds as they pass over their heads. The young, or squabs, as they are called, are in great request as a delicacy in spring; they are very tender, of course, and generally very plump, for the little creatures begin to fatten the moment they break through the shell, and are soon in good order. They are not thought very healthy food, however, when eaten repeatedly in succession. There is a tradition that the Indians, at the time of the year when they lived chiefly on these birds, were not in a healthy condition.

Tuesday, 28th.–The great final spring thaw going on. Our winter deluge of snow is sinking into the earth, softening her bosom for the labors of the husbandman, or running off into the swollen streams, toward the sea. Cloudy sky with mist on the hills, in which the pines look nobly; the older trees especially, half revealed, half shrouded, seem giant phantoms, standing about the hill-sides. The simple note of the robin is heard through the gloom–a cheering sound in these dull hours; perched on the topmost boughs of the trees, they are taking an observation, looking out for a convenient building notch.

Wednesday, 29th.–Lovely day; soft clear sunshine, and delightful air from the west playing in the leafless branches, and among the green threads of the pine foliage. It is not surprising that the pines, when they

> "Wake up into song,
> Shaking their choral locks,"

should make more melody than other trees; the long slender leaves are quivering in the breeze this afternoon like the strings of an instrument, but they are so minute that at a little distance we only remark the general movement of the tufted branches.

The whole country is brown again, save here and there a narrow line of snow under some fence on the hills, or a patch marking a drift which all the storms of winter have helped to pile up.

Nothing can look more dismal than the lake just now; its surface is neither snow, ice, nor water, but a dull crust which gives it a sullen expression quite out of character with the landscape generally, such a day as this; the sun is warming the brown hills, the old pines, and hemlocks with a spring glow after their long chill, but not a smile can be drawn from the lake which grows more dark and gloomy every hour. As if to show us what we lose, there is just one corner open near the outlet, and it is beautiful in blended shades of coloring, rose and blue, clear and soft, as the eye of Spring.

Our little river runs full and swift, spread over the banks to nearly twice its usual width; the water is a fine light green, quite different from its darker summer tint of transparent gray. It is singular that snow and ice in large quantities should always change the color of a stream which they have helped to fill; but so it is: all the waters which flow from the glaciers in Switzerland have a peculiar tint. With us, this effect is seen for a few days only, when the ice first breaks up in spring. Saw a caterpillar this afternoon, the first that has crossed our path.

Thursday, 30th. – The song-sparrows and blue-birds are here, and have been with us several days. The robins are getting quite numerous; they seem to come in detachments, or possibly they only pass from one neighborhood to another in flocks. Their note is very pleasant, and after the silent winter, falls with double sweetness on the ear. Their portly persons and warm red jackets make them very conspicuous flying about among the naked branches, or running over the wilted grass. They are more frequently seen on the ground than any other bird we have, excepting the sparrow, and it is amusing to watch the different gait of the two. The sparrow glides along with great agility and ease; whether in the grass or on the gravel, his movement is light and free: but robin usually makes more fuss; he runs by starts, drops his head, raises his tail, moves rapidly for a few feet, and then stops suddenly, repeating the same course of manœuvres until he takes flight. The European robin is a smaller bird than ours, and lives through the year as far north as England, cheering his native fields with a simple lay even during the cold weather: his habits are different from those of our own bird; he builds in grassy banks, and has a trick of scraping dead leaves together before his door, probably with the idea of concealing his nest. With us, robin never builds on the ground; his nest is placed in trees, where, from its size, it is very conspicuous; once in awhile, however, he builds about a house, but in such a case usually places his nest in some spot shaded by a vine or the branches of a tree. For two summers in succession, we had a nest on a window-sill of the second story, and this spring two pairs seem to be building about the eaves; but in all these instances, the spots chosen are screened by Virginia creepers. Then again with us, robin is only musical early in spring; the rest of the year he is a very silent bird. Some few occasionally linger through the cold weather as far north as the Mohawk, but this seems accidental; many take a south-eastern direction toward the sea-shore, and many more go still farther south to a milder climate. They are with us, however, eight or nine months of the year—honest, homely creatures, running about the grass-plots and paths around our doors, so that they are everywhere considered as friends of the house. I have seen it asserted that the early colonists gave to the gaudy oriole the name of "English robin," showing how fondly memory colored all they had left behind, since one bird is very plain in his plumage, the other remarkably brilliant. The name of robin, however, has now attached itself decidedly to the large red-breasted thrush, with which we are all familiar; and although differing in many respects from the Robin Redbreast of Europe, yet with the name he also inherits the favor of his kinsman, getting all the credit in this part of the world of watching over the Babes in the Woods, picking berries to feed them, and gathering leaves for their covering. This afternoon, as we saw the robins running over the graves in the churchyard, or perched on a tombstone looking at us with those large thoughtful eyes of theirs, we came to the conclusion that our own Redbreast must be quite as capable of a good deed, as his European brother. At this season, we seldom pass the churchyard without finding robins there—they probably have many nests among the trees.

Friday, 31st.— The garden hyacinths, and daffodils, and common lilies are beginning to show their leaves in the flower-borders, and the periwinkle is almost in blossom: this is one of the very earliest flowers to open with us. The blue hyacinths soon follow, though they will scarcely bloom yet this fortnight. The snowdrop seldom opens here before the middle or third week of April, remaining in flower until the tulips fade, early in June; it would seem less hardy with us than in its native climate, for in England it blooms in February, and it has been found by M. de Candolle on the mountains of Switzerland with its flowers actually encased in snow and ice.

One hears a great deal about the sudden outburst of spring in America, but in this part of the country, the earlier stages of the season are assuredly very slow, and for many weeks its progress is gradual. It is only later in the day, when the buds are all full, and the flowers ready to open, that we see the sudden gush of life and joyousness, which is indeed at that moment, almost magical in its beautiful effects. But this later period is a brief one; we have scarcely time to enjoy the sudden affluence of spring, ere she leaves us to make way for summer, and people exclaim at the shortness of the season in America. Meanwhile, spring is with us in March, when we are yet sitting by the fireside, and few heed her steps; now she betrays her presence in the sky, now in the waters, with the returning birds, upon some single tree, in a solitary plant, and each milder touch gives pleasure to those who are content to await the natural order of things.

Saturday, April 1st.—Fresh maple sugar offered for sale to-day; it is seldom brought to market as early as this. A large amount of this sugar is still made in our neighborhood, chiefly for home consumption on the farms. In the villages, where foreign groceries are easily procured, it is eaten more as a dainty than in any other way; the children are very fond of it, and most grown persons like a bit now and then, its peculiar flavor making it pleasant when taken by itself, though it becomes a defect when used for sweetening food. In the spring, a little of it is not thought unhealthy, from a fancy that it purifies the blood; probably it is neither better nor worse in this respect than any other sugar. With our farmers, however, it is a matter of regular household consumption, many families depending on it altogether, keeping only a little white sugar for sickness; and it is said that children have often grown up in this county without tasting any but maple sugar. Maple molasses is also very much used, some persons preferring it to that of the cane, as it has a peculiar flavor which is liked with puddings, or buckwheat cakes.

Some farmers have a regular "sugar-bush," where none but maples are suffered to grow; and on the older farms you occasionally pass a beautiful grove of this kind, entirely clear of under-wood, the trees standing on a smooth green turf. More frequently, however, a convenient spot is chosen in the woods where maples are plenty. The younger trees are not tapped, as they are injured by the process; it is only after they have reached a good size—ten or twelve inches in diameter—that they are turned to account in this way; twenty years at least must be their age, as they rarely attain to such a growth earlier; from this period they continue to yield their sap freely until they decay. It is really surprising that any tree should afford to lose so much of its natural nourishment without injury; but maples that have been tapped for fifty years or more, are just as luxuriant in their foliage and flowers, as those that are untouched. The amount of sap yielded by different trees varies—some will give nearly three times as much as others; the fluid taken from one tree is also much sweeter and richer than that of another, as there seems to be a constitutional difference between them.

From two to five pounds of sugar are made from each tree, and four or five gallons of sap are required to every pound. The fluid begins to run with the first mild weather in March; its course, however, is checked by a hard frost, until a thaw again sets it in motion; some years it continues to flow at intervals until the last of April, so that a regular early spring gives less time for the work than a backward season, when the sap runs later; the usual period, however, for sugar-making, is about two weeks—one year more, another less.

This sugar is made more easily than any other; both the beet and the cane require much more expense and labor. The process with the maple is very simple, and consists merely in collecting the sap and boiling it; neatness and attention are alone necessary to make the sugar of the best quality. A hole is first bored into the trunk, from one to three feet from the ground; a hatchet or chisel is sometimes used for this purpose, but neat farmers prefer a small auger, less than half an inch in diameter, by which means the bark is not injured, closing again over the opening in two or three years. After the hole has been bored, a small trough or "spile," as the country people call it, is inserted; this is usually made of a branch of alder or sumach, which is sharpened at one end and the pith taken out for two or three inches to receive the sap; from that point it is hollowed into an open trough, which rests upon the sap-bucket at the foot of the tree. These buckets are a regular article of manufacture in the country; they are made of pine, or at times of bass-wood, and sell at twenty cents a piece. They are left standing one at the foot of each tree, to receive the sap as it flows, the little stream of sweet and limpid fluid running more or less freely, according to the state of the weather and the character of the tree; twelve quarts are sometimes taken in twenty-four hours from one tree, while others scarcely yield a third as much. The buckets are watched, of course, and emptied from time to time, the sap being carried to the boiler, which is often placed over a furnace upon an arch of bricks; often one large iron boiler is used, but pans of tin are thought preferable, as they give less color and taste to the sugar. This carrying the sap to the boiler is a laborious part of the process, and some farmers have all their lesser spouts connected with a large trough leading to a common receptacle near the furnace; the buckets, however, are more generally used. Two or three hundred trees are frequently tapped in the same wood, and as the sap is running, the fires are burning, and the sugar is boiling all together, day and night, it is a busy moment at the "bush." The persons at work there, usually eat and sleep on the spot until their task is done; and it is a favorite rallying place with the children and young people of the farms, who enjoy vastly this touch of camp life, to say nothing of the new sugar, and a draught of fresh sap now and then. The sap, however, is not thought a wholesome drink, differing in this respect from the juice of the cane, which is consid-

ered particularly healthy, both man and beasts growing fat on the plantations during the seasons of working among the ripe canes. When the work
at the "bush" is fairly commenced, the boiler is filled up from time to time
with fresh sap during the first four-and-twenty hours; after that, the fluid is
permitted to thicken to a syrup about half the sweetness of molasses; it is
then taken off and left to cool and settle. About twelve hours later, it is again
put over to clarify—the white of two eggs, one quart of milk, and half an
ounce of saleratus are allowed to fifty pounds of sugar—and the syrup is not
permitted to boil until the scum has all risen to the surface and been removed. After this clarifying has been attended to, the syrup boils until on
the point of graining, as it is called, or in rustic parlance, "sugaring down;"
it is then taken from the fire and placed in tin pans to cool and form the
"grain;" when this process of graining has thoroughly commenced, the new
sugar is placed in moulds to drain—the harder particles adhering together
as the sugar, the liquid portion, or molasses, dropping into a receptacle for
the purpose. Of course, as soon as the boiler has been emptied it is filled up
with new sap, and the same process is repeated until the season has passed,
or the amount required is made.

There are at present farms in this county where two or three thousand
pounds of sugar are prepared in one season. Formerly much of our sugar
was sent to Albany and New York, and a portion is still sold there to the confectioners. During the early history of the county, half a century since, rents
were usually paid in produce—wheat, potash, sugar, &c., &c.—for the convenience of the tenants, and it is on record that in one year sixty thousand
pounds were received in this way by the leader of the little colony about this
lake; a portion of it was refined and made into pretty little specimen loaves
at a sugar-house in Philadelphia, and it was quite as white and pure as that
of the cane. The common sugar about the country is as light as that usually
received from the West Indies, and the farmers have a simple domestic process by which it is often made quite clear; a clean wet flannel is placed over
the cake while draining, and gradually imbibes the coloring matter, being
washed and changed every morning until the sugar has become quite white;
if it has been neatly made and clarified, three or four days will whiten it thoroughly. No doubt there are maples enough about the country to supply the
whole population of the Republic, if necessary, but the sugar of the cane can
now be procured so easily, and so cheap, from the West Indies and the
southern parts of our own country, that there is little motive for making that
of the maple an article of commerce. Maple sugar sells in the village this

year for nine cents a pound, and good Havana for six cents. The farmers, however, are willing to turn their trees to account for their own use, as it saves them some cash, and requires but little outlay or labor.

A story is told in the village of a Scotch stocking-weaver, who some years since bought a farm near the lake, and the first spring after his arrival in the country was so successful with his maple trees, that in the midst of his labors he came into the village and gave large orders for sap-buckets, pans, furnaces, &c. The good folk were rather surprised at the extent of these preparations, and inquiries were made about this grand sugar-bush. They were told by their new neighbor that as yet he had tapped only a small number of trees, but he intended soon to go to work in earnest among the maples, and, indeed, had quite made up his mind, "canny Scot," as he was, to "give up farming altogether, and keep to sugar-making all the year round;"—a plan which, it may be imagined, tickled the fancy of Jonathan not a little, knowing the ways of maples as he did. Many other trees are tapped for their juices in different parts of the world—the pines for their turpentine, as we all know, and the celebrated cow-tree of South America for its nourishing fluid, yielding vegetable milk, as it were, in regions where the milk of domestic animals seems to have been unknown; and still farther South, on this great continent, they prepare from the sap of the Palm of Chili, a syrup of the consistency of honey, using it as an article of food. In Northern Europe, the birch sap is made into a drink which they call birch-wine, and in this country vinegar is occasionally made in the same way. In the Crimea, the Tartars regularly make sugar from the fine walnut-trees on the shores of the Black Sea. So says Dr. Clarke in his Travels. The lime or basswood also yields a saccharine fluid. Our own hickory is thought to have the sweetest and richest sap of any tree in the woods, and we have heard of superior sugar being made in small quantities from it by certain New England housewives. It would not be generally available for the purpose, however, as the amount of sap yielded is very small.

According to the last general Census, the whole amount of maple sugar made during one year in this county, with a population of 49,658, was 351,748 pounds, or nearly eight pounds to each individual. The whole amount of sugar made in the State, was 10,048,109 pounds. The census does not specify the different kinds of sugar, but it is so well known that no other sort but maple is made in our part of the country, as a manufacture, that it is scarcely worth while to subtract anything from the general reports on account of some experiments here and there, in corn or beet sugar. Taking the reports then, as they stand, we find that there are forty-nine counties in which maple sugar is manufactured, and nine counties in the immediate neighborhood of New York, where none is made. The largest amount made in one county, is reported from St. Lawrence, upwards of 848,000 pounds among a population of 56,000; Chatauque comes very near this, however, giving 839,000 pounds for 47,000 persons. There are nine counties making more than we do; Putnam reports the smallest amount, only 73 pounds, probably the produce of one "bush." The whole amount of various sugars made in the country during the year 1839–40, was upwards of 155,000,000 of pounds; since then, this quantity has nearly doubled, and it is supposed that about half the sugar now consumed by us, is manufactured within our own borders. Of course, a very great proportion comes from the cane plantations of Louisiana, &c., &c.; probably some beet and corn sugar in small quantities may be included in the calculations, but the tables of the last census did not specify the different varieties made in each State; and our only guide in forming an opinion as to the total amount of maple sugar made in the country, must be the respective geographical limits of the cane and the maple. Sugar of one sort or another is made in almost every State; Delaware and the District of Columbia are the only exceptions. We understand that maple sugar is made in Virginia and Kentucky, the first reporting 1,541,843, the last 1,399,835 pounds of sugar; probably this is in a very great measure from the maple. If we give about one-fifth of the whole amount, or some 31,000,000 of pounds to maple sugar, probably we shall not be very far from the truth; we are inclined to believe this calculation rather below than above the mark. From being almost entirely consumed on the ground where it is made, this sugar, however, attracts public attention much less than it would do if it were an article of commerce to the same extent.

Monday, 3d.—Delightful day; first walk in the woods, and what a pleasure it is to be in the forest once more! The earlier buds are swelling perceptibly— those of the scarlet maple and elm flowers on the hills, with the sallows and alders near the streams. We were struck more than usual with the mosses and lichens, and the coloring of the bark of the different trees; some of the chestnuts, and birches, and maples show twenty different shades, through grays and greens, from a dull white to blackish brown. These can scarcely vary much with the seasons, but they attract the eye more just now from the fact that in winter we are seldom in the woods; and at this moment, before the leaves are out, there is more light falling on the limbs and trunks than in summer. The ground mosses are not yet entirely revived; some of the prettiest varieties feel the frost sensibly, and have not yet regained all their coloring.

The little evergreen plants throw a faint tinge of verdure over the dead leaves which strew the forest; in some spots, there is quite a patch of them, but in other places they scarcely show at all. We have many in our woods, all pleasant little plants; their glossy leaves have generally a healthy character, and most of them bear pretty and fragrant blossoms at different seasons. Some ferns have been preserved, as usual, under the snow; though they are sensitive to the frost, yet in favorable spots they seem to escape until the snow falls and shields them, preserving them through the winter in a sort of half evergreen state, like some other garden and field plants. This year there are more of these fern leaves than usual, and they are pleasing, though flattened to the ground by the snow which has been weighing them down.

Nothing like a flower in all the wide woods. But the ground laurel is in bud and will blossom before long; we raked up the dead leaves to look for it, and some of the buds are very large and promising.

The robins, and sparrows, and blue-birds were singing very sweetly as we came home toward evening; there are many more now in the village than in the woods. The wheat is looking green; the other fields are still brown. Every day the lake grows more dull and gloomy.

Tuesday, 4th.—The frogs were heard last night for the first time this season.

Wednesday, 5th.—First seed sown in the garden to-day; peas, beets, onions, &c., &c.

Friday, 7th.—Bright sun, but cool air, which keeps back the swelling buds; and if these come out too soon they are in great danger of being injured by frost. The ice is still in the lake, and knowing ones say we never have warm weather until the waters are open. There is no current in our lake, or so little at least, it is scarcely perceptible; not enough to carry the ice off, and it melts slowly away. Heavy rains are a great help in getting rid of it, and after an opening is once made in the weak crust, a high wind will work upon it like magic, dashing it into fragments, and piling it on the shores, when it vanishes in a very short time. We have known the lake well covered, and men walking upon the ice at two o'clock, when at four on the same day—thanks to a high wind—the waters were entirely free. For some days now the ice has been lying quite detached from the shores, looking all the more unsightly for the narrow border of clear blue water encircling the gloomy island.

Explored a sunny bank in the woods, with the hope of finding a stray ground laurel, but we saw only the buds. Berries were very plenty; it was a perfect bed of the squaw-vine and partridge berry. Stout young pines threw their branches over the bank, and the warm afternoon sun pouring upon trees and plants, brought out strongly the aromatic odors of both; the air was highly scented with this fresh, wild perfume of the forest. A wood of evergreens is generally fragrant; our own pines and cedars are highly so; even the fallen pine leaves preserve their peculiar odor for some time. There is an ancient allusion to the fragrance of the cedar of Lebanon, in the last chapter of the prophet Hosea, who lived in the eighth century before the Christian era; speaking of the mercies God had in store for his people, he says, "I will be as the dew unto Israel; he shall grow as the lily, and cast forth his roots as Lebanon. His branches shall spread, and his beauty shall be as the olive-tree, and his smell as Lebanon."

The little partridge plant is also very aromatic. Like the orange-tree, this humble plant bears fruit and flowers together; its white cups hanging side by side with the coral berries through the mild weather, from early in May to the sharpest frosts in October. It is true these plants grow in groups, and, although side by side, fruit and flower may belong to different stems; but we have seen the berries and fresh blossoms on the same stalk. There is no period of the year when you may not find the berries, but they are in season late in autumn and in the succeeding spring. The snow under which they lie for months ripens them, though they are perhaps more spicy in the autumn. Their form when perfect is remarkable for a fruit; it has five sharp drooping points at the apex, and within these lies, as it were, a second smaller rose-colored berry, containing the tiny seed; they are seldom found in this mature state until a year old, and it is in June that the berries break open and drop the seed. The birds are very fond of this berry, and some eat the spicy little seeds while they reject the fleshy part. A pair of Florida nonpareils, kept in a cage in the village, used to delight in these.

The squaw-vine, with its long creeping branches, is a constant companion of the partridge berry the year round, common in all the woods. Its pretty rounded leaflets are regularly strung in pairs on thread-like vines, often a yard or more in length, with here and there a large red berry in their midst; these last are edible, though insipid. The flowers are slender delicate pink bells, pale without, deep rose-color within; they are very fragrant, and oddly enough the two blossoms form but one large berry, the fruit being marked with a double face, as it were, bearing the remains of the two calices.

It would seem that among our evergreen plants a larger proportion are fragrant than among their deciduous companions; it cannot, however, be the strength of the plant which gives it this additional charm, for what is so sweet as the mignionette, or the European violet, both fragile plants?

Saturday, 8th.—Delightful day. A white-breasted nut-hatch among the trees on the lawn; these active, amusing birds are resident in the State, but one cannot vouch for their remaining all winter among our hills, as we have never yet observed them in cold weather. It is not a very common bird here, but may possibly be found in the woods by those who look for it through the year. We were amused by watching our little visitor this morning; he never touched the spray, always alighting on the trunk, or on a principal limb, running nimbly up some distance, and then flying off to another in ceaseless movement, without a moment's intermission. This bird has other peculiar habits. He sleeps with his head downwards, and he is said to have one quality rare among his race; he is a curious little rogue, and seems desirous of observing your own odd ways, while you are watching his; then, he is a remarkably good husband, taking a vast deal of pains to feed and amuse his wife, and listening to all her remarks and observations in the most meritorious manner. For several days we have observed this nut-hatch running over the same trees, probably in search of some particular insect, or eggs, just now in season for them.

Sunday, 9th.—Six o'clock, P.M.—The lake has been opening all day. The ice began to break up early in the morning; between the time of going to church and returning, we found great changes; and now, so far as the eye can reach, the blue waters are once more quite free. The day has been cool; wind from the north-west.

Monday, 10th.—Lovely weather; air warm and soft. The open lake very beautiful. A decided green tinge rising upon the earth; the wheat-fields are always the first to show the pleasant change as they revive after the severe winter frosts; then the grass begins to color in the orchards, about the roots of the apple-trees, and patches brighten in sunny sheltered spots, along the roadsides, and about the springs. This year, the first grass that turned green within view, was beneath a tuft of young locusts, and it now continues some shades brighter than all about it, though for what reason one cannot say. Possibly it may be owing to the fact that the locust leaves decay soon after falling, and thus nourish the grass; all traces of them soon disappear; this is also the case with the foliage of the apple, while that of many other trees lies about the roots for months, or is blown away by the winds. The cattle, both cows and horses, seem partial to the grass beneath the locusts; it is amusing to watch them make their way in and out among a grove of young locusts armed with thorns; they don't like these at all, but still the grass tempts them in, and after feeding there, you may see them backing very carefully out again. Some of the trees have a touch of life upon their branches, though no green is yet perceptible; but the bark on the young twigs looks glossy, and the spray thickens with the swelling buds; the elm and soft maple flowers, the catkins of the alder and poplars, and the downy heads of some of the sallow tribe are budding.

Charming walk. Went out with the hope of finding some flowers, but were unsuccessful; none of the buds were open enough to show the coloring of a blossom. Saw two butterflies on the highway—a brown, and a black and yellow. The cedar birds have come; they winter in the State, but never, I believe, among our hills. Although disappointed in our search for flowers, the view of the lake was enjoyment enough for one day; standing on the hill-side within the woods, we looked down beneath an archway of green branches, and between noble living columns of pine and hemlock, upon the blue waters below, as though we were gazing at them through the elaborate mouldings of a great Gothic window—a fine frame for any picture. Several boats were moving about, and there was a sparkling ripple playing in the sunshine, as though the waters enjoyed their freedom.

Tuesday, 11th.—Coming in from a walk this afternoon, we found a beautiful oriole perched upon the topmost bough of a locust on the lawn; no doubt he had just alighted after his journey, for they travel singly and by day, the males appearing first. The new comers among the birds often perch in that way, with an observing look, on their first arrival. It is early for orioles, but we gave our guest a hearty welcome, with an invitation to build near the house; we seldom fail to have one of their hanging nests on our narrow lawn, and some years two families have built here. Our visitor looked brilliantly handsome, as he sat high on the leafless tree, in his coat of golden red and black; but in spite of their fanciful costume, the orioles are just as well behaved as the robins—harmless, innocent birds, bearing an excellent character. We all know how industrious and skilful they are in building; both work together at weaving the intricate nest, though the wife is the most diligent. They are particularly affectionate to their young; if any accident befalls the brood, they grieve so earnestly that they actually forget to eat, returning repeatedly to the spoiled nest, as if in hopes of yet finding some one of their little flock. Their voices are remarkably deep and clear, but they have few notes; those few they will sometimes vary, however, by imitating their neighbors, betraying an inclination to mimicry. One taste they share in common with the humming-bird, and some others; they like flowers, the apple blossoms especially, feeding on them as long as they last, and even commencing their feast before the buds are well open. From the moment they arrive, you see them running about the apple branches, as if already on the watch, and so long as the trees are in bloom, you may hear their full, clear voices in the orchards at most hours of the day. Probably they like other flowers also, since the apple-trees are not indigenous here, and they must have begun to feed upon some native blossoms of the forest; they are occasionally seen in the wild cherry-trees, and are said to be partial to the tulip-trees also; but these last do not grow in our neighborhood. Mr. Wilson says the Baltimore oriole is not found in the pine countries, and yet they are common birds here—regular members of our summer flock; and we have remarked they are very often seen and heard among the pines of the church-yard; it is quite a favorite haunt of theirs.

The orchard oriole, a much plainer bird, is a stranger here, though common at no great distance. If they visit us at all, it must be rarely; we have never yet seen them about the lake.

Wednesday, 12th.—On one of the hills of Highborough, several miles from the village, there is a point where, almost every spring, a lingering snow-bank is seen long after the country generally looks pleasant and life-like. Some years it lies there in spite of warm rains, and south winds and sun-shine, until after the first flowers and butterflies have appeared, while other seasons it goes much earlier. Time gives greater consistency and powers of endurance to ice and snow, just as a cold heart grows more obdurate with every fruitless attempt to soften its fountains; old snow in particular, wears away very slowly—as slowly as an old prejudice! This handful of ice lying so late on Snow-Patch Hill, would doubtless prove, in a colder region, or among higher hills, the commencement of a glacier, for it is precisely on this principle that glaciers are formed and continue to extend until they stretch at last into the flowery meadows, as in Switzerland, where you find straw-berries and ice in the same field. Let a snow-bank harden into ice by suc-cessive thaws and frosts, pass through one summer, and the next year it will be more than doubled in bulk, continuing to increase in size, and conse-quently in strength, until it bids defiance to the greatest heats of summer. It is in this way, that from the higher peaks of the Alps and Andes, covered with these vast ice mantles, five thousand years old, glaciers stretch far down into the region of grass and flowers, increasing rather than diminishing every year, since what is lost in summer seldom equals what is added in winter.

Thursday, 13th.—A solitary goldfinch on the lawn. They winter about New York, but seldom return here in large numbers before the 1st of May.

A brown creeper has been running over the locusts on the lawn for sev-eral days; it is unusual to see them in the village, but this bird remained so long that his identity was clearly settled. The little fellow continued for an hour or more among the same trees visited previously by the nut-hatch, and during that time he was not still a second. Always alighting on the trunk near the roots, he ascended to the top; then taking flight, alighted at the roots of the next, repeating again and again the same evolutions with untiring rapidity. If he found the insects he was in search of, he must have swallowed them without much ceremony, for he never seemed to pause for the purpose of eating. Probably, like the nut-hatches, these birds neglect the smaller limbs of a tree because their prey is not found there.

Friday, 14th.—Rainy morning. Passing through one of the village streets this afternoon, we saw a robin's nest in a very low and exposed position. The honest creatures must have great confidence in their neighbors, which, it is to be hoped, will not be abused. It was in the corner of an out-building facing the street, and so near the side-walk, that it looked as though one could shake hands with the inmates across the paling. It was entirely unscreened; a stray branch of a neighboring locust projected, indeed, above it; but if the robins expect the foliage to shelter them, at this early day, they have made a sad miscalculation. The mother bird was on the nest as we passed, sitting, of course; she slowly moved her large brown eyes toward us as we stopped to watch her, but without the least expression of fear;—indeed, she must see the village people coming and going all day long, as she sits there on her nest.

What a very remarkable instinct is that of a sitting bird. By nature the winged creatures are full of life and activity, apparently needing little repose, flitting the livelong day through the fields and gardens, seldom pausing except to feed, to dress their feathers, or to sing;—abroad, many of them, before dawn, and still passing to and fro across the darkening sky of the latest twilight;—capable also, when necessary, of a prolonged flight which stretches across seas and continents. And yet there is not one of these little winged mothers but what will patiently sit, for hour after hour, day after day, upon her unhatched brood, warming them with her breast—carefully turning them—that all may share the heat equally, and so fearful lest they should be chilled, that she will rather suffer hunger herself than leave them long exposed. That it is no unusual drowsiness which comes over them at this time, rendering the duty more easy, is evident, for you seldom find them sleeping; their bright eyes are usually open, and they look, indeed, quite thoughtful, as though already reflecting about their little family. The male among some tribes occasionally relieves his mate by taking her place awhile, and among all varieties he exerts himself to bring her food, and to sing for her amusement. But altogether, this voluntary imprisonment of those busy, lively creatures is a striking instance of that generous enduring patience which is a noble attribute of parental affection.

There are many instances in which a temporary change of habit, or of character, as it were, is produced by the same powerful feeling, where the careless become watchful, the timid bold, the weak strong, under its influence. The eagle, the chief among his race, is a striking instance of this when he lowers his lordly wings to bear a burden in behalf of his young. This peculiar tenderness of the eagle, in bearing its young on the back, is entirely opposed to the common habits of birds, who almost invariably carry their less precious burdens, their food, or the materials for their nests in their bills, or their claws. Whether the eagles in this part of the world resort to the same practice one cannot say; that the Eastern eagle does so we feel assured, for it is implied in two striking passages of Holy Scripture. The Almighty Jehovah who has vouchsafed to represent himself to man in the paternal character, as conveying to our minds the strongest idea of his compassionate providence, when addressing his people of old, was pleased to employ this image: "Ye have seen what I did to the Egyptians, and how I bear you on eagles' wings, and brought you unto myself." And, again, the inspired Prophet, when singing the salvation of Israel through the merciful care of the Almighty, says: "As an eagle stirreth up her nest, fluttereth over her young, spreadeth abroad her wings, taketh them, beareth them on her wings, so the Lord alone did lead him"–as we read in the Song of Moses, in Deuteronomy.

Saturday, 15th.–Cool rain, at intervals, for the last day or two; pleasant again this afternoon. Walked in the woods looking for flowers; went some distance in vain, but at last near the summit of the hill we found a bunch of fresh ground laurel, the first wild blossoms of the year to us, and prized accordingly; there were many more in full bud, but no other open.

Since we were last in the woods, the squirrel-cups (*hepaticus*) have sprung up; their modest little lilac cups, in half-open buds, are hanging singly here and there over the dead leaves, and very pretty they are in this stage of their short life; they have a timid, modest look, hanging leafless from their downy stalks, as if half afraid, half ashamed of being alone in the wide woods; for their companion, the ground laurel, remains closely wrapped in the withered leaves. It cannot be said that either of these plants is fairly in bloom; they are only opening–a slow process with the arbutus, but a rapid one with the hepatica. The mosses are in great beauty now; several varieties are in flower, and exquisitely delicate; the dark brownish moss, with its white-capped flowers and tiny red stalk, and a dainty companion of light green, with a blossom of the same tint, are in perfection. Wherever we went, they were so abundant, and so beautiful in their spring freshness, as to delight the eye.

Fresh grass butter from the farm to-day.

Monday, 17th.—A few white-bellied swallows sailing over the village yesterday; but one swallow does not make a summer, nor can a dozen either; we must expect cool weather yet. These little birds are in favor in the New York markets, after they have fattened themselves upon the whortleberries in the autumn; for unlike their kindred tribes of the swallow and martin race, who live wholly, it is believed, on insects, these are berry-eaters also. They are said to be peculiar to this continent.

Tuesday, 18th.—The fishing-lights enliven the lake now, of an evening, and they are often seen well into the night. They are spearing pickerel, a good fish, though inferior to some others in our lake. Formerly, there were no pickerel here, but some years since they were introduced from a smaller sheet of water, ten or twelve miles to the westward, and now they have become so abundant that they are the most common fish we have—taken at all seasons and in various ways. They are caught in summer, by "trolling," a long line being thrown out and drawn in from the stern by the fisherman, who stands, while an oarsman rows the boat quietly along; during the warm weather, one may see at almost any hour of the morning or afternoon, some fishing skiff passing slowly to and fro in this way, one man at the oars, one at the line, trolling for pickerel. In the evening, they carry on the sport with lights in the bows of the boats, to attract the fish; they are often speared in this way, and we have heard of their being shot with a pistol, which seems what a sailor might call a "lubberly" way of attacking fish—certainly, honest Jack would not have approved of this unfishermanlike proceeding. In the winter, the pickerel are also caught through holes cut here and there in the ice—lines with baited hooks being secured to the ice and left there—the fisherman returning from time to time to see what success his snares have had. The boys call these contrivances "tip-ups," from the bit of stick to which the line is attached, falling over when the fish bite. The largest pickerel caught here, are said to weigh about six pounds.

Wednesday, 19th.—The great spring house-cleaning going on in the village just now, and a formidable time it is in most families, second only as regards discomfort, to the troubles of moving. Scarce an object about a house seems in its proper place—topsy-turvy is the order of the day; curtains and carpets are seen hanging out of doors, windows are sashless, beds are found in passages, chairs are upside down, the ceiling is in possession of the whitewash

brush, and the mop "has the floor," as reporters say of Hon. M.C.'s. Meanwhile, the cleaners, relentless as Furies, pursue the family from room to
room, until the last stronghold is invaded, and the very cats and dogs look
wretched. Singular as it may appear, there are some active spirits in the
country—women spirits, of course—who enjoy house-cleaning: who confess
that they enjoy it. But then there are men who enjoy an election, and it was
settled ages ago that there is no arguing upon tastes. Most sensible people
would be disposed to look upon both house-cleaning and elections, as among
the necessary evils of life—far enough from its enjoyments. One would like
to know from which ancestral nation the good people of this country inherit
this periodical cleaning propensity; probably it came from the Dutch, for
they are the most noted scourers in the Old World, though it is difficult to
believe that such a sober, quiet race as the Hollanders, could have carried
on the work with the same restlessness as our own housewives. We are
said to have taken the custom of moving on May-day, from our Dutch forefathers, and I believe there is no doubt of that fact; but then we may rest
assured that a whole town would not set about moving the same day in Holland. In that sensible, prudent land, not more, perhaps, than a dozen house-
holders at a time, are expected to sacrifice comfort and furniture by such a
step. On the Zuyder Zee, it probably takes a family at least a year to make
up their minds to move, and a year more to choose a new dwelling. But see
what this custom has become under the influence of *go-aheadism!* May-day,
for ages associated with rhymes, sweet blossoms, gayety, and kindly feeling,
has become the most anti-poetical, dirty, dusty, unfragrant, worrying, scolding day in the year to the Manhattanese. So it is with this cleaning process.
Most civilized people clean their dwellings: many nations are as neat as ourselves; some much neater than we are; but few, indeed, make such a fuss
about these necessary labors; they contrive to manage matters more quietly.
Even among ourselves, some patriotic women, deserving well of their country, have made great efforts to effect a change in this respect, within their
own sphere, at least; but alas! in each instance they have, we believe, suc-
cumbed at length to general custom, a tyrant that few have the courage to
face, even in a good cause.

    It must be confessed, however, that after the great turmoil is over—when
the week, or fortnight, or three weeks of scrubbing, scouring, drenching are
passed, there is a moment of delightful repose in a family; there is a refreshing consciousness that all is sweet and clean from garret to cellar; there is a
purity in the household atmosphere which is very agreeable. As you go
about the neighborhood, the same order and cleanly freshness meet you as

you cross every threshold. This is very pleasant, but it is a pity that it should be purchased at the cost of so much previous confusion—so many petty annoyances.

Friday, 21st.—Fresh lettuce from the hot-beds.

Saturday, 22d.—The sky cloudy, with April showers, but we ventured to take a short walk. There were never more brown flowers on the elms; it is unusual to see them in such very great abundance; the trees are thickly clothed with them. The soft maple is also showing its crimson blossoms. The grass is growing beautifully; there is a perceptible difference from day to day, and it is pleasant to note how the cattle enjoy the fresh, tender herbage of the pastures after the dry fodder of the barn-yard. We followed the Green Brook through the fields into the woods; on its banks gathered some pretty pink bells of the spring beauty.

The barn-swallows have made their appearance, and the flocks of the white-billed swallows seem to have increased by new arrivals.

Monday, 24th.—The young leaves on the lilacs, currants, and some early roses and honeysuckles, are springing—the first branches to look green. In the woods the young violet and strawberry leaves look fresh and tender among the withered herbage, and the older evergreens.

Tuesday, 25th.—Charming day. Went into the woods this afternoon to gather a harvest of trailing arbutus. It takes many to make a pretty bunch, for the leaves are large and often in the way, so that one is obliged to use the scissors freely when making them into a nosegay. The plant stretches its vine-like, woody branches far and wide over the hill-sides in thick patches; its large, strong, rounded leaves grow in close tufts—small and large together—and, although tough in texture, they are often defective in rusty spots, especially the old leaves which have been lying under the snow; in summer, they are brighter and more perfect. The flowers grow in clusters at the end of the stems, from two to a dozen, or fifteen in a bunch, pink or white, larger or smaller, varying in size, number, and tint; they are not very much unlike the blossom of a hyacinth, though scarcely so large, and not curled at the edges. They are very fragrant; not only sweet, but with a wild freshness in the perfume, which is very agreeable. Our search began in an old pine grove, on the skirts of the village, but we found nothing in flower there; the soil is good, and there is no want of young plants of various kinds, which will blossom by-and-bye, but at present there are no flowers to be gathered there. In the adjoining wood, we had no better luck; it is a dense growth of young hemlocks and pines, where nothing else thrives—much the darkest and gloomiest about the village; the sunshine never seems to penetrate the shade enough to warm the earth, which is covered with rusty pine leaves. We climbed to higher ground, but no arbutus was there; still we persevered, and at last, near the top of the hill, some remarkably fine clusters were discovered, and from that moment they were found in abundance. They seem often to open first on the hill-tops, but they are in full bloom now in many places.

There is more than usual interest in gathering these flowers, from their peculiar habits. One may easily pass over ground where they abound without observing them, unless one knows their tricks of old; for they often play hide and go seek with you, crouching about old stones, and under dead leaves, and among mosses. But here and there you may see a pretty fresh cluster peeping out from among last year's withered herbage, as though it bloomed from lifeless stalks; and when you stoop to gather it, raking away the dead leaves, you find a dozen bunches in near neighborhood under the faded covering. Perhaps half these sweet flowers lie closely shrouded in this way under the fallen foliage of the forest. After coming at length to the right ground, this afternoon, we were very successful; they are in full season, and never were finer–large and very fragrant. Several bunches of those we gathered, were growing so prettily, that it seemed a pity to pull them; some showing their fragrant heads among rich mosses, while others were hooded in large withered leaves of the oak, chestnut, and maple. The sun had dropped low while we were busy at our pleasant task, but we lingered a moment to look down upon the village as it lay in the valley below, the picture of cheerful quiet, and upon the lake, with sweet evening tints playing over the water; and then descending the hill at a quick pace, we succeeded in reaching the village before the sun had quite set.

Not a single squirrel-cup was seen on our path to-day, yet they abound in many places.

Wednesday, 26th.–The young plants in the gardens are beginning to show in those beds which were made early; peas, beets, &c., &c. The good people of the village are many of them busy now with their gardens, and pleasant, cheerful work it is. From the time of Adam down, it has always looked well to see man, or woman either, working in a garden. In a village, one sees the task going on regularly in all the little neighborhood, at the same moment. We thought of poor —— ——, who told his worthy mother he should like to live to see them make garden once more in the village–poor fellow, he has been in his grave these five weeks.

Thursday, 27th.–Long, pleasant walk. A humming-bird flew past us, the first we had seen.

Followed an old wood road for some distance. Squirrel-cups in abundance; though very regular in other respects, these little flowers are not all colored alike: some are white, others pink, lilac, or grayish blue. They are a nice little flower, with a modest, unobtrusive air, which is very engaging. When they first appear, they shoot up singly, each blossom alone on its downy stalk; but now they have gained courage, standing in little groups, gleaming gayly above the withered foliage. Their young downy leaves do not show yet, although a few of last year's growth are found, in a half-evergreen state. One often sees these flowers at the foot of trees, growing on their roots, as it were; and perhaps it is this position, which, added to their downy, furred leaves and stems, has given them the name of squirrel-cups—a prettier name, certainly, for a wood flower, than liverwort, or its Latin version, hepatica.

The small yellow violets are springing up; they also show their golden heads before their leaves are out. It seems singular that the flower, which is the most precious and delicate part of the plant, should ever be earlier than the leaf, yet it is the case with many plants, great and small; among trees it is very common. Doubtless there is a good reason for it, which one would like to know, as the learned in such matters have probably found it out.

The arbutus is now open everywhere in the woods and groves. How pleasant it is to meet the same flowers year after year! If the blossoms were liable to change—if they were to become capricious and irregular—they might excite more surprise, more curiosity, but we should love them less; they might be just as bright, and gay, and fragrant under other forms, but they would not be the violets, and squirrel-cups, and ground laurels we loved last year. Whatever your roving fancies may say, there is a virtue in constancy which has a reward above all that fickle change can bestow, giving strength and purity to every affection of life, and even throwing additional grace about the flowers which bloom in our native fields. We admire the strange and brilliant plant of the green-house, but we love most the simple flowers we have loved of old, which have bloomed many a spring, through rain and sunshine, on our native soil.

Radishes from the hot-beds to-day.

Thursday, 27th.—A flock of the rusty black-bird or grakles about the village; they have been roving to and fro several days. We generally see these birds for a short time in autumn and spring, but they do not remain here. They move in flocks, and attract attention whenever they are in the neighborhood, by perching together on some tree. Half those now here are brown; both the females and the younger males being of this color: there is a great difference, also, between the males and females, as regards size.

All kinds of black-birds are rare here; they are said to have been very numerous indeed at the settlement of the country, but have very much diminished in numbers of late years. And yet, they are still very common in some of the oldest parts of the country, where they are a very great annoyance to the farmers. These rusty grakles are northern birds; the common blackbird, occasionally seen here in small parties, comes from the south. The red wing black-bird or starling, we have never seen in this county; it may possibly be found here, but certainly is not so common as elsewhere. Nor is the cow-bunting often seen with us; and as all these birds are more or less gregarious, they soon attract attention wherever they appear. They are arrant corn thieves, all of them. It is odd, that although differing in many respects, these birds of black plumage, with the crow at their head, have an especial partiality for the maize.

Saturday, 29th.–The tamaracks are putting forth their bluish green leaves, the lightest in tint of all their tribe; the young cones are also coming out, reminding one somewhat of small strawberries by their color and form, but they soon become decidedly purple, then green, and at last brown. The tamarack is very common about the marshy grounds of this county, attaining its full height in our neighborhood. There are many planted in the village, and in summer they are a very pleasant tree, though inferior to the European larch. Some individuals become diseased and crooked–a great fault in a tree, whose outline is marked by nature with so much regularity–though the same capricious broken line often becomes a beauty in wood of a naturally free and careless growth. This defect is much more common among transplanted tamaracks, than with those you find growing wild in the low grounds.

May 1st.–Cloudy sky; showery; not so bright as becomes May-day. Nevertheless, we managed to seize the right moment for a walk, with only a little sprinkling at the close. It would not do to go into the woods, so we were obliged to be satisfied with following the highway. By the rails of a meadow fence, we found a fine border of the white puccoon; these flowers, with their large, pure white petals, look beautifully on the plant, but they soon fall to pieces after being gathered, and the juice in their stalks stains one's hands badly. We gathered a few, however, by way of doing our Maying, adding to them some violets scattered along the road-side, and a bunch of the golden flowers of the marsh marigold, which enticed us off the road into a low, boggy spot, by their bright blossoms; a handsome flower, this– the country people call it cowslip, though differing entirely from the true plant of that name.

The golden willows are coming into leaf. The weeping willow is not seen here, our winters are too severe for it. Some persons think, that by watching a young tree carefully, and giving it several years to take root, without being discouraged by its slow growth, it would in time become acclimated; the experiment is now going on, but its success is very doubtful. At present, there is no weeping willow within some distance of us, excepting a couple of young nurslings in gardens of the village. Not that we are too far north for this tree, since it is found, even on this continent, in a higher latitude than our own, which is 42° 50′; but the elevation of this highland valley above the sea, usually called 1200 feet, gives us a cooler climate than we should otherwise have. The native willows of America are numerous, but they are all small trees, many mere bushes; the tallest in our own neighborhood, are about five-and-twenty feet high. The golden willow of Europe, however, is common here, and thrives very well, attaining its full size; some of these in the village are very handsome trees; they are now just putting out their first tender green leaflets, which, as they grow larger, take a much graver color.

When we read of those willows of Babylon, in whose shade the children of Israel sat down and wept, thousands of years ago, we naturally think of the weeping willow which we all know to be an Asiatic tree. But the other day, while reading an observation of a celebrated Eastern traveller, the idea suggested itself, that this common impression might possibly be erroneous. The present desolation of the country about Babylon is well known; the whole region, once so fertile, appears now to be little better than a desert, stripped alike of its people, its buildings, and its vegetation, all of which made, in former times, its surpassing glory and its wealth. If at one moment of a brief spring, grass and flowers are found upon those shapeless ruins, a scorching sun soon blasts their beauty; as for trees, these are so few that they scarcely appear in the general view, though, on nearer observation, some are found here and there. One of these, described by Mr. Rich, as an evergreen, like the lignum-vitæ, is so old that the Arabs say it dates with the ruins on which it stands, and it is thought that it may very possibly be a descendant of one of the same species in the hanging gardens of Nebuchadnezzar, which are supposed to have occupied the same site. Immediately on the banks of the river, there is also said to be a fringe of jungle, and here willows are growing; but they are not described as the weeping willow. Speaking of the Euphrates, Sir Robert Ker Porter says: "Its banks were hoary with reeds, and the *gray ozier willows* were yet there, on which the captives of Israel hung up their harps." Now it is scarcely probable that a writer of the merit of Sir R. Porter, familiar with the weeping willow, as he must have been, would describe that beautiful tree as a *gray ozier*. Several other travellers also speak of the fringe of jungle on the Euphrates, and the *ozier* growing there. Not one of several we have been looking over, mentions the noble weeping willow; on the contrary, the impression is generally left that the trees are insignificant in size, and of an inferior variety. If such be really the case, then, and the term *gray ozier* be correct—if willows are growing to-day where willows are known to have stood ages since—is it not natural to suppose that both belonged to the same species? Such is the view Sir R. Porter has taken, whatever variety the trees may belong to. He supposes them to be the same which shaded the captives of Israel. Altogether, after reading the passage of this distinguished traveller, one feels some misgivings lest the claim of the weeping willow, in connection with the 137th Psalm, prove unfounded. One would like to see the proofs clearly made out in behalf of the weeping willow. The assertion, that it is the tree of the Psalmist is universally made, but we have never yet seen a full and complete account of the grounds for this opinion; and, so far as we can discover, no such statement has yet been published. Probably, however, the question may be very easily settled by those who have learning and books at command.

Oziers are incidentally made mention of by very ancient authors in connection with Babylon. The framework of the rude boats, described by Herodotus, was of ozier. This at least is the word given in the translation, and many modern travellers assure us that oziers are now applied to the same purpose by the boatmen of Mesopotamia. Another evidence that this kind of willow was formerly common on that ground, is found in the ruins themselves. M. Beauchamp, in the account of his investigations of the remains of Babylon, during the last century, says: "The bricks are cemented with bitumen. Occasionally layers of oziers in bitumen are found." Other travellers speak of reeds also in the bitumen; so that the plant, and the tree, named by Sir R. Porter, as now found on the banks of the Euphrates—the ozier and the reed—are thus proved, by the most clear and positive evidence, to have also existed there in ancient times.

Two versions of the 137th Psalm have been given to the Christian world by the Church of England, and they differ in some minor points of the translations. That in the Psalter of the Prayer Book was one of the earliest works of the Reformation, taken from the Septuagint, in the time of Archbishop Cranmer. It does not name the tree on which the Israelites hung their harps. "By the waters of Babylon we sat and wept when we remembered thee, O Sion. As for our harps, we hanged them up upon the *trees* that are therein. For they that led us away captive required of us then a song and melody in our heaviness. Sing us one of the songs of Sion." The translation in the Holy Bible, made later, from the original, approaches still nearer to the simple dignity of the Hebrew: "By the waters of Babylon there we sat down, yea, we wept when we remembered Zion. We hanged our harps upon the *willows* in the midst thereof. For there, they that carried us away captive required of us a song; and they that wasted us required of us mirth, saying, Sing us one of the songs of Zion."

The two translations of this noble Psalm, also differ slightly in their last verses. In the Prayer Book, these verses stand as follows: "O, daughter of Babylon, wasted with misery, yea, happy shall he be that rewardeth thee, as thou hast served us. Blessed shall he be that taketh thy children and dasheth them against the stones." The translation of the Holy Bible, by closer adherence to the original, in a single phrase becomes more directly prophetic in character: "O, daughter of Babylon, *who art to be destroyed (or wasted)*, happy shall he be that rewardeth thee, as thou hast served us. Happy shall he be that taketh and dasheth thy little ones against the stones."

To the utmost has this fearful prophecy been fulfilled: Babylon has been destroyed; the cruelties with which she visited Jerusalem were repaid her in full by the awful justice of the Almighty, and the happy fame of her Persian conqueror has long been firmly fixed in history. What sublime, prophetic power in those simple words—"who art to be destroyed"—when addressed by the weeping captive to the mighty city, then in the height of her power and her pride! That destruction has long since been complete; Babylon is wasted indeed; and we learn with interest from the traveller, that beside her shapeless ruins, stand the "gray ozier willows, on which the captives of Israel hung up their harps;" mute and humble witnesses of the surrounding desolation.

Wednesday, 3d.—Pleasant walk on the open hill-side. Sweet, quiet day; if the leaves were out, they would not stir, for the winds are all asleep. Walking over pasture-ground, we did not find many flowers: only a few violets here and there, and some young strawberry flowers, the first fruit-bearing blossom of the year. The fern is coming up, its woolly heads just appearing above ground, the broad frond closely rolled within; presently the down will grow darker, and the leaves begin to uncurl. The humming-birds, and some of the many warblers, use the wool of the young fern-stalks to line their nests.

The valley looked pleasantly from the hill-side this afternoon; the wheat-fields are now very brilliant in their verdure, some of a golden green, others of a deeper shade. Nearly half the fields are ploughed this season, and the farms look like new-made gardens. As we stood on the quiet, open down, a sweet song, from a solitary bird, broke the stillness charmingly: it came from the edge of a bare wood above, but we could not see the little singer.

The beech-bushes have a comical look at this season, growing many together, and huddling their dead leaves so tenaciously about their lower branches, they put one in mind of a flock of bantam chickens, with well feathered legs; one would think these warm May-days, they would be glad to throw off their winter furbelows.

Thursday, 4th.—Potatoes planted in the garden to-day. First mess of asparagus. Also, ice at table.

The chimney-swallows have come in their usual large numbers, and our summer flock of swallows is now complete. Of the six more common varieties of this bird found in North America,[1] we have four in our neighborhood, and the others are also found within a short distance of us.

The white-bellied swallows came first to the village this year; they are generally supposed to be rather later than the barn-swallows. This pretty bird has been confounded with the European martin; but it is peculiar to America, and confined, it would seem, to our part of the continent, for their summer flight reaches to the fur countries, and they winter in Louisiana. It is said to resemble the water-martin of Europe in many of its habits, being partial to the water, often perching and roosting on the sedges; they are very numerous on the coast of Long Island, but they are also very common in this inland county. Occasionally, you see them on the branches of trees, which is not usual with others of their tribe.

The barn-swallow resembles, in many respects, the European chimney-swallow; yet it is, in fact, a different variety—entirely American. Where the European bird is white, ours is bright chestnut. They are one of the most numerous birds we have; scarcely a barn in the country is without them; they seldom choose any other building for their home. They are very busy, cheerful, happy tempered creatures, remarkably peaceable in their disposition, friendly to each other, and to man also. Though living so many together, it is remarkable that they do not quarrel, showing what may be done in this way by sensible birds, though very sensible men and women seem, too often, to feel no scruples about quarrelling themselves, or helping their neighbors to do so. They are often seen at rest on the barn roofs, and just before leaving us for a warmer climate, they never fail to collect out of doors on the fences and plants. They go as far north as the sources of the Mississippi, and winter far beyond our southern boundary.

The chimney-swallow is also wholly American. The European bird, which builds in chimneys, is very different in many respects, placing its nest frequently in other situations, while our own is never known, under any circumstances, to build elsewhere. Before the country was civilized, they lived in hollow trees; but now, with a unanimity in their plans which is very striking, they have entirely deserted the forest, and taken up their abode in our chimneys. They still use twigs, however, for their nests, showing that they were originally a forest bird; while many others, as the robin and the oriole, for instance, gladly avail themselves of any *civilized* materials they find lying about, such as strings, thread, paper, &c., &c. Our chimney swift has no beauty to boast of; it is altogether plain, and almost bat-like in appearance, but, in its way, it is remarkably clever and skilful. It is as good at clinging to a bare wall, or the trunk of a tree, as the woodpecker, its tail being shaped like that of those birds, and used for the same purpose, as a support. The air is their peculiar element; here they play and chase the insects, and feed and sing after their fashion, with an eager, rapid twitter; they have little to do with the earth, and the plants, and the trees, never alighting, except within a chimney. They feed entirely on the wing, supplying their young also, when they are able to fly, in the same manner, and they seem to drink flying as they skim over the water. A cloudy, damp day is their delight, and one often sees them out in the rain. How they provide the twigs for their nests, one would like to know, for they are never observed looking for their materials on the ground, or about the trees;—probably they pick them up as they skim the earth. Their activity is wonderful, for they are on the wing earlier and later than any other of their busy tribe. Often of a summer's evening one sees them pass when it is quite dark—near nine o'clock—and the next morning they will be up, perhaps, at three; they are said, indeed, to feed their young at night, so that they can have but little rest at that season. Some persons shut up their chimneys against them, on account of the noise, which keeps one awake at times; and they have a trick of getting down into rooms through the fire-place, which is troublesome to neat housekeepers; the greatest objection against them, however, is the rubbish they collect in the chimneys. Still one cannot quarrel with them; for their rapid wheeling flight, and eager twitter about the roof of a house, gives it a very cheerful character through the summer. They will not build in a flue that is used for fire, but mind the smoke so little that they go in and out, and put up their nests in an adjoining flue of the same chimney. They remain later than the barn-swallow, go farther north in spring, and winter beyond the limits of our northern continent.

The purple martin is another bird belonging to our Western World, entirely different from the martin of Europe; it is a bird of wide range, however, over this continent, reaching from the Equator to the northern fur countries. The largest of its tribe, it is a very bold, courageous creature, attacking even hawks and eagles when they come into its neighborhood; but it is always very friendly and familiar with man. Mr. Wilson mentions that now only the white man builds his martin-house for these friends of his, but the negroes on the southern plantations put up long canes with some contrivance to invite them to build about their huts; and the Indians also cut off the top branch of a sapling, near their wigwams, and hang a gourd or calabash on the prongs for their convenience. Although these birds are so common in most parts of the country, yet they are comparatively rare with us. Formerly they are said to have been more numerous, but at present so little are they known, that most people will tell you there are none about the village. On making inquiries, we found that many persons had never even heard their name. Bird-nesting boys know nothing of them, while farmers and gardeners, by the half dozen, told us there were no martins about. We stopped before an out-building, the other day, with a martin-house in the gable, and asked if there were any birds in it. "There are no martins in this neighborhood," was the answer, adding that they had been seen some dozen miles off. Again, passing through a barn-yard, we asked a boy if there were any martins there. "Martins?" he inquired, looking puzzled. "No, marm; I never heard tell of such birds hereabouts." The same question was very often asked, and only, in two or three instances, received a different answer; some elderly persons replying that formerly there certainly were martins here. At length, however, we discovered a few, found their abode, and observed them coming and going, and a little later, we saw others on a farm about two miles from the village; still, their numbers must be very small when compared with the other varieties which everybody knows, and which are almost constantly in sight through the warm weather. It is possible that the flock may have been diminished, of late years, by some accidental cause; but such, at least, is the state of things just now.

The pretty little bank-swallow, another very common and numerous tribe, is entirely a stranger here, though found on the banks of lakes and rivers at no great distance; we have seen them, indeed, in large flocks, among the sand-hills near the Susquehannah, just beyond the southern borders of the county. This is the only swallow common to both hemispheres, and it is of this bird that M. de Châteaubriand remarks he had found it everywhere, in all his wanderings over Asia, Africa, Europe, and America.

That the cliff-swallow should also be a stranger here, is not at all remarkable; a few years since, there were none east of the Mississippi. In 1824, a single pair first appeared within the limits of New York, at a tavern near Whitehall, a short distance from Lake Champlain; shortly after Gov. De Witt Clinton introduced them to the world at large by writing a notice of them; they are now rapidly increasing and spreading themselves over the country. The Rocky Mountains seem to have been their great rallying ground; they are found there in great numbers; and as the Prince of Canino observes, they have advanced eastward to meet the white man. These new-comers remain but a short time, about six weeks in June and July, and then disappear again, taking flight for tropical America. They are entirely unknown in Europe, or any part of the Old World. They have more variety in their markings than most swallows.

Friday, 5th.—Fine shower last night, with thunder and lightning; everything growing delightfully. Such days and nights as these, in early spring, the effect produced on vegetation, by electricity and rain together, is really wonderful. M. de Candolle, the great botanist, mentions an instance in which the branches of a grape-vine grew, during a thunder shower, no less than an inch and a quarter in the course of an hour and a half! Really, at that rate, one might almost *see* the plant grow.

The young buds are coming out beautifully; the tufts of scarlet flowers on the soft maples are now daintily tipped with the tender green of the leaf-buds in their midst, and the long green flowers of the sugar maple have come out on many trees; yesterday, there were none to be seen. White blossoms are opening in drooping clusters, also, on the naked branches of the June-berry; this is a tree which adds very much to the gayety of our spring; it is found in every wood, and always covered with long pendulous bunches of flowers, whether a small shrub or a large tree. There is one in the churchyard of great beauty, a tree perhaps five-and-thirty feet in height; and standing among evergreens as it does, it looks beautifully at this season, when covered with its pendant white blossoms. There is a tree in Savoy, called there, the amelanchier, near of kin to this of ours. The poplar, or poppels as the country people call them, are already half-leaved. How rapid is the advance of spring at this moment of her joyous approach! And how beautiful are all the plants in their graceful growth, the humblest herb unfolding its every leaf in beauty, full of purpose and power!

Saw a little blue butterfly on the highway. Gathered a fine bunch of pink ground laurel, unusually large and fragrant, they have quite out-lasted the squirrel-cups, which are withered. Saw a fine maroon moose-flower—its three-leaved blossom as large as a tulip–the darkest and largest of our early spring flowers.

Saturday, 6th.–Warm, soft day. The birds are in an ecstasy. Goldfinches, orioles, and blue-birds enliven the budding trees with their fine voices and gay plumage; wrens and song-sparrows are hopping and singing about the shrubbery; robins and chipping-birds hardly move out of your way on the grass and gravel, and scores of swallows are twittering in the air, more active, more chatty than ever;–all busy, all happy, all at this season more or less musical. Birds who scarcely sing, have a peculiar cry, heard much more clearly and frequently at this season, than any other;–the twittering of the swallows, for instance, and the prolonged chirrup of the chipping-bird, so like that of the locust, when heard from the trees. The little creatures always enjoy a fine day extremely, but with more zest during this their honeymoon, than at any other season. Our summer company have now all arrived, or, rather, our runaways have come back; for it is pleasant to remember that these are really at home here, born and *raised,* as the Kentuckians say, in these groves, and now have come back to build nests of their own among their native branches. The happiest portion of their bird-life is passed with us. Many of those we see flitting about, at present, are doubtless building within sight and sound of our windows; some years we have counted between forty and fifty nests in our own trees, without including a tribe of swallows. Many birds like a village life; they seem to think man is a very good-natured animal, building chimneys and roofs, planting groves, and digging gardens for their especial benefit; only, they wonder not a little, that showing as he does a respectable portion of instinct, he should yet allow those horrid creatures–boys and cats–to run at large in his domain.

Monday, 8th.– On many of the sugar maples the long flowers are hanging in slender green clusters, while on others they have not yet come out; and year after year we find the same difference between various individuals of the same species of maple, more marked, it would seem, among these than with other trees. Some are much in advance of others, and that without any apparent cause–trees of the same age and size growing side by side, varying this way, showing a constitutional difference, like that observed in human beings among members of one family. Frequently the young leaves of the sugar maple are only a day or two behind the flowers; they begin to appear, at least, at that time, but on others, again, they wait until the blossoms are falling. These green flowers hanging in full clusters on long filaments, give a pleasing character to the tree, having the look of foliage at a little distance. Generally they are a pale green, but at times, on some trees, straw-color. The sugar maples, unlike many other flowering trees, do not blossom young; the locusts, amelanchiers, fruit trees generally, &c., &c., blossom when mere shrubs three or four feet high; but the sugar maple and the scarlet maple are good-sized trees before they flower. There are many about the village which are known to be twenty years old, and they have not yet blossomed.

The American maples—the larger sorts, at least—the sugar, the scarlet, and the silver maples, are assuredly very fine trees. A healthful luxuriance of growth marks their character; regular and somewhat rounded in form when allowed to grow in freedom, their branches and trunks are very rarely distorted, having almost invariably an easy upward inclination more or less marked. The bark on younger trees, and upon the limbs of those which are older, is often very beautifully mottled in patches or rings of clear grays, lighter and darker—at times almost as white as that on the delicate birches. The northern side of the branches is usually with us much more speckled than that toward the south. They are also very cleanly, free from troublesome vermin or insects. Few trees have a finer foliage; deep lively green in color, while the leaves are large, of a handsome form, smooth and glossy, and very numerous; for it is a peculiarity of theirs, that they produce every year many small shoots, each well covered with leaves. When bare in winter, one remarks that their fine spray is decidedly thicker than that of many other trees. To these advantages they add their early flowers in spring, and a beautiful brilliancy of coloring in the autumn. The European maple, a different tree entirely, comes into leaf after the elm, and is even later than the ash; but those of this part of the world have the farther merit of being numbered among the earlier trees of the forest.

Nor does the luxuriant beauty of the maple mislead us as to its properties; it is a highly valuable wood. We should be very thankful for its sugar, if that imported from other regions could not be procured; to the Indians it was very precious, one of the very few luxuries known to them. In winter, it ranks with the better sorts of fuel for heat and a cheerful blaze, and the different kinds are employed for very many useful and ornamental purposes. A large amount of furniture of the better sort is made of the various maples. A few years back, maple ranked next to mahogany for these purposes, but lately black walnut has been more in favor. With the exception of the ash-leaved variety, a Western tree, all the American maples are said to be found in this county. The moose-wood,[2] a small tree of graceful, airy growth, and bearing the prettiest flowers of the tribe, to whose young shoots the moose is said to have been so partial; the mountain maple, a shrub growing in thick clumps with an upright flower, the scarlet maple, the silver, the sugar, and the black sugar maples, are all included among our trees. They all, except the shrubby mountain maple, yield a portion of sweet sap, though none is so liberal in the supply as the common sugar maple. The very largest trees of this kind in our neighborhood are said to be about three feet in diameter, and those of forest growth attain to a great height, from sixty to eighty feet; but the common maples about the country are rarely more than eighteen inches in diameter, and forty or fifty feet high.[3] As their wood is usually sound and healthy, they probably attain to the age of the elm, or ash, &c., &c., but we have never heard any accurate calculations on the subject.

Tuesday, 9th.– The lake very beautiful; there is often, at this time of the year, a delicacy and softness in the waters, produced, no doubt, by the atmosphere of a still spring day, which is in beautiful harmony with the season.

A pleasant hour toward evening, pacing to and fro under a mild, cloudy sky, near the bridge; the birds seem to have collected there for our especial amusement, but in reality, were attracted, no doubt, by some insects from the water; it was a greater gathering than we have seen this spring, and several among the party were of more interest than usual. Swallows by scores, chimney, barn, and white-bellied, were sailing about us in ceaseless motion, now passing above, now below the bridge, often so near that we might almost have touched them. A Phœbe-bird sat quietly on a maple branch within a stone's throw, giving us a song ever and anon, as we passed up and down; they have a trick of sitting in that way on the same twig, at no great distance from their nest, and they are much given to build about bridges. Robins were there, of course, they are never out of sight at this season; sparrows were stealing in and out of the bushes, while goldfinches and blue-birds were coming and going. But these were all familiar; it was a couple of little birds fluttering about the blossoms of a red maple, that chiefly attracted our attention, from their novelty; their yellow, and red, and brown markings, and peculiar quick, restless movements among the branches, were new to us. They were half an hour in sight, and several times we stood very near the maples where they were feeding; one of them flew away, but the other remained, coming nearer and nearer, from branch to branch, from tree to tree, until he reached the fence by which we stood. We were very anxious to discover what bird it was, for under such circumstances, it is tantalizing not to be able to settle the question. We supposed, at first, that they were strangers, on their way north, for about this time, many such transient visitors are passing northward, and only loitering here and there by the way. It is not usual, however, for such birds to travel in pairs, and these seemed mated, for after one had flown away down the river, the other showed a strong determination to take the same course, as though there might be the beginning of a nest in that direction. He made a motion toward taking flight, then observing us, stopped; we stood quite still in the walk, the bird sitting on the branch for a minute or more. Then again he made a movement, and took flight in the direction which crossed our path; but, silly little fellow that he was, after flying a yard or two, which brought him immediately before us, where we might easily have struck him with a parasol, his courage failed: he continued fluttering on the spot, or rather lying-to in the air, as a sailor might say, when, awkwardly changing his direction, he flew back to the very branch he had quitted. An unusual manœuvre this, for a bird; and strangely enough, he repeated this proceeding twice, seeming very anxious to follow his companion down the river, and yet dreading to pass so near such formidable creatures as ourselves. Again he took flight, again he paused and fluttered just before us, again returned to the branch he had left. Silly little thing, he might easily have soared far above us, instead of passing so near, or sitting on a branch where we could have killed him a dozen times over, if wickedly inclined; but he behaved so oddly, that had we been either snakes or witches, we should have been accused of fascinating him. Again, the third time, he took flight, and passing near us as quickly as possible, his heart no doubt beating terribly at the boldness of the feat, he succeeded at last in crossing the bridge, and we soon lost sight of him among the bushes on the bank. But while he sat on the branch, and especially as he twice fluttered with distended wings before us, we saw his markings very plainly; they came nearer to those of the yellow red-poll than any other bird of which we could obtain a plate. This is a southern bird, scarcely supposed to breed so far north, I believe, and it is quite possible that the strangers may have been some other variety. The yellow red-poll, however, is said to be very partial to the maple flowers, and these were found feeding on the maple blossoms, hopping from one tree to another.

This pretty stranger had scarcely flown away, when a great awkward kingfisher rose from the river, passing above the bridge, screaming with surprise when he found a human creature nearer than he had supposed; he also flew down the river. Then a party of chicadees alighted among the alder bushes. These were followed by a couple of beautiful little kinglets, ruby crowns, among the smallest of their race; and while all these lesser birds were moving about us, a great hawk, of the largest size, came along from the lake, and continued wheeling for some time over a grove of pines in an adjoining field. We were not learned enough to know what variety of hawk this was, but every other bird of that numerous flock—robins, sparrows, swallows, ruby crowns, blue-birds, goldfinch, Phœbe-bird, chicadee, kingfisher, and the doubtful yellow red-poll—were all varieties peculiar to America.

Wednesday, 10th.—More or less rainy and showery for the last day or two. It has thus far been raining steadily all day, which does not happen very often; the fires are lighted again. Much too wet for walking, but it is pleasant to watch the growth of things from the windows. The verdure has deepened several shades during the last four-and-twenty hours; all the trees now show the touch of spring, excepting the locusts and sumachs, in which the change is scarcely perceptible. Even the distant forest trees now show a light green coloring in their spray, and the ploughed fields, sown with oats some ten days since, are changing the brown of the soil for the green of the young blades.

The rain seems to disturb the birds very little, they are hopping about everywhere in search of their evening meal.

Thursday, 11th.—Black and white creepers in the shrubbery; they are a very pretty bird, so delicately formed. A large party of purple finches also on the lawn; this handsome bird comes from the far north at the approach of severe weather, and winters in different parts of the Union, according to the character of the season; usually remaining about Philadelphia and New York until the middle of May. Some few, however, are known to pass the summer in our northern counties; and we find that a certain number also remain about our own lake, having frequently met them in the woods, and occasionally observed them about the village gardens, in June and July. Their heads and throats are much more crimson than purple just now, and they appear to great advantage, feeding in the fresh grass, the sun shining on their brilliant heads; more than half the party, however, were brown, as usual, the young males and females being without the red coloring. They feed in the spring upon the blossoms of flowering trees; but this afternoon they were eating the seeds out of decayed apples scattered about the orchards.

Also saw again one of the strange birds—yellow red-polls—we watched near the bridge, but could not approach as near as at the first interview; he was in our own garden among the beds, apparently eating insects as well as maple blossoms.

Walked in the woods. The fly-honeysuckle is in full leaf, as well as in flower; it is one of our earliest shrubs. We have several varieties of the honeysuckle tribe in this State. The scarlet honeysuckle, so common in our gardens, is a native plant found near New York, and extending to the southward as far as Carolina. The fragrant woodbine, also cultivated, is found wild in many woods of this State; the yellow honeysuckle grows in the Catskill Mountains; a small variety with greenish yellow flowers, and the hairy honeysuckle with pale yellow blossoms and large leaves, are among our plants. There are also three varieties of the fly-honeysuckle, regular northern plants, one bearing red, another purple, another blue berries; the first is very common here, found in every wood; there is said to be a plant almost identical with this in Tartary.

Friday, 12th.—The aspens are in leaf, and look beautifully on the hill-side, their tremulous foliage being among the very earliest to play in the spring breezes, as their downy seeds are the first of the year to fly abroad; these are as common in the wood at one moment in the spring, as the thistle-down later in the season among the fields; one often sees them lying in little patches along the highway, looking like a powdering of snow-flakes. The birds of some more delicate tribes use this down to line their nests—the humming-bird, for instance. We have been looking and inquiring for the Tackamahac, the great northern or balsam poplar; it is found at Niagara and on Lake Champlain, but the farmers about here seem to know nothing of it. This is a tree of some interest, from the fact that it preserves its size longer than any other wood as it approaches the pole, and the greater portion of the drift-wood in the arctic seas belong to this species. On the northwest coast, it is said to attain a very great size, one hundred and sixty feet in height, and twenty feet in diameter! Poplars, through their different varieties, appear to stretch far over the globe, some being found in the heart of the warm countries of Southern Europe and Asia, others on the skirts of the Arctic regions. The wood used for architectural purposes in the sultry plains of Mesopotamia is said to be almost wholly a variety of the poplar, a native of Armenia, which is the region of the peach.

Saturday, 13th.—It still continues showery, in spite of several attempts to clear. We have had much more rain than usual lately. A high gust came sweeping down the valley this afternoon, driving the rain in heavy sheets before the face of the hills, while pines and hemlocks were tossing their arms wildly on the mountain-tops, and even the bare locusts bent low before the wind; white-caps were rolling with much more power than usual in our placid lake; the garden-walks and the roads were flooded in a moment, and pools formed in every hollow on the lawn; the water literally poured down upon us as if from some other receptacle than the clouds. Let us hope this is the closing shower, for one longs to be abroad in the woods again.

Monday, 15th.—Beautiful day. Long drive and walk in the hills and woods.

While we have been housed in the village, how much has been going on abroad! The leaves are opening rapidly, many of the scarlet maples have their foliage quite formed and colored, though scarcely full-sized yet. The old chestnuts and oaks are in movement, the leaves of the last coming out quite pinkish, a bit of finery of which one would hardly suspect the chiefs of the forest, but so it was in Chaucer's time:

> "Every tree well from his fellowes grewe
> With branches broad; laden with leaves newe,
> That springen out against the sunne's sheene,
> Some very red, and some a glad light greene."

Very many of the trees open their leaf-buds with a warm tint in the green; either brown, or pink, or purplish. Just now, the leaves of the June-berry are dark reddish brown, in rich contrast with its white pendulous flowers. Some of the small oak leaves, especially those of the younger trees, are the deepest crimson; the sugar maples are faintly colored; the scarlet maples, on the contrary, are pure green, seeming to have given all their color to the flowers; the mountain maples are highly colored, and the bracts of the moosewood are quite rosy, as well as some of their leaves. Elms seem to be always green, and so are the beeches; the black birch is faintly tinged with russet at first, the others are quite green. The ashes and hickory are a very light green. It is said that this tenderness and variety of tint in the verdure, so charming in spring as we know the season, belongs especially to a temperate climate. In tropical countries, the buds, unguarded by bracts like our own, are said to be much darker; and in arctic regions, the young leaves are also said to be of a darker color. One would like to know if this last assertion be really correct, as it seems difficult to account for the fact.

Flowers are unfolding on all sides—in the fields, along the road-side, by the fences, and in the silent forest. One cannot go far, on any path, without finding some fresh blossoms. This is a delightful moment everywhere, but, in the woods, the awakening of spring must ever be especially fine. The chill sleep of winter in a cold climate is most striking within the forest; and now we behold life and beauty awakening there in every object; the varied foliage clothing in tender wreaths every naked branch, the pale mosses reviving, a thousand young plants arising above the blighted herbage of last year in cheerful succession, and ten thousand sweet flowers standing in modest beauty, where, awhile since, all was dull and lifeless.

Violets are found everywhere; the moose-flowers are increasing in numbers; young strawberry blossoms promise a fine crop of fruit; the whortleberry-cups are hanging thickly on their low branches, and the early elders are showing their dark, chocolate flower-buds, which we should never expect to open white. The ferns are also unrolling their long-colored fans. We gathered some ground laurel, but the squirrel-cups are forming their seed.

Tuesday, 16th.—Warm, cloudy day. The weather clears slowly, but the air is delightful, so soft and bland. Strolled away from the village in quiet fields by the river, where sloping meadows and a border of wood shut one out from the world. Sweetly calm; nothing stirring but the river flowing gently past, and a few solitary birds flitting quietly to and fro, like messengers of peace. The sunshine is scarcely needed to enhance the beauty of May. The veil of a cloudy sky seems, this evening, to throw an additional charm over the sweetness of the season.

At hours like these, the immeasurable goodness, the infinite wisdom of our Heavenly Father, are displayed in so great a degree of condescending tenderness to unworthy, sinful man, as must appear quite incomprehensible—entirely incredible to reason alone—were it not for the recollection of the mercies of past years, the positive proofs of experience; while Faith, with the holy teaching of Revelation, proclaims "the Lord, the Lord God, merciful and gracious, long-suffering, and abundant in mercy and goodness." What have the best of us done to merit one such day in a lifetime of follies, and failings, and sins? The air we breathe so pure and balmy, the mottled heavens above so mild and kindly, the young herb beneath our feet so delicately fresh, every plant of the field decked in beauty, every tree of the forest clothed in dignity, all unite to remind us, that, despite our own unworthiness, "God's mercies are new every day."

Perhaps some of us have carried heavy hearts about with us during the month of May. There is sorrow on earth amid the joys of spring as at other seasons, but at this gracious and beautiful period the works of the Great Creator unite in themselves to cheer the sad. Often during hours of keen regret, of bitter disappointment, of heavy grief, man is called upon to acknowledge how powerless is the voice of his fellow-man when offering consolation. It seems as though at such moments the witty become dull, the eloquent tedious, the wise insipid, so little are they enabled to effect. Not, indeed, that true friendship has no balm to offer the afflicted; the sympathy of those we love is ever precious, and God forbid we should despise one kindly feeling, one gentle word. But as the days roll onward amid the sorrows, the strifes, the deceits, the cares which beset our path, it must often happen that the full measure of our grief—it may be of our weakness—will be known to our Maker only. We often need much more than sympathy.

The wisest and greatest among us often require guidance, support, strength; and for these, when they fail on earth, we must look above. Blessed is the Christian who has then at hand the Word of God, with its holy precepts, its treasures of eternal comfort. How often to hearts, long since passed into dust, have its sacred pages proved the one source of light when all else was darkness! And, from the Book of Life, let the mourner turn to the works of his God; there the eye, which has been pained with the sight of disorder and confusion, will be soothed with beauty and excellence; the ear, wearied with the din of folly and falsehood, will gladly open to sounds of gentle harmony from the gay birds, the patient cattle, the flowing waters, the rustling leaves. It was not merely to gratify the outer senses of man that these good gifts were bestowed on the earth; they were made for our hearts, the ever-present expression of love, and mercy, and power. When the spirit is harassed by the evils of life, it is then the works of God offer to us most fully the strengthening repose of a noble contemplation; it is when the soul is stricken and sorrowful that it turns to the wise, and beautiful, smile of the creation for a clearer view of peace and excellence:

> "Vernal delight and joy, able to drive
> All sadness but despair."

Christian men of ancient times were wont to illustrate the pages of the Holy Scriptures with choice religious paintings and delicate workmanship; they sent far and wide for the most beautiful colors; they labored to attain the purest lines, the most worthy expression, the most noble design. Not a page did they leave unadorned, not a letter where each was formed by the hand, but showed the touch of a master;—not a blank leaf nor a margin, but bore some delicate traces of pious labors. And thus, to-day, when the precious Book of Life has been withdrawn from the cloisters and given to us all, as we bear its sacred pages about in our hands, as we carry its holy words in our hearts, we raise our eyes to the skies above, we send them abroad over the earth, alike full of the glory of Almighty Majesty,—great and worthy illuminations of the written Word of God.

Coming home through the fields, we found an old pine stretched its entire length on the grass; it must have lain there for years, slowly mouldering away, for it was decayed throughout and fallen asunder in many places so as to follow the curving surface of the ground, but the whole line was entire, and measuring it with a parasol, we made its height to be more than a hundred feet, although something was wanting at the summit. Its diameter, without the bark, was less than two feet.

Wednesday, 17th.—Pleasant weather. In our early walk, before breakfast, we found many of the bob'links playing over the meadows, singing as they flew, their liquid, gurgling medley falling on the ear, now here, now there. These birds build on the ground among the grass or grain, but often perch on the trees. They are one of the few birds about us who sing on the wing, and are almost wholly meadow-birds, rarely coming into the village. Saw summer yellow-birds also, more wholly golden, and of a deeper color than the goldfinch, but not so prettily formed.

Many young leaves are dotting the trees now, spray and foliage both showing. The woods are quite green; the rapidity with which the leaves unfold between sunrise and sunset, or during a night, is truly wonderful! The long, graceful catkins are drooping from the birches, and the more slender clusters are also in flower on the oaks. The beeches are behind most forest trees, but the leaves and some of the flowers are coming out here and there. It is given as a general rule, that those trees which keep their leaves longest in autumn are the earliest in spring, but the beech is a striking exception to this; preserving its withered leaves tenaciously even through the winter, but putting out the new foliage after many of its companions are quite green. The Comptonia or sweet-fern is in flower, the brown, catkin-like blossoms are nearly as fragrant as the foliage; it is the only fern we have with woody branches.

Evening, 9 o'clock.—The frogs are keeping up a vigorous bass, and really, about these times, they often perform the best part of the concert. Just at this season, the early morning and late evening hours are not the most musical moments with the birds; family cares have begun, and there was a good deal of the nursery about the grove of evergreens in the rear of the house, to-night. It was amusing to watch the parents flying home, and listen to the family talk going on; there was a vast deal of twittering and fluttering before settling down in the nest, husband and wife seemed to have various items of household information to impart to each other, and the young nestlings made themselves heard very plainly; one gathered a little scolding, too, on the part of some mother-robins. Meanwhile, the calm, full bass of the frogs comes up from the low grounds with a power that commands one's attention, and is far from unpleasing. It reminds one of the oboe of an orchestra.

Thursday, 18th.—The violets abound now, everywhere, in the grassy fields, and among the withered leaves of the forest; many of them grow in charming little tufts, a simple nosegay in themselves; one finds them in this way in the prettiest situations possible, the yellow, the blue, and the white. A pretty habit, this, with many of our early flowers, growing in little sisterhoods, as it were; we rarely think of the violets singly, as of the rose, or the lily; we always fancy them together, one lending a grace to another, amid their tufted leaves.

There are many different varieties. Botanists count some fifteen sorts in this part of the country, and with one or two exceptions, they are all probably found in our neighborhood. There are some eight different kinds of the blue, or purple, or gray, these colors often changing capriciously; three more are yellow; three more again are white, and one is parti-colored or tri-color; the blue and purple are the largest. Some of these are very beautiful, with every grace of color or form one could desire in a violet, but not one is fragrant. It seems strange, that with all the dewy freshness and beauty of their kind, they should want this charm of the violet of the Old World; but so it is. Still, they are too pleasing and too common a flower to find fault with, even though scentless. The European violet, however, is not always fragrant; some springs they are said to lose their odor almost entirely; the English violet, at least, which has been attributed to the dryness of the season.

Our yellow varieties are great ornaments of the spring, and very common, though not so abundant or large as the purple; one kind, the earliest, grows in little companies of bright, golden blossoms, which are often out before the leaves.

> "Ere rural fields their green resume,
> Sweet flower, I love in forest bare
> To meet thee, when thy faint perfume
> Alone is in the virgin air."

Another is much larger, and grows singly.

The white are quite small, but singularly enough, one of these is fragrant, though the perfume is not so exquisite as that of the European violet; the sweet, white kind are sometimes gathered as late as August. The tri-color is a large and solitary plant, and I have known it fragrant, though it does not appear to be always so. The violets of the Western Prairies are said to be slightly fragrant, although the other flowers of that part of the country have generally no perfume.

Friday, 19th.—Fine, bright weather. The apple-trees are in blossom—they opened last night by moonlight; not one was in flower yesterday, now the whole orchard is in bloom. The orioles have been running over the fresh flowers all the morning, talking to each other, meanwhile, in their clear, full tones. Delightful walk in the evening. We went down to the Great Meadow, beyond Mill Island; the wood which borders it was gay with the white blossoms of the wild cherries and June-berry, the wild plum and the hobble-bush, all very common with us. The evening air was delicately perfumed throughout the broad field, but we could not discover precisely the cause of the fragrance, as it did not seem stronger at one point than at another; it was rather a medley of all spring odors. The June-berry is slightly fragrant, something like the thorn.

We found numbers of the white moose-flowers, the great petals of the larger sorts giving them an importance which no other early flower of the same date can claim. There are several varieties of these flowers; they are quite capricious as regards coloring and size, some being as large as lilies, others not half that size; many are pure white, others dark, others again are flushed with pale pink, or lilac, while one kind, with white petals, is marked about the heart with rich carmine tracery. Now you find one pendulous, while another by its side bears its flowers erect. Botanists call them all *Trilliums*, and a countrywoman told me, the other day, they were all "moose-flowers." Each variety, however, has a scientific name of its own, and some are called nightshades; others wake-robins, both names belonging properly to very different plants. The true English wake-robin is an arum. The difference in their fruit is remarkable. The flowers, so much alike to the general observer, are succeeded by berries of two distinct characters: some resemble the hips of sweet-briar in color and size, though terminating in a sharp point; others bear a dark, purple fruit, strongly ribbed, but rounded in character. I have seen these as large as the common cherry. But although very similar in their growth, leaves, and petals, the hearts of the plants differ very materially, a very simple solution of what at first strikes one as singular. We found only the white flowers, this evening, growing on the skirts of the field. It is rare to meet them beyond the woods, as they disappear before cultivation; and these looked as though they had just stepped out of the forest to take a peep at the world.

The border of an old wood is fine ground for flowers. The soil is usually richer than common, while the sun is felt there with greater power than farther within the shady bounds. One is almost sure of finding blossoms there at the right season. In such spots we also meet a mingled society of plants which it is interesting to note. The wild natives of the woods grow there willingly, while many strangers, brought originally from over the Ocean, steal gradually onward from the tilled fields and gardens, until at last they stand side by side upon the same bank, the European weed and the wild native flower.

These foreign intruders are a bold and hardy race, driving away the prettier natives. It is frequently remarked by elderly persons familiar with the country, that our own wild flowers are very much less common than they were forty years since. Some varieties are diminishing rapidly. Flowers are described to us by those on whom we can place implicit reliance, which we search for, in vain, to-day. The strange pitcher-plant is said to have been much more common, and the moccasin-flower abounded formerly even within the present limits of the village. Both are now rare, and it is considered a piece of good luck to find them. The fragrant azalea is also said to have colored the side-hills in earlier times, on spots where they are now only found scattered here and there.

Saturday, 20th.—The cat-birds are mewing about the grounds. They have been here some little time, usually stealing upon us unawares. They are as common here as elsewhere, and as partial to the society of man. A pair of these birds built for several successive years in an adjoining garden, and became quite fearless and familiar, always seeming pleased when the owner of the garden appeared to work there, according to his custom, giving him a song by way of greeting, and fluttering about close at hand as long as he remained. Last year the family moved away, but we still see the cat-birds on the same spot, quite at home. Whether they are the same pair or not one cannot say.

Some persons do not admire the cat-bird, on account of his sober plumage; but the rich shaded grays of his coat strike us as particularly pleasing, and his form is elegant. His cry, to be sure, is odd enough for a bird, and sometimes when he repeats it twenty times in succession in the course of half an hour, one feels inclined to box his ears. It is the more provoking in him to insult us in this way, because some of his notes, when he chooses, are very musical—soft and liquid—as different as possible from his harsh, grating cry. Like his cousin, the mocking-bird, he often deserves a good shaking for his caprices, both belonging to the naughty class of "birds who can sing, and won't sing," except when it suits their fancy.

The cat-bird is a great bather, like the goldfinch. He is said to use the cast-off skins of snakes to line his nest, whenever he can find them. He leaves us in October, and winters on the Gulf of Mexico.

Monday, 22d.—The apple-blossoms are charmingly fragrant now; they have certainly the most delightful perfume of all our northern fruit-trees.

The later forest-trees are coming into leaf; the black walnuts, butternuts, sumachs, hickories, ashes, and locusts. Trees with that kind of pinnated foliage seem to be later than others. The locust is always the last to open its leaves; they are just beginning to show, and a number of others, which partake of the same character of foliage, have only preceded them by a week or so. The springs are all running beautifully clear and full now. Corn planted to-day.

Tuesday, 23d.—The small, yellow butterflies are fluttering about. These are much the most numerous of their tribe; with us among the earliest to appear in spring, and the latest to retreat before the frosts in autumn.

Wednesday, 24th.—Warm and pleasant. The woods may now be called in leaf, though the foliage is still a tender green, and some of the leaves are not full-sized. The maples, however, so numerous in our woods, have already acquired their deep, rich summer verdure. The young shoots have started on the hemlocks, each twig being tipped with tender green, a dozen shades lighter than the rest of the foliage. These delicate light touches are highly ornamental to the tree, and give it a peculiar beauty half through the summer, for they take the darker shade very slowly. The difference between the greens of the two years' growth is more striking on the hemlock than on any other evergreen remembered, at this moment, either the pine, the balsam, or the Norway fir.

The hemlock spruce is a very common tree in this part of the country, and an imposing evergreen, ranking in height with the tallest oaks, and ashes, and elms of the forest. They are frequently met with eighty feet high. The other day, walking in the woods, we measured one which had just been felled, and it proved a hundred and four feet in height, and three feet two inches in diameter, without the bark. When young bushes, only a few feet high, they are beautiful, especially when tipped with the delicate green of the young spring shoots; their horizontal branches often sweeping the ground, look as though they had no other object in view than to form beautiful shrubbery, very different in this respect from the young pines, which have a determined upright growth from the first, betraying their ambition to become trees as early as possible. The usual verdure of the hemlock is very dark and glossy, lying in double rows flat upon the branches. The younger spray often hangs in loose drooping tufts, and the whole tree is more or less sprinkled with pretty little cones which are very ornamental. As the hemlock grows older, it becomes often irregular, dead limbs projecting here and there, well hung with long drooping lichens of light green, which give it a venerable aspect. Altogether it is the most mossy tree we have.

Some of the hemlocks have a much closer and more compressed upright growth than those commonly met with; so that one is almost tempted to believe there are two distinct varieties. Near the Red Brook, there is a young wood of these close-growing hemlocks, all having the same character; but

I believe it only accidental. Occasionally, but much more rarely, the same thing is seen among the pines.

The hemlock is chiefly used here for tanning, the bark being often stripped off from fine trees, which are then left to decay standing. The timber is sometimes used for joists. Since the custom of making plank roads has commenced, the farmers are beginning to look with more favor upon their hemlock-trees, as this is the only wood used for the purpose, wherever it can be procured. A vast amount of hemlock timber must have already been worked up for our highways, and for paving village side-walks; and probably all that is left will soon be appropriated to the same purposes. Trees, sixteen inches in diameter, are now selling in our neighborhood for a dollar a-piece standing, when taken by the hundred. Pine-trees, standing, sell for five dollars, although they often produce forty dollars' worth of lumber. The porcupine is said to have been very partial to the leaves and bark of the hemlock for food.

Friday, 25th.—Beautiful day. The flowers are blooming in throngs. Our spring garland becomes fuller and richer every day. The white cool-wort[4] is mingled in light and airy tufts with the blue and yellow violets. The low-cornel is opening; its cups are greenish now, but they will soon bleach to a pure white. The elegant silvery May-star is seen here and there; by its side the tall, slender mitella, while warm, rose-colored gay-wings are lying among the mosses, and each of these flowers has an interest for those who choose to make their acquaintance.

Who at first glance would think that the low-cornel, growing scarce half a span high, is cousin-german to the dogwood, which boasts the dignity of a tree? A most thrifty little plant it is, making a pretty white flower of its outer cup—which in most plants is green—and after this has fallen, turning its whole heart to fruit; for wherever we now see one of the simple white blossoms in its whorl of large green leaves, there we shall find, in August, a cluster of good-sized scarlet berries. I have counted sixteen of these in one bunch, looking like so many coral beads. Although each plant stands singly, they are very freely scattered about the wood, a hardy plant, growing far to the northward wherever pine-trees are found.

The May-star[5] is remarkable for its elegance, a delicate star-like blossom of the purest white standing like a gem in a setting of leaves, fine in texture and neatly cut. Some persons call this chick wintergreen, a name which is an insult to the plant, and to the common sense of the community. Why, it is one of the daintiest wood-flowers, with nothing in the world to do with chicks, or weeds, or winter. It is not the least of an evergreen, its leaves withering in autumn, as a matter of course, and there is not a chicken in the country that knows it by sight or taste. Discriminating people, when they find its elegant silvery flower growing in the woods beside the violet, call it May-star; and so should everybody who sees it.

The cool-wort grows in patches upon many banks within the woods, or near them. It is a very pretty flower from its light airy character, and the country people employ its broad, violet-shaped leaves for healing purposes. They lay them, freshly gathered, on scalds and burns, and, like all domestic receipts of the sort, they never fail of course, but "work like a charm;" that is to say, as charms worked some hundred years ago. It is the leaves only that are used in this way, and we have seen persons who professed to have been much benefited by them.

The slender mitella, or fringe-cup, or false sanicle—one does not like a false name for a flower—hangs its tiny white cups at intervals on a tall, slender, two-leaved stalk; a pretty, unpretending little thing, which scatters its black seeds very early in the season. It is one of the plants we have in common with Northern Asia.

As for the May-wings,[6] or "gay-wings," they are in truth one of the gayest little blossoms we have; growing low as they do, and many of their winged flowers together, you might fancy them so many warm lilac, or deep rose-colored butterflies resting on the mosses. They are bright, cheerful little flowers, seldom found singly, but particularly social in their habits; twin blossoms very often grow on the same stalk, and at times you find as many as four or five; we have occasionally gathered clusters of a dozen or eighteen blossoms in one tuft, upon three or four stalks. They bloom here in profusion on the borders of the woods, by the road-side, and in some fields; we found them a day or two since, mingled with the dandelions, in a low meadow by the river; but they are especially fond of growing among the mosses, the most becoming position they could choose, their warmly-colored flowers lying in brilliant relief upon the dark rich ground-work. How beautiful is this exquisite native grace of the flowers, seen in all their habits and positions! They know nothing of vanity, its trivial toils and triumphs! In unconscious, spontaneous beauty, they live their joy-giving lives, and yet how all but impossible for man to add to their perfection in a single point! In their habits of growth, this innate grace may be particularly observed; there is a unity, a fitness, in the individual character of each plant to be traced most closely, not only in form, or leaf, and stem, but also in the position it chooses, and all the various accessories of its brief existence. It is this that gives to the field and wood flowers a charm beyond those of the garden. Pass through the richest and most brilliant parterre in the country, with every advantage which labor, expense, science, and thought can bestow, and you will find there no one plant that is not shorn of some portion of its native grace, a penalty which it pays for the honors of culture. They are richer perhaps, more gorgeous, the effect of the whole is more striking, but singly, they are not so wholly beautiful. Go out in the months of May and June into the nearest fields and groves, and you shall see there a thousand sweet plants, sowed by the gracious hand of Providence, blooming amid the common grass, in crevices of rude rocks, beside the trickling springs, upon rough and shaggy banks, with a freedom and a simple modest grace which must ever be the despair of gardeners, since it is quite inimitable by art, with all its cunning.

Saturday, 26th.– Charming day; walked in the woods. Accidentally breaking away a piece of decayed wood from the dead trunk of a tree, we found a snake coiled within; it seemed to be torpid, for it did not move; we did, however – retreating at once, not caring to make a nearer acquaintance with the creature.

There are not many snakes in the neighborhood; one seldom sees them either in the fields or the woods, though occasionally they cross our path. The most common are the harmless little garter snakes, with now and then a black-snake. Not long since, the workmen at the Cliffs were making a road, and two of them taking up a log to move it, a large black-snake, astonished to find his dwelling in motion, came hurrying out; he was said to have been three or four feet in length. But I have never yet heard of any persons being injured by a snake in this neighborhood; most of these creatures are quite harmless – indeed, of the sixteen varieties found in the State, only two are venomous, the copper-head and the rattlesnake.

There is a mountain in the county, the Crumhorn, where rattlesnakes formerly abounded, and where they are said to be still found, but fortunately, these dangerous reptiles are of a very sluggish nature, and seldom stray from the particular locality which suits their habits, and where they are generally very numerous. An instance is on record, quoted by Dr. De Kay, in which three men, who went upon Tongue Mountain, on Lake George, for the purpose of hunting rattlesnakes, destroyed in two days eleven hundred and four of these venomous creatures! They are taken for their fat, which is sold at a good price.

We found this afternoon a very pretty little butterfly, pink and yellow; it seemed to be quite young, and scarcely in full possession of its powers yet; we thought it a pity to interfere with its happy career, but just begun, and left it unharmed as we found it.

"Thus the fresh clarion, being readie dight,
    Unto his journey did himself addresse,
And with good speed began to take his flight
    Over the fields in his frank lustinesse;
And all the champaine o'er he soared light,
    And all the country wide he did possesse;
Feeding upon his pleasures bounteouslie,
    That none gainsaid, nor none did him envie."

Monday, 28th.—Cloudy day. Pleasant row on the lake. The country, as seen from the water, looked charmingly, decked in the flowery trophies of May. Many of the fruit-trees are still in blossom in the orchards and gardens, while the wild cherries and plums were drooping over the water in many spots. The evening was perfectly still, not a breath to ruffle the lake, and the soft spring character of the hills and fields, bright with their young verdure, had stolen over the waters. Swallows were skimming about busily. We met several boats; one of them, filled with little girls in their colored sun-bonnets, and rowed by an older boy, looked gayly as it passed. We landed and gathered the singular flower of the dragon arum, or Indian turnip, as the country folk call it, violets also, and a branch of wild cherry.

Tuesday, 29th.—Among all the varieties of birds flitting about our path during the pleasant months, there is not one which is a more desirable neighbor than the house-wren. Coming early in spring, and going late in autumn, he is ready at any time, the season through, to give one a song. Morning, noon, or evening, in the moonshine, or under a cloudy sky, he sings away out of pure joyousness of heart. They are pretty little creatures, too, nicely colored, and very delicate in their forms. For several summers we had a nest built under the eaves of a low roof projecting within a few feet of a window, and many a time our little friend, perched on a waving branch of the Virginia creeper, would sing his sweetest song, while the conversation within doors was hushed to hear him. His return has been anxiously watched for, this spring, but in vain. If in the neighborhood, he no longer builds in the same spot.

But the wrens have many merits besides their prettiness and their sweet voice. They are amusing, cheerful little creatures, and they are very true-hearted, moreover. The parents are particularly attentive to each other, and kind to their family, which is a large one, for they raise two broods during the summer. Unlike other birds, they do not discard their children, but keep an eye on the first set, while making ready for the younger ones. Nor are the

young birds themselves eager to run off and turn rovers; they all live together in little family parties through the season, and in autumn you frequently see them in this way, eight or ten together, feeding on the haws of
the thorn-bushes, of which they are very fond.

He is a very great builder, also, is the wren. He seems to think, like that
famous old Countess of yore, Bess of Shrewsbury, that he is doomed to
build for his life. Frequently while his mate is sitting, he will build you several useless nests, just for his own gratification; singing away all the time,
and telling his more patient mate, perhaps, what straws he picks up, and
where he finds them. Sometimes, when he first arrives, if not already mated,
he will build his house, and then look out for a wife afterwards. It is a pity
they should not stay with us all winter, these pleasant little friends of ours,
like the European wren, who never migrates, and sings all the year round.
It is true, among the half dozen varieties which visit us, there is the winter
wren, who remains during the cold weather in some parts of the State; but
we do not see him here after the snow has fallen, and at best he appears
much less musical than the summer bird. Our common house-wren is a
finer singer than the European bird; but he flies far to the southward, in winter, and sings Spanish in Mexico and South America. It is quite remarkable
that this common bird, the house-wren, though passing North and South
every year, should be unknown in Louisiana; yet Mr. Audubon tells us such
is the case.

The mandrakes, or May-apples, are in flower. They are certainly a handsome plant, as their showy white flower is not unlike the water-lily. Some
people eat their fruit—boys especially—but most persons find it insipid. This
common showy plant growing along our fences, and in many meadows, is
said also to be found under a different variety in the hilly countries of Central Asia. One likes to trace these links, connecting lands and races, so far
apart, reminding us, as they do, that the earth is the common home of all.

Thursday, 30th.—The springs are all full to overflowing, this season. Some
trickling down the hill-sides, through the shady woods, many more sparkling
in the open sunshine of the meadows. Happily for us, they flow freely here.
We forget to value justly a blessing with which we are so richly endowed,
until we hear of other soils, and that within the limits of our own country,
too, where the thirsty traveller and his weary beast count it a piece of good
fortune to find a pure wholesome draught at the close of their day's toil.

This is decidedly a spring county. Mineral waters of powerful medicinal
qualities are scattered about within a circuit of twenty miles from the lake.
There are several within the limits of the village itself, but these have little

strength. Others farther off have long been used for their medicinal properties—vile messes to taste—and sending up an intolerable stench of sulphur,
but beautifully clear and cool. There is a salt spring also at no great distance
from the lake, said to be the most easterly of the saline springs in this part
of the country, and at a distance of some eighty miles from the great salt
works of Onondaga.

A portion of our waters are hard, touched with the limestone, through
which they find their way to the surface; but there are many more possess-
ing every good quality that the most particular housewife can desire for
cooking her viands, or bleaching her linen. Near the farm-house doors you
frequently see them falling from a wooden pipe into a trough, hollowed out
of the trunk of a tree, the rudest of fountains; and the same arrangement is
made here and there, along the highway, for the benefit of the traveller and
his cattle.

One likes to come upon a spring in a walk. This afternoon we were seldom out of sight of one. We counted more than a dozen distinct fountain-
heads within a distance of a mile. One filled a clear, sandy pool, on level
grassy ground, near the bank of the river; another, within the forest, lay in
a little rocky basin, lined with last year's leaves; another fell in full measure
over a dark cliff, moistening a broad space of the rock, which, in winter, it
never fails to cover with a sheet of frost-work. More than one lay among the
roots of the forest trees; and others, again, kept us company on the highway,
running clear and bubbling through the ditches by the road-side. There is
a quiet beauty about them all which never fails to give pleasure. There is a
grace in their purity—in their simplicity—which is soothing to the spirit;
and, perhaps among earth's thousand voices, there is none other so sweetly
humble, so lowly, yet so cheerful, as the voice of the gentle springs, passing
on their way to fill our daily cup.

When standing beside these unfettered springs in the shady wood, one
seems naturally to remember the red man; recollections of his vanished
race linger there in a more definite form than elsewhere; we feel assured
that by every fountain among these hills, the Indian brave, on the hunt or
the war-path, must have knelt ten thousand times, to slake his thirst, and
the wild creatures, alike his foes and his companions, the tawny panther, the
clumsy bear, the timid deer and the barking wolf, have all lapped these
limpid waters during the changing seasons of past ages. Nay, it is quite possible there may still be springs in remote spots among the hills of this region,
yet untasted by the white man and his flocks, where the savage and the beast
of prey were the last who drank. And while these recollections press upon

us, the flickering shadows of the wood seem to assume the forms of the wild
creatures which so lately roamed over these hills, and we are half persuaded
that the timid doe or the wily catamount is again drawing near to drink from
the fountain at our feet—we hear the crash of a dry branch, or the rustling of
leaves, and we start as though expecting to see the painted warrior, armed
with flint-headed arrows and tomahawk of stone, gliding through the wood
toward us. It was but yesterday that such beings peopled the forest, beings
with as much of life as runs within our own veins, who drank their daily
draught from the springs we now call our own; yesterday they were here, to-
day scarce a vestige of their existence can be pointed out among us.

Friday, 31st.—Thunder-shower this afternoon, everything growing finely.
The blackberry-bushes, very common here, are coming into flower along
the road-sides and fences. The white thorn is also blooming; there is a rustic elegance about its clusters which leads one readily to admit its claims as
a favorite of the poets—the form of this flower is so simple, and the colored
heads of the stamens are so daintily pretty; it has been opening for several
days, and many of the bushes, or trees rather, are in full flower. In this hilly
climate, it blossoms late, still it saves its credit as the flower of May; in the
rural districts of England, "the May" is said to be a common name for the
hawthorn.

Walked about the shrubbery with the hope of finding a rose open, but our
search was fruitless. Last year a few of the early kind bloomed in May, but
the present season is more backward. With us, the roses scarcely belong to
spring, we should rather date our summer from their unfolding; the bushes
were never more full of buds, however, and some of these are beginning to
disclose their coloring; but the greater number are still closely shut within
their fringed cups. Later in the season, we become critical—we reject the
full-blown flower for the half-open bud, but just now we are eager to feast
our eyes upon a rose—a true, perfect rose—with all her beauties opening to
the light, all her silken petals unfolding in rich profusion about her fragrant
heart.

Summer

Friday, June 1st.—Beautiful day. Pleasant walk. The whole country is green at this moment, more so than at any other period of the year. The earth is completely decked in delicate verdure of varied shades: the fruit-trees have dropped their blossoms, and the orchards and gardens are green; the forest has just put on its fresh foliage, the meadows are yet uncolored by the flowers, and the young grain-fields look grassy still. This fresh green hue of the country is very charming, and with us it is very fugitive, soon passing away into the warmer coloring of midsummer.

The cedar-birds have been very troublesome among the fruit blossoms, and they are still haunting the gardens. As they always move in flocks, except for a very short period when busy with their young, they leave their mark on every tree they attack, whether in fruit or flower. We saw them last week scattering the petals in showers, to get at the heart of the blossom, which, of course, destroys the young fruit. They are very much their own enemies in this way, for no birds are greater fruit-eaters than themselves; they are even voracious feeders when they find a berry to their taste, actually destroying themselves, at times, by the numbers they swallow.

There are two closely-allied varieties of this bird, very similar in general appearance and character, one coming from the extreme north, while the other is found within the tropics. Both, however, meet on common ground in the temperate regions of our own country. The larger sort—the Bohemian wax-wing—is well known in Europe, though so irregular in its flights, that in former times its visits were looked upon by superstitious people as the forerunner of some public calamity. Until lately, this bird was supposed to be unknown on the Western continent; but closer observation has shown that it is found here, within our own State, where it is said to be increasing. It bears a strong general resemblance to the cedar-bird, though decidedly larger, and differently marked in some points. It is supposed to breed very far north in arctic countries. Both birds are crested, and both have a singular appendage to their wings, little red, wax-like, tips at the extremity of their secondary wing-feathers. These vary in number, and are not found on all individuals, but they are quite peculiar to themselves. The habits of the two varieties are, in many respects, similar: they are both berry-eaters, very gregarious in their habits, and particularly affectionate in their dispositions toward one another; they crowd as near together as possible, half a dozen often sitting side by side on the same branch, caressing one another, and even feeding one another out of pure friendliness. They have been called chatterers in the Old World, but in fact they are very silent birds, though fussy and active, which perhaps made people fancy they were chatty creatures also.

The Bohemian wax-wing is rather rare, even in Europe; and yet it is believed that a small flock were in our own neighborhood this spring. On two different occasions we remarked what seemed very large cedar-birds *without* the white line about the eye, and *with* a white stripe on the wings; but they were in a thicket both times, and not being at liberty to stay and watch them, it would not do to assert positively that these were the Bohemian wax-wing. Learned ornithologists, with a bird in the hand, have sometimes made great mistakes on such matters, and, of course, unlearned people should be very modest in expressing an opinion, especially where, instead of one bird in the hand, they can only point to two in a bush. As for the cedar-birds, everybody knows them; they are common enough throughout the country, and are also abundant in Mexico. They are sold in the markets of our large towns, in the autumn and spring, for two or three cents a piece.

Saturday, 2d.– Cloudy morning, followed by a charming afternoon. Long walk. Took a by-road which led us over the hills to a wild spot, where, in a distance of two or three miles, there is only one inhabited house, and that stands on the border of a gloomy swamp, from which the wood has been cut away, while two or three deserted log-cabins along the road only make things look more desolate. We enjoyed the walk all the more, however, for its wild, rude character, so different from our every-day rambles. Passed several beautiful springs in the borders of the unfenced woods, and saw several interesting birds. A handsome Clape, or golden-winged woodpecker, a pretty wood-pewee, and a very delicate little black-poll warbler, this last rare, and entirely confined to the forest; it was hopping very leisurely among the flowery branches of a wild cherry, and we had an excellent opportunity of observing it, for on that wild spot it was not on the look-out for human enemies, and we approached, unobserved, placing ourselves behind a bush. These three birds are all peculiar to our part of the world.

The rude fences about several fields in these new lands were prettily bordered with the Canadian violet, white and lilac; the chinks and hollows of several old stumps were also well garnished with these flowers; one does not often see so many together.

Upon one of these violets we found a handsome colored spider, one of the kind that live on flowers and take their color from them; but this was unusually large. Its body was of the size of a well-grown pea, and of a bright lemon color; its legs were also yellow, and altogether it was one of the most showy colored spiders we have seen in a long time. Scarlet, or red ones still larger, are found, however, near New York. But, in their gayest aspect, these creatures are repulsive. It gives one a chilling idea of the gloomy solitude of a prison, when we remember that spiders have actually been petted by men shut out from better companionship. They are a very common insect with us, and on that account more annoying than any other that is found here. Some of them, with great black bodies, are of a formidable size. These haunt cellars, and barns, and churches, and appear occasionally in inhabited rooms. There is a black spider of this kind, with a body said to be an inch long, and legs double that length, found in the Palace of Hampton Court, in England, which, it will be remembered, belonged to Cardinal Wolsey, and these great creatures are called "Cardinals" there, being considered by some people as peculiar to that building. A huge spider, by-the-by, with her intricate web and snares, would form no bad emblem of a courtier and diplomatist, of the stamp of Cardinal Wolsey. He certainly took "hold with his hands, in kings' palaces," and did his share of mischief there.

Few people like spiders. No doubt these insects must have their merits and their uses, since none of God's creatures are made in vain; all living things are endowed with instincts more or less admirable; but the spider's plotting, creeping ways, and a sort of wicked expression about him, lead one to dislike him as a near neighbor. In a battle between a spider and a fly, one always sides with the fly, and yet of the two, the last is certainly the most troublesome insect to man. But the fly is frank and free in all his doings; he seeks his food openly, and he pursues his pastimes openly; suspicions of others or covert designs against them are quite unknown to him, and there is something almost confiding in the way in which he sails around you, when a single stroke of your hand might destroy him. The spider, on the contrary, lives by snares and plots; he is at the same time very designing and very suspicious, both cowardly and fierce; he always moves stealthily, as though among enemies, retreating before the least appearance of danger, solitary and morose, holding no communion with his fellows. His whole appearance corresponds with this character, and it is not surprising, therefore, that while the fly is more mischievous to us than the spider, we yet look upon the first with more favor than the last; for it is a natural impulse of the human heart to prefer that which is open and confiding to that which is wily and suspicious, even in the brute creation. The cunning and designing man himself will, at times, find a feeling of respect and regard for the guileless and generous stealing over him, his heart, as it were, giving the lie to his life.

Some two or three centuries since, when people came to this continent from the Old World in search of gold, oddly enough, it was considered a good sign of success when they met with spiders! It would be difficult to say why they cherished this fancy; but according to that old worthy, Hakluyt, when Martin Frobisher and his party landed on Cumberland Island, in quest of gold, their expectations were much increased by finding there numbers of spiders, "which, as many affirm, are signes of great store of gold."

They fancied that springs also were abundant near minerals, so that we may, in this county, cherish great hopes of a mine—if we choose.

Monday, 4th.—Very warm yesterday and to-day. Thermometer 83 in the shade at noon. Walked in the evening. The corn-fields are now well garnished with scare-crows, and it is amusing to see the different devices employed for the purpose. Bits of tin hung upon upright sticks are very general; lines of white twine, crossing the field at intervals near the soil, are also much in favor, and the crows are said to be particularly shy of this sort of network; other fields are guarded by a number of little whirligig windmills. One large field that we passed evidently belonged to a man of great resources in the way of expedients; for, among a number of contrivances, no two were alike: in one spot, large as life, stood the usual man of straw, here was a tin pan on a pole, there a sheet was flapping its full breadth in the breeze, here was a straw hat on a stick, there an old flail, in one corner a broken tin *Dutch oven* glittered in the sunshine, and at right angles with it was a tambourine! It must needs be a bold crow that will venture to attack such a camp.[7] It is strange how soon these creatures find out where maize has been planted. For two or three weeks, at this season, they are very troublesome until the grain has outgrown its seed character, and taken root. They do not seem to attack other grains much;—at least, scare-crows are never seen in other fields.

The chipmucks, or ground-squirrels, are also very mischievous in the maize-fields; and the blue-jay follows the same bad example occasionally. In autumn, the king-birds, in addition to the others, attack the ripe grain also, so that the maize has many enemies.

A thunder-shower passed over the village in the afternoon, and in the course of an hour the thermometer fell 20 degrees.

Tuesday, 5th.—Charming, cloudless day; fresh air from the west rustling among the new leaves. Stroll in the woods; flowers blooming abundantly. The wood betony, with its yellow heads, makes quite a show this season; there is more of it than usual, and it is quite ornamental on that account.

The different varieties of Solomon's seal—all elegant plants—are now in bloom. The wise King of Israel must have set his stamp upon many roots in these western forests; for the flowers of the tribe are very numerous here, especially the false spikenard, the delicate two-leaved Solomon's seal, or bead-ruby, and the Clintonia, with yellow lily-like flowers and large blue berries. The tufted convallaria bifolia, or bead-ruby, is one of our most common wood plants, very much like that of Europe, although the flowerets are larger. It is singularly slow in the progress of its fruit. The cluster of berries forms early in June, but requires all summer to ripen; at first they are green and opaque, like wax; then, in July, they become speckled with red; in August the spots spread, and the whole berry is red; and, later still, in September, it takes a beautiful ruby color, and is nearly transparent; in which condition we have seen them as late as the first of December. The false spikenard goes through much the same process, but its fruit is more frequently blasted, and the name of bead-ruby is here confined to the smaller two-leaved plant. The pretty little lily of the valley, that charming flower of the gardens, grows wild in the Southern Alleghanies, but it is not found among the plants of these northernmost ridges of the chain.

We were walking in a beautiful grove where the wood had been only partially cleared, leaving many fine trees standing, mingled with the stumps of others long since felled. The mossy roots of these mouldering old stumps are choice places for the early flowers; one often finds the remains of an old oak, or pine, or chestnut, encircled by a beautiful border of this kind, mosses and flowers blended together in a way which art can never equal. During many successive springs, we have been in the habit of watching the flowers as they unfold upon these mossy hillocks. As usual, they are now daintily sprinkled with blossoms, for the soil is rich as possible in such spots. We amused ourselves with counting the different kinds of flowers growing on several of these little knolls. In one instance, we found fifteen different plants, besides the grasses, in a narrow circle about the swelling roots, six or eight feet in breadth; around another we counted eighteen varieties; another showed twenty-two; and a fourth had six-and-twenty kinds. The groundwork is usually made up of mosses of three or four varieties and shades, all very beautiful, and blended with these are the silvery leaves of the pearly ever-lastings. Violets, blue, white, and yellow, grow there, with rosy gay-wings,[8] cool-wort, fairy-cup, or mitella, low-cornel, May-star, strawberry, dew-drop, bead-ruby, squaw-vine, partridge-plant, pipsissiwa, pyrolas, loose-strife, ground-laurel, innocence, Michaelmas daisies of several kinds, per-haps the coptis, or gold-thread, and three or four ferns. Such are the plants often found in these wild, posy patches, about old stumps, in half-cleared woods. Of course, they are not all in flower together; but toward the prime of the spring, one may at times find nearly a dozen kinds in blossom at the same moment. These are all native plants, gathering, as if out of affection, about the roots of the fallen forest trees.

Wednesday, 6th.—Coolish this morning. Chilly people have lighted their parlor fires. Last year we had strawberries the 6th of June, but the present season is more backward. Good walking weather to-day.

It is a pleasing part of the elegance of May, in a temperate climate, that few of the coarser weeds show themselves during that month; or, rather, at that early day, they do not appear in their true character. They are, of course, very troublesome to gardeners from the first, but they do not then obtrude themselves upon general attention. The season advances with great rapidity, however, and already these rude plants are beginning to show themselves in the forms by which we know them. The burdock and nettle, and thistle, &c., &c., are growing too plentifully under fences, and in waste spots; chickweed and purslane, &c., &c., spring up in the paths and beds so freely and so boldly, that it is the chief labor of the month to wage war upon their tribe.

It is remarkable that these troublesome plants have come very generally from the Old World; they do not belong here, but following the steps of the white man, they have crossed the ocean with him. A very large proportion of the most common weeds in our fields and gardens, and about our build-ings, are strangers to the soil. It will be easy to name a number of these:—such, for instance, as the dock and the burdock, found about every barn and out-building; the common plantains and mallows—regular path-weeds; the groundsel, purslane, pigweed, goose-foot, shepherd's-purse, and lamb's-quarters, so troublesome in gardens; the chickweed growing everywhere; the pimpernel, celandine, and knawel; the lady's thumb and May-weed; the common nettles and teazel; wild flax, stickseed, burweed, doorweed; all the mulleins; the most pestilent thistles, both the common sort and that which is erroneously called the Canada thistle; the sow thistles; the chess, corn-cockle, tares, bugloss, or blue-weed, and the pigeon-weed of the grain-fields; the darnel, yarrow, wild parsnip, ox-eye daisy, the wild garlic, the acrid buttercup, and the acrid St. John's wort of the meadows; the nightshades, Jerusalem artichoke, wild radish, wild mustard, or charlock, the poison hem-lock, the henbane,—ay, even the very dandelion,[9] a plant which we tread un-der foot at every turn. Others still might be added to the list, which were en-tirely unknown to the red man, having been introduced by the European race, and are now choking up all our way-sides, forming the vast throng of foreign weeds. Some of these have come from a great distance, travelling round the world. The shepherd's-purse, with others, is common in China, on the most eastern coast of Asia. One kind of mallows belongs to the East Indies; another to the coast of the Mediterranean. The gimson weed, or Datura, is an Abyssinian plant, and the Nicandra came from Peru. It is sup-posed that the amaranths or greenweeds, so very common here, have also been introduced, though possibly only from the more southern parts of our own country.

Some few American plants have been also carried to Europe, where they have become naturalized; but the number is very small. The evening prim-rose, and the silkweed, among others, have sowed themselves in some parts of the Old World, transported, no doubt, with the tobacco, and maize, and potato, which are now so widely diffused over the Eastern continent, to the very heart of Asia. But even at home, on our own soil, the amount of native weeds is small when compared with the throngs brought from the Old World. The wild cucumber, a very troublesome plant, the great white con-volvolus, the dodder, the field sorrel, the pokeweed, the silkweed, with one or two plantains and thistles, of the rarer kinds, are among the most impor-tant of those whose origin is clearly settled as belonging to this continent. It is also singular that among those tribes which are of a divided nature, some being natives, others introduced, the last are generally the most numerous; for instance, the native chickweeds, and plantains, and thistles, are less com-mon here than the European varieties.

There are other naturalized plants frequent in neglected spots, about farm-houses, and along road-sides, which have already become so common as to be weeds; the simples and medicinal herbs, used for ages by the good-wives of England and Holland, were early brought over, and have very generally become naturalized,—catnip, mint, horehound, tansy, balm, com-frey, elecampane, &c., &c.,—immediately take root, spreading far and wide wherever they are allowed to grow. It is surprising how soon they become firmly established in a new settlement; we often observe them in this new county apart from any dwelling. At times we have found them nearly a mile from either garden or house. The seeds of naturalized plants seem, in many cases, to have floated across our lake upon the water; for we have found the European mint and catnip growing with the blue gentian immediately on the banks where the woods spread around in every direction for some distance.

The word weed varies much with circumstances; at times, we even apply it to the beautiful flower or the useful herb. A plant may be a weed, because it is noxious, or fetid, or unsightly, or troublesome, but it is rare indeed that all these faults are united in one individual of the vegetable race. Often the unsightly, or fetid, or even the poisonous plant, is useful, or it may be interesting from some peculiarity; and on the other hand, many others, troublesome from their numbers, bear pleasing flowers, taken singly. Upon the whole, it is not so much a natural defect which marks the weed, as a certain impertinent, intrusive character in these plants; a want of modesty, a habit of shoving themselves forward upon ground where they are not needed, rooting themselves in soil intended for better things, for plants more useful, more fragrant, or more beautiful. Thus the corn-cockle bears a fine flower, not unlike the mullein-pink of the garden, but then it springs up among the precious wheat, taking the place of the grain, and it is a weed; the flower of the thistle is handsome in itself, but it is useless, and it pushes forward in throngs by the way-side until we are weary of seeing it, and everybody makes war upon it; the common St. John's wort, again, has a pretty yellow blossom, and it has its uses also as a simple, but it is injurious to the cattle, and yet it is so obstinately tenacious of a place among the grasses, that it is found in every meadow, and we quarrel with it as a weed.

These noxious plants have come unbidden to us, with the grains and grasses of the Old World, the evil with the good, as usual in this world of probation—the wheat and tares together. The useful plants produce a tenfold blessing upon the labor of man, but the weed is also there, ever accompanying his steps, to teach him a lesson of humility. Certain plants of this nature—the dock, thistle, nettle, &c., &c.—are known to attach themselves especially to the path of man; in widely different soils and climates, they are still found at his door. Patient care and toil can alone keep the evil within bounds, and it seems doubtful whether it lies within the reach of human means entirely to remove from the face of the earth one single plant of this peculiar nature, much less all their varieties. Has any one, even of the more noxious sorts, ever been utterly destroyed? Agriculture, with all the pride and power of science now at her command, has apparently accomplished but little in this way. Egypt and China are said to be countries in which weeds are comparatively rare; both regions have long been in a high state of cultivation, filled to overflowing with a hungry population, which neglects scarce a rood of the soil, and yet even in those lands, even upon the banks of the Nile, where the crops succeed each other without any interval throughout the whole year, leaving no time for weeds to extend themselves; even there, these noxious plants are not unknown, and the moment the soil is abandoned, only for a season, they return with renewed vigor.

In this new country, with a fresh soil, and a thinner population, we have not only weeds innumerable, but we observe, also, that briers and brambles seem to acquire double strength in the neighborhood of man; we meet them in the primitive forest, here and there, but they line our roads and fences, and the woods are no sooner felled to make ready for cultivation, than they spring up in profusion, the first natural produce of the soil. But in this world of mercy, the just curse is ever graciously tempered with a blessing; many a grateful fruit, and some of our most delightful flowers, grow among the thorns and briers, their fragrance and excellence reminding man of the sweets as well as the toils of his task. The sweet-briar, more especially, with its simple flower and delightful fragrance, unknown in the wilderness, but moving onward by the side of the ploughman, would seem, of all others, the husbandman's blossom.

Thursday, 7th.—There was an alarm of frost last evening, and cautious people covered their tender plants, but no harm was done. It happens frequently, that late in May or early in June, we have a return of cool weather for a day or two, with an alarm about frost, at a very critical moment, when all our treasures are lying exposed; some seasons, much mischief is done to the gardens and crops, but frequently the alarm passes over and we are spared the evil. It seldom happens, even after heavy frosts at such unseasonable times, that the blight is half as severe as people at first suppose; things usually turn out much better than our fears, the plants reviving and yielding a portion of their fruits, if not a full crop. Happily, this year we have had nothing of the kind—the cool moment came earlier—before vegetation was sufficiently advanced to be injured. To-day the air is very pleasant and summer-like.

Walked on Hannah's Height; gathered azaleas in abundance; they are in their prime now, and very beautiful; we have known them, however, to blossom three weeks earlier. Our Dutch ancestors used to call these flowers *Pinxter Blumejies,* from their being usually in bloom about Whit-Sunday; under this name, they figured annually at the great holyday of the negroes, held in old colonial times at Albany and New Amsterdam. The blacks were allowed full liberty to frolic, for several days in Whitsun-week, and they used to hold a fair, building booths, which they never failed to ornament with the *Pinxter Blumejies*. The flowers are very abundant this year, and their deep rose-colored clusters seem to light up the shady woods.

We were in good luck, for we found also a little troop of moccasin plants in flower; frequently, the season has passed without our seeing one, but this afternoon we gathered no less than eighteen of the purple kind, the *Cyprepedium acaule* of botanists. The small yellow, the large yellow, and the showy ladyslipper have also been found here, but they are all becoming more rare.

Friday, 8th.–Rainy morning. It appears that yesterday we missed a fine sight: about dawn it was foggy; a large flock of wild pigeons passing over the valley, became bewildered in the mist, and actually alighted in the heart of the village, which we have never known them to do before. The trees in the churchyard, those in our own grounds, and several other gardens, were loaded with them; unfortunately, no one in the house was aware of their visit at the time. At that early hour, the whole village was quiet, and only a few persons saw them. They were not molested, and remained some little time, fluttering about the trees, or settling on them in large parties. When the fog rose, they took flight again. What a pity to have missed so unusual a sight!

Saturday, 9th.–Charming day. Pleasant row on the lake, which looks very inviting this warm weather; the views are always pleasing: hills and forests, farms and groves, encircling a beautiful sheet of water.

There is certainly no natural object, among all those which make up a landscape, winning so much upon our affection, as water. It is an essential part of prospects, widely different in character. Mountains form a more striking and imposing feature, and they give to a country a character of majesty which cannot exist without them; but not even the mountains, with all their sublime prerogative, can wholly satisfy the mind, when stripped of torrent, cascade, or lake; while, on the other hand, if there be only a quiet brook running through a meadow in some familiar spot, the eye will often turn, unconsciously, in that direction, and linger with interest upon the humble stream. Observe, also, that the waters in themselves are capable of the highest degree of beauty, without the aid of any foreign element to enhance their dignity; give them full sway, let them spread themselves into their widest expanse, let them roll into boundless seas, enfolding the earth in their embrace, with half the heavens for their canopy, and assuredly they have no need to borrow from the mountain or the forest.

Even in a limited water-view, there is a flow of life, a ceaseless variety, which becomes a perpetual source of delight; every passing hour throws over the transparent countenance of the lake, or river, some fresh tint of coloring, calls up some new play of expression beneath the changing influences of the sun, the winds, the clouds, and we are all but cheated into the belief that the waters know something of the sorrows and joys of our own hearts; we turn to them with more than admiration—with the partiality with which we turn to the face of a friend. In the morning, perhaps, we behold the waves charged with the wild power of the storm, dark and threatening, and the evening sun of the same day finds the flood lulled to rest, calmly reflecting the intelligent labors of man, and the sublime works of the Almighty, as though in conscious repose.

Our own highland lake can lay no claim to grandeur; it has no broad expanse, and the mountains about cannot boast of any great height, yet there is a harmony in the different parts of the picture which gives it much merit, and which must always excite a lively feeling of pleasure. The hills are a charming setting for the lake at their feet, neither so lofty as to belittle the sheet of water, nor so low as to be tame and commonplace; there is abundance of wood on their swelling ridges to give the charm of forest scenery, enough of tillage to add the varied interest of cultivation; the lake, with its clear, placid waters, lies gracefully beneath the mountains, flowing here into a quiet little bay, there skirting a wooded point, filling its ample basin, without encroaching on its banks by a rood of marsh or bog.

And then the village, with its buildings and gardens covering the level bank to the southward, is charmingly placed, the waters spreading before it, a ridge of hills rising on either side, this almost wholly wooded, that partly tilled, while beyond lies a background, varied by nearer and farther heights. The little town, though an important feature in the prospect, is not an obtrusive one, but quite in proportion with surrounding objects. It has a cheerful, flourishing aspect, yet rural and unambitious, not aping the bustle and ferment of cities; and certainly one may travel many a mile without finding a village more prettily set down by the water-side.

A collection of buildings always shows well rising immediately from the water; the liquid plain, in its mobile play of expression, and the massive piles of building, with the intricate medley of outline which make up the perspective of a town, when brought naturally into one view, form an admirable contrast, the mind unconsciously delighting in the opposite characters of these chief objects of the scene, each heightening, and yet relieving, the beauty of the other.

Monday, 11th.–Warm day, with soft, hazy sunshine; this sort of atmosphere is always especially fine in a hilly country, shading all the distances so beautifully, from the nearest wooded knoll, to the farthest height. Walked to the Cliffs; found the views very fine. The woods are in great beauty, the foliage very rich, without having lost, as yet, anything of its spring freshness. The hemlocks are still clearly marked with their lighter and darker greens of different years' growth. The old cones are hanging on the pines; many of these remain on the trees all summer. There were very few flowers in the wood where we walked, though I do not know why this should be so; it was composed of fine chestnut and beech, of primitive growth, mingled, as usual, with evergreens. The young seedling forest trees are now springing up everywhere, taking the place of the fading violets. On some of the little beeches and aspens, the growth of one or two seasons, we found the new leaves colored in tender pink, or a shade of red, which is remarkable in trees which do not show any traces of this coloring at other times; even in autumn their brightest tint is usually yellow.

The fire-flies are gleaming about the village gardens this evening–the first we have seen this year.

Tuesday, 12th.–Fine day. The roses are opening at length; they are a fortnight later than last year. This morning we were delighted to find a few May-roses in full bloom; by evening, others will have unfolded–to-morrow, many more will have opened–and in a few days, the village gardens will be thronged with thousands of these noble flowers.

How lavishly are the flowers scattered over the face of the earth! One of the most perfect and delightful works of the Creation, there is yet no other form of beauty so very common. Abounding in different climates, upon varying soils–not a few here to cheer the sad, a few there to reward the good–but countless in their throngs, infinite in their variety, the gift of measureless beneficence–wherever man may live, there grow the flowers.

Wednesday, 13th.–Pale, hazy sunshine. Heard of a dish of wild strawberries; we have not yet seen them ourselves.

Thursday, 14th.–The whip-poor-wills are now heard every evening, from some particular points on the skirts of the village. They arrive here about the first week in May, and continue their peculiar nocturnal note until toward the last of June: "most musical, most melancholy" of night-sounds known in our region. From some houses on the bank of the lake and near the river, they are heard every night; probably the sound comes over the water from the wooded hills beyond, for they are said to prefer high and dry situations. Once in a while, but not very frequently, they come into the village, and we have heard them when they must have been in our own grounds. It is only natural, perhaps, that some lingering shade of superstition should be connected with this singular bird—so often heard, so seldom seen; thousands of men and women in this part of the world have listened to the soft wailing whistle, from childhood to old age, through every summer of a long life, without having once laid their eyes on the bird. Until quite lately, almost every one believed the night-hawk and the whip-poor-will to be the same, merely because the first is often seen by daylight, while the last, which much resembles it, is wholly nocturnal, and only known to those who search for him in the shady woods by day, or meet him by moonlight at night. These birds will soon cease their serenading; after the third week in June, they are rarely heard, in which respect they resemble the nightingale, who sings only for a few weeks in May and June; early in September, they go to the southward. Forty years since, they are said to have been much more numerous here than they are to-day.

Friday, 15th.—Very warm; various sorts of weather in the course of the day. Cloudy morning, brilliant mid-day, and in the afternoon a sudden shower. It rained heavily, with thunder and lightning, for an hour, then cleared again, and we had a charming evening.

Saw a number of humming-birds—they are particularly partial to the evening hours. One is sure to find them now toward sunset, fluttering about their favorite plants; often there are several together among the flowers of the same bush, betraying themselves, though unseen, by the trembling of the leaves and blossoms. They are extremely fond of the Missouri currant—of all the early flowers, it is the greatest favorite with them; they are fond of the lilacs also, but do not care much for the syringa; to the columbine they are partial, to the bee larkspur also, with the wild bergamot or Oswego tea, the speckled jewels, scarlet trumpet-flower, red clover, honeysuckle, and the lychnis tribe. There is something in the form of these tube-shape blossoms, whether small or great, which suits their long, slender bills, and possibly, for the same reason, the bees cannot find such easy access to the honey, and leave more in these than in the open flowers. To the lily the humming-bird pays only a passing compliment, and seems to prefer the great tiger-lily to the other varieties; the rose he seldom visits; he will leave these stately blossoms any day for a head of the common red clover, in which he especially delights. Often of a summer's evening have we watched the humming-birds flitting about the meadows, passing from one tuft of clover to another, then resting a moment on a tall spear of timothy grass, then off again to fresh clover, scarcely touching the other flowers, and continuing frequently in the same field until the very latest twilight.

Mr. Tupper, in his paper on "Beauty," pays a pretty compliment to the humming-bird. Personifying Beauty, he says, she

"Fluttereth into the tulip with the humming-bird."

But, although these little creatures are with us during the tulip season, it may be doubted if they feed on these gaudy blossoms. On first reading the passage, this association struck us as one with which we were not familiar; had it been the trumpet-flower, nothing would have been more natural, for these dainty birds are forever fluttering about the noble scarlet blossoms of that plant, as we all know, but the tulip did not seem quite in place in this connection. Anxious to know whether we had deceived ourselves, we have now watched the humming-birds for several seasons, and, as yet, have never seen one in a tulip, while we have often observed them pass these for other flowers. Possibly this may have been accidental, or other varieties of the humming-bird may have a different taste from our own, and one cannot positively assert that this little creature never feeds on the tulip, without more general examination. But there is something in the upright position of that flower which, added to its size, leads one to believe that it must be an inconvenient blossom for the humming-bird, who generally seems to prefer nodding or drooping flowers, if they are at all large, always feeding on the wing as he does, and never alighting, like butterflies and bees, on the petals. Altogether, we are inclined to believe that if the distinguished author of Proverbial Philosophy had been intimate with our little neighbor, he would have placed him in some other native plant, and not in the Asiatic tulip, to which he seems rather indifferent. The point is a very trifling one, no doubt, and it is extremely bold to find fault with our betters; but in the first place, we are busying ourselves wholly with trifles just now, and then the great work in question has been a source of so much pleasure and advantage to half the world, that no one heeds the misplaced tulip, unless it be some rustic bird-fancier. By supposing the flower of the *tulip-tree* to be meant, the question would be entirely settled to the satisfaction of author, reader, and humming-bird also, who is very partial to those handsome blossoms of his native woods.

It is often supposed that our little friend seeks only the most fragrant flowers; the blossoms on the Western Prairies, those of Wisconsin at least, and probably others also, are said to have but little perfume, and it is observed that the humming-bird is a stranger there, albeit those wilds are a perfect sea of flowers during the spring and summer months. But the amount of honey in a plant has nothing to do with its perfume, for we daily see the humming-birds neglecting the rose and the white lily, while many of their most favorite flowers, such as the scarlet honeysuckle, the columbine, the lychnis tribe, the trumpet flower, and speckled jewels, have no perfume at all. Other pet blossoms of theirs, however, are very fragrant, as the highly-scented Missouri currant, for instance, and the red clover, but their object seems to be quite independent of this particular quality in a plant.

The fancy these little creatures have for perching on a dead twig is very marked; you seldom see them alight elsewhere, and the fact that a leafless branch projects from a bush, seems enough to invite them to rest; it was but yesterday we saw two males sitting upon the same dead branch of a honey-suckle beneath the window. And last summer, there chanced to be a little dead twig, at the highest point of a locust-tree, in sight from the house, which was a favorite perching spot of theirs for some weeks; possibly it was the same bird, or the same pair, who frequented it, but scarcely a day passed without a tiny little creature of the tribe being frequently seen there. Perhaps there may have been a nest close at hand, but they build so cunningly, making their nests look so much like a common bunch of moss or lichen, that they are seldom discovered, although they often build about gardens, and usually at no great height; we have known a nest found in a lilac-bush, and sometimes they are even satisfied with a tall coarse weed; in the woods, they are said to prefer a white oak sapling, seldom building, however, more than ten feet from the ground.

Though so diminutive, they are bold and fearless, making very good battle when necessary, and going about generally in a very careless, confident way. They fly into houses more frequently than any other bird, sometimes attracted by plants or flowers within, often apparently by accident, or for the purpose of exploring. The country people have a saying that when a humming-bird flies in at a window he brings a love message for some one in the house; a pretty fancy, certainly, for Cupid himself could not have desired a daintier *avant courier*. Unfortunately, this trick of flying in at the windows is often a very serious and fatal one to the poor little creatures themselves, whatever felicity it may bring to the Romeo and Juliet of the neighborhood; for they usually quiver about against the ceiling until quite stunned and exhausted, and unless they are caught and set at liberty, soon destroy themselves in this way. We have repeatedly known them found dead in rooms little used, that had been opened to air, and which they had entered unperceived.

They are not so very delicate in constitution as one might suppose. Mr. Wilson remarks that they are much more numerous in this country than the common wren is in England. It is well known that we have but one variety in this part of the continent; there is another in Florida, and there are several more on the Pacific coast, one reaching as far north as Nootka Sound. They frequently appear with us before the chimney-swallows, and I have seen one about our own flower-borders, during a mild autumn, as late as the first of December; they usually disappear, however, much earlier, remaining, perhaps, a month or six weeks later than the swallows. They winter in the tropics, and are said to make their long journeys in pairs, which looks as though they mated for life, like some other birds.

Saturday, 16th.—Warm; thermometer 79 in the shade at five o'clock. Long drive down the valley toward evening. The farms are looking very pleasantly: the young grain waving in the breeze is headed, but not yet colored; the meadows are becoming tinged with their own proper blossoms, the red sorrel flowers, golden buttercups, daisies, and clover appearing successively, until the whole field is gay. The crops generally look very well, promising a good return to the husbandman for his labor. In low grounds, about the brooks, the purple flags are now blooming in profusion, and the thorn-trees are still in flower on many banks.

There is a tradition that during the war of the Revolution the long spines of the thorn were occasionally used by the American women for pins, none of which were manufactured in the country; probably it was the cockspur variety, which bears the longest and most slender spines, and is now in flower. The peculiar condition of the colonies rendered privations of this kind a great additional evil of that memorable struggle; almost everything in the shape of the necessaries and luxuries of life came then from the Old World. Several native plants were prepared at that time to take the place of the prohibited *souchong* and *bohea;* the "New Jersey tea," for instance, a pretty shrub, and the "Labrador tea," a low evergreen with handsome white flowers. Certainly it was only fair that the women should have their share of privations in the shape of pins and tea, when Washington and his brave army were half clad, half armed, half starved, and never paid; the soldiers of that remarkable war, both officers and men, if not literally using the spines of the thorn-tree, like their wives, often went about looking something like Spenser's picture of Despair:

> "His garments naught but many ragged clouts,
> With *thorns* together pinned, and patched was."

In some farm-houses where much knitting and spinning is going on, one occasionally sees a leafless branch of a thorn-bush hanging in a corner, with a ball of yarn on each spine: quite a pretty, rustic device. We saw one the other day which we admired very much.

Monday, 18th.—Lovely day; thermometer 82 in the shade at dinner-time. The wild roses are in flower. We have them of three varieties: the early rose, with reddish branches, which seldom blooms here until the first week in June; the low rose, with a few large flowers; and the tall many-flowered swamp rose, blooming late in the summer. They are quite common about us, and although the humblest of their tribe, they have a grace all their own; there is, indeed, a peculiar modesty about the wild rose which that of the gardens does not always possess. There is one caprice of the gardening art to-day which a rustic finds it difficult to admire, and that is the tall grafted tree roses taking a form which nature assuredly never yet gave to a rose-bush. The flowers themselves may be magnificent as flowers, but one stares at them with curiosity, one does not turn to them with affection; moreover, they look as though they enjoyed being stared at, thereby losing much of their attractiveness; in short, they are not thoroughly rose-like. It is a cruel thing in a gardener to pervert, as it were, the very nature of a plant, and one could sooner forgive the clipping a yew-tree into a peacock, according to the quaint fancy of our forefathers, than this stripping the modest rose of her drapery of foliage—it reminds one of the painful difference between the gentle, healthy-hearted daughter of home, the light of the house, and the meretricious dancer, tricked out upon the stage to dazzle and bewilder, and be stared at by the mob. The rose has so long been an emblem of womanly loveliness, that we do not like to see her shorn of one feminine attribute; and modesty in every true-hearted woman is, like affection, a growth of her very nature, whose roots are fed with her life's blood. No; give back her leaves to the rose, that her flowers may open amid their native branches. This veil of verdure, among whose folds the starry blossoms bud, and bloom, and die, has been given to every plant—the lowly dew-drop, as well as the gorgeous martagon; nay, it is the inheritance of the very rudest weeds; and yet the rose, the noblest flower on earth, you would deprive of this priceless grace!

We are very fortunate in having the wild roses about our own haunts; they are not found everywhere. M. de Humboldt mentions that in his travels in South America he never saw one, even in the higher and cooler regions, where other brambles and plants of a temperate climate were common.

Tuesday, 19th.—Fine strawberries from the fields this evening for tea. Warm, bright weather; thermometer 85—lovely evening, but too warm for much exercise. Strolled in the lane, enjoying the fragrant meadows, and the waving corn-fields on the skirts of the village.

A meadow near at hand would seem to give more pleasure than a corn-field. Grain, to appear to full advantage, should be seen at a little distance, where one may note the changes in its coloring with the advancing season, where one may enjoy the play of light when the summer clouds throw their shadows there, or the breezes chase one another over the waving lawn. It is like a piece of shaded silk which the salesman throws off a little, that you may better appreciate the effect. But a meadow is a delicate embroidery in colors, which you must examine closely to understand all its merits; the nearer you are, the better. One must bend over the grass to find the blue violet in May, the red strawberry in June; one should be close at hand to mark the first appearance of the simple field-blossoms, clover, red and white, buttercup and daisy, with the later lily, and primrose, and meadow-tuft; one should be nigh to breathe the sweet and fresh perfume, which increases daily until the mowers come with their scythes.

The grasses which fill our meadows are very many of them foreign plants; among these are the vernal-grass, which gives such a delightful fragrance to the new-mown hay. The timothy is also an imported grass; so is the meadow-grass considered as the best of all for pasture; the orchard-grass much esteemed also; and the canary-grass, which yields a seed for birds. Some of the most troublesome weeds of this tribe are naturalized, as the dar-nel in pastures, the chess or cheat of the grain-fields; quaking-grass, quitch-grass, yard-grass, and crab-grass, also. Altogether, there are some thirty va-rieties of these imported grasses enumerated by botanists in this part of the country.

A number more are common to both continents, like the Vanilla-grass, often gathered for its perfume, and which in Northern Europe is called holy-grass, from its being scattered before church-doors on holydays; and the manna-grass, bearing sweet grains, which are eaten in Holland and some other countries; the dent-grasses, also, good for cattle, several of which are natives, while others have been introduced. There seem to be some twenty varieties which thus belong to both continents.

In addition to the preceding, there are upwards of a hundred more grasses belonging strictly to the soil; many of these are mere weeds, though others are very useful. Among the native plants of this kind are nimble-will, a great favorite with the Kentucky farmers, and found as far east as this State; several useful kinds of fescue-grass, and soa, one of which has something of the fragrance of the vernal-grass, and the reed canary-grass, of which the ribbon-grass of gardeners is a variety; the salt grasses of the coast, also, very important to the sea-shore farmers. Among the native plants of this tribe we have the wild oat, wild rye, wild barley, mountain rice, and wild rice, found in many of the waters of this State, both fresh and brackish.

Altogether, of some hundred and fifty grasses, about one-fifth of the number seem of foreign origin; but if we consider their importance to the farmer, and the extent of cultivated soil they now cover, we must take a different view of them; probably in this sense the native grasses scarcely rank more than as one to four in our meadows and cultivated lands.

The clovers, also, though thoroughly naturalized, are most of them imported plants: the downy "rabbit-foot," or "stone-clover," the common red variety; the "zig-zag," and the "hop clovers," are all introduced. The question regarding the white clover has not been clearly settled, but it is usually considered, I believe, as indigenous, though some botanists mark the point as doubtful. The buffalo clover found in the western part of this State, and common still farther westward, is the only undoubtedly native variety we possess.

Wednesday, 20th.—Very warm day; thermometer 93 in the shade at three o'clock. The locust flowers are perfuming the village; one perceives their fragrance within doors, throughout the house. In many parts of the country these beautiful trees have been very much injured of late years by a worm called the *borer,* which is very destructive wherever it appears. In the pleasant villages at the westward, where locusts are so much in favor for planting in the streets, they have been very much injured, and their blighted branches give quite a melancholy look to some of these towns. Fortunately for us, the trees in our neighborhood are yet unscathed; these *borers* have not, I believe, appeared anywhere in the county.[10]

Thursday, 21st.—Extremely warm; thermometer 92. Happily, there have been pleasant western breezes through these warm days. Strolled about the village in the evening; saw an old neighbor of threescore and fifteen at work in his garden, hoeing his dozen corn-hills, and weeding his cucumber vines.

One always loves a garden; labor wears its pleasantest aspect there. From the first days of spring, to latest autumn, we move about among growing plants, gay flowers, and cheerful fruits; and there is some pretty change to note by the light of every sun. Even the narrowest cottage patch looks pleasantly to those who come and go along the highway; it is well to stop now and then when walking, and look over the paling of such little gardens, and note what is going on there.

Potatoes, cabbages, and onions are grown here by every family as first requisites. Indian corn and cucumbers are also thought indispensable, for Americans of all classes eat as much maize as their Indian predecessors. And as for cucumbers, they are required at every meal of which a thorough-going Yankee partakes, either as salad in summer, or pickled in winter. We sometimes see men about the villages eating them unseasoned like apples. Peas and beans rank next in favor; some of each are generally found in the smallest gardens. Beets, turnips, and carrots are not so very common; they are not thought absolutely necessary; one sees gardens without them. Rad-ishes do not thrive well in this soil, but the light green leaves of the lettuce are seen everywhere. There is usually a pumpkin-vine running about the corn-hills, its large yellow flowers and golden fruit showing, as a matter of course, below the glossy leaves of the maize; a part of the fruit is made into pies, the rest goes to the cow or pig. Sometimes you find squashes, also, in these small gardens, with a few tomatoes, perhaps; but these last are difficult to raise here, on account of the occasional frosts of May.

Flowers are seldom forgotten in the cottage garden; the widest walk is lined with them, and there are others beneath the low windows of the house. You have rose-bushes, sun-flowers, and holly-hocks, as a matter of course; generally a cluster of pinks, bachelor's buttons, also, and a sweet pea, which is a great favorite; plenty of marigolds, a few poppies, large purple china asters, and a tuft of the lilac phlox. Such are the blossoms to be seen before most doors; and each is pretty in its own time and place; one has a long-standing regard for them all, including the homely sun-flower, which we should be sorry to miss from its old haunts. Then the scarlet flowering bean, so intimately connected with childish recollections of the hero Jack and his wonderful adventure, may still be seen flourishing in the cottage garden, and it would seem to have fallen from a pod of the identical plant celebrated in nursery rhyme, for it has a great inclination for climbing, which is gen-erally encouraged by training it over a window. We do not hear, however, of any in these parts reaching the roof in a single night's growth. You must go to the new lands on the prairies for such marvels now-a-days. They tell a wonderful story of a cucumber-vine somewhere beyond the great lakes, in the last "new settlement," probably; the seed having been sowed one evening in a good bit of soil, the farmer, going to his work next morning, found it not only out of the ground, but grown so much that he was curious to mea-sure it; "he followed it to the end of his garden, over a fence, along an In-dian trail, through an oak opening, and then seeing it stretch some distance beyond, he went back for his horse, but while he was saddling old Bald the vine had so much the advantage of him that it reached the next clearing before he did; there he left it to go back to dinner; and how much farther it ran that day Ebenezer could not tell for certain."

We have no such wonders hereabouts; and even the ambitious bean seldom reaches higher than a low roof; nor is its growth always sufficiently luxuriant to shade the window, for it often shares that task with a morning-glory. The plan of these leafy blinds is a pretty one, but they are too often trained in stiff and straight lines; a poetical idea, *tirée à quatre épingles*. Frequently we see a cottage with a door in the centre, and one window on each side, and vines trained over the sashes in this way, which gives it an odd look, like a house in green spectacles, as it were. When hop-vines are used for screening the windows, which is often the case, the plant is not so easily restrained; and throwing out its luxuriant branches right and left, takes care of itself.

Currants are almost the only fruit seen in the smaller gardens of our neighborhood; even gooseberries are not so general; both raspberries and strawberries grow wild here in such profusion that few persons cultivate them. Currants, by-the-by, both black and red, are also native plants; the black currant is by no means rare in this State, and very much resembles the varieties cultivated in gardens; the wild red currant is chiefly confined to the northern parts of the country, and it is precisely like that which we cultivate. Both purple and green gooseberries are also found wild in our woods.

It is often a matter of surprise and regret that fruit should not be more cultivated among us in gardens of all sizes; but the indifferent common cherry is almost the only fruit-tree found here in cottage gardens. Even the farmers neglect cherries, and plums, and pears, surprisingly. Peaches and grapes seldom ripen here in the open air; they might probably be cultivated as wall fruit, but it is so easy now to procure them by railroad from other counties, that few persons care to try experiments of this kind. Peaches, and melons, and plums, brought from a distance, are carried about the village for sale, throughout the season, as a matter of course.

There is, unhappily, a very serious objection to cultivating fruit in our village gardens; fruit-stealing is a very common crime in this part of the world; and the standard of principle on such subjects is as low as it well can be in our rural communities. Property of this kind is almost without protection among us; there are laws on the subject, but these are never enforced, and of course people are not willing to throw away money, and time, and thought, to raise fruit for those who might easily raise it for themselves, if they would take the pains to do so. There can be no doubt that this state of things is a serious obstacle to the cultivation of choice fruit in our villages; horticulture would be in a much higher condition here if it were not for this evil. But the impunity with which boys, and men, too, are allowed to commit thefts of this kind, is really a painful picture, for it must inevitably lead to increase a spirit of dishonesty throughout the community.

It is the same case with flowers. Many people seem to consider them as public property, though cultivated at private expense. It was but the other day that we saw a little girl, one of the village Sunday-scholars, moreover, put her hand within the railing of a garden and break off several very fine plants, whose growth the owner had been watching with care and interest for many weeks, and which had just opened to reward his pains. Another instance of the same kind, but still more flagrant in degree, was observed a short time since: the offender was a full-grown man, dressed in fine broadcloth to boot, and evidently a stranger; he passed before a pretty yard, gay with flowers, and unchecked by a single scruple of good manners, or good morals, proceeded to make up a handsome bouquet, without so much as saying by your leave to the owner; having selected the flowers most to his fancy, he arranged them tastefully, and then walked off with a free and jaunty air, and an expression of satisfaction and self-complacency truly ridiculous under the circumstances. He had made up his nosegay with so much pains, eyed it so tenderly as he carried it before him, and moved along with such a very mincing and dainty manner, that he was probably on the way to present himself and his trophy to his sweetheart; and we can only hope that he met with just such a reception as was deserved by a man who had been committing petty larceny. As if to make the chapter complete, the very same afternoon, the village being full of strangers, we saw several young girls, elegantly flounced, put their hands through the railing of another garden, facing the street, and help themselves in the same easy manner to their neighbor's prettiest flowers: what would they have thought if some one had stepped up with a pair of scissors and cut half a yard from the ribbon on their hats, merely because it was pretty, and one had a fancy for it? Neither the little girl, nor the strangers in broadcloth and flounces, seem to have learned at common school, or at Sunday school, or at home, that respect for the pleasures of others is simple good manners, regard for the rights of others, common honesty.

No one who had a flower border of his own would be likely to offend in this way; he would not do so unwittingly, at least; and if guilty of such an act, it would be premeditated pilfering. When people take pains to cultivate fruits and flowers themselves, they have some idea of their value, which can only be justly measured by the owner's regard for them. And then, moreover, gardening is a civilizing and improving occupation in itself; its influences are all beneficial; it usually makes people more industrious, and more amiable. Persuade a careless, indolent man to take an interest in his garden, and his reformation has begun. Let an idle woman honestly watch over her own flower-beds, and she will naturally become more active. There is always work to be done in a garden, some little job to be added to yesterday's task, without which it is incomplete; books may be closed with a mark where one left off, needlework may be thrown aside and resumed again; a sketch may be left half finished, a piece of music half practiced; even attention to household matters may relax in some measure for a while; but regularity and method are constantly required, are absolutely indispensable, to the well-being of a garden. The occupation itself is so engaging, that one commences readily, and the interest increases so naturally, that no great share of perseverance is needed to continue the employment, and thus labor becomes a pleasure, and the dangerous habit of idleness is checked. Of all faults of character, there is not one, perhaps, depending so entirely upon habit as indolence; and nowhere can one learn a lesson of order and diligence more prettily and more pleasantly than from a flower-garden.

But another common instance of the good effect of gardening may be mentioned:—it naturally inclines one to be open-handed. The bountiful returns which are bestowed, year after year, upon our feeble labors, shame us into liberality. Among all the misers who have lived on earth, probably few have been gardeners. Some cross-grained churl may set out, perhaps, with a determination to be niggardly with the fruits and flowers of his portion; but gradually his feelings soften, his views change, and before he has housed the fruits of many summers, he sees that these good things are but the free gifts of Providence to himself, and he learns at last that it is a pleasure, as well as a duty, to give. This head of cabbage shall be sent to a poor neighbor; that basket of refreshing fruit is reserved for the sick; he has pretty nosegays for his female friends; he has apples or peaches for little people; nay, perhaps in the course of years, he at length achieves the highest act of generosity—he bestows on some friendly rival a portion of his rarest seed, a shoot from his most precious root! Such deeds are done by gardeners.

Horticulture is not carried on upon a great scale anywhere in this county. We regret that this should be so. A large garden, where taste and knowledge have full scope, is indeed a noble work, full of instruction and delight. The rare trees and plants brought with toil, and cost, and patience, from distant regions; the rich variety of fruits and vegetables; the charming array of flowers, are among the most precious and the most graceful trophies of commerce, and industry, and adventure. Such gardens, whether public or private, are always desirable in a neighborhood. They are among the best gifts of wealth, and scatter abroad too many benefits to deserve the doubtful name of a luxury. If we have none near enough to bring good to our own rural village, it is at least pleasant to remember that other communities are more fortunate than ourselves. When one cannot enjoy some particular good thing one's self, a very little charity, and a very little philosophy, lead one to be glad, at least, that others may profit by it.

A very striking proof of the civilizing effect of large gardens may be seen any day in the great towns on the Continent of Europe, whether in France, Italy, Germany, &c., &c. In those old countries, where grounds of this kind have been more or less open to the public for generations, the privilege is never abused by any disgraceful act. The flowers, the trees, the statuary, remain uninjured year after year; it never seems to occur to the most reckless and abandoned to injure them. The general population of those towns is, in many respects, inferior to our own; but in this particular point their tone of civilization rises far above the level of this country.

Friday, 22d.—Still very warm; thermometer 90 in the shade. Although the heat has been greater and more prolonged than usual in this part of the country, still there is a sort of corrective in our highland air which is a great relief; the same degree of the thermometer produces much more suffering in the lower counties, particularly in the towns. Extreme lassitude from the heat is seldom felt here; and our nights are almost always comparatively cool, which is a very great advantage.

Saturday, 23d.—Bright, warm day; thermometer 89. Fine air from the west.

Pleasant walk in the evening. Met a party of children coming from the woods with wild flowers. In May or June, one often meets little people bringing home flowers or berries from the hills; and if you stop to chat with them, they generally offer you a share of their nosegay or their partridge-berries; they are as fond of these last as the birds, and they eat the young aromatic leaves also. Their first trip to the woods, after the snow has gone, is generally in quest of these berries; a week or two later, they go upon the hills for our earliest flowers—ground-laurel and squirrel-cups; a little later, they gather violets, and then again, the azalea, or "wild honeysuckle," as they call it, to which they are very partial.

But, though pleased with the flowers, the little creatures seldom know their names. This seems a pity; but we have often asked them what they called this or that blossom in their hands, and they seldom could give an answer, unless it happened to be a rose, perhaps, or a violet, or something of that sort, familiar to every one. But their elders are generally quite as ignorant as themselves in this way; frequently, when we first made acquaintance with the flowers of the neighborhood, we asked grown persons–learned, perhaps, in many matters–the common names of plants they must have seen all their lives, and we found they were no wiser than the children or ourselves. It is really surprising how little the country people know on such subjects. Farmers and their wives, who have lived a long life in the fields, can tell you nothing on these matters. The men are even at fault among the trees on their own farms, if these are at all out of the common way; and as for the smaller native plants, they know less about them than Buck or Brindle, their own oxen. Like the children, they sometimes pick a pretty flower to bring home, but they have no name for it. The women have some little acquaintance with herbs and simples, but even in such cases they frequently make strange mistakes; they also are attracted by the wild flowers; they gather them, perhaps, but they cannot name them. And yet, this is a day when flower borders are seen before every door, and every young girl can chatter largely about "bouquets," and the "Language of Flowers" to boot.

It is true, the common names of our wild flowers are, at best, in a very unsatisfactory state. Some are miscalled after European plants of very different characters. Very many have one name here, another a few miles off, and others again have actually, as yet, no English names whatever. They are all found in botanical works under long, clumsy, Latin appellations, very little fitted for every-day uses, just like the plants of our gardens, half of which are only known by long-winded Latin polysyllables, which timid people are afraid to pronounce. But, annoying as this is in the garden, it is still worse in the fields. What has a dead language to do on every-day occasions with the living blossoms of the hour? Why should a strange tongue sputter its uncouth, compound syllables upon the simple weeds by the way-side? If these hard words were confined to science and big books, one would not quarrel with the roughest and most pompous of them all; but this is so far from being the case, that the evil is spreading over all the woods and meadows, until it actually perverts our common speech, and libels the helpless blossoms, turning them into so many "précieuses ridicules." Happy is it for the rose that she was named long ago; if she had chanced to live until our day, by some prairie stream, or on some remote ocean island, she would most assuredly have been called Tom, Dick, or Harry, in Greek or Latin.

Before people were overflowing with science–at a time when there was some simplicity left in the world, the flowers received much better treatment in this way. Pretty, natural names were given them in olden times, as though they had been called over by some rural party—cherry-cheeked maidens, and merry-hearted lads—gone a-Maying, of a pleasant spring morning. Many of those old names were thoroughly homely and rustic, such as the ox-eye, crow-foot, cowslip, butter-cup, pudding-grass, which grew in every meadow; then there was the hare-bell, which loved to hang its light blue bells about the haunts of the timid hare; the larkspur; the bindweed, winding about shrubs and bushes; the honeysuckle, which every child has stolen many a time from the bees; spicy gilliflowers, a corruption of July-flowers, from the month in which they blossomed; daffadowndillies, a puzzle for etymologists; pennyroyal; holly-hock, or holy-oak, as it was sometimes written; paigle, another name for cowslips; primrose, from the early season when the flower blooms; carnation, or "coronation," from the custom of wearing them in wreaths. These last were also called *sops-in-wine,* from their being thrown into wine to improve its flavor, a custom which seems to have prevailed formerly in England; the old Greeks had a practice of the same kind, for l'Abbé Bartholemi tells us that they threw roses and violets into their wine-casks, for the purpose of flavoring their wines. May not this ancient custom prove the origin of the common French phrase—*le bouquet du vin?*

There were other names, again, given to the plants in those good old times, showing a touch of quaint humor—like Bouncing-Bet, Ragged-Robin, bachelor's-button, snap-dragon, foxglove, monks-hood. Others bore names which showed there had been lovers in the fields—like Sweet-Cicely, Sweet-William, heart's-ease, pansies, truelove. Even mere personal names, such as are so often given to-day, were far better managed then—as for instance, Herb-Robert, Good King-Henry, Marietts, Bartram, Angelica. Others, again, were imaginative or fanciful—as morning-glory, night-shade, flag, loose-strife, wake-robin, simpler's-joy, thrift, speedwell, traveller's-joy, snow-drop, winter's pale foundling, wayfaring-tree, eye-bright, shepherd's-purse, pink meaning *eye,* in Dutch, like the French *œillet;* marigold, lady's-smock—from the white leaves of these flowers blooming in the grass, like bleaching linen; the wall-flower, which loved the shade of knightly banners and pennons, and still clings faithfully to falling ruins; king's-spears, flower-gentle, goldilocks, yellow-golds, the flower de luce, flower of light, which great painters have placed in the hands of saintly personages in many a noble work of art; the sweet-daisy or day's-eye, the "eye of day," as Chaucer has called it.

After such names as these, ought we not to be thoroughly ashamed of appellations like Batschia, Schoberia, Buchnera, Goodyera, Brugmannsia, Heuchera, Scheuzeria, Schizanthus, and as many more to match as you please? Names remarkably well adapted to crocodiles, and rattlesnakes, and scorpions, but little suited, one would think, to the flowers gentle of the field. There is a modest little blossom known to all the world as having been highly honored in different countries. *La Marguerite* was probably first named in the *chansons* of some lover troubadour, some noble brother-in-arms, perhaps, of him who sang Blanche of Castille so sweetly:

> "Las! si j'avais pouvoir d'oublier
> Sa beauté, son bien-dire
> Et son très-doux regarder,
> Finirait mon martyre!"

We may well believe it to have been some such knightly poet who first felt the charm of that simple flower, and blending its name and image with that of his lady-love, sang: "*Si douce est la Marguerite!*" So long as knights wore arms, and couched lances in behalf of ladies fair, so long was la Marguerite a favored flower of chivalry, honored by all *preux chevaliers;* knight and squire bore its fame over the sea to merry England, over Alps and Pyrenees also; in Spain it is still *la Margarita;* in Italy, *la Margherettina.* The Italians, by-the-by, have also a pretty rustic name of their own for it, *la pratellina,* the little fielding. And now, when the old towers of feudal castles are falling to the ground, when even the monumental statues of knight and dame are crumbling into dust where they lie in the churches, now at this very day, you may still find the name of *la Marguerite* upon the lips of the peasant girls of France; you may see them measuring the love of their swains by the petals of these flowers, pulling them, one after another, and repeating, as each falls, *un peu, beaucoup, passionément, pas du tout;* the last leaflet deciding the all-important question by the word that accompanies it; alas! that it must sometimes prove *pas du tout!* Oddly enough, in Germany, the land of sentiment and *Vergiessmeinnicht,* this flower of love and chivalry has been degraded into——shall we say it,——*Gänseblume,*–Goose-blossom! Such, at least, is one of its names; we hasten, however, to call it, with others, *Masliebe,* or love-measure: probably from the same fancy of pulling the petals to try lovers' hearts by. In England, the Saxon *daisy* has always been a great favorite with rural poets and country-folk, independently of its knightly honors, as *la*

Marguerite. Chaucer, as we all know, delighted in it; he rose before the sun, he went a-field, he threw himself on the ground to watch the daisy —

> "To seen this flour so yong, so fresh of hew,
> ————————till it unclosed was
> Upon the smal, soft, swete gras."

Now can one believe that if the daisy, or the *Marguerite,* had been called *Caractacussia,* or *Chlodovigia,* it would have been sung by knightly troubadours and minstrels, in every corner of feudal Europe? Can you fancy this flower, "so yong, so fresh of hew," to have delighted Chaucer, under the title of *Sirhumphreydavya,* or *Sirwilliamherschellia,* or *Doctorjohnsonia?* Can you imagine the gentle Emilie, in the garden gathering flowers —

> "To make a sotel garland for her hed,
> While as an angel, hevonlich, she song:—"

Can you imagine this gentle creature, or any other, of whom it might be said,

> "Her cheare was simple as bird in bower,
> As white as lilly, or rose in rise:"

Can you picture to yourself *such* maidens, weaving in their golden tresses, *Symphoricarpus vulgaris, Tricochloa, Tradescantia, Calopogon?* &c., &c. Or conceive for a moment some Perdita of the present day, singing in her sweetest tones:

> "Here's flowers for you —
> Pyxidanthera, Rudbeckia, Sclerolepis,
> Escholtzia, that goes to bed with the sun," &c., &c.

Fancy her calling for fragrant blossoms to bestow on her young maiden friends: "Spargonophorus, Rhododendron, Sabbatia, Schizea, Schollera, Schistidium, Waldsteinia, and the tall Vernonia, Noveborences," &c., &c. Do you suppose that if she had gone on in that style, Florizel would have whispered: "When you speak sweet, I'd have you do it ever?" No, indeed! he would have stopped his ears, and turned to Mopsa and Dorcas. Fancy poor Ophelia prattling to Laertes about the wreath she had woven; instead of her "rosemary," and "pansies," and "herb-o'grace," hear her discourse about "Plantanthera Blepharoglottis, or Psycodes, Ageratum, Syntheris, Houghtoniana, Banksia, and Jeffersonia," &c., &c. Could her brother in that case have possibly called her "O, rose of May, dear maid, kind sister, sweet

Ophelia?" No, indeed! And we may rest assured, that if the daisy, the *douce Marguerite,* had borne any one of these names, Chaucer would have snapped his fingers at it. We may feel confident that Shakspeare would then have showed it no mercy; all his fairies would have hooted at it; he would have tossed it to Sycorax and Caliban; he would not have let either Perdita or Ophelia touch it, nor Miranda, with her *très doux regarder,* look at it once.

Neither daisy, nor cowslip, nor snow-drop is found among the fields of the New World, but blossoms just as sweet and pretty are not wanting here, and it is really a crying shame to misname them. Unhappily, a large number of our plants are new discoveries—new, at least, when compared with Chaucer's daisy, Spenser's coronation flower, or Shakspeare's "pansies and herb-o'-grace"—and having been first gathered since the days of Linnæus, as specimens, their names tell far more of the musty hortus siccus, than of the gay and fragrant May-pole. But if we wish those who come after us to take a natural, unaffected pleasure in flowers, we should have names for the blossoms that mothers and nurses can teach children before they are "in Botany;" if we wish that American poets should sing our native flowers as sweetly and as simply as the daisy, and violets, and celandine have been sung from the time of Chaucer or Herrick, to that of Burns and Wordsworth, we must look to it that they have natural, pleasing names.

Monday, 25th.—Pleasant day; much cooler; thermometer 75. Yesterday, Sunday, we had a shower, which has very much refreshed the air for us here. No thunder or lightning, however, in spite of the previous heat. Long walk this afternoon. Passing through a wheat-field, heard a full chorus of crickets and other insects; they have begun their summer song in earnest. Goldfinches were flying about in little flocks; they are very social creatures, always pleased to be together.

Tuesday, 26th.—Fine day; soft breeze from the north, the wind much warmer than usual from that quarter. Thermometer 78. Walked in the woods. The dogmackie is in flower, and being so common, its white blossoms look very cheerfully in the woods. These flowering shrubs, which live and bloom in shady groves, are scarcely ever touched by the sunbeams; but they are none the less beautiful for the subdued light which plays about them. The dogmackie, like others of the same family, is also called arrow-wood; probably their branches and stems have been employed, at some period or other in the history of arms, for making arrows. We have never heard whether the Indians used the wood in this way.

It was a pretty sight, coming home, to see the women and children scattered about the meadows, gathering wild strawberries. This delightful fruit is very abundant here, growing everywhere, in the woods, along the road-sides, and in every meadow. Happily for us, the wild strawberries rather increase than diminish in cultivated lands; they are even more common among the foreign grasses of the meadows than within the woods. The two varieties marked by our botanists are both found about our lake.

This wild harvest of fruit, a blessing to all, is an especial advantage to the poor; from the first strawberries in June, there is a constant succession until the middle of September. In a week or two we shall have raspberries: both the red and the black varieties are very abundant, and remarkably good. Then come the blackberries—plenty here as in the neighborhood of Falstaff; the running kind, or vine-blackberry, bearing the finest fruit of all its tribe, and growing abundantly on Long Island and in Westchester, is not, however, found in our hills. Whortleberries abound in our woods, and on every waste hill-side. Wild gooseberries are common, and last summer we met a man with a pail of them, which he was carrying to the village for sale. Wild plums are also common, and frequently brought to market. The large purple flower of the rose-raspberry yields a fruit of a beautiful color and pleasant, acid taste, but it is seldom eaten in quantities. Wild grape-vines are very common, and formerly the fruit used to be gathered for sale, but of late years we have not seen any. All these lesser kinds of wild fruits, strawberries, raspberries, blackberries, and whortleberries, are gathered, to a very great extent, for sale; women, children, and occasionally men also, find it a profitable employment to bring them to market; an industrious woman has made in this way, during the fruit season, thirty dollars, without neglecting her family, and we have known an old man who made forty dollars in one summer; children also, if well disposed, can easily support themselves by the same means. Strawberries sell in the village at a shilling a quart; blackberries for three or four cents; raspberries, and whortleberries also, from three to five cents a quart.

Wednesday, 27th.—Charming day; thermometer 80. Towards sunset strolled in the lane.

The fields which border this quiet bit of road are among the oldest in our neighborhood, belonging to one of the first farms cleared near the village; they are in fine order, and to look at them, one might readily believe these lands had been under cultivation for ages. But such is already very much the character of the whole valley; a stranger moving along the highway looks in vain for any striking signs of a new country; as he passes from farm to farm in unbroken succession, the aspect of the whole region is smiling and fruitful. Probably there is no part of the earth, within the limits of a temperate climate, which has taken the aspect of an old country so soon as our native land; very much is due, in this respect, to the advanced state of civilization in the present age, much to the active, intelligent character of the people, and something, also, to the natural features of the country itself. There are no barren tracts in our midst, no deserts which defy cultivation; even our mountains are easily tilled—arable, many of them, to their very summits—while the most sterile among them are more or less clothed with vegetation in their natural state. Altogether, circumstances have been very much in our favor.

While observing, this afternoon, the smooth fields about us, it was easy, within the few miles of country in sight at the moment, to pick out parcels of land in widely different conditions, and we amused ourselves by following upon the hill-sides the steps of the husbandman, from the first rude clearing, through every successive stage of tillage, all within range of the eye at the same instant. Yonder, for instance, appeared an opening in the forest, marking a new clearing still in the rudest state, black with charred stumps and rubbish; it was only last winter that the timber was felled on that spot, and the soil was first opened to the sunshine, after having been shaded by the old woods for more ages than one can tell. Here, again, on a nearer ridge, lay a spot not only cleared, but fenced, preparatory to being tilled; the decayed trunks and scattered rubbish having been collected in heaps and burnt. Probably that spot will soon be ploughed, but it frequently happens that land is cleared of the wood, and then left in a rude state, as wild pasture-ground; an indifferent sort of husbandry this, in which neither the soil nor the wood receives any attention; but there is more land about us in this condition than one would suppose. The broad hill-side, facing the lane in which we were walking, though cleared perhaps thirty years since, has continued untilled to the present hour. In another direction, again, lies a field of new land, ploughed and seeded for the first time within the last few weeks; the young maize plants, just shooting out their glossy leaves, are the first crop ever raised there, and when harvested, the grain will prove the first fruits the earth has ever yielded to man from that soil, after lying fallow for thousands of seasons. Many other fields in sight have just gone through the usual rotation of crops, showing what the soil can do in various ways; while the farm before us has been under cultivation from the earliest history of the village, yielding every season, for the last half century, its share of grass and grain. To one familiar with the country, there is a certain plea-

sure in thus beholding the agricultural history of the neighborhood unfolding before one, following upon the farms in sight these progressive steps in
cultivation.

The pine stumps are probably the only mark of a new country which
would be observed by a stranger. With us, they take the place of rocks,
which are not common; they keep possession of the ground a long while—
some of those about us are known to have stood more than sixty years, or
from the first settlement of the country, and how much longer they will last,
time alone can tell. In the first years of cultivation, they are a very great
blemish, but after a while, when most of them have been burnt or uprooted,
a gray stump here and there, among the grass of a smooth field, does not
look so very much amiss, reminding one, as it does, of the brief history of
the country. Possibly there may be something of partiality in this opinion,
just as some lovers have been found to admire a freckled face, because the
rosy cheek of their sweetheart was mottled with brown freckles; people generally may not take the same view of the matter, they may think that even
the single stump had better be uprooted. Several ingenious machines have
been invented for getting rid of these enemies, and they have already done
good service in the county. Some of them work by levers, others by wheels;
they usually require three or four men and a yoke of oxen, or a horse, to
work them, and it is really surprising what large stumps are drawn out of the
earth by these contrivances, the strongest roots cracking and snapping like
threads. Some digging about the stump is often necessary as a preliminary
step, to enable the chain to be fastened securely, and occasionally the axe is
used to relieve the machine; still, they work so expeditiously, that contracts
are taken to clear lands in this way, at the rate of twenty or thirty cents a
stump, when, according to the old method, working by hand, it would cost,
perhaps, two or three dollars to uproot a large one thoroughly. In the course
of a day, these machines will tear up from twenty to fifty stumps, according
to their size. Those of the pine, hemlock, and chestnut are the most difficult
to manage, and these last longer than those of other trees. When uprooted,
the stumps are drawn together in heaps and burnt, or frequently they are
turned to account as fences, being placed on end, side by side, their roots
interlocking, and a more wild and formidable barrier about a quiet field
cannot well be imagined. These rude fences are quite common in our neighborhood, and being peculiar, one rather likes them; it is said that they last
much longer than other wooden fences, remaining in good condition for
sixty years.

But although the stumps remaining here and there may appear to a stranger the only sign of a new country to be found here, yet closer observation will show others of the same character. Those wild pastures upon hill-sides, where the soil has never been ploughed, look very differently from other fallows. Here you observe a little hillock rounding over a decayed stump, there a petty hollow where some large tree has been uprooted by the storm; fern and brake also are seen in patches, instead of the thistle and the mullein. Such open hill-sides, even when rich and grassy, and entirely free from wood or bushes, bear a kind of heaving, billowy character, which, in certain lights, becomes very distinct; these ridges are formed by the roots of old trees, and remain long after the wood has entirely decayed. Even on level ground there is always an elevation about the root of an old tree and upon a hill-side, these petty knolls show more clearly as they are thrown into relief by the light; they become much bolder, also, from the washing of the soil, which accumulates above, and is carried away from the lower side of the trunk, leaving, often, a portion of the root bare in that direction. Of course, the older a wood and the larger its trees, the more clearly will this billowy character be marked. The tracks of the cattle also make the formation more ridge-like, uniting one little knoll with another, for when feeding, they generally follow one another, their heads often turned in one direction, and upon a hill-side they naturally take a horizontal course, as the most convenient. Altogether, the billowy face of these rude hill-sides is quite striking and peculiar, when seen in a favorable light.

But there are softer touches also, telling the same story of recent cultivation. It frequently happens, that walking about our farms, among rich fields, smooth and well worked, one comes to a low bank, or some little nook, a strip of land never yet cultivated, though surrounded on all sides by ripening crops of eastern grains and grasses. One always knows such places by the pretty native plants growing there. It was but the other day we paused to observe a spot of this kind in a fine meadow, near the village, neat and smooth, as though worked from the days of Adam. A path made by the workmen and cattle crosses the field, and one treads at every step upon plantain, that regular path-weed of the Old World; following this track, we come to a little runnel, which is dry and grassy now, though doubtless at one time the bed of a considerable spring; the banks are several feet high, and it is filled with native plants; on one side stands a thorn-tree, whose morning shadow falls upon grasses and clovers brought from beyond the seas, while in the afternoon, it lies on gyromias and moose-flowers, sarsaparillas and cahoshes, which bloomed here for ages, when the eye of the red man alone beheld them. Even within the limits of the village spots may still be found on the bank of the river, which are yet unbroken by the plough, where the trailing arbutus, and squirrel-cups, and May-wings tell us so every spring; in older regions, these children of the forest would long since have vanished from all the meadows and villages, for the plough would have passed a thousand times over every rood of such ground.

The forest flowers, the gray stumps in our fields, and the heaving surface of our wild hill-sides, are not, however, the only waymarks to tell the brief course of cultivation about us. These speak of the fallen forest; but here, as elsewhere, the waters have also left their impression on the face of the earth, and in these new lands the marks of their passage are seen more clearly than in older countries. They are still, in many places, sharp and distinct, as though fresh from the workman's hand. Our valleys are filled with these traces of water-work; the most careless observer must often be struck with their peculiar features, and it appears remarkable that here, at an elevation so much above the great western lakes, upon this dividing ridge, at the very fountain head of a stream, running several hundred miles to the sea, these lines are as frequent and as boldly marked as though they lay in a low country subject to floods. Large mounds rise like islands from the fields, their banks still sharply cut; in other spots a depressed meadow is found below the level of the surrounding country, looking like a drained lake, enclosed within banks as plainly marked as the works of a fortification; a shrunken brook, perhaps, running to-day where a river flowed at some period of past time. Quite near the village, from the lane where we were walking this evening, one may observe a very bold formation of this kind; the bank of the river is high and abrupt at this spot, and it is scooped out into two adjoining basins, not unlike the amphitheatres of ancient times. The central horn, as it were, which divides the two semicircles, stretches out quite a distance into a long, sharp point, very abrupt on both sides. The farther basin is the most regular, and it is also marked by successive ledges like the tiers of seats in those ancient theatres. This spot has long been cleared of wood, and used as a wild pasture; but the soil has never yet been broken by the plough, and we have often paused here to note the singular formation, and the surprising sharpness of the lines. Quite recently they have begun to dig here for sand; and if they continue the work, the character of the place must necessarily be changed. But now, as we note the bold outline of the basin, and watch the lines worked by the waters ages and ages since, still as distinct as though made last year, we see with our own eyes fresh proofs that we are in a new country, that the meadows about us, cleared by our fathers, are the first that have lain on the lap of the old earth, at this point, since yonder bank was shaped by the floods.

Thursday, 28th.—Thunder shower about sunrise; it continued raining until the afternoon. The shower was much needed, and every one is rejoicing over the plentiful supply.

Walked in the afternoon, though the sky was still cloudy and threatening. Obliged to follow the highway, for the woods are damp and dripping, and the grass matted after the heavy rain. But our walk proved very pleasant. It is not always those who climb in search of a commanding position, nor those who diverge from the beaten track at the beck of truant fancy, who meet with the most enjoyment. The views beneath a sober sky were still beautiful. The village lay reflected in the clear, gray waters, as though it had nothing else to do this idle afternoon but to smile upon its own image in the lake; while the valley beyond, the upland farms of Highborough, opposite, and the wooded hills above us, were all rich in the luxuriant greens and showery freshness of June. Many crows were stirring; some passing over us with their heavy flight, while others were perched on the blasted hemlocks just within the verge of the wood. They are very partial to this eastern hill; it is a favorite haunt of theirs at all seasons. Many of the lesser birds were also flitting about, very busy, and very musical after the rainy morning; they make great havoc among the worms and insects at such times, and one fancies that they sing more sweetly of a still evening, after a showery day, than at other moments. Some of the goldfinches, wrens, song-sparrows, and blue-birds, seemed to surpass themselves as they sat perched on the rails of the fences, or upon the weeds by the road-side.

There was scarcely a breath of air stirring. The woods lay in calm repose after the grateful shower, and large rain-drops were gathered in clusters on the plants. The leaves of various kinds receive the water very differently: some are completely bathed, showing a smooth surface of varnished green from stem to point—like the lilac of the garden, for instance;—on others, like the syringa, the fluid lies in flattened transparent drops, taking an emerald color from the leaf on which they rest; while the rose and the honeysuckle wear those spherical diamond-like drops, sung by poets, and sipped by fairies. The clover also, rose among the grasses, wears her crystals as prettily as the queen of the garden. Of course, it is the different texture of the leaves which produces this very pleasing effect.

Friday, 29th.—Very pleasant. Sunshine, with a warm mist on the hills; most beautiful effects of light and shade playing about the valley.

The sweet-briar is now in full blossom. It is one of the pleasantest shrubs in the whole wide world. With us it is not so very common as in most of the older counties, growing chiefly at intervals along the road-side, and in fields which border the highways. One never sees it in the woods, with the wild roses, and other brambles. The question as to its origin is considered as settled, I believe, by botanists, and, although thoroughly naturalized in most parts of the country, we cannot claim it as a native.

That old worthy, Captain Gosnold, the first Englishman who set foot in New England, landed on Cape Cod, as far back as 1602; he then proceeded to Buzzard Bay, and took up his quarters, for a time, in the largest of the Elizabeth Islands, where the first building, raised by English hands in that part of the continent, was put together. The object of his voyage was to procure a cargo of the sassafras root, which, at that time, was in high repute for medicinal purposes, and a valuable article of commerce. In relating his voyage, besides the sassafras which he found there in abundance, he mentions other plants which he had observed: the thorn, honeysuckle, wild pea, strawberries, raspberries, and grape-vines, all undoubtedly natives; but he also names the eglantine, or sweet-briar, and the tansy, both of which are generally looked upon as naturalized on this continent. Perhaps the worthy captain had his head so full of sassafras, as to care little for the rest of the vegetation, and he may have mistaken the wild rose for the eglantine, and some other plant for tansy. His wild pea was probably one of our common vetches.

Some of the most beautiful sweet-briars in the world are found growing wild along the road-sides about Fishkill, on the Hudson. They are partial to the neighborhood of the cedars which are common there, and clinging to those trees, they climb over them, untrained, to the height of twenty feet or more. When in flower the effect is very beautiful, their star-like blossoms resting on the foliage of the cedars, which is usually so dark and grave.

Saturday, 30th.– Charming weather. First dish of green peas from the garden to-day.

Came home from our walk with the village cows, this evening. Some fifteen or twenty of them were straggling along the road, going home of their own accord to be milked. Many of these good creatures have no regular pasture the summer through, but are left to forage for themselves along the road-sides, and in the unfenced woods. They go out in the morning, without any one to look after them, and soon find the best feeding ground, generally following this particular road, which has a long reach of open woods on either side. We seldom meet them in any number on the other roads. They like to pasture in the forest, where they doubtless injure the young trees, being especially fond of the tender maple shoots. Sometimes we see them feeding on the grass by the way-side, as soon as they have crossed the village bridge; other days they all walk off in a body, for a mile or more, before they begin to graze. Toward evening, they turn their heads homeward, without being sent for, occasionally walking at a steady pace without stopping; at other times, loitering and nibbling by the way. Among those we followed, this evening, were several old acquaintances, and probably they all belonged to different houses; only two of them had bells. As they came into the village, they all walked off to their owners' doors, some turning in one direction, some in another.

Of course, those cows that feed in fenced pastures are sent for, and it is only those who forage for themselves who come and go alone, in this way.

Monday, July 2d.– Clear, and cooler. New potatoes to-day. Pleasant drive, in the afternoon, on the lake shore. The midsummer flowers are beginning to open. Yellow evening primrose, purple rose-raspberry; the showy willow-herb, with its pyramid of lilac flowers; the red and the yellow lilies. We observed, also, a handsome strawberry blite, with its singular fruit-like crimson heads; this flower is not uncommon in new lands, in the western part of the State, and is probably a native, though precisely similar to that of Europe. The track over which we passed this afternoon, and where we found the blite, has been recently opened through the forest.

Observed many birds. The goldfinches were in little flocks as usual, and purple-finches flew across our road more than once; quarrelsome king-birds were sitting on the shrubs and plants along the bank, watching the wild bees, perhaps; for they are said to devour these as greedily as those of the hive. Some of them were skimming over the lake in pursuit of other game, being very partial also to the tribe of water insects. Saw another bird not often met with, a red-start; unlike the European red-start, which often builds about houses, the American bird of the same tribe is very shy, and only seen in the forest. The one we observed this evening was flitting about in a young grove upon the borders of a brook; his red and black plumage, and flirting tail, showing here and there among the foliage.

Tuesday, 3d.–* * * * We had, for several weeks, been planning a visit to Farmer B—'s; our good friend, his step-mother, having given us a very warm invitation to spend the day with her. Accordingly, we set off in the morning, after breakfast, and drove to the little village of B— Green, where we arrived about noon. Here the coachman stopped to water his horses, and make some inquiries about the road.

"Do you know where B—'s folks live?" he asked of a man in the yard.

"Yes, sir; B—'s folks live three miles from here."

"Which road must I take?"

"Straight ahead. Turn to the left when you come to the brick school-house; then take the right when you get to the gunsmith's shop, and any of the neighbors about will tell you which is B—'s house."

The directions proved correct. We soon reached the school-house; then came to the gunsmith's shop, and a few more turnings brought us in sight of the low, gray farm-house, the object of our morning's drive. Here a very cordial and simple greeting awaited us, and we passed the day most agreeably.

*   *   *   *   *

How pleasantly things look about a farm-house! There is always much that is interesting and respectable connected with every better labor, every useful or harmless occupation of man. We esteem some trades for their usefulness, we admire others for their ingenuity, but it seems natural to like a farm or a garden beyond most workshops. It needs not to be a great agricultural establishment with scientific sheds and show dairies—for knowledge and experience are necessary to appreciate the merits of such a place;—a simple body, who goes to enjoy and not to criticise, will find enough to please him about any common farm, provided the goodman be sober and industrious, the housewife be neat and thrifty.

From the window of the room in which we were sitting, we looked over the whole of Mr. B—'s farm; the wheat-field, corn-field, orchard, potato-patch, and buckwheat-field. The farmer himself, with his wagon and horses, a boy and a man, were busy in a hay-field, just below the house; several cows were feeding in the meadow, and about fifty sheep were nibbling on the hillside. A piece of woodland was pointed out on the height above, which supplied the house with fuel. We saw no evergreens there; the trees were chiefly maple, birch, oak, and chestnut; with us, about the lake, every wood contains hemlock and pine.

Finding we were interested in rural matters, our good friend offered to show us whatever we wished to see, answering all our many questions with the sweet, old smile peculiar to herself. She took us to the little garden; it contained potatoes, cabbages, onions, cucumbers, and beans; a row of currant-bushes was the only fruit; a patch of catnip, and another of mint, grew in one corner. Our farmers, as a general rule, are proverbially indifferent about their gardens. There was no fruit on the place besides the apple-trees of the orchard; one is surprised that cherries, and pears, and plums, all suited to our hilly climate in this county, should not receive more attention; they yield a desirable return for the cost and labor required to plant and look after them.

Passing the barn, we looked in there also; a load of sweet hay had just been thrown into the loft, and another was coming up the road at the moment. Mr. B——worked his farm with a pair of horses only, keeping no oxen. Half a dozen hens and some geese were the only poultry in the yard; the eggs and feathers were carried, in the fall, to the store at B——Green, or sometimes as far as our own village.

They kept four cows; formerly they had had a much larger dairy; but our hostess had counted her threescore and ten, and being the only woman in the house, the dairy-work of four cows, she said, was as much as she could well attend to. One would think so; for she also did all the cooking, baking, washing, ironing, and cleaning for the family, consisting of three persons; besides a share of the sewing, knitting, and spinning. We went into her little buttery; here the bright tin pans were standing full of rich milk; everything was thoroughly scoured, beautifully fresh, and neat. A stone jar of fine yellow butter, whose flavor we knew of old, stood on one side, and several cheeses were in press. The wood-work was all painted red.

While our kind hostess, on hospitable thought intent, was preparing something nice for tea, we were invited to look about the little sitting-room, and see "farm ways" in that shape. It was both parlor and guest-chamber at the same time. In one corner stood a maple bedstead, with a large, plump feather bed on it, and two tiny pillows in well-bleached cases at the head. The walls of the room were whitewashed, the wood-work was unpainted, but so thoroughly scoured, that it had acquired a sort of polish and oak color. Before the windows hung colored paper blinds. Between the windows was a table, and over it hung a small looking-glass, and a green and yellow drawing in water colors, the gift of a friend. On one side stood a cherry bureau; upon this lay the Holy Bible, and that its sacred pages had been well studied, our friend's daily life could testify. Near the Bible lay a volume of religious character from the Methodist press, and the Life of General Marion. The mantel-piece was ornamented with peacocks' feathers, and brass candle-sticks, bright as gold; in the fireplace were fresh sprigs of asparagus. An open cupboard stood on one side, containing the cups and saucers, in neat array, a pretty salt-cellar, with several pieces of cracked and broken crockery, of a superior quality, preserved for ornament more than use.

Such was the "square room," as it was called. It opened into the kitchen, and as our dear hostess was coming and going, dividing her time between her biscuits and her guests, very impartially, at last we asked permission to follow her, and sit by her while she was at work, admiring the kitchen quite as much as we did the rest of her neat dwelling. The largest room in the house, and the one most used, it was just as neat as every other corner under

the roof. The chimney was very large, according to the approved old custom, and it was garnished all about with flat-irons, brooms, brushes, holders, and cooking utensils, each in its proper place. In winter, they used a
stove for cooking, and in the very coldest weather, they kept two fires burning, one in the chimney, another in the stove. The walls were whitewashed.
There was a great deal of wood-work about the room—wainscoting, dressers,
and even the ceiling being of wood—and all was painted dark red. The ceiling of a farm-kitchen, especially if it be unplastered, as this was, is often a
pretty rustic sight, a sort of store-place, all kinds of things hanging there on
hooks or nails driven into the beams; bundles of dried herbs, strings of red
peppers and of dried apples hanging in festoons, tools of various kinds, bags
of different sorts and sizes, golden ears of seed-corn ripening, vials of physic
and nostrums for man and beast, bits of cord and twine, skeins of yarn and
brown thread just spun, and lastly, a file of newspapers. The low red ceiling
of Farmer B——'s kitchen was not quite so well garnished in July as we have
seen it at other times, still, it was by no means bare, the festoons of apples,
red peppers, and Indian corn being the only objects wanting. By the window hung an ink bottle and a well-fingered almanac, witty and wise, as
usual. A year or two since, an edition of the almanac was printed without
the usual prognostics regarding the winds and sunshine, but it proved a
complete failure; an almanac that told nothing about next year's weather nobody cared to buy, and it was found expedient to restore these important
predictions concerning the future snow, hail, and sunshine of the county.
Public opinion demanded it.

A great spinning-wheel, with a basket of carded wool, stood in a corner,
where it had been set aside when we arrived. There was a good deal of spinning done in the family; all the yarn for stockings, for flannels, for the cloth
worn by the men, for the colored woolen dresses of the women, and all the
thread for their coarse toweling, &c., &c., was spun in the house by our hostess, or her grand-daughter, or some neighbor hired for the purpose. Formerly, there had been six step-daughters in the family, and then, not only all
the spinning, but the weaving and dying also, were done at home. They
must have been notable women, those six step-daughters; we heard some
great accounts of days' spinning and weaving done by them. The presses
and cupboards of the house were still full to overflowing with blankets, white
and colored flannels, colored twilled coverlets for bedding, besides sheets,
table-cloths, and patched bed-quilts, all their own work. In fact, almost all
the clothing of the family, for both men and women, and everything in the
shape of bedding and toweling used by the household, was home-made.

Very few dry-goods were purchased by them; hats and shoes, some light materials for caps and collars, a little ribbon, and a printed calico now and then, seemed to be all they bought. Nor was this considered at all remarkable; such is the common way of living in many farmers' families. It has been calculated that a young woman who knows how to spin and weave can dress herself with ease and comfort, as regards everything necessary, for twelve dollars a year, including the cost of the raw materials; the actual allowance for clothing made by the authorities of this county, to farmers' daughters, while the property remained undivided, has been fifteen dollars, and the estimate is said to have included everything necessary for comfort, both winter and summer clothing. The wives and daughters of our farmers are very often notable, frugal women—perhaps one may say that they are usually so until they go from home. With the young girls about our villages, the case is very different; these are often wildly extravagant in their dress, and just as restless in following the fashions as the richest fine lady in the land. They often spend all they earn in finery.

Very pretty woolen shawls were shown us, made by our friend's stepdaughters, after Scotch patterns; several families of Scotch emigrants had settled in the neighborhood some thirty years since, and had furnished their friends with the patterns of different plaids; whether these were Highland or Lowland, we could not say. Some of their twilled flannels were also remarkably good in quality and color, but these are apt to shrink in washing. They are quite skilful dyers in scarlet, orange, green, blue, and lilac. With the maple leaves, they dye a very neat gray for stockings, but most of their coloring materials were purchased in the villages, dye-stuffs being an important part of the stock in trade of all our country druggists. Most of the spinning and weaving was in cotton or wool; the clothing and bedding was wholly of cotton or woolen materials. A certain amount of tow was used for toweling, bagging, smock frocks and pantaloons, for summer working clothes for the men. From time to time, a little flax was raised, especially to make linen, chiefly for a few finer towels and tablecloths, the luxuries of the household.

Those who live in our large towns, where they buy even their bread and butter, their milk and radishes, have no idea of the large amount of domestic goods, in wool and cotton, made by the women of the rural population of the interior, even in these days of huge factories. Without touching upon the subject of political economy, although its moral aspect must ever be a highly important one, it is certainly pleasant to see the women busy in this way, beneath the family roof, and one is much disposed to believe that the home system is healthier and safer for the individual, in every way. Home, we may rest assured, will always be, as a rule, the best place for a woman; her labors, pleasures, and interests, should all centre there, whatever be her sphere of life.

The food of the family, as well as their clothing, was almost wholly the produce of their own farm; they dealt but little with either grocer or butcher. In the spring, a calf was killed; in the fall, a sheep and a couple of hogs; once in a while, at other seasons, they got a piece of fresh meat from some neighbor who had killed a beef or a mutton. They rarely eat their poultry—the hens were kept chiefly for eggs, and their geese for feathers. The common piece of meat, day after day, was corned pork from their pork-barrel; they usually kept, also, some corned beef in brine, either from their own herd, or a piece procured by some bargain with a neighbor. The bread was made from their own wheat, and so were the hoe-cakes and griddle-cakes from the Indian meal and buckwheat of their growth. Butter and cheese from their dairy were on table at every meal, three times a day. Pies were eaten very frequently, either of apples, pumpkins, dried fruits, or coarse minced-meat; occasionally they had pie without any meat for their dinner; puddings were rare; Yankee farmers generally eating much more pastry than pudding. Mush and milk was a common dish. They ate but few eggs, reserving them for sale. Their vegetables were almost wholly potatoes, cabbage, and onions, with fresh corn and beans, when in season, and baked beans with pork in winter. Pickles were put on table at every meal. Their sugar and molasses was made from the maple, only keeping a little white sugar for company or sickness. They drank cider from their own orchard. The chief luxuries of the household were tea and coffee, both procured from the "stores," although it may be doubted if the tea ever saw China; if like much of that drunk about the country, it was probably of farm growth also.

While we were talking over these matters, and others of a more personal nature, with our gentle old hostess, several visitors arrived;—probably, on this occasion, they came less to see the mistress of the house than her carriage-load of strange company. Be that as it may, we had the pleasure of making several new acquaintances, and of admiring some very handsome strings of gold beads about their necks; a piece of finery we had not seen in a long while. Another fashion was less pleasing. We observed that a number of the women in that neighborhood had their hair cropped short like men, a custom which seems all but unnatural. Despite her seventy years and the rheumatism, our hostess had her dark hair smoothly combed and neatly rolled up under a nice muslin cap, made after the Methodist pattern. She was not one to do anything unwomanly, though all B—Green set the fashion.

A grand-daughter of our hostess, on a visit at the farm, had been in the meadow picking strawberries, and now returned with a fine bowl full, the ripest and largest in the field. The table was set; a homespun table-cloth, white as snow, laid upon it, and every vacant spot being covered by something nice, at four o'clock we sat down to tea. Why is it that cream, milk, and butter always taste better under the roof of a farm-house than elsewhere? They seem to lose something of their peculiar sweetness and richness after passing the bounds of the farm, especially if they have been rattled over the pavement of a large town to market. Country-made bread, too, is peculiar; not so light, perhaps, nor so white as that of the baker's, but much sweeter, and more nourishing. Our farmers' wives often use a little potato or Indian meal with their wheat, which gives the bread additional sweetness and *body*, as the *gourmets* call it, in speaking of their wines. With such strawberries and cream, such bread and butter, we could not do justice to half the good things on table. The cup-cake and ginger-bread, the biscuits and cheese, the various kinds of sweetmeats and stewed apples, the broiled ham and pickles, the apple-pie and mince-pie, were thrown away upon us. Our hostess put the nicest bits on a whole row of little plates and saucers before each guest, and after a long drive, one can make a very substantial meal; still, we could not eat up all the good things, and our friend was scarcely satisfied with the result, although we flattered ourselves we had been doing wonders. But such strawberries and cream, such bread and butter, ought to be enough to satisfy any reasonable tea-drinker.

As we had a drive of several miles before us, we were obliged to say good-bye early in the afternoon, taking leave of our venerable friend with those feelings of unfeigned regard and respect which the good and upright alone excite.

After such a pleasant day, we had a charming drive home, including even the long and slow ascent of Briar Hill. The birds, perched on the rails and bushes, sung us cheerfully on our way. As we stopped at the tavern, at the little hamlet of Old Oaks, to water the horses, we found a long row of empty wagons and buggies, drawn up before the house, betokening a rustic merry-making in honor of the eve of the "Fourth." A fiddle was heard from an upper room, and we had scarcely stopped before a couple of youths, in holy-day attire, stepped to the carriage, offering to help us alight, "presuming the ladies had come to the dance." Being informed of their mistake, they were very civil, apologized, and expressed their regrets. "They had hoped the ladies were coming to the ball." We thanked them, but were on our way to—. They bowed and withdrew, apparently rather disappointed at the loss of a whole carriage full of merry-makers, whom they had come out to receive with so much alacrity. Dancing was going on vigorously within; the dry, ear-piercing scrape of a miserable violin was heard playing Zip Coon, accompanied by a shrill boyish voice, half screaming, half singing out his orders: "Gents, forward!"–"Ladies, same!"–"Alla-maine left!"– "Sachay all!"–"Swing to your partners!"–"Fling your ladies opposyte!"– "Prummena-a-de awl!" The directions were obeyed with great energy and alacrity; for the scraping on the floor equalled the scraping on the violin, and the house fairly shook with the general movement.

Half an hour more, over a familiar road, brought us to the village, which we entered just as the sun set.

Wednesday, 4th–Warm and pleasant. The sun, as usual on this day, ushered in by great firing of cannon, and ringing of bells, and hoisting of flags. Many people in the village from the country, all in holyday trim. Public holydays, once in a while, are very pleasant; it does one good to see everybody looking their cleanest and gayest. It is really a cheerful spectacle to watch the family parties in wagon-loads coming into the village at such times; old and young, fathers, mothers, sons, daughters, and babies. Certainly we Americans are very partial to gatherings of all sorts; such an occasion is never thrown away upon our good folk.

There was the usual procession at noon: a prayer, reading the Declaration of Independence, a speech, and dinner. The children of the Sunday-school had also a little entertainment of their own. Frequently there is a large picknick party on the lake, with dancing, in honor of the day, but this year there was nothing of the kind. In the afternoon matters seemed to drag a little; we met some of the country people walking about the village, looking in rather a doubtful state of enjoyment; they reminded us of the inquiry of a pretty little French child at a party of pleasure, where things were not going off very briskly; fixing her large blue eyes earnestly on an elder sister's face, she asked anxiously, "*Eugénie, dis moi donc est ce que je m'amuse?*" About dusk, however, we were enlivened by the ascent of a paper balloon, and fireworks, rockets, serpents, fire-balls, and though not very remarkable, everybody went to see them.

Thursday, 5th.–Fine day. The locust-trees are in great beauty. Their foliage never attains its full size until the flowers have fallen; it then has an aftergrowth, the leaves become larger and richer, taking their own peculiar bluish-green. The lower branches of a group of young locusts before the door are now sweeping the grass very beautifully. These trees have never been trimmed; is not the common practice of trimming our locusts a mistake, unless one wishes for a tall tree at some particular point? Few of our trees throw out their branches so near the ground as to sweep the turf in this way, and wherever the habit is natural, the effect is very pleasing. With the locusts, it is their large pinnated leaves which cause the branches to droop in this way, or perhaps the ripening pods add their weight also, for it is only about midsummer, or just at this season, that they bend so low as to touch the grass; the same branches which are now hanging over the turf, in winter rise two or three feet above it.

The three-thorned acacia, or honey locust, as it is sometimes called, if left to its natural growth, will also follow the same fashion, its lower branches drooping gracefully, until their long leaves sweep the grass. There is a young untrimmed tree of this kind in the village, a perfect picture in its way, so prettily branched, with its foliage sweeping the ground. As a general thing, are not all our trees too much trimmed in this country?

Friday, 6th.—Warm, half-cloudy day; light, fitful airs, which set the leaves dancing here and there without swaying the branches. Of a still, summer's day, when the foliage generally is quiet, the eye is at times attracted by a solitary leaf, or a small twig dancing merrily, as though bitten by a tarantula, to say nothing of aspen leaves, which are never at rest. The leaves of the maples, on their long stalks, are much given to this trick; so are the white birches, and the scarlet oaks, and so is the fern also. This fluttering is no doubt caused by some light puff of air setting the leaf in motion, and then dying away without any regular current to follow its course; the capricious movement continues until the force of the impulse is exhausted, and the giddy leaf has tired itself out. At times the effect is quite singular, a single leaf or two in rapid movement, all else still and calm; and one might fancy Puck, or some other mischievous elf, sitting astride the stem, shaking his sides with laughter at the expense of the bewildered spectator.

Saturday, 7th.—Clear, warm weather. Thermometer 78 in the shade.

The rose-bushes about the village gardens are suffering from the same blight which attacked them last year; it has not, however, done so much mischief this season, nor have its ravages been so general. Those bushes which stand alone, surrounded by grass, escaped in many cases; those in our neighborhood have been attacked, and the richer the earth, the more they seem to have suffered.

Monday, 9th.—Brilliant, warm weather. Thermometer 80 in the shade.

Walked in the woods; went in search of the large two-leaved orchis, a particular plant, which we have watched for several years, as it is something of a rarity, having been seen only in two places in the neighborhood. We found the large, shining leaves lying flat on the ground, in the well-known spot, but some one had been there before us and broken off the flower-stalk. The leaves of this orchis are among the largest and roundest in our woods.

The handsome, large purple-fringed orchis is also found here, but we have not seen it this summer. The country people call it soldier's plume; it is one of our most showy flowers.

Tuesday, 10th.—Warm, cloudless weather. Thermometer 84 in the shade. Pleasant row on the lake toward sunset.

The water is beautifully clear; as we rowed along we could see what was going on far below the surface. The fish kept out of view; we only observed a few small perch. The soil of the lake, if one may use the phrase, varies much in character; along the eastern shore one looks down upon a pavement of rounded gray stones, with here and there the wreck of a dead tree, lying beneath the waves it once shaded; coasting the western bank, one finds reaches of clean sand, with a few shells of fresh water mussels scattered about, and colorless leaves of last year's growth, oak and chestnut, lying near them still undecayed. Then, again, in other places, the bottom is muddy, and thickly covered with a growth of aquatic plants of various kinds. There must be a good number of these plants in our lake, judging from those we have already gathered or seen. They vary much in their construction; all springing as they do from the same watery nursery, one might expect them to be much like each other, and to differ decidedly from those of the fields; but such is not the case. Some are thick and rough, like the reeds, the water-lilies, and the pickerel-weed; but others are as fine and delicate in their foliage as those that grow in the air. Many of those which raise their flowers above the water bear handsome blossoms, like the lilies, the purple pickerel-weed, and the brilliant water-marigold, or Beck's-bidens, which is found in Canaderaga Lake, about twelve miles from us; others are dull and unsightly, and some of these form an ugly patch in shallow spots, near our wharf, for a few weeks in August.

But this fringe of reeds and plants is only seen here and there in shallow spots; a few strokes of the oar will carry a boat at once into water much too deep to be fathomed by the eye. The depth of the lake is usually given at a hundred and fifty feet. It has no tributaries beyond a few nameless brooks, and is chiefly fed by springs in its own bosom. Of course, where such is the case, the amount of water varies but little; it has never overflowed its banks, and when the water is called low, a stranger would hardly perceive the fact.

This afternoon we rowed across Black-bird Bay, and followed the shady western bank some distance. Landed and gathered wild flowers, meadow-sweet, white silk-weed, clematis, and Alleghany vine, *adlumia*. This is the season for the climbing plants to flower; they are usually later than their neighbors. The Alleghany vine, with its pale pink clusters and very delicate foliage, is very common in some places, and so is the common clematis.

Observed, also, several vines of the glycine, *Apios tuberosa,* though its handsome purple flowers have not yet appeared. This plant has been recently carried to Europe by a French gentleman, sent out to this country by his government for scientific purposes. He supposes that it may be introduced as a common article of food, to take, in some measure, the place of the potato. The root has a pleasant taste, and is said to be much eaten by some tribes of Indians. A kind of one-seeded pea, growing in the western part of the county, *Psoralea,* was also carried to France, with the view of turning it to account in the same way. This last is not found in our neighborhood; but the glycine, or ground-nut, is not uncommon in our thickets. Whether the plan of making these a part of the common food of France will succeed or not, time alone can decide. It usually takes more than one generation to make a change in national diet. Potatoes were several centuries coming into favor on the Continent of Europe; and during the last scarcity in Great Britain, the Scotch and English did not take very kindly to the Indian corn, although it is certainly one of the sweetest grains in the world. After a change of this kind has once been made, however, and people have become accustomed to the novelty, whatever it may be, there is generally a sort of reaction in its favor, until presently no one can do without it. This has been strikingly the case with potatoes, in the way of food, and with tea and coffee in the way of drinks.

Wednesday, 11th.–Very warm. Thermometer 89 in the coolest position. Bright sunshine, with much air. Long drive in the evening. The chestnuts are in flower, and look beautifully. They are one of our richest trees when in blossom, and being common about the lake, are very ornamental to the country, at this season; they look as though they wore a double crown of sunshine about their flowery heads. The sumachs are also in bloom, their regular yellowish spikes showing from every thicket.

The hay-makers were busy on many farms after sunset this evening. There are fewer mowers in the hay-fields with us than in the Old World. Four men will often clear a field where, perhaps, a dozen men and women would be employed in France or England. This evening we passed a man with a horse-rake gathering his hay together by himself. As we went down the valley, he had just begun his task; when we returned, an hour and a half later, with the aid of this contrivance, he had nearly done his job.

One day, as we were driving along the bank of the lake, a year or two since, we saw, for the first time in this country, several young women at work in a hay-field; they looked quite picturesque with their colored sun-bonnets, and probably they did not find the work very hard, for they seemed to take it as a frolic.

We also chanced, on one occasion, to see a woman ploughing in this county, the only instance of the kind we have ever observed in our part of the world. Very possibly she may have been a foreigner, accustomed to hard work in the fields, in her own country. In Germany, we remember to have once seen *a woman* and *a cow* harnessed together, dragging the plough, while a man, probably the husband, was driving both. I have forgotten whether he had a whip or not. This is the only instance in which we ever saw a woman in harness, though in travelling over Europe, one often sees the poor creatures toiling so hard, and looking so wretched, that one's heart aches for them. We American women certainly owe a debt of gratitude to our countrymen for their kindness and consideration for us generally. Gallantry may not always take a graceful form in this part of the world, and mere flattery may be worth as little here as elsewhere, but there is a glow of generous feeling toward woman in the hearts of most American men, which is highly honorable to them as a nation and as individuals. In no country is the protection given to woman's helplessness more full and free—in no country is the assistance she receives from the stronger arm so general—and nowhere does her weakness meet with more forbearance and consideration. Under such circumstances, it must be woman's own fault if she be not thoroughly respected also. The position accorded to her is favorable; it remains for her to fill it in a manner worthy her own sex, gratefully, kindly, and simply; with truth and modesty of heart and life; with unwavering fidelity of feeling and principle; with patience, cheerfulness, and sweetness of temper—no unfit return to those who smooth the daily path for her.

Thursday, 12th.—Very warm and brilliant weather. Thermometer 90 in the shade. Drive in the evening over the Highborough Hills; the roads very dusty; fortunately, we left the cloud "in our wake," as the sailors say. The young fruits are getting their ruddy color in the orchards and gardens, and the grain is taking its golden tinge. The fields are looking very rich and full of promise.

Friday, 13th.—Very warm. Thermometer 92 in the shade, with much air from the south-west. Though very warm, and the power of the sun great, yet the weather has not been close. We have had fine airs constantly; often quite a breeze. It is, indeed, singular that so much air should collect no clouds.

Drive down the valley in the evening. The new-shorn meadows look beautifully, bordered as they are in many places by the later elder-bushes, now loaded with white flowers. The earlier kind, which blooms in May, more common in the woods, is already ripening its red berries.

About eight o'clock there was a singular appearance in the heavens: a dark bow, very clearly marked, spanned the valley from east to west, commencing at the point where the sun had just set, the sky, at the same time, being apparently cloudless. At one moment two other fainter bows were seen; the principal arch was visible, perhaps, half an hour, fading slowly away with the twilight. Neither of our party remembered to have seen anything like it. In superstitious times it would doubtless have been connected with some public calamity.

Saturday, 14th.—A light shower this morning. Just enough to lay the dust and refresh the air, which now blows cool and moist from the northward. Shaded, vapory sky; most grateful relief after the hot sun and dry air of the last ten days. No thunder or lightning.

Monday, 16th.—Rather cooler; thermometer 79. Fine day. Walked in the woods.

Found many of the Philadelphia, or orange lilies, scattered about singly, as usual. They like to grow in woods and groves, and are often found among the fern. The Canadian, or yellow lily, is also in flower, growing in lower and more open grounds; a bit of meadow-land, on the border of one of our brooks, is now brilliantly colored with these handsome flowers. The very showy Martagon, or Turk's-cap lily, also belongs to our neighborhood. Last summer a noble plant—a pyramid of twenty red blossoms on one stalk—was found growing in a marshy spot on the hill, at the Cliffs.

Brought home a beautiful bunch of these orange lilies, with the leaves of the sweet-fern, and the white flowers of the fragrant early wintergreen.

Tuesday, 17th.—Rambled about Mill Island and the woods beyond. The red wooden grist-mill, standing here, is the oldest and most important of the neighborhood. In dry seasons, when water fails in the lesser streams, grain has been brought here from farms twenty miles distant. This present summer, however, the water has been so low, that the wheels have stopped.

The low saw-mill, on the farther bank, is one of half a dozen within a few miles. It does a deal of work. Some of the logs float down the lake and river; others are drawn here on the snow in winter; but the basin above the dam is generally well filled with them. As the stream runs a mere rivulet now, many of the logs are lodged on the mud, and the mill is idle. We rarely see the river so low.

We are told that for some years after the village was commenced, Mill Island was a favorite resort of the Indians, who, at that time, came frequently in parties to the new settlement, remaining here for months together. The island was then covered with wood, and they seem to have chosen it for their camp, in preference to other situations. Possibly it may have been a place of resort to their fishing and hunting parties when the country was a wilderness. Now they come very seldom, and singly, or in families, craving permission to build a shanty of boughs or boards, in order to ply their trade of basket-makers. They no longer encamp on the island itself, for the oak by the bridge is almost the only tree standing on it, and they still love the woods; but three out of the four families who have been here during the last ten years, have chosen the neighboring groves for their halting-place.

There are already many parts of this country where an Indian is never seen. There are thousands and hundreds of thousands of the white population who have never laid eyes upon a red man. But this ground lies within the former bounds of the Six Nations, and a remnant of the great tribes of the Iroquois still linger about their old haunts, and occasionally cross our path. The first group that we chance to see strike us strangely, appearing as they do in the midst of a civilized community with the characteristics of their wild race still clinging to them; and when it is remembered that the land over which they now wander as strangers, in the midst of an alien race, was so lately their own—the heritage of their fathers—it is impossible to behold them without a feeling of peculiar interest.

Standing at the window, one summer's afternoon, our attention was suddenly fixed by three singular figures approaching the house. More than one member of our household had never yet seen an Indian, and unaware that any were in the neighborhood, a second glance was necessary to convince us that these visitors must belong to the red race, whom we had long been so anxious to see. They came slowly toward the door, walking singly and silently, wrapped in blankets, bareheaded and barefooted. Without knocking or speaking, they entered the house with a noiseless step, and stood silently near the open door. We gave them a friendly greeting, and they proved to be women of the Oneida tribe, belonging to a family who had encamped in the woods the day before, with the purpose of selling their baskets in the village. Meek in countenance, with delicate forms and low voices, they had far more of the peculiarities of the red race about them than one would look for in a tribe long accustomed to intercourse with the whites, and a portion of whom have become more than half civilized. Only one of the three could speak English, and she seemed to do so with effort and reluctance. They were dressed in gowns of blue calico, rudely cut, coarsely stitched together, and so short as to show their broadcloth leggings worked with beads. Their heads were entirely bare, their straight, black hair hanging loose about their shoulders, and, although it was midsummer at the time, they were closely wrapped in coarse white blankets. We asked their names. "Wallee"–"Awa"–"Cootlee"–was the answer. Of what tribe? "Oneida," was the reply, in a voice low and melancholy as the note of the whip-poor-will, giving the soft Italian sound to the vowels, and four syllables to the word. They were delicately made, of the usual height of American women, and their features were good, without being pretty. About their necks, arms, and ankles, they wore strings of cheap ornaments, pewter medals, and coarse glass beads, with the addition of a few scraps of tin, the refuse of some tin-shop passed on their way. One, the grandmother, was a Christian; the other two were Pagans. There was something startling and very painful in hearing these poor creatures within our own community, and under our own roof, declaring themselves heathens! They paid very little attention to the objects about them, until the youngest of the three observed a small Chinese basket on a table near her. She rose silently, took the basket in her hand, examined it carefully, made a single exclamation of pleasure, and then exchanged a few words with her companions in their own wild but musical tongue. They all seemed struck with this specimen of Chinese ingenuity. They asked, as usual, for bread and cold meat, and a supply was cheerfully given them, with the addition of some cake, about which they appeared to care very little. In the mean time a messenger had been sent to one of the shops of the village, where toys and knicknacks for children were sold, and he returned with a handful of copper rings and brooches, pewter medals, and bits of bright ribbons, which were presented to our guests; the simple creatures looking much gratified, as well as surprised, although their thanks were brief, and they still kept up the true Indian etiquette of mastering all emotion. They were, indeed, very silent, and unwilling to talk, so that it was not easy to gather much information from them; but their whole appearance was so much more Indian than we had been prepared for, while their manners were so gentle and womanly, so free from anything coarse or rude in the midst of their untutored ignorance, that we were much pleased with the visit. Later in the day we went to their camp, as they always call their halting-place; here we found several children and two men of the family. These last were evidently full-blooded Indians, with every mark of their race stamped upon them; but, alas! not a trace of the "brave" about either. Both had that heavy, sensual, spiritless expression, the stamp of vice, so painful to behold on the human countenance. They had thrown off the blanket, and were equipped in ragged coats, pantaloons, and beavers, from the cast-off clothing of their white neighbors, with the striking addition, however, of bits

of tin to match those of the squaws. Some of these scraps were fastened
round their hats, others were secured on their breasts and in the button-holes,
where the great men of the Old World wear diamond stars and badges of
honor. They were cutting bows and arrows for the boys of the village, of
ash-wood, and neither of them spoke to us; they either did not, or would not
understand our companion, when addressed in English. The women and
children were sitting on the ground, busy with their baskets, which they make
very neatly, although their patterns are all simple. They generally dye the
strips of ash with colors purchased in the villages from the druggists, using
only now and then, for the same purpose, the juices of leaves and berries,
when these are in season, and easily procured.

Since the visit of the Oneida squaws, several other parties have been in
the village. The very next season a family of three generations made their
appearance at the door, claiming an heredity acquaintance with the master
of the house. They were much less wild than our first visitors, having dis-
carded the blanket entirely, and speaking English very well. The leader and
patriarch of the party bore a Dutch name, given him, probably, by some of
his friends on the Mohawk Flats; and he was, moreover, entitled to write
Reverend before it, being a Methodist minister—the Rev. Mr. Kunkerpott.
He was notwithstanding a full-blooded Indian, with the regular copper-
colored complexion, and high cheekbones; the outline of his face was decidedly Roman, and his long, gray hair had a wave which is rare among
his people; his mouth, where the savage expression is usually most strongly
marked, was small, with a kindly expression about it. Altogether he was a
strange mixture of the Methodist preacher and the Indian patriarch. His son
was much more savage than himself in appearance—a silent, cold-looking
man; and the grandson, a boy of ten or twelve, was one of the most uncouth,
impish-looking creatures we ever beheld. He wore a long-tailed coat twice
too large for him, with boots of the same size, and he seemed particularly
proud of these last, looking at them from time to time with great satisfaction, as he went tottering along. The child's face was very wild, and he was
bareheaded, with an unusual quantity of long, black hair streaming about
his head and shoulders. While the grandfather was conversing about old
times, the boy diverted himself by twirling round on one leg, a feat which
would have seemed almost impossible, booted as he was, but which he
nevertheless accomplished with remarkable dexterity, spinning round and
round, his arms extended, his large black eyes staring stupidly before him,
his mouth open, and his long hair flying in every direction, as wild a looking creature as one could wish to see. We expected every moment that he

would fall breathless and exhausted, like a dancing dervish, supposing that the child had been taught this accomplishment as a means of pleasing his civilized friends; but no, he was only amusing himself, and kept his footing to the last.

Some farther acquaintance with the Indians, who still occupy lands reserved for them by the government in the western part of the State, has only confirmed the impressions produced by these first interviews. Civilization, in its earliest approaches, seems to produce a different effect upon the men and the women, the former losing, and the latter gaining by it. The men, when no longer warriors and hunters, lose their native character; the fire of their savage energy is extinguished, and the dull and blackened embers alone remain. Unaccustomed by habit, prejudice, hereditary instinct, to labor, they cannot work, and very generally sink into worthless, drinking idlers. Many of them are seen in this condition in the neighborhood of their own lands. The women, on the contrary, have always been accustomed to toil while the warriors were idle, and it is much more easy for them to turn from field labors to household tasks, than for the men to exchange the excitement of war and hunting for quiet, regular, agricultural or mechanic pursuits. In the savage state, the women appear very inferior to the men, but in a half-civilized condition, they have much the advantage over the stronger sex. They are rarely beautiful, but often very pleasing; their gentle expression, meek and subdued manner, low, musical voices, and mild, dark eyes, excite an interest in their favor, while one turns with pain and disgust from the brutal, stupid, drunken countenances too often seen among the men. Many a young girl might be found to-day among the half-civilized tribes, whose manner and appearance would accord with one's idea of the gentle Pocahontas; but it is rare, indeed, that a man is seen among them who would make a Powhattan, a Philip, or an Uncas. And yet, unfavorable as their appearance is, there are few even of the most degraded who, when aroused, will not use the poetical, figurative speech, and the dignified, impressive gesture of their race. The contrast between the degraded aspect they bear every day, and these sudden instinctive flashes, is very striking. Instances are not wanting, however, in which men, of purely Indian blood, have conquered the many obstacles in their path, and now command the sympathy and respect of their white brethren by the energy and perseverance they have shown in mastering a new position among civilized men.

The dress of the women is also more pleasing than that of the men, preserving as they do something of a characteristic costume. They are generally wrapped in blankets, and bareheaded, or those of the richer families wear a round beaver, which makes them look a little like the brown peasant girls of Tuscany; they seem to be the only females in the country who do not make a profound study of the monthly fashion-plates. The men are almost always dressed in shabby clothes, cut upon white patterns. The women either dislike to speak English, or they are unable to do so, for they are very laconic indeed in conversation; many of them, although understanding what is said, will only answer you by smiles and signs; but as they do not aim as much as the men at keeping up the cold dignity of their race, this mute language is often kindly and pleasing. Many of those who carry about their simple wares for sale in the neighborhood of their own villages would be remarked for their amiable expression, gentle manner, and low, musical voices. They still carry their children tied up in a blanket at their backs, supporting them by a band passing round the forehead, which brings the weight chiefly upon the head.

It is easy to wish these poor people well; but surely something more may justly be required of us—of those who have taken their country and their place on the earth. The time seems at last to have come when their own eyes are opening to the real good of civilization, the advantages of knowledge, the blessings of Christianity. Let us acknowledge the strong claim they have upon us, not in word only, but in deed also. The native intellect of the red men who peopled this part of America surpassed that of many other races laboring under the curses of savage life; they have shown bravery, fortitude, religious feeling, eloquence, imagination, quickness of intellect, with much dignity of manner; and if we are true to our duty, now at the moment when they are making of their own accord a movement in the path of improvement, perhaps the day may not be distant when men of Indian blood may be numbered among the wise and the good, laboring in behalf of our common country.

It is painful, indeed, to remember how little has yet been done for the Indian during the three centuries since he and the white man first met on the Atlantic coast. But such is only the common course of things; a savage race is almost invariably corrupted rather than improved by its earliest contact with a civilized people; they suffer from the vices of civilization before they learn justly to comprehend its merits. It is with nations as with individuals—amelioration is a slow process, corruption a rapid one.

Wednesday, 18th.—Warm, brilliant weather. Thermometer 89, with much dry air. Walked in the woods.

That ghost-like plant, the Indian-pipe, is in flower, and quite common here—sometimes growing singly, more frequently several together. The whole plant, about a span high, is entirely colorless, looking very much as if it were cut out of Derbyshire spar; the leaves are replaced by white scales, but the flower is large and perfect, and from the root upward, it is wholly of untarnished white. One meets with it from June until late in September; at first, the flower is nodding, when it really looks something like the cup of a pipe; gradually, however, it erects itself as the seed ripens, and turns black when it decays. I have seen a whole cluster of them bordered with black—in half-mourning, as it were—though of a healthy white within this line. It was probably some blight which had affected them in this way.

The pretty little dew-drop, *Dalibarda repens* of botanists, is also in blossom—a delicate, modest little flower, opening singly among dark green leaves, which look much like those of the violet; it is one of our most common wood-plants; the leaves frequently remain green through the winter. The name of dew-drop has probably been given to this flower from its blooming about the time when the summer dews are the heaviest.

The one-sided wintergreen is also in blossom, with its little greenish-white flowers all turned in the same direction; it is one of the commonest plants we tread under foot in the forest. This is a wintergreen region, all the varieties being found, I believe, in this county. Both the glossy pipsissiwa and the pretty spotted wintergreen, with its variegated leaves, are common here; so is the fragrant shin-leaf; and the one-flowered pyrola, rare in most parts of the country, is also found in our woods.

Observed the yellow diervilla or bush-honeysuckle still in flower. The hemlocks still show the light green of their young shoots, which grow dark very slowly.

Thursday, 19th.—Warm, clear day; thermometer 88.

It happens that the few humble antiquities of our neighborhood are all found lying together near the outlet of the lake; they consist of a noted rock, the ruins of a bridge, and the remains of a military work.

The rock lies in the lake, a stone's throw from the shore; it is a smooth, rounded fragment, about four feet high; the waters sometimes, in very warm seasons, leave it nearly dry, but they have never, I believe, overflowed it. There is nothing remarkable in the rock itself, though it is perhaps the largest of the few that show themselves above the surface of our lake; but this stone is said to have been a noted rallying-point with the Indians, who were in the habit of appointing meetings between different parties at this spot. From the Mohawk country, from the southern hunting-grounds on the banks of the Susquehannah, and from the Oneida region, they came through the wilderness to this common rendezvous at the gray rock, near the outlet of the lake. Such is the tradition; probably it is founded in truth, for it has prevailed here since the settlement of the country, and it is of a nature not likely to have been thought of by a white man, who, if given to inventing anything of the kind, would have attempted something more ambitious. Its very simplicity gives it weight, and it is quite consistent with the habits of the Indians, and their nice observation; for the rock, though unimportant, is yet the largest in sight, and its position near the outlet would make it a very natural waymark to them. Such as it is, this, moreover, is the only tradition, in a positive form, connected with the Indians preserved among us; with this single exception, the red man has left no mark here, on hill or dale, lake or stream.

From tradition we step to something more positive; from the dark ages we come to the dawn of history. On the bank of the river are found the ruins of a bridge, the first made at this point by the white man. Among the mountain streams of the Old World are many high, narrow, arches of stone, built more than a thousand years since, still standing to-day in different stages of picturesque decay. Our ruins are more rude than those. In the summer of 1786, a couple of emigrants, father and son, arrived on the eastern bank of the river, intending to cross it; there was no village here then—a single log-cabin and a deserted block-house stood on the spot, however, and they hoped to find at least the shelter of walls and a roof. But there was no bridge over the river, nor boat to ferry them across: some persons, under such circumstances, would have forded the stream; others might have swam across; our emigrants took a shorter course—they made a bridge. Each carried his axe, as usual, and choosing one of the tall pines standing on the bank, one of the old race which then filled the whole valley, they soon felled the tree, giving it such an inclination as threw it across the channel, and their bridge was built—they crossed on the trunk. The stump of that tree is still standing on the bank among the few ruins we have to boast of; it is fast mouldering away, but it has outlasted the lives of both the men who felled the tree—the younger of the two, the son, having died in advanced old age, a year or two since.

The military work alluded to was on a greater scale, and connected with an expedition of some importance. In 1779, when General Sullivan was ordered against the Indians in the western part of the State, to punish them for the massacres of Wyoming and Cherry Valley, a detachment of his forces, under General Clinton, was sent through this valley. Ascending the Mohawk, to what was sometimes called the "portage" over the hills to this lake, they cut a road through the forest, and transporting their boats to our waters, launched them at the head of the lake, and rowed down to the site of the present village. Here they lay encamped some little time, finding the river too much encumbered with flood-wood to allow their boats to pass. To remove this difficulty, General Clinton ordered a dam to be built at the outlet, thus raising the lake so much, that when the work was suddenly opened, the waters rushed through with such power, that they swept the channel clear; by this means, the troops were enabled to pass in their boats from these very sources of the stream to the rendezvous at Tioga Point, a distance of more than two hundred miles, by the course of this winding river. This is the only incident which has connected our secluded lake with historical events, and it is believed that upon no other occasion have troops, on a warlike errand, passed through the valley. Probably in no other instance have so large a number of boats ever floated on our quiet lake, and we can scarcely suppose that a fleet of this warlike character will ever again, to the end of time, be collected here. Some few traces of this military dam may still be seen, though every year they are becoming more indistinct.

Friday, 20th.—Warm; thermometer 85, with high wind from the southward. Light sprinkling showers through the day, barely enough to lay the dust. No thunder or lightning.

The fire-flies flitting about this evening in the rain; they do not mind a showery evening much; we have often seen them of a rainy night, carrying their little lanterns about with much unconcern; it is only a hard and driving shower which sends them home. These little creatures seem to have favorite grounds; there is a pretty valley in the county, about twenty miles from us, where they are very numerous; one sees them dancing over those meadows in larger parties than about our own.

Saturday, 21st.—Fine weather; heat not so great; thermometer 77.

Our little fruit-venders are beginning to bring whortleberries to market; they are very plenty on our hills, being common in the woods, and abundant in half-cleared lands. This little shrub, including all its numerous varieties, spreads over a broad extent of country, growing alike within the forest, in waste lands, upon hills and in swamps; it is well known that on this Western Continent it fills the place held in Europe by the heath. Though much less showy than the golden broom or the purple heather, the European plants of waste grounds, the whortleberry has the higher merit of producing an edible fruit, which we still find very pleasant, though now supplied with so many luxuries of the kind by horticulture. To the poor Indians the whortleberries must have been very precious, yielding fruit for their benefit during three months of the year, more or less.

The northern lights are brilliant this evening; for some months they have been less frequent than usual. We have them, at intervals, during all seasons.

Monday, 23d.—Just at the point where the village street becomes a road and turns to climb the hill-side, there stands a group of pines, a remnant of the old forest. There are many trees like these among the woods; far and near such may be seen rising from the hills, now tossing their arms in the stormy winds, now drawn in still and dark relief against the glowing evening sky. Their gaunt, upright forms standing about the hill-tops, and the ragged gray stumps of those which have fallen, dotting the smooth fields, make up the sterner touches in a scene whose general aspect is smiling. But although these old trees are common upon the wooded heights, yet the group on the skirts of the village stands alone among the fields of the valley; their nearer brethren have all been swept away, and these are left in isolated company, differing in character from all about them, a monument of the past.

It is upon a narrow belt of land, a highway and a corn-field on one side, a brook and an orchard on the other, that these trees are rooted; a strip of woodland connected with the forest on the hills above, and suddenly cut off where it approaches the first buildings of the village. There they stand, silent spectators of the wonderful changes that have come over the valley. Hundreds of winters have passed since the cones which contained the seed of that grove fell from the parent tree; centuries have elapsed since their heads emerged from the topmost wave of the sea of verdure to meet the sunshine, and yet it is but yesterday that their shadows first fell, in full length, upon the sod at their feet.

Sixty years since, those trees belonged to a wilderness; the bear, the wolf, and the panther brushed their trunks, the ungainly moose and the agile deer browsed at their feet; the savage hunter crept stealthily about their roots, and painted braves passed noiselessly on the war-path beneath their shade. How many successive generations of the red man have trod the soil they overshadowed, and then sat down in their narrow graves—how many herds of wild creatures have chased each other through that wood, and left their bones to bleach among the fern and moss, there is no human voice can tell. We only know that the summer winds, when they filled the canvas of Columbus and Cabot, three hundred years ago, came sweeping over these forest pines, murmuring then as we hear them murmur to-day.

There is no record to teach us even the name of the first white man who saw this sequestered valley, with its limpid lake; it was probably some bold hunter from the Mohawk, chasing the deer, or in quest of the beaver. But while towns were rising on the St. Lawrence and upon the sea-board, this inland region lay still unexplored; long after trading-houses had been opened, and fields had been tilled, and battles had been fought to the north, south, east, ay, and even at many points westward, those pines stood in the heart of a silent wilderness. This little lake lay embedded in a forest until after the great struggle of the Revolution was over. A few months after the war was brought to an honorable close, Washington made a journey of observation among the inland waters of this part of the country; writing to a friend in France, he names this little lake, the source of a river, which, four degrees farther south, flows into the Chesapeake in near neighborhood with his own Potomac. As he passed along through a half-wild region, where the few marks of civilization then existing bore the blight of war, he conceived the outline of many of those improvements which have since been carried out by others, and have yielded so rich a revenue of prosperity. It is a pleasing reflection to those who live here, that while many important places in the country were never honored by his presence, Washington has trod the soil about our lake. But even at that late day, when the great and good man came, the mountains were still clothed in wood to the water's edge, and mingled with giant oaks and ashes, those tall pines waved above the valley.

At length, nearly three long centuries after the Genoese had crossed the ocean, the white man came to plant a home on this spot, and it was then the great change began; the axe and the saw, the forge and the wheel, were busy from dawn to dusk, cows and swine fed in thickets whence the wild beasts had fled, while the ox and the horse drew away in chains the fallen trunks of the forest. The tenants of the wilderness shrunk deeper within its bounds with every changing moon; the wild creatures fled away within the receding shades of the forest, and the red man followed on their track; his day of power was gone, his hour of pitiless revenge had passed, and the last echoes of the war-whoop were dying away forever among these hills, when the pale-faces laid their hearth-stones by the lake shore. The red man, who for thousands of years had been lord of the land, no longer treads the soil; he exists here only in uncertain memories, and in forgotten graves.

Such has been the change of the last half century. Those who from childhood have known the cheerful dwellings of the village, the broad and fertile farms, the well-beaten roads, such as they are to-day, can hardly credit that this has all been done so recently by a band of men, some of whom, white-headed and leaning on their staves, are still among us. Yet such is the simple truth. This village lies just on the borders of the tract of country which was opened and peopled immediately after the Revolution; it was among the earliest of those little colonies from the sea-board which struck into the wilderness at that favorable moment, and whose rapid growth and progress in civilization have become a by-word. Other places, indeed, have far surpassed this quiet borough; Rochester, Buffalo, and others of a later date, have become great cities, while this remains a rural village; still, whenever we pause to recall what has been done in this secluded valley during the lifetime of one generation, we must needs be struck with new astonishment. And throughout every act of the work, those old pines were there. Unchanged themselves, they stand surrounded by objects over all of which a great change has passed. The open valley, the half-shorn hills, the paths, the flocks, the buildings, the woods in their second growth, even the waters in the different images they reflect on their bosom, the very race of men who come and go, all are different from what they were; and those calm old trees seem to heave the sigh of companionless age, as their coned heads rock slowly in the winds.

The aspect of the wood tells its own history, so widely does it differ in character from the younger groves waving in gay luxuriance over the valley. In the midst of smooth fields it speaks so clearly of the wilderness, that it is not the young orchard of yesterday's planting, but the aged native pines which seem the strangers on the ground. The pine of forest growth never fails to have a very marked character of its own; the gray shaft rises clear and unbroken by bend or bough, to more than half its great elevation, thence short horizontal limbs in successive fan-like growth surround the trunk to its summit, which is often crowned with a low crest of upright branches. The shaft is very fine from its great height and the noble simplicity of its lines; in coloring, it is a pure clear gray, having the lightest and the smoothest bark of all its tribe, and only occasionally mottled with patches of lichens. The white pine of this climate gathers but few mosses, unless in very moist situations; the very oldest trees are often quite free from them. Indeed, this is a tree seldom seen with the symptoms of a half-dead and decaying condition about it, like so many others; the gray line of a naked branch may be observed here and there, perhaps, a sign of age, but it generally preserves to the very last an appearance of vigor, as though keeping death at bay until struck to the heart, or laid low from the roots. It is true, this appearance may often prove deceptive; still, it is a peculiarity of our pine, that it preserves its verdure until the very last, unlike many other trees which are seen in the forest, half green, half gray, and lifeless.

The pine of the lawns or open groves and the pine of the forest differ very strikingly in outline; the usual pyramidal or conical form of the evergreen is very faintly traced on the short, irregular limbs of the forest tree; but what is lost in luxuriance and elegance is more than replaced by a peculiar character of wild dignity, as it raises its stern head high above the lesser wood, far overtopping the proudest rank of oaks. And yet, in their rudest shapes, they are never harsh; as we approach them, we shall always find something of the calm of age and the sweetness of nature to soften their aspect; there is a grace in the slow waving of their limbs in the higher air, which never fails; there is a mysterious melody in their breezy murmurs; there is an emerald light in their beautiful verdure, which lies in unfading wreaths, fresh and clear, about the heads of those old trees. The effect of light and shade on the foliage of those older forest pines is indeed much finer than what we see among their younger neighbors; the tufted branches, in their horizontal growth, are beautifully touched with circlets of a clear light, which is broken up and lost amid the confused medley of branches in trees of more upright growth. The long brown cones are chiefly pendulous, in clusters, from the upper branches; some seasons they are so numerous on the younger trees as to give their heads a decided brown coloring.

The grove upon the skirts of the village numbers, perhaps, some forty trees, varying in their girth from five or six to twelve feet; and in height, from a hundred and twenty to a hundred and sixty feet. Owing to their unscreened position and their height, these trees may be clearly distinguished for miles, whether from the lake, the hills, or the roads about the country—a land-mark overtopping the humble church-spires, and every object raised by man within the bounds of the valley. Their rude simplicity of outline, the erect, unbending trunks, their stern, changeless character, and their scanty drapery of foliage, unconsciously lead one to fancy them an image of some band of savage chiefs, emerging in a long, dark line from the glen in their rear, and gazing in wonder upon their former hunting-grounds in its altered aspect.

The preservation of those old pines must depend entirely upon the will of their owner; they are private property; we have no right to ask that they may be spared, but it is impossible to behold their hoary trunks and crested heads without feeling a hope that they may long continue unscathed, to look down upon the village which has sprung up at their feet. They are certainly one of the most striking objects in the county, and we owe a debt of gratitude to the hand which has so long preserved them, one of the honors of our neighborhood. It needs but a few short minutes to bring one of these trees to the ground; the rudest boor passing along the highway may easily do the deed; but how many years must pass ere its equal stand on the same spot! Let us pause to count the days, the months, the years; let us number the generations that must come and go, the centuries that must roll onward, ere the seed sown from this year's cones shall produce a wood like that before us. The stout arm so ready to raise the axe to-day, must grow weak with age, it must drop into the grave; its bone and sinew must crumble into dust long before another tree, tall and great as those, shall have grown from the cone in our hand. Nay, more, all the united strength of sinew, added to all the powers of mind, and all the force of will, of millions of men, can do no more toward the work than the poor ability of a single arm; these are of the deeds which time alone can perform. But allowing even that hundreds of years hence other trees were at length to succeed these with the same dignity of height and age, no other younger wood can ever claim the same connection as this, with a state of things now passed away forever; they cannot have that wild, stern character of the aged forest pines. This little town itself must fall to decay and ruin; its streets must become choked with bushes and brambles; the farms of the valley must be anew buried within the shades of a wilderness; the wild deer and the wolf, and the bear, must return from beyond the great lakes; the bones of the savage men buried under our feet must arise and move again in the chase, ere trees like those, with the spirit of the forest in every line, can stand on the same ground in wild dignity of form like those old pines now looking down upon our homes.

Tuesday, 24th. – Thermometer 84 in the shade at three o'clock. Still, clear, and dry; the farmers very anxious for rain.

Pleasant row in the afternoon; went down the river. One cannot go far, as the mill-dam blocks the way, but it is a pretty little bit of stream for an evening row. So near its source, the river is quite narrow, only sixty or eighty feet in breadth. The water is generally very clear, and of greenish gray; after the spring thaws it sometimes has a bluish tint, and late in autumn, after heavy rains, it takes a more decided shade of dark green. It is rarely turbid, and never positively muddy. It has no great depth, except in spots; there are some deep places, however, well known to the boys of the village for feats of diving performed there, certain lads priding themselves upon walking across the bed of the river through these deep spots, while others still more daring are said to have actually played a game of "lap-stone," sitting in what they call the "Deep Hole." In general, the bottom is stony or muddy, but there are reaches of sand also. The growth of aquatic plants is thick in many places, and near the bridge there is a fine patch of water-grasses, which have a beautiful effect seen from above, their long tufts floating gracefully in the slow current of the stream, like the locks of a troop of Mermaids. One of these plants, by-the-by, bears the name of the "Canadian Water-Nymph;" but it is one of the homeliest of its tribe; there are others much more graceful to which the name would be better adapted. It will be remembered that in the northern part of the State there is quite a large stream called Grass River, from the great quantity of these grassy plants growing in its waters.

The older trees on the bank have long since been cut away; but many young elms, maples, ashes, amelanchiers, &c., stand with their roots washed by the water, while grape-vines and Virginia creepers are climbing over them. Wild cherries and plums also line the course of our little river. Sallows and alders form close thickets lower than the forest trees. All our native willows on this continent are small; the largest is the black willow, with a dark bark, about five-and-twenty feet high. It grows some miles farther down the stream. Our alders also are mere bushes, while the European alder is a full-sized tree, tall as their elms or beeches.

Wednesday, 25th.–Warm and clear. Thermometer 83, with fine air.

Long drive. The roads very dusty, but the wind was in our favor, and it is such a busy time with the farmers, that there was little movement on the highway. In the course of a drive of several hours, we only saw three or four wagons.

The farms look very rich with the ripening grains, but rain is much wanted. The Indian corn, and hops, and potatoes, have had more sun than they need. The grass also is much drier than usual in this part of the country; but the trees are in great beauty, luxuriantly green, showing as yet no evil effects from this dry season. The maize is thought to have suffered most; the farmers say the ears are not filling as they ought to do; but the plants themselves look well, and the yellow flowers of the pumpkin-vines lying on the ground help, as usual, to make the corn-fields among the handsomest on the farms.

Vines like the pumpkin, and melon, and cucumber, bearing heavy fruits, show little inclination for climbing; it is well they do not attempt to raise themselves from the earth, since, if they did so, they could not support their own fruit. The fact that they do not seek to climb is a pleasing instance of that beautiful fitness and unity of character so striking in the vegetable world generally; the position in which they are content to lie is the one best calculated to mature their large, heavy gourds; the reflected heat of the earth aiding the sun in the task, while the moisture from the ground does not injure the thick rind, as would be the case with fruits of a more delicate covering.

Thursday, 26th.–Lowering, cloudy morning, with strong breeze from the south-east; one of those skies which promise rain every ten minutes. Dark vapors cover the heavens, and sweep over the hill-tops, but the clouds open, gleams of sunshine come and go, and no rain falls. Long drive in the morning. The mowers are still at work here and there, for there is much hay cut in our neighborhood. The wheat harvest has also commenced, and the crop is pronounced a very good one.

There are certain fancies connected with the wheat-fields prevailing among our farmers, which they are very loth to give up. There is the old notion, for instance, that a single barberry-bush will blight acres of wheat, when growing near the grain, an opinion which is now, I believe, quite abandoned by persons of the best judgment. And yet you see frequent allusions to it, and occasionally some one brings up an instance which he sagely considers as unanswerable proof that the poor barberry is guilty of this crime. In this county we have no barberries; they are a naturalized shrub in America; at least, the variety now so common in many parts of the country came originally from the other hemisphere, and they have not yet reached us. There is another kind, a native, abundant in Virginia; whether this is also accused of blighting the wheat, I do not know.

The deceitful chess, or cheat, is another object of especial aversion to the farmers, and very justly. It is not only a troublesome weed among a valuable crop, but, looking so much like the grain, its deceptive appearance is an especial aggravation. Many of our country folk, moreover, maintain that this plant is nothing but a sort of wicked, degenerate wheat; they hold that a change comes over the grain by which it loses all its virtue, and takes another form, becoming, in short, the worthless chess; this opinion some of them maintain stoutly against all opponents, at the point of scythe and pitchfork. And yet this odd notion is wholly opposed to all the positive laws, the noble order of nature; they might as well expect their raspberry bushes to turn capriciously into blackberries, their potatoes into beets, their lettuce into radishes.

Most of the weeds which infest our wheat-fields come from the Old World. This deceitful chess, the corn-cockle, the Canada thistle, tares, the voracious red-root, the blue-weed, or bugloss, with others of the same kind. There is, however, one brilliant but noxious plant found among the corn-fields of Europe which is not seen in our own, and that is the gaudy red poppy. Our farmers are no doubt very well pleased to dispense with it; they are quite satisfied with the weeds already naturalized. But so common is the poppy in the Old World that it is found everywhere in the corn-fields, along the luxuriant shores of the Mediterranean, upon the open, chequered plains of France and Germany, and among the hedged fields of England. The first wild poppies ever seen by the writer were gathered by a party of American children about the ruins of Netley Abbey, near Southampton, in England.

So common is this brilliant weed among the European grain-fields, that there is a little insect, an ingenious, industrious little creature, who invariably employs it in building her cell. This wild bee, called the upholsterer bee, from its habits, leads a solitary life, but she takes a vast deal of pains in behalf of her young. About the time when the wild poppy begins to blossom, this little insect flies into a corn-field, looks out for a dry spot of ground, usually near some pathway; here she bores a hole about three inches in depth, the lower portion being wider than the mouth; and quite a toil it must be to so small a creature to make the excavation; it is very much as if a man were to clear out the cellars for a large house with his hands only. But this is only the beginning of her task: when the cell is completed, she then flies away to the nearest poppy, which, as she very well knows, cannot be very far off in a corn-field; she cuts out a bit of the scarlet flower, carries it to the nest, and spreads it on the floor like a carpet; again she returns to the blossom and brings home another piece, which she lays over the first; when the floor is covered with several layers of this soft scarlet carpeting, she proceeds to line the sides throughout in the same way, until the whole is well surrounded with these handsome hangings. This brilliant cradle she makes for one little bee, laying only a single egg amid the flower-leaves. Honey and bee-bread are then collected and piled up to the height of an inch; and when this store is completed, the scarlet curtains are drawn close over the whole, and the cell is closed, the careful mother replacing the earth as neatly as possible, so that after she has finally smoothed the spot over, it is difficult to discover a cell you may have seen open the day before.

This constant association with the wheat, which even the insects have learned by instinct, has not remained unheeded by man. Owing to this connection with the precious grain, the poppy of the Old World received, ages ago, all the honors of a classical flower, and became blended with the fables of ancient mythology; not only was it given to the impersonation of Sleep, as one of his emblems, from the well-known narcotic influences of the plant, but it was also considered as sacred to one of the most ancient and most important deities of the system; the very oldest statues of Ceres represent her with poppies in her garlands, blended with ears of wheat, either carried in her hand, or worn on her head. The ancient poets mingled the ears of wheat and the poppy in their verses:

> "The meanest cottager
> *His poppy grows among the corn,*"

says Cowley, in his translation of Virgil; and in our own day Mr. Hood, in his pleasing picture of Ruth, introduces both plants, when describing her beautiful color:

> "And on her cheek an autumn flush,
> *Like poppies grown with corn."*

In short, so well established is this association of the poppy and wheat, by the long course of observation from time immemorial to the present season, that the very *modistes* of Paris, when they wish to trim a straw bonnet with field plants, are careful to mingle the poppy with heads of wheat in their artificial flowers. Fickle Fashion herself is content to leave these plants, year after year, entwined together in her wreaths.

But in spite of this general prevalence of the poppy throughout the grain-fields of the Old World, and its acknowledged claim to a place beside the wheat, it is quite unknown here as a weed. With us this ancient association is broken up. Never having seen it ourselves, we have frequently asked farmers from different parts of the country if they had ever found it among their wheat, and thus far the answer has always been the same; they had never seen the flower out of gardens. Among our cottage gardens it is very common. It is, however, naturalized about Westchester, in Pennsylvania, and may possibly be found in some other isolated spots; but in all this range of wheat-growing country, among the great grain-fields of the Genesee, of Ohio, of Michigan, it is said to be entirely unknown as a field plant.

It must be the comparative severity of the winters which has broken up this very ancient connection in our part of the world; and yet they have at times very severe seasons in France and Germany, without destroying the field poppies.

Friday, 27th.—Cooler; a refreshing shower last evening; no thunder or lightning.

The butterflies are very numerous now; tortoise-shell, black, and yellow, with here and there a blue; large parties of the little white kind, and the tiny tortoise-shell, also, are fluttering about the weeds. The yellow butterflies with pink markings are the most common sort we have here; they are regular roadsters, constantly seen on the highway. Last summer about this time, while driving between Penn-Yan and Seneca Lake, we found these little creatures more numerous than we had ever yet seen them; there had been a heavy rain the day before, and there were many half-dried, muddy pools along the road, which seemed to attract these butterflies more than the flowers in the meadows; they are always found hovering over such spots in summer; but on that occasion we saw so many that we attempted to count them, and in half a mile we passed seventy, so that in the course of a drive of a couple of hours we probably saw more than a thousand of these pretty creatures strung along the highway in little flocks.

There is a singular insect of this tribe, a kind of moth, seen about the flower-beds in the summer months. They are so much like humming-birds in their movements, that many of the country people consider them as a sort of cousin-german of our common rubythroat. We have been repeatedly asked if we had seen these "small humming-birds." Their size, the bird-like form of their body and tail, the rapid, quivering motion of their wings, their habit of feeding on the wing instead of alighting on the flowers, are indeed strangely like the humming-bird. Nevertheless, these are true moths, and there are, I believe, several species of them flitting about our meadows and gardens. The common green potato, or tobacco-worm, is said to become a moth of this kind; and the whole tribe of hawk-moths are now sometimes called humming-bird moths, from these same insects. They are not peculiar to this country, but are well known also in Europe, though not very common there. Altogether, they are singular little creatures; their tongues, with which they extract the honey from the flowers, just as the humming-bird does, are in some cases remarkably long, even longer than their bodies. One of the tribe is said to have a tongue six inches in length, and it coils it up like a watch-spring when not using it.

Saturday, 28th.—Passed the afternoon in the woods.

What a noble gift to man are the forests! What a debt of gratitude and admiration we owe for their utility and their beauty!

How pleasantly the shadows of the wood fall upon our heads, when we turn from the glitter and turmoil of the world of man! The winds of heaven seem to linger amid these balmy branches, and the sunshine falls like a blessing upon the green leaves; the wild breath of the forest, fragrant with bark and berry, fans the brow with grateful freshness; and the beautiful wood-light, neither garish nor gloomy, full of calm and peaceful influences, sheds repose over the spirit. The view is limited, and the objects about us are uniform in character; yet within the bosom of the woods the mind readily lays aside its daily littleness, and opens to higher thoughts, in silent consciousness that it stands alone with the works of God. The humble moss beneath our feet, the sweet flowers, the varied shrubs, the great trees, and the sky gleaming above in sacred blue, are each the handiwork of God. They were all called into being by the will of the Creator, as we now behold them, full of wisdom and goodness. Every object here has a deeper merit than our

wonder can fathom; each has a beauty beyond our full perception; the
dullest insect crawling about these roots lives by the power of the Almighty;
and the discolored shreds of last year's leaves wither away upon the lowly
herbs in a blessing of fertility. But it is the great trees, stretching their arms
above us in a thousand forms of grace and strength, it is more especially the
trees which fill the mind with wonder and praise.

Of the infinite variety of fruits which spring from the bosom of the earth,
the trees of the wood are the greatest in dignity. Of all the works of the creation which know the changes of life and death, the trees of the forest have
the longest existence. Of all the objects which crown the gray earth, the
woods preserve unchanged, throughout the greatest reach of time, their native character: the works of man are ever varying their aspect; his towns and
his fields alike reflect the unstable opinions, the fickle wills and fancies of each
passing generation; but the forests on his borders remain to-day the same
they were ages of years since. Old as the everlasting hills, during thousands
of seasons they have put forth, and laid down their verdure in calm obedience to the decree which first bade them cover the ruins of the Deluge.

But, although the forests are great and old, yet the ancient trees within
their bounds must each bend individually beneath the doom of every earthly
existence; they have their allotted period when the mosses of Time gather
upon their branches; when, touched by decay, they break and crumble to
dust. Like man, they are decked in living beauty; like man, they fall a prey
to death; and while we admire their duration, so far beyond our own brief
years, we also acknowledge that especial interest which can only belong to
the graces of life and to the desolation of death. We raise our eyes and we
see collected in one company vigorous trunks, the oak, the ash, the pine,
firm in the strength of maturity; by their side stand a young group, elm, and
birch, and maple, their supple branches playing in the breezes, gay and fresh
as youth itself; and yonder, rising in unheeded gloom, we behold a skeleton
trunk, an old spruce, every branch broken, every leaf fallen,—dull, still, sad,
like the finger of Death.

It is the peculiar nature of the forest, that life and death may ever be found
within its bounds, in immediate presence of each other; both with ceaseless,
noiseless, advances, aiming at the mastery; and if the influences of the first
be the most general, those of the last are the most striking. Spring, with all
her wealth of life and joy, finds within the forest many a tree unconscious of
her approach; a thousand young plants springing up about the fallen trunk,
the shaggy roots, seek to soften the gloomy wreck with a semblance of the
verdure it bore of old; but ere they have thrown their fresh and graceful

wreaths over the mouldering wood, half their own tribe wither and die with the year. We owe to this perpetual presence of death an impression calm, solemn, almost religious in character, a chastening influence, beyond what we find in the open fields. But this subdued spirit is far from gloomy or oppressive, since it never fails to be relieved by the cheerful animation of living beauty. Sweet flowers grow beside the fallen trees, among the shattered branches, the season through; and the freedom of the woods, the unchecked growth, the careless position of every tree, are favorable to a thousand wild beauties, and fantastic forms, opening to the mind a play of fancy which is in itself cheering and enlivening, like the bright sunbeams which chequer with golden light the shadowy groves. That character of rich variety also, stamped on all the works of the creation, is developed in the forest in clear and noble forms; we are told that in the field we shall not find two blades of grass exactly alike, that in the garden we shall not gather two flowers precisely similar, but in those cases the lines are minute, and we do not seize the truth at once; in the woods, however, the same fact stands recorded in bolder lines; we cannot fail to mark this great variety of detail among the trees; we see it in their trunks, their branches, their foliage; in the rude knots, the gnarled roots; in the mosses and lichens which feed upon their bark; in their forms, their coloring, their shadows. And within all this luxuriance of varied beauty, there dwells a sweet quiet, a noble harmony, a calm repose, which we seek in vain elsewhere, in so full a measure.

These hills, and the valleys at their feet, lay for untold centuries one vast forest; unnumbered seasons, ages of unrecorded time passed away while they made part of the boundless wilderness of woods. The trees waved over the valleys, they rose upon the swelling knolls, they filled the hollows, they crowded the narrow glens, they shaded the brooks and springs, they washed their roots in the lakes and rivers, they stood upon the islands, they swept over the broad hills, they crowned the heads of all the mountains. The whole land lay slumbering in the twilight of the forest. Wild dreams made up its half-conscious existence. The hungry cry of the beast of prey, or the fierce deed of savage man, whoop and dance, triumph and torture, broke in fitful bursts upon the deep silence, and then died away, leaving the breath of life to rise and fall with the passing winds.

Every rocky cliff on the hill-side, every marshy spot on the lowlands, was veiled in living, rustling folds of green. Here a dark wave of pine, hemlock, and balsam ran through a ravine, on yonder knoll shone the rich glossy verdure of oak, and maple, and chestnut; upon the breast of the mountain stood the birch, the elm, and the aspen, in light and airy tufts. Leaves of every tint of green played in the summer sunshine, leaves fluttered in the moonlight, and the showers of heaven fell everywhere upon the green leaves of the unbroken forest.

Sixty years have worked a wonderful change; the forest has fallen upon the lowlands, and there is not a valley about us which has not been opened. Another half century may find the country bleak and bare; but as yet the woods have not all been felled, and within the circle which bounds our view, there is no mountain which has been wholly shorn, none presents a bald front to the sky; upon the lake shore, there are several hills still wrapped in wood from the summit to the base. He who takes pleasure in the forest, by picking his way, and following a winding course, may yet travel many a long mile over a shady path, such as the red man loved.

The forest lands of America preserve to the present hour something that is characteristic of their wild condition, undisturbed for ages. They abound in ruins of their own. Old trees, dead and dying, are left standing for years, until at length they are shivered and broken by the winds, or they crumble slowly away to a shapeless stump. There was no forester at hand to cut them down when the first signs of decay appeared; they had no uses then, now they have no value. Broken limbs and dead bodies of great trees lie scattered through the forests; there are spots where the winds seem to have battled with the woods—at every step one treads on fallen trunks, stretched in giant length upon the earth, this still clad in its armor of bark, that bare and mouldering, stained by green mildew, one a crumbling mass of fragments, while others, again, lie shrouded in beautiful mosses, long green hillocks marking the grave of trees slowly turning to dust. Young trees are frequently found growing upon these forest ruins; if a giant pine or oak has been levelled by some storm, the mass of matted roots and earth will stand upright for years in the same position into which it was raised by the falling trunk, and occasionally a good-sized hemlock, or pine, or beech, is seen growing from the summit of the mass, which in itself is perhaps ten or twelve feet high. We have found a stout tree, of perhaps twenty years' growth, which has sprung from a chance seed, sown by the winds on the prostrate trunk of a fallen pine or chestnut, growing until its roots have stretched down the side of the mouldering log, and reached the earth on both sides, thus holding the crumbling skeleton firmly in its young embrace. The decay of these dead trees is strangely slow; prostrate pines have been known to last fifty years, undecayed, still preserving their sap; and upright gray shafts often remain standing for years, until one comes to know them as familiarly as the living trees. Instances are on record where they have thus remained erect in death for a space of forty years.[11] Amid this wild confusion, we note here and there some mark left by civilized man; the track of wheels, a rude road sprinkled over by withered leaves, or the mark of the axe, sharp and clean, upon a stump close at hand, reminding us how freely and how richly the forest contributes to the wants of our race.

Perhaps two-fifths of the woods in our neighborhood are evergreens, chiefly pine and hemlock; the proportion varies, however, in different spots; occasionally you see a whole mountain-side dark with hemlock and pine, while other hills, again, are almost entirely covered with deciduous trees; more frequently, they are pleasingly mingled in the same wood. Both hemlock and pine grow in all positions, upon the hills, in the valleys, in dry soils, and upon the banks of the streams. The balsam is less common, generally found in marshy spots, in company with its kinsman, of the tamarack, which in summer, at least, has all the appearance of an evergreen. The balsam is a beautiful tree; though not aspiring to the dignity of the pine and hemlock, it shoots up in the most perfect and gradual spire-like form, to a height of thirty or forty feet, remarkable for its elegance; the foliage is very rich in color and quantity. It seems to delight in throwing its image into the pools and tarns about our hills, often standing on their banks, tinging the waters with its own dark green. There is no cedar very near us; the white cedar, or cypress, is found about eight or nine miles to the northward, and still farther in that direction it is very abundant, but along the course of the river, southward from the lake, to a distance of more than a hundred miles, we do not remember to have seen it. We have also but one pine, though that one is the chief of its family; the noble white pine, the pride of the Alleghanies; neither the yellow, the pitch, nor the red pine is known here, so far as one can discover. The arbor vitæ is also unknown. It has been thought by some of our neighbors that the evergreens diminish in numbers as the old woods are cut away, the deciduous trees gaining upon them; but looking about at the young thrifty groves of pine seen in every direction, there does not seem much reason to fear that they will disappear. They shoot up even in the cleared fields, here and there, and we have observed in several instances, that in spots where old pine woods had been cut down, close thickets of young trees of the same kind have succeeded them.

The oak of several varieties, white, black, the scarlet, and the red; the beech, the chestnut; black and white ashes; the lime or bass-wood; the white and the slippery elms; the common aspen, the large-leaved aspen; the downy-leaved poplar, and the balm of Gilead poplar; the white, the yellow, and the black birches, are all very common. The sumach and the alder abound everywhere. But the glossy leaves of the maple are more numerous than any others, if we include the whole family, and with the exception of the western or ash-leaved maple, they all grow here, from the fine sugar maple to the dwarf mountain maple: including them all, then, perhaps they number two for one of any other deciduous tree found here. They sow themselves very freely; in the spring one finds the little seedling maples coming up everywhere. With the exception of the chestnut, the nut trees are not so very common; yet the hickory is not rare, and both the black walnut and the butternut are met with. The sycamore, very abundant to the north of us, on the Mohawk, is rare here; it is found on the banks of a little stream two or three miles to the southward, and that is the only spot in the neighborhood where it has been observed. The pepperidge or sour-gum is found here and there only. The tulip-tree, abundant in most parts of the country, has not been seen within fifteen miles of our lake. The sweet-gum, or liquid-amber, is unknown here. The sassafras, also, is a stranger with us. That beautiful shrub, the laurel, so very common on the Hudson, is missed here; it grows in the county, however, but more than twenty miles to the southward of our village. The handsome flowering dog-wood, so ornamental to the forests in other parts of the State, is also wanting in this neighborhood.

The finest trees about the banks of our lake are remarkable rather for their height than their girth. Belonging to the old forest race, they have been closely pressed on all sides by their fellows, and the trunks rise in a branch-less shaft to a commanding height; their foliage crowns the summit in full masses, and if never devoid of the native graces of each species, still it has not all the beauty developed by the free growth of the open fields. The older ashes, elms, and oaks are striking trees, much more stern and simple than their brethren of the lawns and meadows, all bearing the peculiar character of forest growth. The younger tribe of the woods, from the same cause which gives a stern simplicity to their elders, become, on the other hand, even more light and airy than their fellows in the open ground; shaded by the patriarchs of the forest, they shoot up toward the light in slender gracile stems, throwing out their branches in light and airy spray. So slight and supple are the stems of this younger race, that trees of thirty and forty, ay, even fifty feet in height, often bend low beneath the weight of the winter's snow upon their naked branches; some of them never regain their upright position, others gradually resume it as their trunks gain strength. Upon a wild wood-road near the lake shore there is a natural green archway, formed in this manner by two tall young trees accidentally bending toward each other from opposite sides of the road, until their branches meet over the track; the effect is very pretty, one of those caprices of the forest world, which in older times might have passed for the work of some elfin wood-man.

It is to be feared that few among the younger generation now springing up will ever attain to the dignity of the old forest trees. Very large portions of these woods are already of a second growth, and trees of the greatest size are becoming every year more rare. It quite often happens that you come upon old stumps of much larger dimensions than any living trees about them; some of these are four, and a few five feet or more in diameter. Occasionally, we still find a pine erect of this size; one was felled the other day, which measured five feet in diameter. There is an elm about a mile from the village seventeen feet in girth, and not long since we heard of a bass-wood or linden twenty-eight feet in circumference. But among the trees now standing, even those which are sixty or eighty feet in height, many are not more than four, or five, or six feet in girth. The pines, especially, reach a surprising elevation for their bulk.

As regards the ages of the larger trees, one frequently finds stumps about two hundred years old; those of three hundred are not rare, and occasionally we have seen one which we believed to claim upward of four hundred rings. But as a rule, the largest trees are singled out very early in the history of a settlement, and many of these older stumps of the largest size have now become so worn and ragged, that it is seldom one can count the circles accurately. They are often much injured by fire immediately after the tree has been felled, and in many other instances decay has been at work at the heart, and one cannot, perhaps, count more than half the rings; measuring will help, in such cases, to give some idea; by taking fifty rings of the sound part, and allowing the same distance of the decayed portion for another fifty. But this is by no means a sure way, since the rings vary very much in the same tree, some being so broad that they must have sensibly increased the circumference of the trunk in one year, to the extent, perhaps, of an inch, while in other parts of the same shaft you will find a dozen circles crowded into that space. In short, it is seldom one has the satisfaction of meeting with a stump in which one may count every ring with perfect accuracy. It is said that some of the pines on the Pacific coast, those of Oregon and California, have numbered nine hundred rings; these were the noble Lambert pines of that region. Probably very few of our own white pines can show more than half that number of circles.

It is often said, as an excuse for leaving none standing, that these old trees of forest growth will not live after their companions have been felled; they miss the protection which one gives to another, and, exposed to the winds, soon fall to the ground. As a general rule, this may be true; but one is inclined to believe that if the experiment of leaving a few were more frequently tried, it would often prove successful. There is an elm of great size now standing entirely alone in a pretty field of the valley, its girth, its age, and whole appearance declaring it a chieftain of the ancient race—the "Sagamore elm," as it is called—and in spite of complete exposure to the winds from all quarters of the heavens, it maintains its place firmly. The trunk measures seventeen feet in circumference, and it is thought to be a hundred feet in height; but this is only from the eye, never having been accurately ascertained. The shaft rises perhaps fifty feet without a branch, before it divides, according to the usual growth of old forest trees. Unfortunately, gray branches are beginning to show among its summer foliage, and it is to be feared that it will not outlast many winters more; but if it die to-morrow, we shall have owed a debt of many thanks to the owner of the field for having left the tree standing so long.

In these times, the hewers of wood are an unsparing race. The first colonists looked upon a tree as an enemy, and to judge from appearances, one would think that something of the same spirit prevails among their descendants at the present hour. It is not surprising, perhaps, that a man whose chief object in life is to make money, should turn his timber into bank-notes with all possible speed; but it is remarkable that any one at all aware of the value of wood, should act so wastefully as most men do in this part of the world. Mature trees, young saplings, and last year's seedlings, are all destroyed at one blow by the axe or by fire; the spot where they have stood is left, perhaps, for a lifetime without any attempt at cultivation, or any endeavor to foster new wood. One would think that by this time, when the forest has fallen in all the valleys—when the hills are becoming more bare every day—when timber and fuel are rising in prices, and new uses are found for even indifferent woods—some forethought and care in this respect would be natural in people laying claim to common sense. The rapid consumption of the large pine timber among us should be enough to teach a lesson of prudence and economy on this subject. It has been calculated that 60,000 acres of pine woods are cut every year in our own State alone; and at this rate, it is said that in twenty years, or about 1870, these trees will have disappeared from our part of the country! [12] But unaccountable as it may appear, few American farmers are aware of the full value and importance of wood. They seem to forget the relative value of the forests. It has been reported in the State of New York, that the produce of tilled lands carried to tide-water by the Erie Canal, in one year, amounted to 8,170,000 dollars' worth of property; that of animals, or farm-stock, for the same year, is given at $3,230,000; that of the forests, lumber, staves, &c., &c., at $4,770,000.[13] Thus the forest yielded more than the stock, and more than half as much as the farm lands; and when the comparative expense of the two is considered, their value will be brought still nearer together. Peltries were not included in this account. Our people seldom remember that the forests, while they provide food and shelter for the wildest savage tribes, make up a large amount of the wealth of the most civilized nations. The first rude devices of the barbarian are shaped in wood, and the cedar of Lebanon ranks with the gold of Ophir within the walls of palaces. How much do not we ourselves owe to the forests as regards our daily wants! Our fields are divided by wooden fences; wooden bridges cross our rivers; our village streets and highways are being paved with wood; the engines that carry us on our way by land and by water are fed with wood; the rural dwellings without and within, their walls, their floors, stairways, and roofs are almost wholly of wood; and in this neighborhood the fires that burn on our household hearths are entirely the gift of the living forest.

But independently of their market price in dollars and cents, the trees have other values: they are connected in many ways with the civilization of a country; they have their importance in an intellectual and in a moral sense. After the first rude stage of progress is past in a new country–when shelter and food have been provided–people begin to collect the conveniences and pleasures of a permanent home about their dwellings, and then the farmer generally sets out a few trees before his door. This is very desirable, but it is only the first step in the track; something more is needed; the preservation of fine trees, already standing, marks a farther progress, and this point we have not yet reached. It frequently happens that the same man who yesterday planted some half dozen branchless saplings before his door, will to-day cut down a noble elm, or oak, only a few rods from his house, an object which was in itself a hundred-fold more beautiful than any other in his possession. In very truth, a fine tree near a house is a much greater embellishment than the thickest coat of paint that could be put on its walls, or a whole row of wooden columns to adorn its front; nay, a large shady tree in a door-yard is much more desirable than the most expensive mahogany and velvet sofa in the parlor. Unhappily, our people generally do not yet see things in this light. But time is a very essential element, absolutely indispensable, indeed, in true civilization; and in the course of years we shall, it is to be hoped, learn farther lessons of this kind. Closer observation will reveal to us the beauty and excellence of simplicity, a quality as yet too little valued or understood in this country. And when we have made this farther progress, then we shall take better care of our trees. We shall not be satisfied with setting out a dozen naked saplings before our door, because our neighbor on the left did so last year, nor cut down a whole wood, within a stone's throw of our dwelling, to pay for a Brussels carpet from the same piece as our neighbor's on the right; no, we shall not care a stiver for mere show and parade, in any shape whatever, but we shall look to the general proprieties and fitness of things, whether our neighbors to the right or the left do so or not.

How easy it would be to improve most of the farms in the country by a little attention to the woods and trees, improving their appearance, and adding to their market value at the same time! Thinning woods and not blasting them; clearing only such ground as is marked for immediate tillage; preserving the wood on the hill-tops and rough side-hills; encouraging a coppice on this or that knoll; permitting bushes and young trees to grow at will along the brooks and water-courses; sowing, if need be, a grove on the bank of the pool, such as are found on many of our farms; sparing an elm or two about the spring, with a willow also to overhang the well; planting one or two chestnuts, or oaks, or beeches, near the gates or bars; leaving a few others scattered about every field to shade the cattle in summer, as is frequently done, and setting out others in groups, or singly, to shade the house—how little would be the labor or expense required to accomplish all this, and how desirable would be the result! Assuredly, the pleasing character thus given to a farm and a neighborhood is far from being beneath the consideration of a sensible man.

But there is also another view of the subject. A careless indifference to any good gift of our gracious Maker, shows a want of thankfulness, as any abuse or waste, betrays a reckless spirit of evil. It is, indeed, strange that one claiming to be a rational creature should not be thoroughly ashamed of the spirit of destructiveness, since the principle itself is clearly an evil one. Let us remember that it is the Supreme Being who is the Creator, and in how many ways do we see his gracious providence, his Almighty economy, deigning to work progressive renovation in the humblest objects when their old forms have become exhausted by Time! There is also something in the care of trees which rises above the common labors of husbandry, and speaks of a generous mind. We expect to wear the fleece from our flocks, to drink the milk of our herds, to feed upon the fruits of our fields; but in planting a young wood, in preserving a fine grove, a noble tree, we look beyond ourselves to the band of household friends, to our neighbors—ay, to the passing wayfarer and stranger who will share with us the pleasure they give, and it becomes a grateful reflection that long after we are gone, those trees will continue a good to our fellow-creatures for more years, perhaps, than we can tell.

Quite recently, two instances of an opposite character connected with this subject have accidentally fallen under our notice. At a particular point in the wilds of Oregon, near the bank of the Columbia River, there stood a single tree of great size, one of the majestic pines of that region, and long known as a landmark to the hunters and emigrants passing over those solitary wastes. One of the expeditions sent out to explore that country by the government, arriving near the point, were on the watch for that pine to guide their course; they looked for it some time, but in vain; at length, reaching the spot where they supposed it ought to have stood—a way-mark in the wilderness—they found the tree lying on the earth. It had been felled, and left there to rot, by some man claiming, no doubt, to be a civilized being. The man who could do such an act would have been worthy to make one of the horde of Attila, barbarians who delighted to level to the ground every object over which their own horses could not leap.

Opposed to this is an instance less striking, but more pleasing, and happily much nearer to our own neighborhood. Upon the banks of the Susquehannah, not far from the little village of Bainbridge, the traveller, as he follows the road, observes a very fine tree before him, and as he approaches he will find it to be a luxuriant elm, standing actually in the midst of the highway; its branches completely cover the broad track, sweeping over the fences on either side. The tree stands in the very position where a thorough-going utilitarian would doubtless quarrel with it, for the road is turned a little out of its true course to sweep round the trunk; but in the opinion of most people, it is not only a very beautiful object in itself, but highly creditable to the neighborhood; for, not only has it been left standing in its singular position, but as far as we could see, there was not a single mark of abuse upon its trunk or branches.

Monday, 30th.—Very warm. Thermometer 80 in the house; 89 in the shade without.

Walking in the lane toward evening, saw a couple of meadow-larks in great agitation; perhaps some disaster had befallen their young; it seems rather late for them to have little ones, but they raise two broods in the summer. They were flying from one bush to another, and back again over the same ground, crying as they went quite piteously. These birds build on the ground; their nest is made of different grassy plants, quite cleverly contrived, and almost always placed in a meadow. They are decidedly larger and handsomer than the European sky-lark, but their simple note is not at all remarkable; the female sings a little as she rises and falls, like the wife of the red-wing black-bird. Their flight is very different from that of their European kinsman, being heavy and laborious; they like, however, to perch on the very highest branches of trees, which is singular in birds living so much on the ground, and moving apparently with some effort. Climate seems to affect them but little, for they reach from the tropics to 53' north latitude, and they are resident birds in the lower counties of our own State, though never remaining, I believe, among these hills.

It is to be regretted that neither of the two great singing-birds of the Old World is found in America; that both the sky-lark and the nightingale should be strangers on this side the Atlantic. In some respects the nightingale differs from the common notions regarding it in this country. We have read so much of "plaintive Philomel," that most of us fancy a solitary bird, in the deep recesses of the grove, chanting by moonlight an air "most musical, most melancholy." But this is far from being always the case; the birds sing by daylight at least as often as they do at night, and of a pleasant morning or evening, one may hear a whole choir of them singing cheerfully together. It is said that they never move about in flocks; this may be so, but they certainly live in close neighborhood—a number in the same wood. In the months of May and June, at early dawn, just about the time when the market people and chimney-sweeps are moving about the streets of Paris, the nightingales are heard singing gayly enough, a dozen at a time, perhaps, in the very heart of that great city. They live in the *maronniers,* and lindens, and elms, among the noble gardens of the town, whether public or private, and seem to mind the neighborhood of man as little as the greenlets which flit about the plane-trees of Philadelphia. It is true, that at the same season, you may, if you choose, take a moonlight walk in the country,

> "And the mute silence hist along,
> Lest Philomel will deign a song
> In her sweetest, saddest plight."

And probably this solitary song, owing partly to the moonlight, and partly to the stillness of night, will produce a much deeper effect than the choir you heard in the morning, or at sunset.

It is said that an attempt was made, some years since, to introduce the nightingale into this country, a gentleman in Virginia having imported a number and given them their liberty in the woods. But they seem to have all died; the change of climate and food was probably too great. They are delicate birds; they are said to be very rare in the northern counties of England, and to avoid also the western parts of the island. Still, the nightingale is a bird of passage, and now that the sea-voyage is so much shorter, possibly, if the experiment were repeated, it might succeed. Birds are great travellers, and they have undoubtedly spread themselves over the world as we now find them. Within our own short history, we know of well-accredited instances of changes in their course. In this very State we now have the singular Cliff-swallow, which a few years since was entirely unknown, and the first seen here were a solitary pair. The Cat-birds also are said to have been unknown on the Genesee until several years after the country had been opened. Blue-birds and robins are far more numerous than they used to be, while on the other hand several birds are known to have deserted our neighborhood for regions more to their taste, such as the quail, the kill-deers, the crested woodpeckers, &c., &c.

The sky-lark is more hardy than the nightingale, and possibly might bear our climate better, though not a migratory bird. Of the two, we should perhaps prefer the lark. In the first place, he sings more or less the whole year round, and never deserts his native fields, while the nightingale is only in voice for a few weeks in May and June. And then the habits of the lark are peculiar to himself. There is no act of the eagle so noble in character as the uprising of the lark to greet the sun; it is the very sublime of action. We know nothing within the whole range of nature more eloquent. If we may believe Lafontaine, this bird likes to build his lowly nest in a grain-field—

> "Les alouettes font leur nid
> Dans les blès, quand ils sont en herbe."

The lark of the fable sings wittily, rather than lyrically; but all that the *bonhomme* does with the creatures which people his world of fancy, is so exquisite in its way, that we are entirely satisfied with his bird in the homely, motherly character. It is her husband who is the poet; it is he who sings those noble sunrise odes; she herself is the clever, notable—*mère de famille*—who knows the world, though Lafontaine did not. When the farmer talks of collecting first his neighbors, and then his relations, to cut the grain, she gives herself no concern whatever—why should she? But when the goodman comes with his son, and they decide to begin the work themselves, the point is settled, the lark family must take flight—

> "C'est à ce coup, qu'il faut décamper, mes enfants,
> Et les petits en même temps
> Voletants, se culebutants
> Délogèrent tous, sans trompette."

In this part of the world, Lafontaine would have been compelled to choose some other more humble bird, to teach us so cleverly the useful lesson of self-dependence; but if he had chanced to make acquaintance with the meadow-lark, the grass-bird, the bobolink, or even the modest little song-sparrow, he would have taught either of them, in a trice, to sing with more than all "*l'esprit des Mortemars.*"

There is in this country a lark common to both continents—the horned-lark or shore-lark—a very pretty arctic bird, which in winter goes as far south as Georgia, but we have never heard of it in these highlands. On the coast of Long Island it is quite common. It is said also to breed on the Western prairies.

Tuesday, 31st.—Refreshing shower in the morning; gentle rain, no thunder or lightning; it is remarkable how little electricity we have had this summer. We have often, in common seasons, heavy showers, with very sharp lightning, and thunder which echoes grandly among our hills. We have known the lightning to strike seven times in the course of an hour, in the village and the immediate neighborhood, twice in the lake, and five times on the land; but very happily, no serious accident occurred on that occasion, though one or two persons were stunned. This summer we have hardly seen a flash.

First melons to-day.

Wednesday, August 1st.—Pleasant; walked over Mill Bridge in the afternoon. Gathered a fine bunch of the crimson lobelia by the river-side. What an exquisite shade of red lies on the petals of this brilliant plant! It reminds one that the Russian word for *beauty* and for *red* is said to be the same—*krasnoi*, as M. de Ségur gives it; most of us would probably consider rose-color or blue as more beautiful, but certainly the inimitable, vivid, and yet delicate tint of the lobelia, may claim to be identical with *krasnoi*, or beauty. The blue lobelia, also very handsome in its way, is not found here, though very common on the Mohawk.

Walking through a wood, found hawk-wort and asters in bloom, also a handsome rattlesnake plantain, or Goodyera, with its veined leaves and fragrant spike of white flowers; this is one of the plants formerly thought to cure the bite of the rattlesnake, though little credit is given to the notion now-a-days.

Thursday, 2d.—Long drive down the valley.

There is not a single town of any size within a distance of forty miles, yet already the rural population of this county is quite large. The whole country, within a wide circuit north, south, east and west, partakes of the same general character; mountain ridges, half tilled, half wood, screening cultivated valleys, sprinkled with farms and hamlets, among which some pretty stream generally winds its way. The waters in our immediate neighborhood all flow to the southward, though only a few miles to the north of our village, the brooks are found running in an opposite course, this valley lying just within the borders of the dividing ridge. The river itself, though farther south it becomes one of the great streams of the country, cannot boast of much breadth so near its source, and running quietly among the meadows, half screened by the groves and thickets, scarcely shows in the general view.

The whole surface of the country is arable; very little marsh or bog is found in the lower lands, and there are no barren tracts upon the hills. Rocks rarely break through the surface, except here and there where a low cliff runs along the hill-sides, and these are usually shaded by the forest. This general fertility, this blending of the fields of man and his tillage with the woods, the great husbandry of Providence, gives a fine character to the country, which it could not claim when the lonely savage roamed through wooded valleys, and which it must lose if ever cupidity, and the haste to grow rich, shall destroy the forest entirely, and leave these hills to posterity, bald and bare, as those of many older lands. No perfection of tillage, no luxuriance of produce can make up to a country for the loss of its forests; you may turn the soil into a very garden crowded with the richest crops, if shorn of wood, like Sampson shorn of his locks, it may wear a florid aspect, but the noblest fruit of the earth, that which is the greatest proof of her strength, will be wanting.

Cross-roads occur frequently, and many more are seen in the distance, winding over the hills toward other valleys and other villages. Indeed, the number of roads by which the country is cut up in every direction, crossing each other at short intervals, hither and thither, might alone lead a foreigner to suppose it much older in civilization; and when the great extent of the country and the date of its settlement are remembered, these roads bear very striking testimony to the spirit and activity of the people. It is true that many of them are very imperfectly worked, yet in summer and winter they are all in respectable condition, and many of them as good as need be; these new plank roads, which are just beginning, promise, indeed, to be admirable, and the workmanship, filling up hollows and grading hills, is often quite imposing. It must also be remembered that the climate is much against us in this respect, owing to the deep frosts of winter and sudden thaws of spring, which are enough to injure greatly the best-made roads in the world.

The soil, without being so rich as that farther west, is very good, and the school of agriculture respectable, though scarcely very scientific. A portion of the farmers are graziers and dairymen, and large herds are seen feeding in some pastures. Wool is also a staple of the county, and one cannot go very far without coming upon a flock of sheep, nibbling quietly by themselves, unwatched by dog or shepherd. During the summer months, the cattle of these valleys have generally good cause to be satisfied with their lot; the grass seldom fails, and those excessive heats, accompanied by long parching droughts—almost a matter of course in the lower counties—are seldom felt here; the continued warm weather of this last summer has been something uncommon. But though dryer than usual, our meadows are still greener than those in other parts of the State; we have just heard that two hundred head of cattle, and two thousand head of sheep, have been driven into our county from St. Lawrence, to be pastured here during the drought. Generally, our grass and foliage are refreshed by passing showers, during the warmest weather, and the beauty of the verdure is a source of great pleasure to those who come from the *brown* fields about New York and Philadelphia.

The crops are those which belong naturally to a temperate, hilly country. Wheat, oats, buckwheat, maize, potatoes, and barley are the most common, with some turnips and carrots for fodder. Rye is rather rare. Hop-grounds are frequent, for although this is not much of a beer-drinking community, yet a large amount of hops is carried hence to the sea-ports for European markets. These fields are said to be very profitable for the owners, but they are by no means so pleasing in a landscape as grain or pasture lands. Those two vines, the hop and the grape, so luxuriant and beautiful in their natural state, alike lose much of their peculiar grace, when cultivated in the common way; at a distance, a hop-ground and a vineyard very much resemble each other, though the hop is trained much higher than the grape; the poles and stakes in each case go far toward destroying the beauty of the plants. Both these vines, by-the-by, the grape and the hop, are natives of this part of the country.

The new disease among the potatoes, which has already done so much mischief in past years, has only shown itself this season in some few fields. Generally, the crop looks quite well in our neighborhood. This disease seems to be one of the most singular on record in the vegetable world, unaccountable in its origin, and so very general in both hemispheres; is it not the only instance of such a general and prolonged blight? Probably in time the evil will mercifully be removed, for it scarcely belongs to the nature of vegetable productions to perish entirely and become extinct like tribes of animals.

About a couple of miles from the village there is a very pretty pool in a field near the road, covering, perhaps, an acre or more of ground; marvellous tales were formerly told of its depth, and for a long time people tried to believe it unfathomable; but unfortunately, actual measurement has destroyed the illusion, and it is found to be only five or six feet in depth! All agree, however, that it has become much more shallow since the country has been opened and the woods cut away:

> "Before these fields were shorn and tilled,
>   Full to the brim our rivers flowed;
> The melody of waters filled
>   The fresh and boundless wood.
> And torrents dashed, and rivulets played,
> And fountains spouted in the shade."

But now, as the old Indian sings, these things are changed:

> "The springs are silent in the sun,
>   The rivers by the blackened shore
> With lessening current run."

This little lake, Pappoose Pool, as it is called, looks very prettily as one comes and goes along the highway, with its border of evergreens of various kinds sweeping half round it, and making a fine background to the water, which they color with their dark branches.

Presently, after passing this little pool, one comes to a factory on the bank of a pretty stream of some size, which received its name from the number of oaks standing on its banks in former times; most of these have been felled years ago, and the river now runs among open fields, just beyond the factory, however, a few hoary old trunks are seen rising far above the younger trees and shrubs; but these are sycamores, and with their white bark and scanty branches, they look like lingering ghosts of the fallen forest. The banks of this stream are the only ground in the neighborhood, I believe, where sycamores are found, and there are but a few, scattered here and there, along its track.

The factory, a stone building of some size, with its usual neighbors, a mill and a store, make up a little hamlet, with a cluster of red wooden cottages, and a yellow house for the agent. A couple of thriving maples, good-sized trees, have been left standing in the open space crossed by the road, much to the credit of those who have spared them—"may their shadows never be less!" It is a pity that a few more were not scattered about with a bench or two in the shade; the spot would then make a neat hamlet green.

Some people think that public seats would not answer in our part of the world; it is said that if made of stone they would be cracked and broken, if made of wood chipped and defaced by the knives of the thoughtless men and boys of a country neighborhood. But surely it is time we began to learn a lesson of civilization in this respect; to put things to their proper uses is one of the first precepts of good sense and good manners. Benches were not made to be chipped, nor knives to mutilate and deface with. One would like an experiment of this kind to be fairly tried; if it failed, then it would be time enough to complain; and wherever it succeeds, it must be very creditable to the rural community who carries it out. Travellers in Switzerland remember with pleasure the seats placed at intervals along the road-side in that country for the weary and wayfaring; near Berne these seats are very common indeed, and although they are often found in quiet, secluded spots, the fear of their being injured by the people seems never to have been suggested. Cannot we in this country, where schools, and books, and churches are so common, follow, in this respect, the pleasant, simple custom offered by the example of our fellow-republicans of Berne? These public benches form, indeed, only a part of a general system, the first step toward the open green of the village, the public walks of the larger towns, and the noble gardens of great cities, so happily provided in most countries of Europe, for the health and innocent recreation of the people. Surely it would be very desirable to introduce all these into our own country, and here, where land is cheaper, they ought to be more easily carried out than in the Old World. A bench or two of this description beneath a cluster of trees on a little green in any hamlet, would have a good effect in bringing many a mother out into the open air, with her baby, at odd moments, when it would be good for both to be there; such a play-ground would be better than the dusty street for the children; and if fathers and husbands were content to talk politics under the trees rather than in the smoky, drinking bar-room, it would certainly do them no harm.

Besides this cotton factory at the Twin-Maples, there is another on the opposite side of the valley, upon the main stream; several others are found in different parts of the county, but they are all on a moderate scale.

Another large stone building is seen across the valley, on the brow of an abrupt bank, looking in the distance like an old French *auberge*. It is the county poor-house, and rising in the midst of a prosperous country, tells us that even under the most favorable circumstances, within a young and vigorous society, there must be poor among us, some the victims of their own follies or vices, some the victims of those of others.

The valley becomes broader and more level about four or five miles from the village; a hamlet has grown up here about an Academy, founded early in the history of the county, by a Lutheran clergyman, who has left his name to the spot. Farm-houses and cottages are springing up here along the highway in close neighborhood, for a mile or more. Many of these, painted white, with green blinds, and pleasant door-yards, and a garden adjoining, look very neat and cheerful. Green-house plants, geraniums, callas, cactuses, &c., &c., are seen on these cottage porches at this season; they are much prized during the long winter, and something of the kind is found in many houses. A very broad field, remarkably level for this part of the world, lies on one side of the highway; sugar-maples line the road here, and they bear marks of having been tapped for the sap, thus serving the double purpose of a pleasant, shady avenue, and a sugar bush where the trees are close at hand. A burying-ground lies at one corner of the broad field, and a little meeting-house at the farther point. But the great edifice of the hamlet is of course the Academy, a brick building, colored gray, flanked by wings, with a green before its doors, and a double row of maples, planted in a semicircle, forming its academic shades. The institution was endowed by the Lutheran clergyman, a German by birth, who was the original owner of a small patent covering this spot; the worthy man is said to have been an eccentric character, but he was one of the first preachers of the Holy Gospel, perhaps the very first, in this valley, and his preaching from a cart is one of the local traditions. A little parsonage close at hand is occupied by the principal of the Academy; with its garden, flowers, arbor, and bee-hives, it looks pleasantly from the road-side. Some years since it was a Swedish clergyman who officiated here.

From the summit of a hill on the left, crossed by a country road, there is a fine view over the valley, and the lake in the distance; there are also several little sheets of water, limpid, mountain tarns, among those hills; the stream flowing from one of these forms a modest little cascade. It is rather remarkable that we have so few cascades in this county, abounding as it does with brooks and streams, and lesser lakes lying at different levels; but the waters generally work their way gradually down the hills without taking any bold leaps.

On the opposite side of the valley, a mile or two farther down the stream, there is a singular fissure in the rocks, a sort of ravine, called "The Jambs," where a geologist might perhaps find something to interest him, if one ever found his way here. A low barrow is also observed on that side of the valley, which some persons believe to be artificial; it has very much the character of the Indian mounds in other parts of the country, very regular in its outline, and not larger than many which are known to be the work of the red man; occasionally it is proposed to open it, but no step of the kind has yet been taken. There are, however, very many low knolls about our valley, near the banks of the river, and it is sometimes difficult to decide, from a partial examination, whether they were raised by man, or shaped by floods.

Friday, 3d.—Walked in the woods. Our sweet-fern is a pleasant plant; there is always something very agreeable in a shrub or tree with fragrant foliage; the perfume is rarely sickly, as occasionally happens with flowers; it is almost always grateful and refreshing. These aromatic leaves of the sweet-fern are frequently used in rustic practice to stop bleeding; we have never seen the remedy tried, but have often heard it recommended. Some of our good-wives also make a tea of the leaves, which they say is very strengthening, and good for hemorrhage of the lungs. The plant is also used in home-made beer.

Strictly speaking, the botanists do not call this a fern, but it looks very much as if Adam may have called it so. It is the only plant of the kind, in temperate climates, with a woody stem. The botanical name of Comptonia was given it, after a bishop of London, of the last century, who was a great botanist.

In some of the northern counties of New York, Herkimer and Warren, for instance, acres of wild lands, whole mountain-sides, are covered with this plant, even to the exclusion, in many places, of the whortleberry; in that part of the country it also grows as a weed by the road-side, like the thistles and mulleins. In our own neighborhood it is chiefly confined to the woods.

Saturday, 4th.—Pleasant day. At nine o'clock in the evening set out for a moonlight walk on Mount—. Beautiful night; the rising moon shone through the branches, filling the woods, as it were, with wild fantastic forms never seen by day; one seems at such moments to be moving in a new world, among trees and plants of another creation. The brake had a very peculiar aspect, a faint silvery light lay upon its fronds, even in the shade, giving the idea that in the sunshine they must be much paler in color than their neighbors, which is not the case; the same sort of pale, phosphorescent light gleamed about other plants, and upon the chips and stones in the path.

The views, after leaving the woods, were beautifully clear and distinct. The reflections in the lake below were strangely perfect for a night scene; village, woods, and hills lay softly repeated on the bosom of the flood, as though it were dreaming by night of objects dear and familiar by day. One might have counted the trees and the fields; even the yellow coloring of the grain-fields beside the green meadows was distinctly given.

As the night winds rose and fell with a gentle murmuring sough, the deep bass of the frogs, and the higher notes of the insect throng, continued in one unbroken chaunt. What myriads of those little creatures must be awake and stirring of a fine summer night! But there is a larger portion of the great family on earth in movement at night, than we are apt to remember; because we sleep ourselves, we fancy that other creatures are inactive also. A number of birds fly at night besides the owls, and night-hawks, and whip-poor-wills; very many of those who come and go between our cooler climate and the tropics, make their long journeys lighted by the moon or the stars. The beasts of prey, as is well known, generally move at night. Of the larger quadrupeds belonging to this continent, the bears, and wolves, and foxes, are often in motion by starlight; the moose and the deer frequently feed under a dark sky; the panther is almost wholly nocturnal; the wary and industrious beaver also works at night; that singular creature, the opossum, sleeps in his tree by day and comes down at night. The pretty little flying-squirrel wakes up as twilight draws on; our American rabbit also shuns the day; that pest of the farm-yard, the skunk, with the weasels, rove about on their mischievous errands at night. Some of those animals whose furs are most valued, as the ermine and sable, are nocturnal; so is the black-cat, and the rare wolverine also. Even our domestic cattle, the cows and horses, may frequently be seen grazing in the pleasant summer nights.

Monday, 6th.–Bright, warm day. Thermometer 84.

Heard an oriole among some elms on the skirts of the village this morning; it is rather late for them. We generally see little of them after July; when they have reared their family, and the young have come to days of discretion, these brilliant birds seem to become more shy; they are very apt to leave the villages about that time for the woods. Some few, however, occasionally remain later. But toward the last of this month they already take their flight southward.

A change has come over the bobolinks also–in July they lose those cheerful, pleasant notes with which they enliven the fields earlier in the season; it is true they are still seen fluttering over the meadows from time to time, with a peculiar cry of their own, and the young males acquire a pretty note of their own, which they sing in the morning, but they are already thinking of moving. They are very cheerful birds, and one misses them when they disappear. We seldom see them here in those large flocks common elsewhere; those about us are probably all natives of our own meadows. They travel southward very gradually, visiting first, in large parties, the wild rice-grounds of Pennsylvania and Maryland, where they remain some weeks; in October, they abound in the cultivated rice plantations of Carolina, where they also linger a while, but finally they retreat to the tropical islands. Altogether, few birds are so long on their progress southward.

Tuesday, 7th.—Walked in the Great Meadow. The old trees which bordered this fine field in past years are fast falling before the axe. A few summers back, this was one of the most beautiful meadows in the valley: a broad, grassy lawn of some twenty acres, shut out from the world by a belt of wood sweeping round it in a wide circle; it was favorite ground with some of us, one of those spots where the sweet quiet of the fields, and the deeper calm of the forest, are brought together. On one hand, the trees were of a younger growth, luxuriant and grove-like in aspect, but beyond, the wood rose from the bank of the river in tall, grand columns, of lighter and darker shades of gray. Nothing can be more different than the leafy, bowery border of a common wood, where one scarcely sees the trunks, and the bounds which mark a breach in the ancient forest. The branchless shafts of those aged oaks, pines, chestnuts, hemlocks and ashes, are very impressive objects, forming in such positions a noble forest portal. We have frequently stood upon the highway, perhaps half a mile off, to admire those great trunks lighted up by the sunshine, with which they had so lately made acquaintance; there are few such forest colonnades left in our neighborhood, and this is now falling rapidly before the axeman.

The hoary trunks of the ashes are particularly fine in such situations; they are the lightest in coloring among our larger trees, as the shaft of the hemlocks is the darkest. The ashes of this country very frequently grow in low grounds on the banks of rivers. We have many varieties of this fine tree in the United States: the white, the red, the green or yellow, the blue, and the black, besides the small and very rare flowering ash, only twenty feet high. Of these different kinds, only the white and the black are understood to belong to our highland county; both these are common here, and both are handsome and valuable trees, used for very many mechanical purposes. The white ash, indeed, is said to be as desirable as the hickory—our American tree being considered superior for timber to that of Europe, which it much resembles. When used for fuel, it has the peculiarity of burning nearly as well in a green state as when dry, and the timber also scarcely requires any seasoning. The black ash, more especially a northern tree, is abundant here; it is smaller than the white, and is much used by the Indian basket-makers, being thought rather preferable to the white for their purposes. It is amusing to remember that the small bows and arrows made to-day by the roving Indians as playthings for our boys, are manufactured out of the same wood used for the arms of heroes in the ancient world; many a great warrior besides Achilles has received his death wound from an ashen spear; ashen lances were shivered in the tournaments of chivalrous days, by the stout knights of the middle ages, the Richards and Bertrands, Oliviers and Edwards. At the present day the ash is still used, with the beech, to arm the regiments of modern lancers. Bows, also, were made of the ash, as well as of the yew, in ancient times. For all we know, the bow of William Tell may have been an ashen one. There is one very remarkable association connected with the European ash, which is a hardy tree, clinging to the rocky mountains of Northern Europe. It figures largely in Scandinavian mythology. The ash-tree, Yggdrassil, was their tree of life, or an emblem of the world. It is singular that a sacred tree should be found in the mythology of several different nations of the East; India, Persia, Egypt, and Assyria. We are not told that any particular kind of tree is specified in Eastern mythology; the Scandinavian Sagas, however, are very particular in pointing out the ash as their sacred tree, Yggdrassil. Major Frye, in his translations of Œhlenschlœger, quotes the following passage from the Edda, describing this great ash:

"This ash is the first and greatest of all trees, which spreads its branches over the whole earth. It springs from three roots. Near one of these roots, which pushes the trunk and branches toward Asagard,[14] flows the fountain of Urda, which contains the water of wisdom, and of which Mimer[15] is the guardian. The gods often descend to this spot to sit in judgment on the actions of mankind, and of one another. They interrogate Urda.[16] The second root of Yggdrassil stretches toward the region of the Hrimthusser[17] frost-giants of Utgard.[18] The third root extends below, as far as Niffelheim,[19] and is continually gnawed by the dragon Nidhòg.[20]

"On the branches of this ash dwells an eagle; he knoweth much, and between his eyes sits a Hawk, called Vàderfalner. A squirrel, called Ratatosk, runs up and down the trunk of the ash-tree, and endeavors to excite discord between the eagle and the dragon Nidhòg, who dwells at its root. Four stags spring round the ash-tree and bite its branches: their names are, Dainn, Dvalen, Dunneyr, and Durathzor."

Many versions of this allegory have been given by different Northern writers, and any one who pleases may try his ingenuity on it, as he sits in the shade of the ash-tree. They are all connected with the good and evil in man; with the good and evil above, and about him,—faint gleams of great truths.

Wednesday, 8th.—Very warm; thermometer 86. It is sad to see how many of our springs are wasting away from the drought; in some places where we are accustomed to meet the limpid waters flowing cheerfully through the fields and woods, we now find a parched and thirsty track; at other points, not entirely dry, an ample fountain has dwindled away to a meagre, dropping rill. Rain is much needed.

Thursday, 9th.—Very warm; thermometer 90. Passed the afternoon and evening on the lake. Land and water were both in great beauty; the lake was in that sweet mood when it seems to take pleasure in reflecting every beautiful object; all the different fields, and buildings, and trees, were repeated with fidelity, while the few white clouds floating above were also clearly given below. The waters of our narrow lake are more frequently seen reflecting the village, the hills, and the woods, than the clouds; in still weather they receive much of their coloring from the shores. But this afternoon we noticed several of these visionary islands lying on its bosom, and whenever seen here, they are the more pleasing from our having nothing more substantial in this way; our islands are all of this shadowy character.

On the larger lakes further westward, and in still weather, these cloud islands are often very beautiful; in that more level region the broad expanse of Cayuga and Seneca is very much colored by the skies. Some people find fault with the great size of those islandless lakes; but assuredly, living water is never to be quarrelled with in a landscape; smaller basins with higher banks are no doubt more picturesque, but those ample, limpid lakes are very fine in their way. There is a noble simplicity in their every-day aspect which, on so great a scale, is in itself imposing. The high winds so frequent in that part of the country having full scope over their broad bosoms, often work out fine storm views, while on the other hand the beautiful sunsets of that level region color the waters exquisitely.

Landed at Signal-Oak Point; the noble spring here was quite full, though so many others have failed; while standing near the little fountain, one of our party had the good luck to discover an Indian relic in the gravel, a flint arrow-head. It was very neatly cut, though not of the largest size. One would like to know its little history; it may have been dropped by some hunter who had come to the spring, or been shot from the wood at some wild creature drinking there at the moment. Another of these arrow-heads was found a while since in the gravel of our own walks; they are occasionally turned up in the village, but are already more rare than one would suppose.

Gathered several August flowers on the banks of the brook; the yellow knot-root, or Collinsonia, with its horned blossom; yellow speckled-jewels, more rare with us than the orange kind; purple asters, and a handsome bunch of red berries of the cranberry-tree. We have frequently found the blue gentian growing here, but it is not yet in flower, and the plants have been so much gathered that comparatively few are left.

There is the skeleton of an old oak lying on the gravelly beach of this point, which was well known in the early years of the little colony. Deer were very common here at that time, and of course they were much hunted; these poor creatures, when pursued, always take refuge in the water, if there be a lake or river at hand; and when a party was out hunting in the hills it was a common practice to station some one in the old oak at this spot, which overhung the water, and commanded a view of the lake in its whole length; a set of signals having been agreed on beforehand, the scout in the tree pointed out to the hunters, by this means, the direction taken by the game. Some few years since this signal-oak fell to the ground, and a fragment of it now lies on the shore. This whole grove was formerly very beautiful, composed chiefly of noble oaks of primeval growth, many of them hung with grape-vines, while a pretty clump of wild roses grew at their feet; some of the vines and many of the rose-bushes are still left, but the trees are falling rapidly. They have been recklessly abused by kindling fires against their trunks, using them as chimney shafts, which of course must destroy them. In this way, oaks that might have stood yet for centuries, with increasing beauty, have been wantonly destroyed. Not a season passes that one does not fall, and within the last few years their number has very sensibly diminished. The spot is but a wreck of what it was.

It is a long time since the signal-oak was needed by the hunters, the deer having disappeared from these woods with wonderful rapidity. Within twenty years from the foundation of the village, they had already become rare, and in a brief period later they had fled from the country. One of the last of these beautiful creatures seen in the waters of our lake occasioned a chase of much interest, though under very different circumstances from those of a regular hunt. A pretty little fawn had been brought in very young from the woods, and nursed and petted by a lady in the village until it had become as tame as possible. It was graceful, as those little creatures always are, and so gentle and playful that it became a great favorite, following the different members of the family about, caressed by the neighbors, and welcome everywhere. One morning, after gambolling about as usual until weary, it threw itself down in the sunshine, at the feet of one of its friends, upon the steps of a store. There came along a countryman, who for several years had been a hunter by pursuit, and who still kept several dogs; one of his hounds came to the village with him on this occasion. The dog, as it approached the spot where the fawn lay, suddenly stopped; the little animal saw him, and started to its feet. It had lived more than half its life among the dogs of the village, and had apparently lost all fear of them; but it seemed now to know instinctively that an enemy was at hand. In an instant a change came over it, and the gentleman who related the incident, and who was standing by at the moment, observed that he had never in his life seen a finer sight than the sudden arousing of instinct in that beautiful creature. In a second its whole character and appearance seemed changed, all its past habits were forgotten, every wild impulse was awake; its head erect, its nostrils dilated, its eye flashing. In another instant, before the spectators had thought of the danger, before its friends could secure it, the fawn was leaping wildly through the street, and the hound in full pursuit. The bystanders were eager to save it; several persons instantly followed its track, the friends who had long fed and fondled it, calling the name it had hitherto known, but in vain. The hunter endeavored to whistle back his dog, but with no better success. In half a minute the fawn had turned the first corner, dashed onward toward the lake, and thrown itself into the water. But if for a moment the startled creature believed itself safe in the cool bosom of the lake, it was soon undeceived; the hound followed in hot and eager chase, while a dozen of the village dogs joined blindly in the pursuit. Quite a crowd collected on the bank, men, women, and children, anxious for the fate of the little animal known to them all; some threw themselves into boats, hoping to intercept the hound before he reached his prey; but the plashing of the oars, the eager voices of the men and boys, and the barking of the dogs, must have filled the beating heart of the poor fawn with terror and anguish, as though every creature on the spot where it had once been caressed and fondled had suddenly turned into a deadly foe. It was soon seen that the little animal was directing its course across a bay toward the nearest borders of the forest, and immediately the owner of the hound crossed the bridge, running at full speed in the same direction, hoping to stop his dog as he landed. On the fawn swam, as it never swam before, its delicate head scarcely seen above the water, but leaving a disturbed track, which betrayed its course alike to anxious friends and fierce enemies. As it approached the land, the exciting interest became intense. The hunter was already on the same line of shore, calling loudly and angrily to his dog, but the animal seemed to have quite forgotten his master's voice in the pitiless pursuit. The fawn touched the land—in one leap it had crossed the narrow line of beach, and in another instant it would reach the cover of the woods. The hound followed, true to the scent, aiming at the same spot on the shore; his master, anxious to meet him, had run at full speed, and was now coming up at the most critical moment;

would the dog hearken to his voice, or could the hunter reach him in time to seize and control him? A shout from the village bank proclaimed that the fawn had passed out of sight into the forest; at the same instant, the hound, as he touched the land, felt the hunter's strong arm clutching his neck. The worst was believed to be over; the fawn was leaping up the mountain-side, and its enemy under restraint. The other dogs, seeing their leader cowed, were easily managed. A number of persons, men and boys, dispersed themselves through the woods in search of the little creature, but without success; they all returned to the village, reporting that the animal had not been seen by them. Some persons thought that after its fright had passed over it would return of its own accord. It had worn a pretty collar, with its owner's name engraved upon it, so that it could easily be known from any other fawn that might be straying about the woods. Before many hours had passed a hunter presented himself to the lady whose pet the little creature had been, and showing a collar with her name on it, said that he had been out in the woods, and saw a fawn in the distance; the little animal, instead of bounding away as he had expected, moved toward him; he took aim, fired, and shot it to the heart. When he found the collar about its neck he was very sorry that he had killed it. And so the poor little thing died; one would have thought that terrible chase would have made it afraid of man; but no, it forgot the evil and remembered the kindness only, and came to meet as a friend the hunter who shot it. It was long mourned by its best friend.

This, if not the last chase in our waters, was certainly one of the very latest. The bay crossed by the frightened creature has been called "Fawn Bay," and the fine spring in the field above also bears the name of "Fawn Spring."

Friday, 11th.—Very warm; thermometer 89. The village has not been so dusty for years; of course, walking and driving are less agreeable than usual; and yet the country looks so beautifully that one is unwilling to remain long within doors.

This afternoon, by striking into a narrow cross-road which carried us over the hills, we had a very pleasant drive; the track was quite grassy in places, the shady boughs of an unfenced wood overhung the carriage, and pretty glimpses of the lake and hill-sides opened as we slowly ascended. It may be well at times to come suddenly upon a beautiful view; the excitement of surprise adds in many instances to the enjoyment. Where the country is level and commonplace, the surprise becomes an important element from being less easily attained; after driving through a tame, uninteresting country, if we come suddenly upon a wild nook, with its groves, and brook, and rocks, we no doubt enjoy it the more from the charm of contrast. Where the landscape depends for its merit upon one principal object, as a cascade, a small lake, a ruin, &c., &c., the effect is the same, and it is generally desirable that the best view be seen at once. But as regards hills and mountains, the case is very different, for the gradual ascent is in itself a full source of enjoyment; every turn we reach in the climbing path, every rood we gain in elevation, opens some fresh object of admiration, or throws what we have already seen into a new light; the woods, the farms, the hamlets, ay, whole valleys, great hills, broad rivers, objects with which we are already familiar perhaps, are ceaselessly assuming novel aspects. Even the minute beauties which we note one by one along the ascending pathway, the mountain flower, the solitary bird, the rare plant, all contribute their share of pleasure; the very obstacles in the track, the ravine, the precipice, the torrent, produce their own impression, and add to the exultation with which we reach at length the mountain-top, bringing with us a harvest of glowing sensations gathered by the way, all forming delightful accessories to the greater and more exalted prospect awaiting us at the goal. Between an isolated view, though fine in its way, and the gradual ascent of a commanding height, there lies all the difference we find in the enjoyment of a single ode and that which we derive from a great poem; it is the Lycidas of Milton beside the Othello or Lear of Shakspeare; a sonnet of Petrarch compared with the Jerusalem of Torquato. So at least we thought this afternoon, as we slowly ascended our own modest hills, and remembered the noble mountains of other lands.

The country is looking very rich; the flowery character of summer has not yet faded. Buckwheat crops, in white and fragrant bloom, are lying on half the farms; the long leaves of the maize are still brilliantly green, and its yellow flowers unblighted; late oat-fields here and there show their own pallid green beside recently-cut stubble, which still preserves the golden color of the ripe wheat. In several meadows of the valley mowers were busy, haycocks stood about the fields, and loaded carts were moving about, carrying one back to the labors of midsummer, but these were doubtless crops of seed grass, timothy and clover, and not hay for fodder. The glowing August sunshine was just the light for such a scene, gilding the hanging wood, and filling the valleys with warmth, while a soft haze gave distance and importance to every height.

From the most elevated point crossed by the road we looked over two different valleys, with their several groups of broad hills, and many a swelling knoll. Looking down from a commanding position upon a mountainous country, or looking upward at the same objects, leave very different impressions on the mind. From below we see a group of mountains as pictures in one aspect only, but looking abroad over their massive forms from an adjoining height, we comprehend them much more justly; we feel more readily how much they add to the grandeur of the earth we live on, how much they increase her extent, how greatly they vary her character, climates, and productions. Perhaps the noble calm of these mountain piles will be more impressive from below; but when we behold them from a higher point, blended with this majestic quiet, traces of past action and movement are observed, and what we now behold seems the repose of power and strength after a great conflict. The most lifeless and sterile mountain on earth, with the unbroken sleep of ages brooding over its solitudes, still bears on its silent head the emotion of a mighty passion. It is upon the brow of man that are stamped the lines worn by the care and sorrow of a lifetime; and we behold upon the ancient mountains, with a feeling of awe, the record of earth's stormy history. There are scars and furrows upon the giant Alps unsoftened by the beaming sunlight of five thousand summers, over which the heavens have wept in vain for ages, which are uneffaced by all the influences at the command of Time. This character of former action adds inconceivably to the grandeur of the mountains, connecting them as it does with the mystery of the past; upon a plain we are more apt to see the present only, the mental vision seems confined to the level uniformity about it, we need some ancient work of man, some dim old history, to lead the mind backward; and this is one reason why a monument always strikes us more forcibly upon a plain, or on level ground; in such a position it fills the mind more with itself and its own associations. But without a history, without a monument, there is that upon the face of the mountains which, from the earliest ages, has led man to hail them as the "everlasting hills."

In ancient times, this expression of individual action in the mountains was acknowledged by seer and poet. The fabled wars of the Titans, with the uptorn hills they hurled in their strife with the gods, may probably be traced back to this source, and similar fables in the form given them, by Scandinavian Sagas, are but a repetition of the same idea. We who have the most Holy Bible in our hands, may reverently read there also imagery of the like character. We are told by those familiar with the ancient tongues of the East, that in the early ages of the world the great mountains were all called the "mountains of the Lord." The expression occurs repeatedly in the Pentateuch. But after the supernatural terrors which accompanied the proclamation of the Law in the wilderness, the same idea of mountains paying especial homage to the power of the Creator, seems to have become blended among the Hebrews with recollections of the quaking of Sinai. In the 68th

Psalm, written by King David, when the ark was transported to Mount Zion, there are two different passages in which this grand image occurs:

"The earth shook, the heavens also dropped, at the presence of God; even Sinai itself was moved at the presence of God, at the presence of the God of Israel."

"Why leap ye, ye high hills? This is the hill which God desireth to dwell in; yea, the Lord will dwell in it forever."

The 114th Psalm, supposed to have been composed by a different prophetic writer, is a sublime ode, expressive throughout, in brief and noble language, of the power of God, as shown in the deliverance of the Israelites, and in the miraculous ministry of the earth herself, her floods and her hills, in their behalf:

"The sea saw it, and fled; Jordan was driven back.

"The mountains skipped like rams, and the little hills like lambs.

"What ailed thee, O thou sea, that thou fleddest? Thou Jordan, that thou wast driven back?

"Ye mountains, that ye skipped like rams, and ye little hills like lambs?

"Tremble, thou earth, at the presence of God; at the presence of the God of Sinai!"

The lowly hills about us are but the last surges of a billowy sea of ridges stretching hundreds of miles to the southward, where they rise to a much more commanding elevation, and attain to the dignity of mountains. But even standing upon the humble hills of our own county—all less than a thousand feet in height—we see some of the sights, we hear some of the sounds, we breathe the air, we feel the spirit of a mountain land; we have left the low country; the plains lie beneath us; we touch at least upon the borders of the "everlasting hills."

Saturday, 12th.—Thermometer 87. The birds seem to mind the heat but little. True, the full gush of summer song is over, and the change is decided from May and June; but many of the little creatures sing very sweetly yet. A wren gave us this morning as fine a song as one could wish for, and all his family sing yet. The song-sparrows also are in voice, and so are the greenlets. The goldfinches also sing; we heard one this afternoon as musical as in May; generally, however, their note differs at present from what it was earlier in the season. Their families are now mostly at large, and one sees the birds moving idly about, as if no longer thinking of the nest. At this moment their flight is more irregular than at first; they rise and they drop carelessly with closed wings, moving hither and thither, often changing their course capriciously, and while in motion, they repeat over and over again a series of four notes, with the emphasis on the first. In short, many of our little friends are seen about the fields and gardens yet, and the country is by no means silent, though the most musical season is over. Perhaps one enjoys these occasional songs all the more from their being heard singly, having become more of a favor than in June. But certainly August is not the voiceless month some people seem to fancy it.

Monday, 14th.—Very warm. Thermometer 83 in the shade. It is not often that this valley suffers so much from drought; the last month has been unusually dry. This morning a few light clouds were seen about sunrise, and they were anxiously watched, with the hope of a shower; but as the sun rose, they melted away.

There is no walking out of the woods, and even in the shade of the trees it is close and sultry. Many of the forest trees are getting a parched look, and even the little wood-plants, screened from the direct influence of the sun, looked thirsty and feeble this afternoon.

But if vegetation suffer, the insect world rejoices in this dry, warm weather. Day and night, in the hot noontide sun, and in the brilliant moonlight, there is an unceasing hum about the fields and woods, much fuller in tone than usual. This is very pleasant in its way;—all the more so from being, like the songs of birds, a proof that the little creatures are happy in the passing hours. We are told that insects have, in truth, no voices, and that the sounds we hear from them are produced generally by friction, or by striking together hard substances of different parts of their bodies. But the character of the sound remains the same, however it be produced. No doubt the fly enjoys the idle buzzing of its own wings, the bee the hum which accompanies its thrifty flight, and the loud chirrup of the locust is probably as much an expression of ease and pleasure, as the full gush of song from the breast of his neighbor, the merry wren.

There are said to be very many varieties of locusts in this country. We have but few in our own neighborhood compared with the great numbers found in other counties of this State. The large tree-locusts are only heard with us in the warmest weather.

The Katy-did also, a very common insect elsewhere, is rare here. We have only a few, and their pleasant cry is seldom heard excepting in very warm evenings. During this last week, however, we have been greeted by the locust[21] and the Katy-did also.

Tuesday, 15th.—Very sultry; thermometer 95 in the shade.[22] The sun rose clear and bright; but soon after a few clouds gathered on the hills, and hopes of rain were again awakened. Many anxious eyes were cast upward, but the clouds dispersed, and the heat continued unrelenting.

The geometric spiders are weaving their neat and regular webs about the gardens and out-buildings. The pea-brush and bean-poles are well garnished with them. The earth also is covered with webs, as usual at this season. In France the peasants call these, as they lie spread on the grass, *fils de Marie*—Mary's threads—from some half-religious fancy of olden times.

Sitting in the shade this afternoon, we watched a fierce skirmish between a black wasp and a large spider, who had spun its web among the tendrils of a Virginia creeper. The wasp chanced to alight on the outskirts of the spider's domain, where his legs became partially entangled; he had scarcely touched the leaf when the watchful creature made a rapid dash at him. The antagonists were placed face to face; whether the wasp wounded his enemy one could not say, but after the first touch, the spider instantly retreated several inches, still keeping, however, a bold, undisguised position, her great fixed eyes staring fiercely at the intruder. The wasp was getting more and more entangled in the web; he grew angry, moved his wings and legs rapidly, but to no purpose. Seeing his situation as clearly as the spectator, or probably more so, the spider made another attack, and the adversaries closed in a fierce struggle. The wasp seemed anxious to bring his sting to bear upon the enemy; the spider equally determined to wound her long-legged foe on the head, probably by a bite with her poisonous fangs; now the wasp seemed the sufferer; now again the spider relaxed her hold a little. A fresh assault of the spider was followed by a violent struggle of the wasp, when, suddenly, whether by good luck or good management one could not see, the web broke, the wasp's wings were free; he rose from the leaf, and he carried the spider with him, whether as a captive or a pertinacious enemy, one could not determine; they were soon out of sight. Perhaps the wasp found, before he alighted, that he had "caught a Tartar." About five minutes after the disappearance of the combatants, a wasp alighted on the very same spot where the joust had taken place, and he had a sort of agitated, eager flutter about him. It was either the same individual who had been engaged in the fray, or else a stranger, who, by scent or otherwise, discovered traces of the contest. If it was the hero of the fight, possession of the field of battle and the enemy's country, established his claim as victor; but if only an ally, the fortune of the day still remains in the dark, and, like many other great battles, may be claimed by both parties.

Some of our American wasps are said to hunt spiders, and then enclose them in the cell with their young, who feed upon them. But in the battle this afternoon the spider was clearly the aggressor. These battles between the two races are frequent; but the bees and spiders seem to keep the peace.

We have but few wasps here; our most common kind is this black variety; the large, brown wasps, so abundant elsewhere, are unknown about the village. A smaller variety, called hornets here, are not uncommon. But fortunately for us, the pleasant, thrifty bees far outnumber the other members of their family about our lake.

Wednesday, 16th.–Thermometer 92. The whole country pining for rain; not a drop has fallen here since the last of July.

During these prolonged heats the cattle suffer more, probably, than man. In summer they love the cool shade and refreshing waters, but now the sweet pastures, to which they are accustomed, are blighted and parched, while many a little pool and spring about the fields, well known to them, and where they go of their own accord to drink, they now find entirely wasted away. It is touching to see their patience; and yet, poor creatures, unlike man, they know nothing of hope and their Maker's mercy.

Thursday, 17th.–Rain at last, to our great joy. This morning the sun rose clear; but light clouds were soon seen gathering slowly about the hills, then spreading gradually over the whole sky, and veiling the valley in grateful shade. About noon the first drops fell; the hum of insects, so loud during the last fortnight, suddenly ceased, and was succeeded by the refreshing sound of the rain-drops pattering among the leaves. Most persons thought the long drought and great heat would have been followed by a severe gust and thunder-shower, which is usually the case, but the blessing fell gently and mildly upon us this morning. About a quarter of an hour after it had commenced raining, the sunshine broke through the clouds, and it was feared the sky would clear; happily, another and a fuller cloud came slowly down the lake, pouring a plentiful supply upon us, and it has continued raining all day.

Friday, 18th.–Decidedly cooler. Everything much refreshed by the shower. Still raining this morning.

Saturday, 19th.–Decided change in the weather; thermometer 62, with cool, north wind. This sort of atmosphere is very unfavorable to the scenery; it lowers the hills, narrows the lake, and altogether, the familiar objects of the landscape do not look half so well as when a soft haze hangs upon the hills. The natural features of the country are not on a scale sufficiently grand to rise superior above such accidents of light and shade. Most summers, we have a touch of this sort of weather–sometimes in July, sometimes in August—this sort of cool, matter-of-fact atmosphere, when things look unenjoyable without, and people feel cross at having to close their doors and windows, and sometimes light a fire.

Saw a large flock of barn-swallows hanging in clusters upon the mulleinstalks in a waste field. They are thinking of moving.

Monday, 21st.—Very pleasant again. Walked some distance. The grain harvest is now over, very generally, and cattle are seen feeding among the stubble on many farms.

In this part of the world, although we have once seen a woman ploughing, once found a party of girls making hay with the men of the family, and occasionally observed women hoeing potatoes or corn, we have never yet seen a sight very common in the fields of the Old World: we have never yet met a single gleaner. Probably this is not entirely owing to the prosperous state of the country, for there are many poor among us. "The poor ye have with you always, and whensoever ye will, ye may do them good." In the large towns, who has not seen the wretched creatures who pick up the filthy rags from the rubbish and mud of the streets? Where human beings can earn a livelihood in this way in the cities, gleaning in the fields of the country ought not to surprise one. Even about our villages there are not only many persons in want, a number supported by the public, but there are usually others, also, who may be called regular beggars; men, and women, and children, who had rather beg than work. Let not the accusation be thought a harsh one. There are, even in our small rural communities, fathers and mothers who teach their children to beg, alas! who deliberately encourage their children in thieving and lying, and vice of the foulest kinds. Where such things exist, it cannot be the great prosperity of the country which keeps the gleaner from following in the reaper's steps. Probably there are several reasons why gleaning is not practiced here. Food is comparatively cheap; our paupers are well fed, and those who ask for food, are freely supplied by private charity. Wheat bread, and meat, and butter, and sugar, and tea, and coffee, are looked upon as necessaries, openly asked for by the applicant, and freely bestowed by the giver. This comparative abundance of food in the early days of the different colonies, and the full demand for labor, were probably the reasons why the custom of gleaning was broken up on this side the Atlantic; and the fact that it is not customary, is one reason why it is never thought of to-day. Then, again, our people, generally, are not patient and contented with a little; gleaning would not suit their habit. Many of them, probably, had rather beg than glean.

But although the practice is entirely abandoned on this side the ocean—

in our part of the continent, at least–it prevails very generally in the Old World. In some countries it has been regulated by law; in others it is governed by long-established usage. In some villages of France and Germany, a certain day is fixed in the *commune,* when the gleaning is to begin; sometimes the church-bell rings, in other villages the beat of the drum calls the gleaners to the fields; peasant mothers, with their little children, boys and girls, old and infirm men and women, are seen in little parties moving toward the unfenced fields, and spreading themselves through the yellow stubble. In Switzerland, parties of the very poor, the old and the little ones who cannot earn much, come down from the mountain villages, where grain is not raised, into the more level farms of the lower country, expressly to glean. One never sees these poor creatures without much interest; mothers, children, and the aged make up the greater number of their bands, and humble as the occupation may be, it is yet thoroughly honest, and, indeed, creditable, so far as it shows a willingness to undertake the lowliest task for a livelihood, rather than stand by wholly idle.

There is no country in Europe, I believe, where gleaning is not a general custom, from the most northern grain-growing valleys, to the luxuriant plains of Sicily. Even in fertile Asia, and in the most ancient times, gleaning was a common practice. The sign of the Zodiac, called the Virgin, is said to represent a gleaner, and that carries one back very far. The Mosaic laws contain minute directions for gleaning. While the children of Israel were yet in the wilderness, before they had conquered one field of the Promised Land, they received the following injunctions:

"And when ye reap the harvest of your land, thou shalt not wholly reap the corners of thy field; neither shalt thou gather the gleanings of thy harvest. And thou shalt not glean thy vineyard, neither shalt thou gather every grape of thy vineyard; thou shalt leave them for the poor and the stranger: I am the Lord your God."–Lev. xix.

"When thou cuttest down thine harvest in thy field, and thou hast forgot a sheaf in the field, thou shalt not turn again to fetch it: it shall be for the stranger, for the fatherless, and for the widow: that the Lord thy God may bless thee in all the work of thine hands."–Deut. xxiv.

Whether a custom of this kind already prevailed in the ancient world before the days of Moses, we cannot determine, since the Pentateuch is the oldest authority extant. The earlier books of the sacred writings, Genesis and Exodus, contain nothing on the subject. Some of the precepts of the Mosaic code, however, are known to be merely a confirmation and repetition of those given still earlier, such as those which enjoin sacrifice and circumcision, &c., &c. Many others doubtless flowed first, at the period of the Exodus, from Almighty wisdom and mercy, like the raising of the tabernacle, the establishment of the Levitical Priesthood, &c., &c. The protection of the gleaner may have belonged to either class of precepts; but its minuteness partakes very much of the character of the Hebrew law, and it is quite possible that it may have been first inculcated from the lips of Moses in the wilderness. Whatever be the origin of the custom, it has since spread far and wide; it was a simple form of charity, natural to a primitive age, and during thirty-three hundred years at least, it has prevailed in the world. There is, I believe, no part of the Old World where it has not been more or less practiced, whether in Asia, Africa, or Europe; and it is possible there may be some portions of this continent also where it is customary, though we have never seen any allusion to it by travellers, either in North or South America. Within the limits of our own country, it is believed to be entirely unknown.

One never thinks of gleaning without remembering Ruth. How wholly beautiful is the narrative of sacred history in which we meet her! One of the most pleasing pictures of the ancient world preserved to our day, it is at the same time delightful as a composition. Compare it for a moment with the celebrated episode in the "Seasons," and mark how far above the modern poet stands the ancient Hebrew writer. Undoubtedly, Thomson's imitation is an elegant, graceful, polished pastoral, in charmingly flowing verse, but, as Palemon himself expresses it, the tale is rather "romantic." Lavinia, though "beauty's self," and charmingly modest, is yet, alas! rather doll-like; one doubts if she really suffered very much, with that "smiling patience" in her look, and those "polished limbs," "veiled in a simple robe." And Palemon, "pride of swains," "who led the rural life in all its joy and elegance," "amusing his fancy with autumnal scenes"—we have always had certain misgivings that he was quite a commonplace young squire. It is unwise to be very critical in reading, for one loses much pleasure and instruction by being over-nice and fault-finding in these as in other matters; but really, it was such a bold step in Thomson to remind one of Ruth, that he himself is to blame if the comparison inevitably suggests itself, and as inevitably injures his pretty little English lass. We never look into the Seasons, without wishing that Crabbe had written the gleaning passages.

As for Ruth, the real Ruth, her history is all pure simplicity, nature and truth, in every line. Let us please ourselves by dwelling on it a moment. Let us see Naomi, with her husband and sons, driven by famine into the country of the Moabites; let us hear that the two young men married there, and that, at the end of ten years, the mother and her daughters-in-law were alike widowed. Naomi then determines to return to her own country; both her daughters-in-law set out with her. Orpah and Ruth had alike been faithful to the Jewish family: "The Lord deal kindly with you as ye have dealt with the dead, and with me," says Naomi, as she urges them to leave her and go back to their own friends. Both the young women wept, and both answered, "Surely we will return with thee unto thy people." Naomi again urges their leaving her: "Turn again, my daughters, why will ye go with me?" "And Orpah kissed her mother-in-law, but Ruth clave unto her." This is the first sentence that betrays the difference between the young women; both had been kind and dutiful to their husbands and mother-in-law, but now we see one turning back, and the other *cleaving* to the poor, and aged, and solitary widow. No positive blame is attached to Orpah, but from that instant we love Ruth. Read over her passionate remonstrance with her mother-in-law: "Thy people shall be my people; thy God my God. Where thou diest will I die, and there will I be buried." We follow the two women to Bethlehem, the native town of the family: "And all the city was moved about them, and they said, Is this Naomi?" "And she said, Call me not Naomi, call me Mara, for the Almighty hath dealt very bitterly with me: I went out full, and the Lord hath brought me home again empty." It was at the beginning of the barley harvest when they came to Bethlehem, and now we find Ruth preparing to glean. Probably gleaning was at this time a custom among the neighboring nations also, for the proposal comes from Ruth herself, and not from her Jewish mother-in-law, who merely signifies her assent: "Go, my daughter." The young widow went, and "her hap was, to light upon a part of the field belonging to Boaz." An obsolete word that, "her hap," for she happened. Presently we see the owner of the field coming from Bethlehem, and we hear his salutation to the reapers: "The Lord be with you; and they answered him, The Lord bless thee."

Doubtless, in those ancient times, the people all lived together in towns and villages for mutual protection, as they did in Europe during the middle ages—as they still do, indeed, to the present hour, in many countries where isolated cottages and farm-houses are rarely seen, the people going out every morning to the fields to work, and returning to the villages at night. While looking over his reapers, Boaz remarks a gleaner, a young woman whom he had not yet seen; the other faces were probably familiar to the benevolent man, the poor of his native town, but this was a stranger. Now, it is nowhere said that Ruth was beautiful; very possibly she was not so; we have always been rather disposed to believe that of the two Orpah may have been the

handsome one. The beauty of many women of the Old Testament is mentioned with commendation by the different writers of the sacred books, as
that of Sarah, Rebecca, Rachel, and a number more; but we are nowhere
told that Ruth was "well favored." We read of her devotion to Naomi; of her
gentleness, her humility; of her modesty, for she did not "follow young
men," and all the people knew she was "a virtuous woman;" but not a word
is uttered as to her being fair to look at. The omission is the more marked,
for she is the principal character in a narrative of four chapters. With the exception of Sarah and Esther, no other woman of the Old Testament fills so
large a space; and it will be remembered that the beauty of both Sarah and
Esther is distinctly mentioned. No; with Ruth the attention is wholly fixed
on the moral qualities, and the sacred historian has thus assigned her a place
beside the Christian women of the New Testament, where personal appearance is in no instance even alluded to. May we not, then, please ourselves
with believing that Ruth was not beautiful; that she had merely one of those
faces which come and go without being followed, except by the eyes that
know and love them? Boaz no sooner learns who she is than he gives her a
most kindly welcome: "Hearest thou not, my daughter? Go not to glean in
another field; neither go from hence, but abide here fast by my maidens.
Have I not charged the young men that they shall not touch thee? And
when thou art athirst, go unto the vessels and drink of that which the young
men have drawn." We are not told that Boaz was an old man, but it is implied in several places. He calls Ruth "My daughter," and he is mentioned
as a kinsman of Naomi's husband; he commends her for not following "young
men, whether rich or poor," and there is a certain calmness and dignity in
his manner and conduct throughout the narrative, such as one would naturally connect with the idea of an elderly man. The generous kindness and
the upright simplicity of his conduct toward Ruth are very beautiful. When
the young widow, "falling on her face," asks humbly, "Why have I found
grace in thine eyes, that thou shouldst take knowledge of me, seeing I am a
stranger?" He answers, "It hath fully been showed me all that thou hast
done unto thy mother-in-law, since the death of thy husband;"—"a full reward be given thee of the Lord God of Israel, under whose wings thou art
come to trust." Ruth was poor, and had doubtless met with neglect and
harshness. She was generous and warm-hearted herself, and could justly
value the kindness of others; she thanks the owner of the field, "for that thou
hast comforted me, and for that thou hast spoken friendly unto thine handmaid." The word given here as friendly, is rendered in the margin "to the
heart." The phrase may be a common Hebrew expression, but it has a

strength of feeling characteristic of the speaker. Blessed, indeed, are the lips that "speak to the heart" of the afflicted; and blessed is the sorrowing soul who hears them! Boaz asks the young widow to eat with his people at mealtime: "Eat of the bread, and dip thy morsel in the vinegar." "And she sat beside the reapers, and he reached her parched corn." The vinegar mentioned here is supposed to mean a kind of acid wine frequently named by ancient writers; and the parched corn was probably half-ripe ears of wheat or barley roasted in this way; a common article of food in the East during all ages. "And when she was risen up to glean, Boaz commanded his young men, saying, Let her glean even among the sheaves, and reproach her not. And let fall some of the handfuls of purpose for her, and leave them that she may glean them, and rebuke her not. So she gleaned in the field until even, and beat out that she had gleaned; and it was about an ephah of barley." An ephah was about a bushel of our measure; and barley was a grain highly valued in Judea, where it was much used for food. A bushel seems a large quantity; but it is surprising what full sheaves some of the gleaners will carry home with them, now-a-days, and in fields where no handfuls are dropped on purpose. It was only when Ruth told her mother of her good success that she learned that Boaz was a near kinsman of her former husband, and, consequently, according to the Jewish law, one upon whom she might have claims. Naomi bids her follow the reapers of Boaz according to his wish; and she did so "through the barley-harvest, and through the wheat-harvest, and she dwelt with her mother-in-law." It was at the close of the harvest that Ruth, following Naomi's directions, laid herself down at night, at the feet of Boaz, as he slept on the threshing-floor; an act by which she reminded him of the law that the nearest of kin should marry the childless widow. This act has been very severely commented on. Upon this ground only, M. de Voltaire has not scrupled to apply to Ruth one of the most justly opprobrious words in human language; and several noted skeptics of the English school have given this as one among their objections against the Holy Scriptures.[23] As though in a state of society wholly simple and primitive, we were to judge of Ruth by the rules of propriety prevailing in the courts of Charles II. and Louis XV. Ruth and Boaz lived, indeed, among a race, and in an age, when not only the daily speech, but the daily life also, was highly figurative; when it was the great object of language and of action to give force and expression to the intention of the mind, instead of applying, as in a later, and a degenerate society, all the powers of speech and action to concealing the real object in view. The simplicity with which this peculiarly Jewish part of the narrative is given, will rather appear to the impartial judge a merit. But the

Christian has double grounds for receiving this fact in the same spirit as it is recorded, and upon those grounds we may feel confident that, had Ruth been a guilty woman, or had Boaz acted otherwise than uprightly toward the young widow, neither would have been spared the open shame of such misconduct. The Book of Ruth has always been received by the Church, both Jewish and Christian, as a part of the inspired Scriptures; it must, therefore, be essentially true, and no evil word or deed finds a place in the narrative. Then, again, the impartiality of the sacred biographers, from the first to the last books of the Holy Scriptures, is so very striking, so very peculiar to themselves, so widely different from the eulogies or apologies of uninspired men under similar circumstances, that reason alone requires us to receive each narrative simply as it is given. We read with a feeling of awe of the occasional failings and sins of such men as Noah, Abraham, Aaron, and David; the whole nature of man stands humbled before us, while the mercy of our God rises, indeed, exalted above the heavens! We feel that these passages are laid open to us by the same Omniscient Spirit which searches our own hearts by the same just hand which weighs our own words, and thoughts, and deeds in the balance. And if such men as Abraham, and Aaron, and David were not spared by the inspired pen, why should it screen the Moabitish widow, and the comparatively unimportant Boaz? The writer of the narrative has not, by one word, imputed sin to either. How dare the mind of the reader do so? One may add a word for the skeptic, since this passage has been made a pointed subject of objection by men of that school. There are but three positions which the infidel can take upon the subject: he may, with the Christian, believe the Book of Ruth to be true, in which case he is bound to receive the facts as they are given; he may hold the narrative to be a compound of fiction and truth, and then plain justice requires that those points upon which the Scriptural writers have always shown such marked impartiality be charged to the side of truth, and he is at liberty to doubt any other passage of the book rather than this particular one; he may, lastly, declare the book to be, in his opinion, wholly fictitious; in this case he is bound, by common sense, to receive the narrative precisely as it is written, since it is a broad absurdity to judge fictitious characters otherwise than as they are represented. If he suppose one act or one view beyond what the writer presents or implies, he may as well sit down and compose an entire fabric of his own, and then the world will have one Book of Ruth in the Holy Bible, and another among the works of Mr. A., B., or C.

When Boaz found Ruth lying at his feet, he immediately understood the action as figurative. "And it came to pass at midnight that the man was afraid, and turned himself, and behold a woman lay at his feet."–"And he said, Who art thou? And she answered, I am Ruth, thine handmaid; spread therefore thy skirt," or wing, "over thy handmaid, for thou art a near kinsman." Her whole answer is figurative, like the act. Spreading the skirt, or wing, was a common Hebrew phrase, implying protection, and it is said to be, to this day, a part of the Jewish marriage ceremony. Boaz well knew that the action and the words were intended to remind him of the law, that the "near kinsman" should marry the widow. "And now, my daughter, fear not; I will do thee all that thou requirest: for all the city of my people doth know that thou art a virtuous woman. And now it is true that I am thy near kinsman, howbeit there is a kinsman nearer than I. Tarry this night, and it shall be in the morning, that if he will perform unto thee the part of a kinsman, well; let him do the kinsman's part: but if he will not do the part of a kinsman to thee, then will I do the part of a kinsman unto thee, as the Lord liveth: lie down until the morning." "And she lay at his feet until the morning." When, at dawn, she is going, he bids her bring her veil, and measures six measures of barley in it, saying, "Go not empty unto thy mother-in-law." The occurrences in the concluding chapter, at the gate of the town, are strikingly ancient, oriental, and Jewish. The nearer kinsman declines to fulfill the duties enjoined by the law, he does not wish to buy the "parcel of land," or to marry Ruth, "lest he mar his own inheritance;" he makes over the duty to Boaz, giving him his shoe as a token, a singular and very primitive custom; but we are reading now of times before the date of the Trojan war, chronology having placed these incidents in the fourteenth century before Christ. Boaz then calls upon all present to be witnesses to the contract by which he engaged to buy the land, and to marry the widow. "And all the people that were in the gate, and the elders, said, We are witnesses. The Lord make the woman that is come into thine house like Rachel, and like Leah, which two did build the house of Israel: and do thou worthily in Ephratah, and be famous in Bethlehem." Probably before the six measures of barley were eaten, Ruth entered the house of Boaz as his wife. Naomi went with her; and in time Ruth gave a grandson to the aged widow: "And Naomi took the child, and laid it in her bosom, and became nurse unto it." "And the women said unto her, He shall be unto thee the restorer of thy life, and a nourisher of thine old age, for thy daughter-in-law *which loveth thee, which is better to thee than seven sons*, hath borne him." This child became in the course of years the grandfather of David; Ruth received the honor coveted by every Jewish woman – she was one in the line between Sarah and the Blessed Virgin, the mother of our Lord. It was undoubtedly to record her place in the sacred genealogy, or rather for the sake of that genealogy, that the book was written, and has received a place in the Holy Scriptures.

We have meanwhile strayed a wide way from our own ungleaned fields; but the history of Ruth is in itself so very beautiful, and it is so full of interest, as connected with a very remote antiquity, beyond the reach of the oldest Greek literature, that one never turns to it without pleasure. While plodding on our daily round of duties, if the eye fall by chance upon a picture of some great old master, we gladly linger a moment to enjoy its beauty and excellence; and thus the noble devotion of Ruth, seen amid the ancient frame-work of the sacred historian, never fails to delight the imagination, to refresh the mind, to strengthen the heart, whenever we turn to it from the cares of our own path through life.

Tuesday, 22d.—Pleasant; walked in the woods. Gathered a fine bunch of ferns. All the plants of this kind growing in our neighborhood belong, I believe, to the common sorts. We have none of the handsome climbing-fern here, with its palmate leaves; it is found nearly as far north as this, but nearer the coast, and on lower ground. The walking-fern, also, another singular variety, rooting itself like the banyan, from the ends of its long entire leaves, is a stranger here, though found within the State. The maiden-hair, with its very delicate foliage, and polished brown stem, is the prettiest variety we have near us.

Wednesday, 23d.—The swallows have left the chimneys. This evening they were flying over the grounds in parties, as though preparing to take leave. There was something peculiar in their movement; they were flying quite low, through the foliage of the trees, and over the roof of the house, returning again and again, upon their former track. We watched them for more than an hour, while they kept up the same evolutions with much more regularity than usual; perhaps they were trying their wings for the journey southward.

It is amusing to look back to the discussions of naturalists during the last century, upon the subject of the migration of swallows: a number of them maintained that these active birds lay torpid during the cold weather in caves and hollow trees; while others, still more wild in their theories, supposed that swallows went under water and passed the winter in the mud, at the bottom of rivers and pools! Grave and learned were the men who took sides in this question, for and against the torpid theory. One might suppose that it would have required a great amount of the clearest evidence to support a notion so opposed to the general habits of those active birds; but the facts that among the myriads of swallows flitting about Europe, one was occasionally found chilled and torpid, that swallows were frequently seen near the water, and that during the mild days of autumn a few stragglers appeared again, when they were supposed to revive, made up the chief part of what was urged in favor of these notions. It would be difficult to understand how sensible people could be led to maintain such opinions, were it not that men, both learned and unlearned, often show a sort of antipathy to simple truths. Thomson, in the Seasons, alludes to this strange notion; speaking of the swallows, he says:

> "Warn'd of approaching winter, gathered, play
> The swallow people; and toss'd wide around
> O'er the calm sky, in convolution swift,
> The feather'd eddy floats; rejoicing once
> *Ere to their wintry slumbers they retire;*
> *In clusters clung, beneath the mould'ring bank,*
> *And where, unpierc'd by frost, the cavern sweats.*
> Or rather into warmer climes convey'd
> With other kindred birds of season,
> There they twitter cheerful."

He seems rather to have inclined himself to the better opinion.[24]

In ancient times the swallows were very naturally included among other migratory birds; there is said to be an old Greek ode in which the return of the swallow is mentioned. The Prophet Jeremiah has an allusion to the wandering of the swallow, which he includes among other migratory birds: "Yea, the stork in the heavens knoweth her appointed times, and the turtle, and the crane, and the *swallow,* observe the time of their coming; but my people know not the judgment of the Lord."–Jer., viii. 7. Indeed, it is but just to the common sense of man to say that the obvious fact of the migration of those swift-winged birds seems only to have been doubted during a century or so; and among the achievements of our own age may be numbered that of a return to the simple truth on this point of ornithology. We hear nothing now-a-days of the mud or cave theories.

Thursday, 24th.–Brilliant day. Passed the afternoon on the lake. The views were very beautiful. Downy seeds of various kinds, thistle, dandelion, &c., &c., were thickly strewed over the bosom of the lake; we had never before observed such numbers of them lying on the water.

Saw a crane of the largest size flying over the lake, a mile or two to the northward of our boat. A pair of them have been about the lake all summer; they are said to be the large brown crane. We found one of their young this afternoon lying dead upon the bank of a brook, to which we gave the name of Crane Brook on this occasion. It was a good-sized bird, and seemed to have been killed in a fight with some winged enemy, for it had not been shot. As for the boldness of calling the brook after it, the pretty little stream had no name before; why not give it one?

Last summer a pair of eagles built their nest on one of the western hills, which we ventured to call Eagle Hill, on the same principle. These noble birds are occasionally seen hovering over the valley, though not often.

Measured an old grape-vine in the glen, near Crane Brook; it proved to be seven inches in circumference.

Friday, 25th.—Observed the chimney-swallows again this evening wheeling in a low flight over the roof, and through the foliage of the trees. It looked as though they were taking leave of us. They have deserted the chimneys, but we have not discovered where they pass the night. Perhaps in the hollow trees in the woods, for there are many such at hand. Mr. Wilson says, it frequently happens that these birds make their general rendezvous when they first come, and just before they leave, in the chimneys of the Court-House, if there be one in the place; they seem to find out that such chimneys are little used. But we have never heard of the swallows honoring our own Court-House in this way.

Saturday, 26th.—Again we observed the chimney-swallows, flying over the house and through the trees, just as they have done these four or five evenings. Perhaps there is some particular insect among the leaves which attracts them just now.

Saw a few barn-swallows also, this afternoon; but most of these seem to have left us already.

Monday, 28th.—About sunset this evening observed many night-hawks flying over the village.

We happened once to see a large flight of these birds. We were travelling a short distance north of the Mohawk, at this very date, the 28th of August, when, about an hour before sunset, a number of large birds were seen rising from a wood to the eastward, all moving slowly in a loose, straggling flock, toward the south-west. They proved to be night-hawks; and they continued passing at intervals until an hour after sunset. They seemed to heed each other very little, being seldom near together, but all were aiming in the same direction. We must have seen several hundreds of them, in the course of the two hours they were in sight.

Tuesday, 29th.—The swallows have moved their parade-ground this evening. We missed them about the house, but found them wheeling over the highway, near the bridge, the very spot where we first saw them in the spring.

Wednesday, 30th.—Walked in the woods. Observing an old branchless trunk of the largest size, in a striking position, where it looked like a broken column, we walked up to examine it. The shaft rose, without a curve or a branch, to the height of perhaps forty feet, where it had been abruptly shivered, probably in some storm. The tree was a chestnut, and the bark of a clear, unsullied gray; walking round it, we saw an opening near the ground, and to our surprise found the trunk hollow, and entirely charred within, black as a chimney, from the root to the point where it was broken off. It frequently happens that fire steals into the heart of an old tree, in this way, by some opening near the roots, and burns away the inside, leaving merely a gray outer shell. One would not expect the bark to be left in such cases, but the wood at the heart seems more inflammable than the outer growth. Whatever be the cause, such shafts are not uncommon about our hills, gray without, charred within.

There is, indeed, much charred wood in our forests; fires which sweep over the hills are of frequent occurrence here, and at times they do much mischief. If the flames are once fairly kindled in dry weather, they will spread in all directions as the wind varies, burning sometimes for weeks together, until they have swept over miles of woodland, withering the verdure, destroying the wood already cut, and greatly injuring many trees which they do not consume. Several years since, in the month of June, there was quite an extensive fire on the eastern range of hills; it lasted for ten days or a fortnight, spreading several miles in different directions. It was the first important fire of the kind we had ever seen, and of course we watched its progress with much interest; but the spectacle was a very different one from what we had supposed. It was much less terrible than the conflagration of buildings in a town; there was less of power and fierce grandeur, and more of treacherous beauty about the flames as they ran hither and thither along the mountain-side. The first night after it broke out we looked on with admiration; one might have thought it a general illumination of the forest, as the flames spread in long winding lines, gaining upon the dark wood every moment, up and down, and across the hill, collecting here and there with greater brilliancy about some tall old tree, which they hung with fire like a giant lustre. But the next day the sight was a sad one indeed: the deceitful brilliancy of the flames no longer pleased the eye; wreaths of dull smoke and hot vapors hung over the blighted trees, and wherever the fire had wandered there the fresh June foliage was utterly blasted. That night we could no longer take pleasure in the spectacle; we could no longer fancy a joyous illumination. We seemed rather to behold the winding coils of some fiery serpent gliding farther and farther on its path of evil; a rattling, hissing sound accompanying its movement, the young trees trembling and quivering with agitation in the heated current which proclaimed its approach. The fresh flowers were all blighted by its scorching breath, and with its forked tongue it fed upon the pride of the forest, drying up the life of great trees, and without waiting to consume them, hurrying onward to blight other groves, leaving a blackened track of ruin wherever it passed.

Some fifty years since a fire of this kind is said to have spread until it enclosed within its lines the lake and the valley, as far as one could see, surrounding the village with a network of flame, which at night was quite appalling in its aspect. The danger, however, was not so great as it appeared, as there was everywhere a cleared space between the burning forest and the little town. At times, however, very serious accidents result from these fires; within a few days we have heard of a small village, in the northern part of the State, in St. Lawrence county, entirely destroyed in this way, the flames gaining so rapidly upon the poor people that they were obliged to collect their families and cattle in boats and upon rafts, in the nearest pools and streams.

Of course, more or less mischief is always done; the wood and timber already cut are destroyed, fences are burnt, many trees are killed, others are much injured, the foliage is more or less blighted for the season; the young plants are killed, and the earth looks black and gloomy. Upon the whole, however, it is surprising that no more harm is done. On the occasion of the fire referred to in these woods, we found the traces of the flames to disappear much sooner than we had supposed possible. The next season the smaller plants were all replaced by others; many of the younger trees seemed to revive, and a stranger passing over the ground to-day would scarcely believe that fire had been feeding on those woods for a fortnight only a few seasons back. A group of tall, blasted hemlocks, on the verge of the wood, is the most striking monument of the event. The evergreens generally suffer more than other trees, and for some cause or other the fire continued busy at that point for several days. We repeatedly passed along the highway at the time, with the flames at work on either side. Of course, there was no danger, but it looked oddly to be driving quietly along through the fire. The crackling of the flames was heard in the village, and the smell of smoke was occasionally quite unpleasant.

A timely rain generally puts a stop to the mischief; but parties of men are also sent out into the woods to "fight the fire." They tread out the flames among the dry leaves by trampling them down, and they rake away the combustible materials, to confine the enemy to its old grounds, when it soon exhausts itself. The flames spread more frequently along the earth, than from tree to tree.

Thursday, 31st.—The water-lilies are still in blossom; opening quite early in the season, they continue to flower until the frost cuts them off. We found numbers of them in Black-bird Bay this evening.

Our water-lilies in this lake are all of the yellow kind. The fragrant white lily is not known to grow either in the lake, or in any of the little pools and marshy spots very near. It is, however, to be found a short distance to the northward of our own waters.[25] The yellow variety is common enough about the neighborhood.

The roots of this yellow lily were a favorite repast with the moose, and no doubt those great, unwieldy animals have often stood in the shallow water of the little bay we now call after the black-birds, feeding on the lilies, which must have always grown there.[26] The beaver, also, was very partial to these plants, and as he was no stranger here in Indian times, probably he may often have been at this spot taking his share of the lilies. But it is now more than fifty years since these plants have bloomed only for man, and the bees, and the black-birds. The last, probably, heed them very little, although they are near neighbors, generally haunting the low point which forms the bay, whenever they visit our neighborhood.

One of the noblest plants of our country belongs to this tribe of the water-lilies: the Nelumbo, or sacred bean, or water-chinquapin, as it is sometimes called. Its great leaves are from one to two feet broad, and its pale yellow blossom about half a foot in diameter. It is chiefly in our western waters that the Nelumbo is found; in this part of the country it is much more rare. There is, however, one locality in our own State where it grows, and that is on the northern frontier, Sodus Bay, Lake Ontario. It is also found at one point in the Connecticut, and in the Delaware, below Philadelphia. Wherever it is seen, it attracts attention, from the great size of the leaves and the blossom.

This noble flower belongs to a very celebrated family; it calls cousin with the famous Hindoo and Egyptian Lotus, being one of the varieties of that tribe. In Hindoo and Egyptian fable, these plants were held very sacred, as emblems of the creation. In Hindostan, the lotus was an attribute of Ganga, the goddess of the Ganges, and was supposed to have been produced by Vishnu, before the earth was created, and when its first petals unfolded, they discovered the deity Brama lying within. In Egypt, the flower was sacred to Isis, believed to have been given her by Osiris, and was associated with their own sacred river, the Nile; it was also the emblem of Upper Egypt, as the papyrus was of Lower Egypt. Very many traces of these ancient superstitions are still seen blended with the architecture, bas-reliefs, paintings, &c., &c., and whatever remains to us of those nations. There appear to have been several kinds of lotus represented on the ancient Egyptian monuments. One was white, with a fruit like that of the poppy; another bore blue flowers, with the same fruit; the third, and the most celebrated, is mentioned by Herodotus as the lily-rose, and was also called the flower of Antinous; the blossom was of a beautiful red, and the fruit like the rose of a watering-pot, with large seeds like filberts. These are all said to be found at present in India, but what is singular, the finest, the lily-rose, has now disappeared from Egypt, where it was formerly in such high consideration. The blue variety is still found there.

At the present day, the lotus is more honored in Asia than in Egypt. The Hindoos still consider it a sacred flower. In Ceylon, they have a variety which they call Nelumbo, whence our own name. A number of varieties are said to be found in China, where it is also sacred; this does not prevent the Chinese from eating it, however, and it is much cultivated by them as an article of food. The seeds of the Lien Wha, as they call it, are of the form and size of an acorn, and are considered more delicate than almonds; the root, also, is boiled; or sliced raw, and served with ice in summer; or laid up in salt and vinegar for winter use.

These fine plants seem to have an aversion to the soil or climate of Europe; it is said that the ancient Romans attempted to cultivate them in Italy, without success, and that modern European horticulturists have also failed in their efforts to cultivate them in hot-houses. And yet, in this part of the world, the Nelumbo grows in the icy waters of Lake Ontario. Both the large seeds, and the root of our American variety, are said to be very pleasant to the taste—the latter is not unlike the sweet potato.

Autumn

Friday, September 1st.—Glorious night. The moon rose early in the evening, with unusual splendor, ascending into a cloudless sky, with a brilliancy and power in her light quite remarkable. The stars were all pale and dim. The blue of the sky and the green of the trees were clearly seen; even the character of the foliage on the different trees was plainly marked. The lake and hills might have been almost as well known to a stranger as by day. The whole village was like a brilliantly-lighted room; one knew their acquaintances in the street, and could distinguish their different dresses. Within doors, the moonbeams poured a flood of silvery light through the windows; lamps and candles seemed needless; one could go all about the house without their assistance, and we read both letters and papers with ease.

The frogs were singing in full chorus, and the insect world was wide awake, humming in every field. It seemed really a shame to close one's eyes upon such a night. Indeed, there was nothing this evening of the calm, still, dreamy character of common moonlight, but rather an animating, exciting power in the fullness of light, which seemed to rival the influence of the busy day.

Saturday, 2d.—Saw a few barn-swallows about a farm-yard, some miles from the village. The chimney-swallows have not yet disappeared. The goldfinches are scouring the fields and gardens in flocks, feasting upon the ripe seeds; at this moment, they have a little chatty note, which is very pleasant, though scarcely musical; but as they all seem to be talking at once, they make a cheerful murmur about the thickets and fields.

Monday, 4th.—Many of the maple leaves are now covered with brilliant crimson patches, which are quite ornamental; these are not the autumnal change in the color of the leaf itself, for that has not yet commenced, but little raised patches of crimson, which are quite common upon the foliage of our maples in August and September. Many persons suppose these to be the eggs of some insect; but they are, I believe, a tiny parasitic vegetable, of the fungus tribe, like that frequently seen on the barberry, which is of a bright orange color. The insects who lay their eggs in leaves, pierce the cuticle of the leaf, which distends and swells over the young insect within; but the tiny parasitic plants alluded to are not covered by the substance of the leaf, they rise above it, and are quite distinct from it. Those on the maple are the most brilliant of any in our woods.

The leaves of the wych-hazel are frequently covered with large conical excrescences, which are doubtless the cradle of some insect; over these, the cuticle of the leaf itself rises, until it grows to a sharp-pointed extremity. Some leaves show a dozen of these excrescences, and few bushes of the wych-hazel are entirely free from them. Occasionally, one finds a good-sized shrub where almost every leaf has been turned to account in this way, the whole foliage bristling with them. Indeed, there is no other tree or bush in our woods so much resorted to by insects for this purpose as the wych-hazel; all the excrescences bear the same form, so that they probably belong to the same insect, which must be a very common one, judging from the provision made for the young. But so little attention has yet been paid to entomology in this country, that we have not been able to discover, from any books within reach, what little creature it is which crowds the wych-hazel leaves in this way.

Those excrescences made by insects are probably always injurious to the plant, the little creatures generally feeding on the juices of the foliage, which they often destroy; but the tiny parasitic plants of the Æcidium tribe are comparatively harmless, and they are frequently ornamental.

Tuesday, 5th.—A party of chimney-swallows were seen wheeling over the highway, near the bridge, this afternoon.[27]

Wednesday, 6th.—Delightful weather. Long walk. The Michaelmas daisies and golden-rods are blooming abundantly in the fields and woods. Both these common flowers enliven the autumn very much for us, growing freely as they do in all soils and situations, for, unlike the more delicate wild flowers of spring, they are not easily driven from the ground, growing as readily in the fields among foreign grasses as in their native woods. By their profusion, their variety, and their long duration, from midsummer to the sharpest frosts of autumn, they console us for the disappearance of the earlier flowers, which, if more beautiful, are more fragile also.

The golden-rod is a fine showy plant in most of its numerous forms. There are said to be some ninety varieties in North America, and about a third of these belong to our own part of the continent, the Middle States of the Union. Of this number, one, with a pyramidal head, has fragrant leaves.

Another is common to both Europe and America; this is one of the smaller and insignificant kinds, but the only plant of the family found on both continents. Perhaps the golden-rods are not quite so luxuriant with us, as in the lower counties; the larger and more showy kinds seem more abundant in the valley of the Mohawk than upon our hills. Still, they are common enough here, lining all the fences just now. The silver-rod, or *Solidago bicolor,* abounds in our neighborhood; the bees are very fond of it; at this season, and even much later, you often find them harvesting the honey of this flower, three or four bees on one spike.

As for the Michaelmas daisies, they can scarcely thrive better anywhere than in our own region—common as possible in all the fields and woods. There would seem to be a greater variety among these flowers than in any other family except the grasses; botanists count some hundred and thirty American asters, and of these, about one-fourth belong to this part of the country. The difference between many of these is very slight, scarcely perceptible to the casual observer; but others, again, are very strongly marked. We all note that some are quite tall, others low; that some bear very small blossoms, others large and showy flowers; some are white, others pinkish, others grayish, those purple, these blue. Their hearts vary also in color, even upon the same plants, according to the age of the different flowers, the centre being either yellow, dark reddish purple, or pale green; and this enlivens the clusters very much. The leaves, also, are widely different in size and form. All this variety, added to their cheerful abundance, gives interest to this common flower, and makes it a favorite with those who live in the country. They remain so long in bloom, that toward the close of the season, the common sorts may all be found together. Some of the handsomer kinds, large, and of a fine purple color, delight in low, moist spots, where, early in September, they keep company, in large patches, with the great bur-marigold, making a rich contrast with those showy golden blossoms.

It is well known that both the golden-rods and asters are considered characteristic American plants, being so much more numerous on this continent than in the Old World.

Another flower, common in our woods just now, is the Bird-bell, the Nabalus of botanists. There are several varieties of these; the taller kinds are fine plants, growing to a height of four or five feet, with numerous clusters of pendulous, straw-colored bells, strung along their upper branches. If the color were more decided, this would be one of our handsomest wild flowers; its numerous blossoms are very prettily formed, and hung on the stalks with peculiar grace, but they are of a very pale shade of straw color, wanting the brilliancy of warmer coloring, or the purity of white petals. These plants are sometimes called lion's-foot, rattlesnake-root, &c., but the name of Bird-bell is the most pleasing, and was probably given them from their flowering about the time when the birds collect in flocks, preparatory to their flight southward, as though the blossoms rung a warning chime in the woods, to draw them together. The leaves of the Bird-bell are strangely capricious in size and shape, so much so at times, that one can hardly credit that they belong to the same stalk; some are small and simple in form, others are very large and capricious in their broken outline. Plants are sometimes given to caprices of this kind in their foliage, but the Bird-bell indulges in far more fancies of this sort than any other with which we are acquainted in this neighborhood.

Yellow Gerardias are in flower still in the woods, and so is the Hawk-wort. The blue Gentian is also in bloom now; though not common, it is found in spots about the lake.

We gathered, this afternoon, some flowers of the partridge-berry and squaw-vine, the only spring blossoms still found in the woods. Directly in the path, as we were going up Mount—, we also found a large dragon's-claw, or corallarhiza; its brown stalk and flowers measured about fifteen inches in height, and it was divided into eight leafless branches.

Thursday, 7th.—Cooler. Went down to the great meadow for lady's tresses, which grow there plentifully. Pretty and fragrant, these flowers are not unlike an autumn lily of the valley; one is puzzled to know why they should be called lady's tresses—possibly from the spiral twist of the flowers on the stalk. Gathered also a fine bunch of purple asters, and golden bur-marigolds; these last were slightly fragrant.

This evening we kindled our autumn fires.

Friday, 8th.—Lovely day; warm, silvery mist, gradually clearing to soft sunshine. Passed a charming morning at the Cliffs. The wych-hazel is in bloom; brown nuts and yellow flowers on the same twig. Gathered some speckled-jewels, partridge-berry, and squaw-vine blossoms. Found a purple rose-raspberry in flower; it is always pleasant to meet these late flowers, unlooked-for favors as they are. A year or two since the wild roses on this road flowered in September, a second bloom; and the same season a number of our earlier garden roses bore flowers the second time as late as the 16th of September.

Blackberries still very plenty, and sweet; they have not brought any to the village lately, people seem tired of them. Found also a few red raspberries, whortleberries, and the acid rose-berry. This is a land of berries; a large portion of our trees and plants yield their seed in this form. Among such are the several wild cherries, and plums, the amelanchiers and dog-woods, the mountain ash, the sumachs, and the thorns; all the large bramble tribe, with their pleasant fruits, roses, raspberries, the blackberry, and the gooseberry; the numerous whortleberries, and bilberries, viburnums, and honeysuckles, spikenards, and cohoshes; pokeweed, the trilliums, the convallarias, and the low cornel, clintonia, and medeola; the strawberry, the partridge plant, and squaw-vine, &c., &c. These are all common, and very beautiful while in season. Without going at all out of our way this morning, we gathered a very handsome bunch of berries, some of a dark purple, others light, waxy green, these olive, those white, this scarlet, that ruby color, and others crimson, and pale blue. The berry of the round-leaved dog-wood is of a very delicate blue.

The snowberry, so very common in our gardens, is a native of this State, but I have never heard of its being found in this county.

The birds were feasting upon all these berries at the Cliffs; saw quite a gathering of them in a sumach grove, robins, blue-birds, sparrows, gold-finches, cat-birds, wild pigeons, and woodpeckers; there were several others also perched so high that it was not easy to decide what they were. The little creatures were all very active and cheerful, but quite songless; a chirrup, or a wild call, now and then, were the only sounds heard among them.

Saturday, 9th.–Pleasant morning in the woods. Much amused by squirrels. First found a little chipmuck, or ground squirrel, sitting on a pile of freshly-cut chestnut rails, at a wild spot in the heart of the woods. The little creature saw us as we approached, and took a seat not far from him; he moved quickly a few yards and then resumed his sitting position, with his face toward us, so as to watch our movements. He was holding something in his fore paws, which he was eating very busily; it was amusing to watch him taking his dinner; but we were puzzled to know what he was eating, for it was evidently no chestnut, but covered with down, which he brushed away from his face, now and then, quite angrily. For nearly ten minutes he sat there, looking toward us from time to time; but we were curious to know what he was eating, and moved toward him, when he vanished among the rails; he left a bit of his dinner, however; this proved to be the heart of a head of half-ripe thistle, in which the seed had not yet formed; it looked very much like a miniature artichoke, and he seemed to enjoy it exceedingly. Returning to our seat, he reappeared again upon the rails. Presently a beautiful red squirrel made his appearance, in the notch of a tall old pine, perhaps fifty feet from the ground; a hemlock had been uprooted, and in falling its head had locked in this very notch, its root was near the spot where we were sitting. This squirrel is very fond of the cones of the hemlock, and other firs, and perhaps he had run up the half-prostrate trunk in quest of these; at any rate, he took this road downward. He paused every few steps to utter the peculiar cry which has given them the name of chickaree, for they often repeat it, and are noisy little creatures. He came deliberately down the whole length of the trunk, chatting and waving his beautiful tail as he moved along. After leaving the tree he played about, here and there, apparently in quest of nuts, and he frequently came very near us of his own accord; once we might have struck him with ease, by stretching out our parasols. His large eyes were beautiful. This kind of squirrel eats most of our grains, wheat, rye, buckwheat. He swims quite well, and is found as far south as the mountains of Carolina. His fur is thought the best among his tribe.

Passing under a chestnut-tree by the road-side, we had farther occasion to observe how fearless the squirrels are in their interviews with mankind. A little fellow was cutting off chestnut burs with his teeth, that they might drop on the ground; he had already dropped perhaps a dozen bunches; after a while he came down, with another large cluster of green burs in his mouth, with these he darted off into the woods, to his nest, no doubt. But he soon came back, and taking up another large cluster from the ground, ran off again. This movement he repeated several times, without being at all disturbed, though he evidently saw us standing a few yards from him. These gray squirrels are common in every wood, and they say that one of them is capable of eating all the nuts yielded by a large tree; one of them had been known to strip a butternut-tree, near a house, leaving only a very meagre gleaning for the family. These little creatures sometimes undertake the most extraordinary journeys; large flocks of them set out together upon a general migration. Some forty years since a great migration of this kind took place among the gray squirrels, in the northern part of this State, and in crossing the Hudson above Albany, very many of them were drowned. This was in the year 1808.

There is another larger gray squirrel not so common, called the fox squirrel, measuring two and a half feet in length.

The black squirrel is small, only a foot long; its fur is of a glossy jet black. We saw one this summer, but at a distance from our lake. They are nowhere very common, and are rather a northern variety, not seen south of Pennsylvania. There is a deadly feud between these and the gray squirrels, and as their enemies are the largest and the most numerous, they are invariably driven off the nutting-grounds when both meet. The two kinds are said never to remain long together in the same neighborhood.

These, with the flying squirrel, make up all the members of their family found in our State. The pretty little flying squirrels are quite small, about nine inches long. They are found here and there through this State, and indeed over the Union, and in Mexico also. They live in hollow trees, but we have never had the good luck to meet one in our rambles. They are seldom seen, however, in the daytime, dozing away until twilight.

Monday, 11th.—Church-yards are much less common in this country than one might suppose, and to judge from the turn things are taking now, it seems probable this pious, simple custom of burying about our churches, will soon become obsolete. As it is, the good people of many rural neighborhoods must make a day's journey before they can find a country church-yard in which to read Gray's Elegy. A great proportion of the places of worship one sees here have no graves near them. In the villages they make part of the crowd of buildings with little space about them; nor does it follow that in the open country, where land is cheaper, the case is altered; you pass meeting-houses standing apart, with broad fields spreading on all sides, but no graves at hand. Some distance beyond, perhaps, you will come to a square enclosure, opening into the highway, and this is the cemetery of the congregation. Small family burying-grounds, about the fields, are very common; sometimes it is a retired spot, neatly enclosed, or it may be only a row of graves in one corner of the meadow, or orchard. Walking in the fields a while since, we were obliged to climb a stone wall, and on jumping down into the adjoining meadow, we found we had alighted on a grave; there were several others lying around near the fence, an unhewn stone at the head and foot of each humble hillock. This custom of burying on the farms had its origin, no doubt, in the peculiar circumstances of the early population, thinly scattered over a wide country, and separated by distance and bad roads from any place of public worship. In this way the custom of making the graves of a family upon the homestead gradually found favor among the people, and they learned to look upon it as a melancholy gratification to make the tombs of the departed members of a family near the dwelling of the living. The increase of the population, and the improvement of the roads on one hand, with the changes of property, and the greater number of villages on the other, are now bringing about another state of things. Public cemeteries for parishes, or whole communities, are becoming common, while the isolated burial-places about the farms are more rare than they used to be.

The few church-yards found among us are usually seen in the older parishes; places of worship, recently built, very rarely have a yard attached to them. The narrow, crowded, abandoned church-yards, still seen in the heart of our older towns, have become, in the course of time, very striking monuments to the dead. Nowhere is the stillness of the grave so deeply impressive; the feverish turmoil of the living, made up of pleasure, duty, labor, folly, sin, whirling in ceaseless movement about them, is less than the passing winds, and the drops of rain to the tenants of those grounds, as they lie side by side, in crowded but unconscious company. The present, so full, so fearfully absorbing with the living, to the dead is a mystery; with those mouldering remains of man the past and the future are the great realities. The stillness, the uselessness if you will, of the old church-yard in the heart of the bustling city, renders it a more striking and impressive *memento mori* than the skull in the cell of a hermit.

We hear from time to time plans for changes which include the breaking up of those old church-yards in the towns. We are told that those old graves are unsightly objects; that a new square on the spot would be more agreeable to the neighborhood; that a street at this particular point would be a very convenient thoroughfare, and would make A, B, or C richer men by some thousands. Such are the motives usually urged in defence of the act:— embellishment, convenience, or gain. But which of these is of sufficient force to justify the desecration of the tomb? Assuredly necessity alone can excuse the breach of equity, of decency, of good faith, and good feeling involved in such a step. Man is the natural guardian of the grave; the remains of the dead are a solemn deposit entrusted to the honor of the living. In the hour of death we commend our souls into the hands of our Maker; we leave our bodies to the care of our fellow-creatures. Just so long, therefore, as each significant mound bears a trace of its solemn character, just so long should it be held sacred by the living. Shall we, in a Christian land, claim to have less of justice, less of decency and natural feeling, than the rude heathen whose place on the earth we have taken; a race who carefully watched over the burial-places of their fathers with unwavering fidelity? Shall we seek to rival the deed of the brutal wrecker who strips the corpse of the drowned man on the wild shore of the ocean when no honest arm is near? Shall we follow in the steps of the cowardly thief who prowls in the darkness about the field of battle to plunder the lifeless brave? Shall we cease to teach our children that of all covetousness, that which would spoil the helpless is the most revolting? Or, in short, shall we sell the ashes of our fathers that a little more coin may jingle in our own pockets?

It matters little that a man say he should be willing his own grave should be broken up, his own bones scattered to the winds; the dead, whom he would disturb, might tell a different tale could their crumbling skeletons rise up before him, endowed once more with speech. There was a great man who, if we may believe the very solemn words on his tomb, has spoken in this instance, as in ten thousand others, the strong, natural language of the human heart:

"Good friend, for Jesus' sake forbeare
To dig the dust enclosed here;
Blest be he that spares these stones,
And curst be he that moves my bones."

In this new state of society—in this utilitarian age—it behooves us, indeed, to be especially on our guard against any attack upon the tomb; the same spirit which, to-day, stands ready to break open the graves of a past generation, to-morrow, by carrying out the same principle, may deny decent burial to a brother. It may see useless expense in the shroud, waste of wood in the coffin, usurpation of soil in the narrow cell of the deceased. There is, indeed, a moral principle connected with the protection of the grave, which, if given up, must inevitably recoil upon the society by whom it has been abandoned.

The character of a place of burial, the consideration or neglect it receives, the nature of the attention bestowed on it, are all intimately connected with the state of the public mind on many important subjects. There is very little danger in this country of superstitions connected with the grave. What peril there is lies on the other side. Is there no tendency to a cold and chilling indifference upon such subjects among our people? And yet a just consideration of Death is one of the highest lessons that every man needs to learn. Christianity, with the pure wisdom of Truth, while it shields us on one hand from abject, cowardly fear, on the other hand is ever warning us alike against brutal indifference, or the confidence of blind presumption. With all the calmness of Faith, with all the lowliness of Humility, with all the tenderness of Charity, and with the undying light of heavenly Hope at her heart, the Christian Church sits watching beside the graves of her children.

The oldest tomb belonging to the good people of this little town lies within the bounds of the Episcopal Church-yard, and bears the date of 1792. It was a child who died of the small-pox. Close at hand is another stone bearing a date two years later, and marking the grave of the first adult who fell among the little band of colonists, a young man drowned while bathing in the lake—infancy and youth were buried before old age. At the time these graves were dug, the spot was in a wild condition, upon the border of the forest, the wood having been only partially cut away. In a few years other members of the little community died, one after another, at intervals, and they were also buried here, until the spot had gradually taken its present character of a burying-ground. The rubbish was cleared away, place was made for those who must follow, and ere many years had passed, the brick walls of a little church rose within the enclosure, and were consecrated to the worship of the Almighty, by the venerable Bishop Moore. And thus this piece of ground was set apart for its solemn purposes, while shaded by the woods, and ere it had been appropriated to common uses: the soil was first broken by the spade of the grave-digger, and Death is the only reaper who has gathered his harvest here. The spot soon lost its forest character, however, for the older trees were all felled; possibly some among them may have been used as timber in building the little church. Happily, at the time of clearing the ground, a few young bushes were spared from the axe, and these having been left to grow at will, during the course of half a century, have become fine flourishing trees. The greater number are pines, and a more fitting tree for a Christian church-yard than the white pine of America could scarcely be named. With all the gravity and unchanging character of an evergreen, they have not the dull gloom of the cypress or the yew; their growth is noble, and more than any other variety of their tribe, they hold murmuring communion with the mysterious winds, waving in tones of subdued melancholy over the humble graves at their feet. A few maples and elms, and a fine amelanchier, appear among them, relieving their monotonous character. Some of these have been planted for that purpose, but the pines themselves are all the spontaneous growth of the soil. Judging from their size, and what we know of their history, they must have sprung up from the seed about the time when the first colonists arrived — contemporaries of the little town whose graves they overshadow.

The tombs themselves have all a natural interest for the people of the place, but there are none to attract the attention of a stranger. One of the earlier Missionaries in these parts of the country is buried here among his flock; he came into the woods a young man, passed a long life in preaching the Gospel among the different hamlets about, and died at last much respected and esteemed for his simplicity of character and faithful performance of the duties of his sacred office. One day, as he was walking through the church-yard with a brother clergyman, he pointed out a spot beneath two pines, expressing a wish to lie there, when the work of life should be over. Years after this conversation, he died in another parish, and was buried there; but he was nominal rector of this church at the time, and his friends were aware that he wished his body removed to this ground. Steps were accordingly taken, his remains were brought here, and laid in a grave selected by one of the vestry. A simple monument of white marble was raised to his memory by the different parishes he had founded in the county. Some years later, the clergyman to whom the old Missionary had pointed out the spot where he wished to be buried, happened to preach here, and passing through the church-yard, he paused to look at the monument, observing that he was pleased to find his friend had been laid in the very spot chosen by himself so long before; and it was only then the parish learned that their old rector had pointed out this same position for his grave, a vestryman having chosen it without being aware of the fact. Thus the wish of the old servant of God was unconsciously fulfilled by those who were ignorant of it.

> "The dead in Christ, they rest in hope,
>   And o'er their sleep sublime,
> The shadow of the steeple moves,
>   From morn, to vesper chime.
> On every mound, in solemn shade,
>   Its imaged cross doth lie,
> As goes the sunlight to the west,
>   Or rides the moon on high."

Tuesday, 12th.–Delightful walk. Many flocks of birds in movement, wheeling in the sunshine, or alighting upon the trees and fences. Saw a large hawk in full flight before a few king-birds–a common sight enough. Crows, also, when they meet the stout-hearted king-birds in the corn-fields, which they frequently do at this season, are sure to retreat before their spirited enemy. Even the eagle is worsted by them at times, and keeps out of their way.

The butterflies were enjoying the bright, warm day. We observed one, a common yellow butterfly, who had been soaring very high; he came down from the top of a tall pine, growing on high ground, and made a long descent to the glen below, without pausing. Generally, these little creatures fly low. In England, they have a handsome butterfly, which they call the "Emperor;" he lives entirely on the tallest forest trees, and never descends to the ground, his exalted position having been the cause of his receiving the title; I do not know whether we have any in this country with the same habits.

The woods, generally, are green as midsummer–but a small shrub here and there is faintly touched with autumnal colors.

Wednesday, 13th.–Bright and pleasant. Slight touch of frost in the clear moonlight of last night, the first we have had this autumn. It has left no traces, and seems only to have fallen in spots; even the tomato-vines in the garden are untouched.

As we were standing on the wharf, we observed bur-marigolds growing in a spot usually covered with water the year round. The lake has been very low lately, but this particular spot can only have been out of water three or four weeks at the utmost, and here we have plants already grown up and in flower. They are annuals, I believe.

Thursday, 14th.—Rainy, cheerless day. Short walk toward evening. Saw a couple of snail-shells, in a tuft of fern, by the road-side. How much less common are these land-snails in our part of the world than in Europe; in the Old World, you find them in the fields and gardens at every turn, but here we only see one now and then, and chiefly in the woods.

Friday, 15th.—Strong wind from the south, rustling with a full, deep sough through the trees. The locusts, as their branches bend before the wind, show their pods prettily—some clusters bright yellow, others a handsome red, as they are more or less ripe. The Virginia creepers are turning cherry color; they are always the first leaves to change.

Saturday, 16th.—Pleasant, soft weather. The farmers are ploughing and sowing grain, and have been doing so for some days; they are earlier than they used to be with their autumn seed-time. The buckwheat fields are turning red, and will soon be cut. The maize-stalks are drying and withering as the ears ripen; on some farms, they are harvesting both crops—red buckwheat sheaves, and withered corn-stalks, are standing about the fields. All through the summer months, the maize-fields are beautiful with their long glossy leaves; but when ripe, dry and colorless, they will not compare with the waving lawns of other grains. The golden ears, however, after the husk has been taken off, are perhaps the noblest heads of grain in the world; the rich piles now lying about the fields are a sight to rejoice the farmer's heart.

The great pumpkins, always grown with maize, are also lying ripening in the sun; as we have had no frost yet, the vines are still green. When they are harvested and gathered in heaps, the pumpkins rival the yellow corn in richness; and a farm-wagon carrying a load of husked corn and pumpkins, bears as handsome a load of produce as the country yields. It is a precious one, too, for the farmer and his flocks.

Cattle are very fond of pumpkins; it is pleasant to see what a feast the honest creatures make of them in the barn-yard; they evidently consider them a great dainty, far superior to common provender. But in this part of the world, not only the cattle, but men, women, and children—we all eat pumpkins. Yesterday, the first pumpkin-pie of the season made its appearance on table. It seems rather strange, at a first glance, that in a country where apples, and plums, and peaches, and cranberries abound, the pumpkin should be held in high favor for pies. But this is a taste which may probably be traced back to the early colonists; the first housewives of New England found no apples or quinces in the wilderness; but pumpkins may have been raised the first summer after they landed at Plymouth. At any rate, we know that they were soon turned to account in this way. The old Hollander, Van der Donck, in his account of the New Netherlands, published in 1656, mentions the pumpkin as being held in high favor in New Amsterdam, and adds, that the English colonists—meaning those of New England—"use it also for pastry." This is probably the first printed allusion to the pumpkin-pie in our annals. Even at the present day, in new Western settlements, where the supply of fruit is necessarily small at first, pumpkins are made into preserves, and as much pains are taken in preparing them, as though they were the finest peaches from the markets of Philadelphia and Baltimore. When it is once proved that pumpkin-pies were provided for the children of the first colonists by their worthy mothers, the fact that a partiality for them continued long after other good things were provided, is not at all surprising, since the grown man will very generally be found to cherish an exalted opinion of the pies of his childhood. What bread-and-milk, what rice-puddings, can possibly equal the bread-and-milk, the rice-puddings of the school-boy? The noble sex, especially, are much given to these tender memories of youthful dainties, and it generally happens, too, that the pie or pudding so affectionately remembered, was home-made; you will not often find the confectioner's tart, bought with sixpence of pocket-money, so indelibly stamped in recollections of the past. There is at all times a peculiar sort of interest about a simple home-made meal, not felt where a *cordon-bleu* presides; there is a touch of anxiety in the breast of the housekeeper as to the fate of the boiled and roast, the bread and paste, preserves and other cates, which now changes to the depression of a failure, now to the triumph of brilliant success, emotions which are of course shared, in a greater or less degree, by all who partake of the viands, according to the state of the different appetites, and sensibilities. But this ghost of the school-boy pie, this spectral plum-pudding, sitting in judgment upon the present generation of pies and puddings, when it takes possession of husband, brother, or father, has often proved the despair of a housekeeper. In such a case, no pains-taking labors, no nice mixing of ingredients, no careful injunctions to cook or baker, are of any use whatever; that the pie of to-day can equal the pie of five-and-twenty years since, is a pure impossibility. The pudding is tolerable, perhaps—it does pretty well—they are much obliged to you for the pains you have taken—yes, they will take a little more—another spoonful, if you please—still, if they must speak with perfect frankness, the rice-pudding, the plum tart, the apple-pie they are now eating, will no more compare with the puddings, and tarts, and pies eaten every day in past times at their good mother's table, than—language fails to express the breadth of the comparison! Such being man's nature, apropos of pies and puddings, it follows, of course, that the pumpkin-pies eaten by the first tribe of little Yankee boys were never equalled by those made of peaches and plums in later years, and the pumpkin-pie was accordingly promoted from that period to the first place in pastry, among all good Yankees. Probably the first of the kind were simple enough; eggs, cream, brandy, rose-water, nutmegs, ginger, and cinnamon, are all used now to flavor them, but some of these ingredients must have been very precious to the early colonists, too valuable to be thrown into pies.

Probably there was also another reason why the pumpkin-pie was so much in favor in New England: it had never made part of Christmas cheer: it was not in the least like the mince-pie, that abomination of their stern old fathers. We hardly know whether to laugh or to cry, when we remember the fierce attacks made upon the roasted boar's-head, the mince-pies, and other good things of that kind, by the early Puritans; but when we recollect the reason of this enmity, we mourn over the evils that prejudice brings about in this world. Strange, indeed, that men, endowed with many Christian virtues, should have ever thought it a duty to oppose so bitterly the celebration of a festival in honor of the Nativity of Christ! Happily, Time, the great ally of Truth, has worked a change in this respect; Christmas is kept throughout the country, and mince-pies are eaten with a quiet conscience and very good appetite by everybody. And what is vastly to the credit of the community, while all have returned to the mince-pie, all are quite capable of doing justice to a good pumpkin-pie also, and by a very happy state of things, the rival pastries are found on the same tables, from Thanksgiving to Ash-Wednesday. Mince-pies are even more in favor in this country than in England; some people eat them all the year round; I have been offered a slice on the eve of the 4th of July. Those made by the farmers' wives about the country are, however, very coarse imitations of the real thing; their paste is made with lard, and always heavy; coarsely-hashed meat, and apples, and suet, with a little spice, are the chief ingredients, and a dish more favorable to dyspepsia could not easily be put together.

Monday, 18th.—A pair of the golden-winged woodpeckers, or clapes, as many persons call them, have been on the lawn all the afternoon. These large woodpeckers often come into the village, especially in the spring and autumn, and they are frequently seen on the ground, running their bills into the grass in quest of ants and their eggs, which are favorite food with them. They are handsome birds, differing in some respects from the other wood-peckers, and peculiar to North America, although two kindred varieties of golden-winged woodpeckers are found about the Cape of Good Hope. But they have no bird in Europe at all like ours.

Besides the clape, we frequently see the downy woodpecker, and the hairy woodpecker, in the village; the first is the smallest of its tribe in America, and the second, which is a little larger, differs from it chiefly in the red band on its head. Both these birds make holes innumerable in the trunks of many trees, not only for insects, but for the sake of the sap also, which they drink; they are called sap-suckers by the country people, on that account. Frequently one sees a tree completely riddled, by a succession of these holes, which go round the trunk in regular rings, many of the circles lying close together; Mr. Wilson says that they are often so near together, that one may cover eight or ten of these holes with a silver dollar. Both these smaller woodpeckers are often seen on the rails of fences hunting for insects; and both remain here through the winter.

The handsome red-head, one of the migratory woodpeckers, is much more rare in our neighborhood than it used to be, but it is still found here, and we have seen them in the village. They are naturally sociable birds. A hundred miles to the westward, they are very numerous, even at the present day.

The large pileated woodpecker, or log-cock, a resident in Pennsylvania through the winter, is said to have been occasionally seen here of late years; but we have never observed it ourselves. It is quite a forest bird.

Besides these, there are the red-bellied, and the yellow-bellied, coming from the south, and rarely seen in this part of the State. The arctic and the banded woodpeckers, coming from the north, are occasional visitors, but we have never met them.

Tuesday, 19th.—Mild, soft weather lately; to-day, high gust, with rain. Those leaves that had at all loosened their hold, locusts and Virginia creepers, are flying before the wind. The apples, blown off, are lying under the trees, scattered in showers over the green grass.

Saw a flock of wild pigeons; they have not been very numerous in our neighborhood lately, but every year we have a few of them. These birds will go a great distance for food, and their flight is astonishingly rapid. A pigeon of this kind is said to have been killed in New York during the rice season, with undigested Carolina rice in its crop; and as they require but twelve hours for digestion, it is supposed that the bird was only a few hours on his journey, breakfasting on the Santee, and dining on the Hudson. At this rate, it has been calculated that our passenger-pigeon might go to Europe in three days; indeed, a straggler is said to have been actually shot in Scotland. So that, whatever disputes may arise as to the rival merits of Columbus and the Northmen, it is very probable that American pigeons had discovered Europe long before the Europeans discovered them.

Thursday, 21st.—Equinox. Warm; showery as April. Sunshine, showers, and rainbows succeeding each other through the day. Beautiful effect of light on the hills; a whole mountain-side on the lake shore bathed in the tints of the rainbow, the colors lying with unusual breadth on its wooded breast. Even the ethereal green of the bow was clearly seen above the darker verdure of the trees. Only the lower part of the bow, that which lay upon the mountain, was colored; above, the clouds were just tinged where they touched the brow of the hill, then fading away into pale gray.

Ice at table still. We Americans probably use far more ice than most people; the water for drinking is regularly iced, in many houses, until late in the autumn, when the frost cools the springs for us out of doors.

Friday, 22d.—Mushrooms are springing up by the road-side and in pasture-grounds; they are not so numerous as last year, however, when the fungus tribe abounded. Mushrooms are not much eaten in our country neighborhood; people are afraid of them, and perhaps they are right. Certainly, they should never be eaten unless gathered by a person who understands them thoroughly. In France, they are not allowed to be offered for sale, I believe, until inspected by an officer appointed for the purpose. There is a good old Irish mother who supplies one or two houses in the village when they are in season, and she understands them very well.

The Indians of this part of the continent ate mushrooms. Poor creatures, they were often reduced to great extremities for food, from their want of forethought, feeding upon lichens, *tripe de roche,* and everything edible which grew in the forest. But mushrooms seem to have been considered by them as a great delicacy. A Chippewa, when speaking with Major Long on the subject of a future life, gave the following account of the opinions prevailing among his people: "In this land of souls, all are treated according to their merits." "The wicked are haunted by the phantoms of the persons or things they have injured; thus, if a man has destroyed much property, the phantoms of the wrecks of this property obstruct his passage wherever he goes; if he has been cruel to his dogs, they also torment him after death; the ghosts of those whom during his lifetime he has wronged, are there permitted to avenge their wrongs." "Those who have been good men are free from pain; they have no duties to perform; their time is spent in dancing and singing, and they feed *upon mushrooms,* which are very abundant." Thus, mushrooms appear to be the choice food of the Chippewa heroes in the happy hunting-grounds.

Saturday, 23d.—Lovely evening; soft and mild, windows open; the sun throwing long shadows on the bright grass of the lawn. But for a light touch of autumn here and there, we might have believed ourselves at midsummer.

The last melons were eaten to-day. The grapes are ripening; many years we lose them by frost, either in the spring, or early in the autumn. Cold injures them less, however, at this season than in spring.

A large flock of black and white creepers running about the apple-trees, up and down, and around the trunk and branches; they are pretty, amusing little creatures, like all birds of that habit.

Monday, 25th.—Showery again. The woods are still green, but some trees in the village are beginning to look autumn-like. And yet we have had no frost of any consequence. Though an active agent in effecting the beautiful autumnal changes in the foliage, frost does not seem indispensable; one finds that the leaves turn at a certain time, whether we have had frost or not. The single trees, or groves, and the borders of a wood, seem to be touched first, while the forest generally still preserves its verdure. The Virginia creepers, whether trained upon our walls, hanging about the trees in the woods, or tangling the thickets on the banks of the river, are always the first to show their light, vivid crimson, among the green of the other foliage. A maple here and there generally keeps them company, in scarlet and yellow.

The pines are thickly hung with dark-brown cones, drooping from their higher branches. This is also the moment when their old leaves fall, and there is more yellow among their foliage this autumn than usual, probably owing to the dry weather we have had. Near at hand, these rusty leaves impair their beauty, but at a little distance, they are not observed. The hemlocks effect the change in their foliage imperceptibly, at least they seldom attract attention by it; nor do their fallen leaves lie in rusty, barren patches on the earth, beneath the trees, like those of the pine.

Saw a pretty sight: a party of robins alighted on the topmost boughs of a group of young locusts near the house, and sipped up the rain-drops gathered on the leaves; it was pretty to see them drinking the delicate drops, one after another. Smaller birds joined them—sparrows, probably, and drank also. Birds often drink in this way, but one seldom sees a whole flock sipping at the same time. It is said that the fine pinnated grouse, now becoming a very rare bird in this State, drinks only in this way, refusing water from a vessel, or a spring, but eagerly drinking when it trickles down in drops.

Tuesday, 26th.—A fine bunch of woodcock, with several partridges, and a brace of wood-ducks, brought to the house. The woodcock is less common here than the partridge, or the ruffed grouse rather, as we should call it; but all our game-birds are rapidly diminishing in numbers. By the laws of the State every county is enabled to protect its own property of this kind, by including any wild animal, or bird, or fish within the list of those which can only be destroyed at certain seasons; the county courts deciding the question in each case. Hitherto more attention has been paid to the preservation of game on Long Island than in any other part of this State; and although so near New York, although the laws are very imperfectly administered in these, as in some other respects, yet the efforts of the Long Islanders have succeeded in a degree at least. The deer, for instance, are said to be actually increasing there, and until lately they have preserved more game-birds than in most other counties; they still have, or had quite lately, a few of the fine pinnated grouse. In this county very little attention has been paid to this subject, and probably everything of the kind will soon disappear from our woods. The reckless extermination of the game in the United States would seem, indeed, without a precedent in the history of the world. Probably the buffaloes will be entirely swept from prairies, once covered with their herds, by this generation.[28]

The wood-ducks brought in this morning were both drakes, but young, and consequently they had not acquired their beautiful plumage. We had one for dinner; it was very delicate; a canvas-back could scarcely have been more so. These ducks are summer visitors to our lake. Unlike others of their family, they build nests in trees. They are said to be one of the two most beautiful species in the world, the other being the Mandarin Duck of China. Ours are chiefly confined to the fresh waters of the interior, being seldom found on the sea-shore. They are said frequently to build in the same tree for several seasons. Mr. Wilson gives a pleasing account of a nest he had seen on the banks of the Tuckahoe River, New Jersey:—"The tree was an old grotesque white oak, whose top had been torn off by a storm. In this hollow and broken top, and about six feet down, on the soft, decayed wood, lay thirteen eggs, snugly covered with down, doubtless taken from the breast of the bird. The eggs were of the highest polish, fine in the grain, greatly resembling old polished ivory. This tree had been occupied, probably by the same pair, for four successive years in breeding-time; the person who gave me the information, and whose house was within twenty or thirty yards of the tree, said that he had seen the female, the spring preceding, carry down thirteen young, one by one, in less than ten minutes. She caught them in her bill by the wing, or the back of the neck, and landed them safely at the foot of the tree, when she afterward led them to the water. Under this same tree, at the time I visited it, a large sloop lay on the stocks, nearly finished; the deck was not more than twelve feet distant from the nest, yet notwithstanding the presence and the noise of the workmen, the ducks would not abandon their old breeding-place, but continued to pass out and in, as if no person had been near. The male usually perched on an adjoining limb, and kept watch while the female was laying, and also often while she was sitting. A tame goose had chosen a hollow space at the root of the same tree, to lay and hatch her young in."

The feathers of these beautiful birds are said to be frequently used by the Indians to ornament their calumet, or Pipe of Peace; the head and neck of the wood-duck are frequently seen covering the stem of the pipe.

Owing to the richness of its plumage, Linnæus gave this bird the name of the Bridal Duck, *Anas Sponsa,* and it is singular that the bird which approaches nearest to ours, the Mandarin Duck of China, figures regularly in the marriage procession of the Chinese; not, however, from its beauty, but as an emblem of conjugal fidelity, for which good quality they are remarkable. A story is told of a female in the aviary of a European gentleman at Macao, who all but starved herself to death when her husband was carried off, and would probably have died had he not been found and restored to her. The joy of both at meeting was extreme, and the husband celebrated his return by putting to death a rival drake who had been trying, but in vain, to console his mourning partner. We have never heard whether our own birds are remarkable for the same good quality or not, but their returning to the same nest for years, looks, at least, as if they mated for life.

Wednesday, 27th.—Decided white frost last night. The trees show it perceptibly in a heightened tint of coloring, rising here and there; some single maples in the village streets are vividly crimson. But the general tint is still green.

Many birds flying about in parties. Some of the goldfinches still wear their summer colors, yellow and black. Walking in the lane, we came upon a large mixed flock, feeding on the thistles and silkweed of an adjoining field which is overrun with these weeds. There were goldfinches, blue-birds, sparrows, robins; and perched in a tree, at no great distance, were several meadow-larks apparently attracted by the crowd, for they sat quietly looking on. Altogether there must have been several hundreds in the flock, for there were frequently six or eight hanging upon one thistle-stalk. Some were feeding busily; others were flitting about, now on the fences, now in the road. It was a gay, pretty sight. We disturbed them, of course, passing in their midst; but they did not seem much alarmed. Taking flight, as we came close upon them, they alighted again on the rails and weeds, a few yards beyond, repeating over and over the same movement as we walked slowly on, until more than half the flock had actually accompanied us in this way a good piece of road, a quarter of a mile. They seemed half convinced that we meant no harm to them. As we reached the end of the lane and turned into the highway, some went back to their feast; others, as it was near sunset, flew away in parties.

The numbers of these autumn flocks vary very much with the seasons; some years they are much more numerous than others. After a cold, late spring, we have comparatively few. Many birds at such times, probably, stop short on their spring journey, remaining farther south; and others, alas! are destroyed by a severe untimely frost. Not long since, early in the season, a large party of blue-birds arrived in the village. We watched them with much interest; their brilliant plumage of silvery blue showing beautifully as they flitted about in the sunshine; and added to their gentle, harmless character and pleasant note, this makes them very desirable birds to have about a house and on a lawn. We observed no less than three pairs building under the eaves, at the time referred to, passing up and down before the windows twenty times a day, and several others were going in and out of holes and chinks of the trees in sight. One night there came a hard frost, followed by a fall of snow; the next day six of these pretty blue-birds were picked up dead in one cluster in our own garden, and several others were said to be lying about the grounds. They seemed to have collected together to warm themselves. That summer we saw very few blue-birds, and the following autumn there was scarcely a large flock of them seen in the neighborhood.

Fine sunset; the evening still and quiet. The lake beautiful in its reflections of the sky. Soft barred clouds were floating above the hills, and the color of each lay faithfully repeated on the water;—pink, violet, gray, and blue in successive fields.

Thursday, 28th.—In our walk, this afternoon, observed a broad field upon a hill-side covered with the white silvery heads of the everlastings. The country people sometimes call these plants "moonshine," and really the effect in the evening upon so broad a field reminded one of moonlight. These flowers deserve the name of "everlasting;" some of them begin to bloom early in the spring, and they continue in blossom until the latest days of autumn. They are extremely common here; one of our characteristic plants.

A noisy flock of blue-jays collected in the wood behind us as we were standing on Mount—. They were hunting for nuts, and chattering like monkeys. Their cry is anything but musical, but they are certainly very handsome birds. There is another kind of jay—the Canada jay—sometimes seen in this State; it is not so fine a bird as the common sort. These birds are said to eat all sorts of things; just now they are frequently mischievous in the maize-fields. They are good mimics, when trained, and a little given to thieving, like the magpie. We do not quarrel with them, however, for they are one of the few birds that pass the winter in our woods: at least, some of their flocks remain here, though others probably go off toward the coast.

Friday, 29th.—Great change in the weather. Chilly, pinching day. The county fair of the Agricultural Society is now going on in the village, which is thronged with wagons and chilly-looking people. Three or four thousand persons, men, women, and children, sometimes attend these fairs; to-day the village is thought more crowded than it has been any time this year; neither the circus, nor menagerie, nor election, has collected so many people as the Fair.

The cattle-show is said to be respectable; the ploughing match and speech were also pronounced creditable to the occasion. Within doors there is the usual exhibition of farm produce and manufactures. The first department consists of butter, cheese, maple sugar, honey, a noble pumpkin, about five feet in circumference; some very fine potatoes, of the Carter and pink-eye varieties, looking as though there were no potato-disease in the world; some carrots and turnips also. Apples were the only fruit exhibited. Some of the butter and cheese was pronounced very good; and both the maple sugar and honey were excellent. Altogether, however, this part of the show was meagre; assuredly we might do much more than has yet been done in this county, with our vegetables and fruits. And a little more attention to the arrangement of the few objects of this kind exhibited at the Fair, is desirable; people take great pains in arranging a room for a public ball or dinner; but an exhibition of this kind is of far more real interest and importance than any meeting for mere amusement. These agricultural fairs are among the most pleasing as well as most important gatherings we country people know of.

The cattle and the domestic manufactures form much the most important features in our fairs. The stock of this county is not thought remarkable, I believe, either one way or the other; but some prizes from the State Society have been distributed among us. Our domestic manufactures, however, are really very interesting, and highly creditable to the housewives of the county. Some of the flannels and carpeting are of excellent quality. A very short time since, before imported carpets were reduced as low in price as they are to-day, a large amount of carpeting was made by families in the inland counties, and some of the best houses were carpeted throughout with domestic manufactures, the wool being raised on the farm, and spun, dyed, and woven in the house, or in the immediate neighborhood. At this moment many such carpets are found in our county, and are probably thought imported by those who are not aware how much work of the kind is done among our rural population. Some are made on the Venetian patterns, like stair carpeting, but others are imitations of ingrain. There is still another kind of carpeting, more humble in quality, much used in the country, rag carpeting, some of which may be seen in every farm-house, and common in the villages also; strips of cotton, woollen, or linen are cut, sewed together, and dyed of different colors, when they are woven with a warp of tow, in Venetian patterns. Some of these are very pretty and neat. One of the best and largest country inns in the interior of this State is almost wholly carpeted in this way. In Europe these rag carpets are not seen, at least not on the common track of travellers, and possibly they are an invention of our great-grandmothers after they had crossed the ocean. Or it may be that they are found in English farm-houses off the common route.

Besides excellent flannels and carpeting, we saw very good shawls, stamped table-covers, blankets, shirting and sheeting, towelling and table linen; leather and morocco; woollen stockings, mittens, gloves, and socks; very neat shoes and boots, on Paris patterns; embroidery, and fancy work of several kinds; some very good broadcloth; pretty plaid and striped woollen materials, for dresses; handsome bed-quilts, of unusually pretty patterns, and well quilted, &c., &c. Altogether this was the most creditable part of the indoor exhibition. Every one must feel an interest in these fairs; and it is to be hoped they will become more and more a source of improvement and advantage in everything connected with farming, gardening, dairy-work, manufacturing, mechanical, and household labors.

The butter and cheese of this county ought to be of the very highest quality. That of our best dairies already commands a high price in the large towns; but with plenty of grass, good spring water in abundance, and a comparatively cool summer climate, there ought not to be a pound of *bad butter* to be found here. Unfortunately, a great deal of a very indifferent kind is made and eaten; and yet bad butter is almost as injurious to health as bad air, of which we hear so much now-a-days. At the taverns it is seldom that one meets with tolerable butter.

Saturday, 30th.—Milder again. There are still many grasshoppers thronging the fields and road-sides of warm days. The turkeys, however, make great havoc among them; these birds fatten very much on the grasshoppers of September.

Monday, October 2d.—Soft, half-cloudy day; something of spring in the atmosphere. The woods also are spring-like in their appearance to-day: many trees are just on the verge of turning, colored in light, delicate greens of every tint; the effect is very beautiful, and strangely like May. But here and there, amid these pleasing varieties of verdure, we find a brilliant flash of scarlet or crimson, reminding us that we are near the close of the year, under the influence of bright autumn, and not of gentle spring.

Drive and walk. Sat upon the cliffs enjoying the view. The day was perfectly still, the lake calm and placid, the reflection of its banks more than usually lovely in its clearness and accuracy; the changing woods, each brilliant tree, the hills, farms, and buildings were all repeated with wonderful fidelity, and all the sweetness of the natural landscape.

Gathered quite a pretty bunch of flowers; asters, everlastings, goldenrods, bird-bell, innocence, pink and yellow fumitory, and a bunch of white blackberry flowers, blooming out of season. Found some of the fruit, also, quite eatable still; a rose-berry also, here and there. Some of the leaves of these bushes, the rose-raspberry, are very large, among the largest leaves we have; measured one this morning of unusual size, twelve inches and a half in breadth. The bush grew in a moist, shady spot.

Many butterflies sailing over the fields. The yellow butterflies are the earliest to come, and the last to leave us; they seem more social in their habits than most of their kind, for you generally see them in parties, often in the meadows, often on the highways. Not long since we saw a troop of these little creatures, a dozen or more, fluttering over a muddy spot in the road, as they often do,—whether to drink or not, I do not know; there was a cottage and a blacksmith-shop close at hand, and a pretty white kitten had strayed out to sun herself. As we came to the spot puss was in the midst of the butterflies at quiet, gentle play with them; they did not seem to mind her good-natured taps at all, avoiding them by flitting about, but without any signs of alarm, still hovering over the same spot; we watched them a moment, and then, fearful that puss might wound some of her little play-fellows, we took her up and set her on the fence.

Heard a cat-bird and jays in the woods. Heard a gun also, boding mischief to partridges or pigeons.

Sat down to look at the water, and a bit of pebbly shore, many feet below. Counted the flowers of a tall mullein spike, which measured thirty-three inches in length; it bore five hundred and seventy flowers, or rather seed-vessels, for it was out of blossom; each of these seed-vessels was filled with tiny dark seed, probably by the hundred, for I had not the time or patience to count these. No wonder that mulleins are common; they must yield fruit ten thousand-fold! The birds do not seem to like their seed; they are not seen feeding on the mullein stalks, as we see them on the thistles every day.

Tuesday, 3d.—Pleasant. The varied greens of yesterday are already gone; light, delicate yellows prevail to-day, and the groves remind us of what we read of the golden gardens of the Incas, in the vale of Cuzco. Scarlet and crimson are increasing also; it seems singular, but the sumachs, which a few days since were a dark reddish purple, are now taking a bright scarlet, a much lighter tint, while the usual progress with the coloring of the foliage is from light to dark. The Virginia creeper is vivid cherry color, as usual, and its leaves are already dropping; they are always the first to fall. The birches are yellow, more so than usual; the elms also; the lime-trees deep orange. The aspens are quite green still, as well as the Lombardy poplars, and the willows.

They are digging the potatoes; the crop is not a bad one in this neighborhood; some of the Carters, especially, are very fine, large and mealy; and there is generally but little of the decay yet. Some of the farmers expect to lose only a fourth of the crop, others more, some few even less. But the disease often shows itself after the potatoes are in the cellar.

Wednesday, 4th.—Sky soft, but cloudy. How rapid are the changes in the foliage at this season! One can almost see the colors growing brighter. The yellows are more decided, the scarlet and crimson spreading farther, with a pink flush rising on many trees where yellow prevails, especially among the maples. Still there is a clear vein of green perceptible; not the verdure of the pine and hemlock, but the lighter greens of the aspens and beeches, with some oaks and chestnuts not yet touched. Indeed, the woods are very beautiful to-day; the general effect is charming, while here and there we note a scarlet maple, a golden birch, so brilliantly vivid that we are really amazed at the richness and beauty of their coloring.

The children are out nutting; it is the chestnuts which are the chief attraction with them—they are very common here. A merry group of boys and girls were chatting away in the "Chestnut Grove" this afternoon, as we passed. Black walnuts are not so frequent, and the butternuts in this immediate neighborhood are rare; in some parts of the county they abound. Beech-nuts are plenty. Hazel-nuts are rare, and our hickory-nuts are not as good as "Thiskytoms" should be. Still, all things with kernels are "nuts" to

boys, and the young rogues make furious attacks upon all the chestnut, walnut, and hickory trees in the neighborhood; they have already stripped the
walnut-trees about the village of all their leaves; these are disposed to fall
early, but the boys beat the branches so unmercifully that they become quite
bare as soon as the fruit is ripe.

A large party of pretty little wrens were feeding on the haws of an old
thorn-tree by the road-side. Perhaps they were winter wrens, which are found
in this State, and remain here through the year. We do not remember, however, to have ever seen a wren in this county, during our coldest months.

Thursday, 5th.—The woods are very fine, under the cloudy sky, to-day.
Scarlet, crimson, pink, and dark red increasing rapidly—gaining upon the
yellows. So much the better; seasons where yellow prevails are far from being our finest autumns. The more crimson and scarlet we have to blend with
the orange and straw colors, the gayer we are. Still, this seems rather a yellow year; for the elms and hickories—which often wither and turn brown,
without much beauty—are very handsome just now, in clear shades of yellow, fluttering in the breeze like gold-leaf; while the chestnuts, birches, wych-
hazel, and many maples, as usual, wear the same colors. Although there are
certain general rules regarding the coloring of the trees, still they vary with
different seasons; some which were red last year may be yellow this autumn,
and others which were dull russet may be bright gold color. The other day
we found a wood-path strewed, at one spot, with pink aspen-leaves; but the
general color of this tree is a decided yellow, nor do I ever remember to
have seen its foliage pink before this instance; still there was no mistake
about the matter, the leaves belonged to the large aspen, and they were
clearly pink. They looked, however, as if they had first turned yellow, and
then a coat of rich warm lake had been laid on afterward. Maples frequently
go through the same process.

Some of the oaks are turning deep red, others scarlet. The ashes are already dark purple. But while most of the foliage is gaining in brilliancy, bare
limbs are already seen here and there; the Virginia creepers are all but
leafless, so are the black walnuts; and the balm of Gilead poplar is losing
its large leaves. Such is Autumn: prodigal in her magnificence, scattering
largesse with a liberal hand, she is yet careless, and regardless of finish in
the lesser details; she flings cloth of gold over the old chestnut, and Tyrian
purple upon the oak; while the neighboring grape-vine hangs a dull and
blighted garland of russet upon the forgotten aspen, still green. Spring has
a dainty hand, a delicate pencil; no single tree, shrub, plant, or weed, is left
untouched by her; but Autumn delights rather in the breadth and grandeur

of her labors, she is careless of details. Spring works lovingly—Autumn, proudly, magnificently.

Friday, 6th.—Beautiful day. House-cleaning going on in the village; happily, the labors of the task at this season are less tremendous and overwhelming than in spring; it is a matter of two or three days, instead of weeks.

The woods are brilliant in the sunshine. There is still a vein of green, however, running through the forest, independently of the pines and firs.

In our stroll this evening we saw several flocks of birds, water-fowl and other smaller birds, moving steadily to the southward. These flocks give much interest to the autumn sky; they are often seen now, but are not common at other seasons—unless, indeed, it be in picture-books, where every landscape is provided with a nondescript flock of its own, quite as a matter of course. Through the spring and summer, the birds live with us, in our own atmosphere, among our own groves and plants, every-day companions; but at this season they soar above us, and we look up at the little creatures with a sort of respect, as we behold the wonderful powers with which they are endowed, sailing in the heavens, over hill and dale, flood and town, toward lands which we may never hope to see.

Saturday, 7th.—Charming weather. The woods on the hills are glorious in the sunshine, the golden light playing about their leafy crests, as though it took pleasure in kindling such rich coloring. The red of the oaks grows deeper, the chestnuts are of a brighter gold color. Still a touch of green in the woods; the foliage of the beech struggles a long time to preserve its verdure, the brownish yellow creeps over it very slowly; most trees turn more rapidly, as though they took pleasure in the change.

Butterflies fluttering about in the sunshine; dragon-flies also, "la demoiselle dorée," as the French call them—strange, that what is a young lady in France should become a dragon across the Channel! Many grasshoppers by the road-sides. Small gnat-like flies abound, in flocks,

> "borne aloft,
> Or sinking, as the light wind lives or dies."

Beautiful moonlight this evening, with a decided frosty feeling in the air. The moon was determined to show us what she could do toward lighting up the autumn foliage at night; the effect was singular, as seen in the trees about the lawn. A dreamy fugitive coloring of scarlet and yellow seemed to be thrown over the sumachs and maples, near the house; and even upon the hills, in spots where the light fell with all its power, the difference between the colored belts of yellow or scarlet, and the darker evergreens, was quite perceptible.

Monday, 9th.—As the sun rose the lake lay buried in mist, which gradually rolled away, with sea-like glimpses of the water. The leaves of the locusts are shrivelled by the frost, and dropping rapidly and silently from the branches; several trees on the lawn will be all but bare to-night. The foliage always falls as much after a sharp frost as from the effect of a high wind; such mornings as this the leaves drop calmly and silently to the earth, but the stormy winds tear them angrily from the trees, and drive them wildly from grove to grove, from field to field, ere they rest beneath their shroud of snow.

The air is quite sharp this morning, and the birds come fluttering about the windows, as though it were more chilly than they liked out of doors; we saw several robins, sparrows, and goldfinches about the windows in different parts of the house. One goldfinch, in full color, flew against the glass pane. One would gladly open to the little creatures, but if we approach the window they are frightened, and fly off again; it is a pity we cannot make them understand they would be very welcome to warm themselves and then fly away at will. Probably they take the house for a respectable sort of cave, where they mean to shelter themselves from the frosty air a while; but as they never come until toward the last of the season, it looks very much as if they wished to say good-bye, and inquire if we have any messages for our friends in Carolina.

A handsome Antiopa butterfly, brown and buff, also came fluttering about a window of the second story several times in the course of the morning, coming and going, as if anxious to find its way in. At last we opened the window, but it was frightened by the noise, and fluttered away. These large and handsome butterflies are longer-lived than many of their companions; they outlive the winter, by clinging to the rafters of barns and out-buildings, or concealing themselves in sheltered crevices of walls, where they remain in a torpid state until the mild weather in spring, when they come out again, and may occasionally be seen flitting about among the leafless and flowerless shrubs of March and April.

Tuesday, 10th.—Mild. Showery morning, bright afternoon. Pleasant walk on the lake-road. The pines are clear green again, having cast their rusty leaves. A few cones also are dropping, but many hang on the trees through the winter.

A few years since, those who followed this road, along the lake shore, frequently met an old man, coming and going in this direction, whose venerable appearance would probably have attracted a stranger's attention. His head was white with the honors of fourscore and upward, yet his tall, slender figure was erect and active, showing few marks of age; and his face was remarkable for a kindly, benevolent expression, a bright, healthy eye, and ruddy complexion. This old man led a singular life, partaking of the retirement and simplicity of that of a hermit, with the active benevolence of a different class of men. With children living in the village, and calling the house of a daughter his home, he loved the quiet solitude of the fields; and, unwilling to be idle, so long as he had strength to work, the good old man applied to the owner of the land in this direction for a spot to till; his request was complied with, and he chose a little patch within a short walk of the village. Early in the morning, before sunrise, he would go out into the woods, frequently remaining out the whole day, only bending his steps homeward toward evening. Often he might be seen at work with his spade or his hoe, about the little field which he was the first man to till; he made a fence of the decayed logs lying about, collected the rubbish and brushwood and burned it, then ploughed, and planted maize and potatoes. Often, when missed from his field, he has been found sitting among the bushes reading his Bible or his hymn-book, or kneeling in prayer. On the hill-side, at no great distance from his little clearing, there is a shallow cave, well known in the neighborhood, and many a summer morning, before the village bell has rung for sunrise, the good old man has been kneeling there, in earnest prayer for the people of the sleeping town at his feet. Much of his time was passed in prayer, in reading the Holy Scriptures, and singing pious hymns, with his pleasant old voice. He always had a smiling, friendly greeting for his acquaintances, and expressed a very warm interest in the children and grandchildren of those he had known in earlier days; he never met a young person of his acquaintance without some solemn words of good advice, and a blessing, given with earnest sincerity. Occasionally he would visit his different friends in the village, and although his object was generally of a charitable or religious nature, yet he loved to talk of past times with those whose memories went back to the first years of the little colony. He had been a miller by trade, and came into the county at an early day, and of course knew much of the history of this rural community. But he had also other recollections of a more ambitious nature; for he had begun life as a soldier, during the troubles of the Revolution, having belonged to the "Jersey line;" and it was with some latent pride that he would relate how he had, more than once, stood sentinel before the tent of General Washington, and seen "His Excellency" go in and out. His recollection of the battle of Long Island, and the celebrated retreat across the East River, was particularly good; his old cheek would flush, and his mild eye grow brighter, as he told the incidents of that day and night; while the listener must needs smile to see the young soldier thus getting the better of the peaceful old solitary. His activity was unusual for such advanced years: a great walker, he never used horse or wagon if he could help it; and at the age of eighty-two he walked forty miles in one day, to visit a friend in the next county. He ate only the simplest food, and never drank anything but water, or a bowl of milk now and then; and this temperance, added to regular exercise and light labor in the fields, with a mind at peace, were no doubt the cause of the good health and activity he enjoyed so late in life. This excellent man was a striking example of what the Holy Scriptures alone may do for the honest, simple heart, who endeavors faithfully to carry out the two great commandments – loving our Maker with all the heart, and doing unto others as we would have others do to us. Full of simple piety and benevolence, temperate, frugal, and industrious, single-minded, and upright in word and deed, his conduct in all these respects was such as to command the respect and veneration of those who knew him. It was like a blessing to meet so good a man in one's daily walks. Such an instance of honorable integrity and simple piety was a strong encouragement to perseverance in duty, among the many examples of a very opposite character – examples of weakness, folly, and sin, which hourly crossed one's path.

Not long since, during the cold weather in winter, the village heard with regret that their venerable old neighbor had fallen on the ice, and broken a leg; from that time he has been compelled to give up his field labors, having become quite infirm. Bowed down with age and debility, his mind often wanders; but on the subject nearest his heart, he is still himself. He may be seen occasionally, of a pleasant day, sitting alone in the lane near his daughter's door, scarcely heeding what passes before him; his eyes closed, his hands clasped, and his lips moving in prayer. If one stops to offer him a respectful greeting, he shakes his head, acknowledging that memory fails him, but he still bestows a blessing with his feeble voice and dim eye – "God bless you, my friend, whoever you be!"

The little patch of ground enclosed by logs, just within the edge of the wood, and the frequent turning-point in our walks, was the good man's clearing. It now lies waste and deserted. A solitary sweet-briar has sprung up lately by the road-side, before the rude fence. This delightful shrub is well known to be a stranger in the forest, never appearing until the soil has been broken by the plough; and it seems to have sprung up just here expressly to mark the good man's tillage. Tall mullein-stalks, thistles, and weeds fill the place where the old husbandman gathered his little crop of maize and potatoes; every season the traces of tillage become more and more faint in the little field; a portion of the log fence has fallen, and this summer the fern has gained rapidly upon the mulleins and thistles. The silent spirit of the woods seems creeping over the spot again.

Wednesday, 11th.—Autumn would appear to have received generally a dull character from the poets of the Old World; probably if one could gather all the passages relating to the season, scattered among the pages of these writers, a very large proportion would be found of a grave nature. English verse is full of sad images applied to the season, and often more particularly to the foliage.

> "The *chilling* autumn, angry winter,"

are linked together by Shakspeare.

> "The *sallow* autumn fills thy laps with leaves,"

writes Collins.

> "O pensive autumn, how I grieve
> Thy sorrowing face to see,
> When languid suns are taking leave
> Of every drooping tree!"

says Shenstone.

> "Ye trees that fade when autumn heats remove,"

says Pope.

> "Autumn, melancholy wight!"

exclaims Wordsworth. And hundreds of similar lines might be given; for very many of the English poets seem to have felt a November chill at their fingers' ends when alluding to the subject.

The writers of France tell much the same tale of Autumn, across the Channel.

> "Plus pâle, que la pâle automne,"

says Millevoye, in his touching lament.

> "la pâle Automne
> D'une main languissante, effeuillant sa couronne,"

writes Delille; and again,

> "Dirai-je à quels désastres,
> De l'Automne orageux nous exposent les astres?"

And again,

> "Voyez comment l'Automne nébuleux
> Tous les ans, pour gémir, nous amène en ces lieux."

St. Lambert tells us of fogs and mists, in his sing-song verses, his "ormeaux, et rameaux, et hameaux."

> "Ces voiles suspendus qui cachent à la terre
> Le ciel qui la couronne, et l'astre qui l'éclaire
> Préparent les mortels au retour des frimas.
> Mais la feuille en tombant, du pampre dépouillé
> Découvre le raisin, de rubis émaillé."

Observe that he was the especial poet of the seasons, and bound to fidelity in their behalf; and yet, painting Autumn during the vintage, he already covers the sky with clouds, and talks of "frimas."

> "Salut, bois couronnés d'en reste de verdure
> Feuillage, jaunissant sur les gazons épars,"

writes M. de Lamartine, in his beautiful but plaintive verses to the season. In Germany we shall find much the same tone prevailing.

> "In des Herbstes welkem Kranze,"

says Schiller; and again,

> "Wenn der Frühlings Kinder sterben,
> Wenn vom Norde's kaltem Hauch
> Blatt und Blume sich entfärben—"

As for the noble poets of Italy, summer makes up half their year; the character of autumn is less decided; she is scarcely remembered until the last days of her reign, and then she would hardly be included among "i mesi gai."

In short, while gay imagery has been lavished upon Spring and Summer, Autumn has more frequently received a sort of *feuille morte* drapery, by way of contrast. Among the older poets, by which are meant all who wrote previously to the last hundred years, these grave touches, in connection with autumn, are particularly common; and instances of an opposite character are comparatively seldom met with.

There were exceptions, however. Such glowing poets as Spenser and
Thomson threw a warmer tint into their pictures of the season. But, strange
to say, while paying her this compliment, they became untrue to nature—
they robbed Summer to deck Autumn in her spoils. They both—British poets, as they were—put off the grain-harvest until September, when in truth
the wheat-sheaf belongs especially to August, in England; that month is
given up to its labors, and it is only the very last sheaves which are gathered
in September. Yet hear what Spenser says:

> "Then came the Automne, all in yellow clad,
> As though she joyed in her plenteous store,
> Laden with fruit that made her laugh full glad;
> Upon her head a wreath, which was enrolde
> With *eares of corne* of every sort, she bore,
> And in her hand *a sickle* she did holde,
> To reap the ripened fruits the earth did yolde."

The ears of corn, and the sickle, were certainly the rightful property of
Summer, who had already been spending weeks in the harvest-field.

Thomson first introduces the season in very much the same livery as
Spenser, as we may all remember:

> "Crown'd with *the sickle,* and *the wheaten sheaf,*
> While Autumn, nodding o'er the yellow plain,
> Comes jovial on;   .   .   .   .   .
>   .   .   .   .   broad and brown, below,
> Extensive harvests hang the heavy head:—"

In classic days Spring was seen crowned with flowers; Summer with grain;
Autumn with fruits; and Winter with reeds. All the four seasons, the Anni
of Roman mythology, took a masculine form. Traces of this may be found
in the gender given to the different seasons, grammatically speaking, in the
principal modern tongues of Europe, for they are chiefly masculine. In Italian, spring, *la primavera,* is feminine; *l'estate, l'autumno, l'inverno,* are masculine; in verse, *il verno* is occasionally used for winter; and the gender of summer is sometimes changed to a feminine substantive, *la state.* In German, *der
Frühling, der Sommer, der Winter, der Herbst,* are all masculine, and so is the
more poetical word, *der Lenz,* for spring; but the Germans, as we all know,
have peculiar notions on the subject of gender, for they have made the sun
feminine, and the moon masculine. The Spaniards have adopted the same
words as the Italians, with the same genders—*la primavera, el verano* or *el es-*

tio, el otoño, el invierno, spring alone being feminine. In French, we have them all masculine, strictly speaking, *le printemps, l'été, l'automne, l'hiver;* but by one of the very few licenses permitted in French grammar, autumn occasionally becomes feminine, in a sense half poetical, half euphonical. Strictly speaking, we are taught that, with an adjective preceding it, autumn, in French, is always masculine.

> "Ou quand sur les côteaux *le vigoureux* Automne
> Etalait ses raisins dont Bacchus se couronne;"

while with the adjective coming after, it is feminine: "une automne délicieuse," says Madame de Sévigné. But this rule is often neglected in verse, by the same writers who are quoted as authority for it, as we have seen in "la pâle automne" of Delille; the feeling and tact of the individual seem to decide the question; and this is one of the very few instances in which such liberty is allowed to the French poet. As might be supposed, the variation becomes a grace; and probably if something more of the same freedom were generally diffused through the language, the poetry of France would have more of that life and spirit which is now chiefly confined to her greater writers in verse. In that case, we should have had more than one Lafontaine to delight us.

In English, thanks to our neuter gender, poets are allowed to do as they choose in this matter; and in many cases they have chosen to represent all three of the earlier seasons in a feminine form—not only spring and summer, but autumn also—as we have just seen in the case of Spenser. Thomson, however, has made Summer a youth, a sort of Apollo:

> "Child of the Sun, refulgent Summer comes
>
> .   .   .   .
>
> He comes attended by the sultry hours,
> And ever fanning breezes on his way."

And his autumn also, "crowned *with the sickle* and the wheaten sheaf," scarcely looks like a female.

In climates still warmer than those of Greece and Rome, the ears of grain might correctly have been woven into the wreath of May. Ruth must have gleaned the fields of Boaz during the month of May, or some time between the Passover and Pentecost—festivals represented by our Easter and Whitsunday—for that was the harvest-time of Judea.

Many of the poets of our mother-speech have, however, followed the examples of Spenser and Thomson, in representing autumn as the season of

the grain-harvest in England. Among others, Keats, who also gives a glowing picture of the season, in those verses, full of poetical images, beginning—

> "Season of mists, and mellow fruitfulness!
> Close bosom friend of the maturing sun."

He then asks, "Who has not often seen thee

> ". . . sitting careless on a granary floor,
> Thy hair soft-lifted by the winnowing wind;
> Or on a half-reaped furrow lain asleep,
> Drows'd with the fume of poppies; while thy hook
> Spares the next swathe, and all its twined flowers!"

But while such poets as Spenser and Thomson give a warmer picture of
the season than many of their contemporaries, on another point, at which
we are looking just now, they do not differ from others—neither of them sees
any beauty in the foliage of the season. It is true, Thomson speaks, in one
line, of

> "Autumn beaming o'er the yellow woods,"

but this seems an accidental epithet, for it does not occur in the descriptive
part of the season. When he is expressly engaged in painting autumn for us,
he tells us of the "tawny copse." Another passage of his commences in a way
which at first leads one to expect some praise of the autumn foliage, for he
speaks of the "many-colored woods." To an American, this immediately
suggests the idea of scarlet and golden tints; but he proceeds in a very different tone—his "many-colored woods" are all sad.

> "Shade deep'ning over shade, the country round
> Imbrown: a clouded umbrage, dusk and dun,
> Of ev'ry hue, from wan declining green
> To sooty dark."

Sober enough, in good sooth. And then he strips the trees amid gloomy fogs
and mists:

> "And o'er the sky the leafy deluge streams;
> Till chok'd and matted with the dreary shower,
> The forest walks at ev'ry rising gale
> Roll wide the wither'd waste."

It would require a general and accurate knowledge of English verse, and a very correct memory, to say positively that no allusion to the beauty of the autumnal woods may be found in the older poets of England; but certainly, if such are to be met with, they do not lie within the range of every-day reading. Are there any such in Milton, skillful as he was in picturing the groves and bowers of Eden?

> "Thick as autumnal leaves that strew the brooks
> In Vallambrosa,"

will occur to the memory; but we have no coloring here. Is there a single line of this nature in Shakspeare, among the innumerable comparisons in which his fancy luxuriated? Shall we find one in the glowing pages of Spenser? In Dryden? In Chaucer, so minute in description, and delighting so heartily in nature–from the humble daisy to the great oaks, with "their leavès newe?" One is almost confident that in these, and every other instance, the answer will prove a negative.

Much the boldest touch of the kind, remembered at present, in European verse, is found in a great French rural writer, Delille; speaking of the woods in Autumn, he says:

> "Le pourpre, l'orangé, l'opale, l'incarnat,
> De leurs riches couleurs étalent l'abondance."

But these lines stand almost alone, differing entirely from other descriptions of the season by himself and many of his countrymen, with whom it has very generally been "*la pâle automne.*" Probably in these lines Delille had some particular season in view. European autumn is not always dull; she has her bright days, and at times a degree of beauty in her foliage. From the more northern countries, as far south as Italy, one may occasionally see something of this kind, reminding one of the season in America. More than a hundred years since, Addison alluded briefly, in his travels, to the beauty of the autumnal woods in Southern Germany, where, indeed, the foliage is said to be finer than in any other part of Europe; but nowhere, I believe, has he given the colored leaves a place in verse. Delille, it must be remembered, was a more modern poet, writing at the close of the last and the commencement of the present century; and just about that time allusions of this kind were finding their way into the literature of Europe.

A very decided change in this respect has indeed taken place within the last fifty or sixty years. English writers, particularly, seem suddenly to have discovered Autumn under a new character; two very different pictures are now given of her; one is still "Autumn, melancholy wight!" while the other bears a much gayer expression. Just now allusions to beautiful "autumnal tints" have become very much the fashion in English books of all sorts; and one might think the leaves had been dyed, for the first time, to please the present generation. In reality, there can hardly have been any change in this respect since the days of Chaucer; whence, then, comes this altered tone?

Some foundation for the change may doubtless be found in the fact, that all descriptive writing, on natural objects, is now much less vague and general than it was formerly; it has become very much more definite and accurate within the last half century. Some persons have attributed this change, so far as it regards England, to the taste for landscape painting, which has been so generally cultivated in that country during the same period. Probably this has had its effect. The partiality for a more natural style in gardening may also have done something toward bringing the public mind round to a natural taste on all rural subjects. It is seldom, however, that a great change in public taste or opinion is produced by a single direct cause only; there are generally many lesser collateral causes working together, aiding and strengthening each other meanwhile, ere decided results are produced. This is perceptible in small matters, as well as in matters of importance. Something more than a mere partiality for landscape painting has been at work; people had grown tired of mere vapid, conventional repetitions, they felt the want of something more positive, more real; the head called for more of truth, the heart for more of life. And so, writers began to look out of the window more frequently; when writing a pastoral they turned away from the little porcelain shepherds and shepherdesses, standing in high-heeled shoes and powdered wigs upon every mantel-piece, and they fixed their eyes upon the real living Roger and Dolly in the hay-field. Then they came to see that it would do just as well, nay, far better, to seat Roger and Dolly under a hawthorn, or an oak of merry England, than to paint them beneath a laurel, or an ilex of Greece or Rome; in short, they learned at length to look at nature by the light of the sun, and not by the glimmerings of the poet's lamp. And a great step this was, not only in art, but in moral and intellectual progress.[29] One of the first among the later English poets, who led the way back into the track of truth, was the simple, kindly, upright Cowper; and assuredly it was a task worthy of a Christian poet—that of endeavoring to paint the works of the Creation in their native dignity, rather than tricked out in conventional devices of man.

Still, all this might have taken place without producing that especial attention to autumn, perceptible in later English writers; that very frequent mention of its softer days and varied foliage, which marks a change of feeling from the "chilling autumn" of Shakspeare, and the foliage "dusk and dun" of Thomson. One is led to believe that the American autumn has helped to set the fashion for the sister season of the Old World; that the attention which the season commands in this country, has opened the eyes of Europeans to any similar graces of the same months in their own climates; the gloom is less heeded by them, while every pleasing touch is noted with gratification. In the same way, we now see frequent allusions to the "Indian summer" by Englishmen, in their own island, where this last sweet smile of the declining year was entirely unheeded until its very marked character in this country had attracted admiration. Our native writers, as soon as we had writers of our own, pointed out very early both the sweetness of the Indian summer, and the magnificence of the autumnal changes. In fact, they must have been dull and blind not to have marked both these features of the season, as we usually enjoy them. And here, indeed, we find the precise extent of the difference between the relative beauty of autumn in Europe and in America: with us it is quite impossible to overlook these peculiar charms of the autumnal months; while in Europe, though not wholly wanting, they remained unnoticed, unobserved, for ages. Had the same soft atmosphere of the "Indian summer" warmed the woods of Windsor, year after year, while Geoffrey Chaucer roamed among their glades, the English would have had a word or a phrase to express the charm of such days, before they borrowed one from another continent. Had the maples, and oaks, and ashes, on the banks of the Avon, colored the waters of that stream, year after year, with their own scarlet, and crimson, and purple, while Will. Shakspeare, the bailiff's son, was shooting his arrows on its banks, we should have found many a rich and exquisite image connected with autumnal hours hovering about the footsteps of Lear and Hamlet, Miranda and Imogen, and Rosalind. Had the woods of England been as rich as our own, their branches would have been interwoven among the masques of Ben Jonson and Milton; they would have had a place in more than one of Spenser's beautiful pictures. All these are wanting now. Perhaps the void may be in a measure filled up for us by great poets of our own; but even then one charm will fail—the mellow light of eld, which illumines the page of the old poet, will be missed; for that, like the rich flavor of old wine, is the gift of Time alone.

In the meanwhile, however, the march of Autumn through the land is not a silent one—it is already accompanied by song. Scarce a poet of any fame among us who has not at least some graceful verse, some glowing image connected with the season; and year after year the song must become fuller, and sweeter, and clearer.

In those parts of this continent which answer to the medium climates of Europe, and where Autumn has a decided character of her own, the season is indeed a noble one. Rich in bounty, ripening the blended fruits of two hemispheres, beauty is also her inalienable dower. Clear skies and cheerful breezes are more frequent throughout her course than storms or clouds. Fogs are rare indeed. Mild, balmy airs seem to delight in attending her steps, while the soft haze of the Indian summer is gathered like a choice veil about her brows, throwing a charm of its own over every feature. The grain-harvest has been given to Summer; of all its treasures, she preserves alone the fragrant buckwheat and the golden maize. The nobler fruits are all hers–the finer peaches and plums, the choicest apples, pears, and grapes. The homely, but precious root-harvest belongs to her–winter stores for man and his herds. And now, when the year is drawing to a close, when the blessings of the earth have been gathered and stored, when every tree and plant has borne its fruits, when every field has yielded its produce, why should the sun shine brightly now? What has he more to ripen for us at this late day?

At this very period, when the annual labors of the husbandman are drawing to a close, when the first light frosts ripen the wild grapes in the woods, and open the husks of the hickory-nuts, bringing the latest fruits of the year to maturity, these are the days when, here and there, in the groves you will find a maple-tree whose leaves are touched with the gayest colors; those are the heralds which announce the approach of a brilliant pageant–the moment chosen by Autumn to keep the great harvest-home of America is at hand. In a few days comes another and a sharper frost, and the whole face of the country is changed; we enjoy, with wonder and delight, a natural spectacle, great and beautiful, beyond the reach of any human means.

We are naturally accustomed to associate the idea of verdure with foliage–leaves should surely be green! But now we gaze in wonder as we behold colors so brilliant and so varied hung upon every tree. Tints that you have admired among the darker tulips and roses, the richer lilies and dahlias of the flower-garden–colors that have pleased your eye among the fine silks and wools of a lady's delicate embroidery–dyes that the shopman shows off with complacency among his Cashmeres and velvets–hues reserved by the artist for his proudest works–these we now see fluttering in the leaves of old oaks, and tupeloes, liquid ambers, chestnuts, and maples!

We behold the green woods becoming one mass of rich and varied coloring. It would seem as though Autumn, in honor of this high holiday, had collected together all the past glories of the year, adding them to her own; she borrows the gay colors that have been lying during the summer months among the flowers, in the fruits, upon the plumage of the bird, on the wings of the butterfly, and working them together in broad and glowing masses, she throws them over the forest to grace her triumph. Like some great festival of an Italian city, where the people bring rich tapestries and hang them in their streets; where they unlock chests of heir-looms, and bring to light brilliant draperies, which they suspend from their windows and balconies, to gleam in the sunshine.

The hanging woods of a mountainous country are especially beautiful at this season; the trees throwing out their branches, one above another, in bright variety of coloring and outline, every individual of the gay throng having a fancy of his own to humor. The oak loves a deep, rich red, or a warm scarlet, though some of his family are partial to yellow. The chestnuts are all of one shadeless mass of gold-color, from the highest to the lowest branch. The bass-wood, or linden, is orange. The aspen, with its silvery stem and branches, flutters in a lighter shade, like the wrought gold of the jeweller. The sumach, with its long, pinnated leaf, is of a brilliant scarlet. The pepperidge is almost purple, and some of the ashes approach the same shade during certain seasons. Other ashes, with the birches and beech, hickory and elms, have their own tints of yellow. That beautiful and common vine, the Virginia creeper, is a vivid cherry-color. The sweet-gum is vermilion. The Viburnum tribe and dog-woods are dyed in lake. As for the maples, they always rank first among the show; there is no other tree which contributes singly so much to the beauty of the season, for it unites more of brilliancy, with more of variety, than any of its companions; with us it is also more common than any other tree. Here you have a soft maple, vivid scarlet from the highest to the lowest leaf; there is another, a sugar maple, a pure sheet of gold; this is dark crimson like the oak, that is vermilion; another is parti-colored, pink and yellow, green and red; yonder is one of a deep purplish hue; this is still green, that is mottled in patches, another is shaded; still another blends all these colors on its own branches, in capricious confusion, the different limbs, the separate twigs, the single leaves, varying from each other in distinct colors, and shaded tints. And in every direction a repetition of this magnificent picture meets the eye: in the woods that skirt the dimpled meadows, in the thickets and copses of the fields, in the bushes which fringe the brook, in the trees which line the streets and road-sides, in those of the lawns and gardens—brilliant and vivid in the nearest groves, gradually lessening in tone upon the farther woods and successive knolls,

until, in the distant back-ground, the hills are colored by a mingled confusion of tints, which defy the eye to seize them.

Among this brilliant display, there are usually some few trees which fade,
and wither, and dry into a homely brown, without appearing to feel the general influence; the sycamores, the locusts, for instance, and often the elms
also, have little beauty to attract the eye, seldom aiming at more than a tolerable yellow, though at times they may be brighter.

Imported trees, transplanted originally from the Old World, preserve, as
a rule, the more sober habits of their ancestral woods; the Lombardy poplar
and the weeping willow are only pale yellow; the apple and pear trees, and
some of the garden shrubs, lilacs, and syringas, and snow-balls, generally
wither, without brilliancy, though once in a while they have a fancy for
something rather gayer than pale yellow or russet, and are just touched with
red or purple.

Other trees, again, from some accident of position or other cause, will remain a clear green, weeks after their companions of the same species are in
full color.

But amid the general gayety, the few exceptions are scarcely observed,
unless they are pointed out, and the beautiful effect of the great picture remains unbroken.

One observes also, that the spirit of the scene is carried out in many lesser
details, for which we are scarcely prepared. Walking through the woods and
fields, you find many of the smaller shrubs very prettily colored, little annuals also, and the seedlings of the forest-trees. The tiny maples especially,
not longer than your finger, with half a dozen little leaflets, are often as delicately colored as blossoms, pink, and red, and yellow. Some of the flowering plants, also, the sarsaparillas and May-stars, with their finely-cut leaves,
are frequently of a soft, clear straw-color. One may make very handsome
bunches of these bright leaves; a branch of the golden chestnut, or aspen, or
birch, a crimson twig from a young oak, another of scarlet maple, a long,
plume-like leaf of the red sumach, with some of the lesser seedlings, and the
prettiest of the wood-plants, make up a bouquet which almost rivals the
dahlias in brilliancy.

Some persons occasionally complain that this period of the year, this brilliant change in the foliage, causes melancholy feelings, arousing sad and sorrowful ideas, like the flush on the hectic cheek. But surely its more natural
meaning is of a very different import. Here is no sudden blight of youth and
beauty, no sweet hopes of life are blasted, no generous aim at usefulness and
advancing virtue is cut short; the year is drawing to its natural term, the sea-

sons have run their usual course, all their blessings have been enjoyed, all our precious things are cared for; there is nothing of untimeliness, nothing of disappointment in these shorter days and lessening heats of autumn. As well may we mourn over the gorgeous coloring of the clouds, which collect to pay homage to the setting sun, because they proclaim the close of day; as well may we lament the brilliancy of the evening star, and the silvery brightness of the crescent moon, just ascending into the heavens, because they declare the approach of night and her shadowy train!

Mark the broad land glowing in a soft haze, every tree and grove wearing its gorgeous autumnal drapery; observe the vivid freshness of the evergreen verdure; note amid the gold and crimson woods, the blue lake, deeper in tint at this season than at any other; see a more quiet vein of shading in the paler lawns and pastures, and the dark-brown earth of the freshly-ploughed fields; raise your eyes to the cloudless sky above, filled with soft and pearly tints, and then say, what has gloom to do with such a picture? Tell us, rather, where else on earth shall the human eye behold coloring so magnificent and so varied, spread over a field so vast, within one noble view? In very truth, the glory of these last waning days of the season, proclaims a grandeur of beneficence which should rather make our poor hearts swell with gratitude at each return of the beautiful autumn accorded to us.

Thursday, 12th.—Rather cool this afternoon. As we were walking to and fro, about twilight, a bat came flickering across our path several times. It was quite a small one, and perhaps inexperienced in life, for most of his kind have already disappeared—we have not seen one for some weeks. There are said to be five different kinds of bats in this State, and we have a good share here. One evening in the month of August, there were no less than five of these creatures in the house at the same time; after a prolonged fight, two of them were routed; the other three kept possession of the ground all night.

Friday, 13th.—Delightful day. Long walk in the woods. Found a few asters and golden-rods, silver-rods, and everlastings, scattered about. The flowers are becoming rare, and chary of their presence; still, so long as the green grass grows, they lie scattered about, one here, another there, it may be in the shady woods, or it may be in the flower-border; reminding one of those precious things which sweeten the field of life—kindly feelings, holy thoughts, and just deeds—which may still be gleaned by those who earnestly seek them, even in the latest days of the great pilgrimage.

The woods are very beautiful; on Mount—the groundwork of the forest was colored red by the many little whortleberry bushes growing there—they are brighter than usual. Here and there we found fresh berries on them, and a white flower among their red leaves. Some of the wych-hazels have lost their foliage entirely, the yellow blossoms hanging on leafless branches.

A number of the trees, in low situations and along the shores of the lake, are quite green still. The alders are all unchanged. So are the apple-trees, lilacs, syringas, the willows and aspens. The poplars are beginning to turn yellowish on their lower branches, their tops are still clear green.

Saturday, 14th.—Pleasant day. Walked some distance along the bank of the river. Gathered handsome berries of the cranberry-tree. Found many vines along the bank in that direction; bitter-sweet, with its red berries; hairy honeysuckle; green-briars, with their dark-blue berries, besides many Virginia creepers and grape-vines. Observed several soft maples of a clear gold-color throughout, while others near them were bright crimson; they are not so often variegated as the sugar maple. Saw a handsome thorn-tree vivid red. The large leaves of the moose-wood are yellow. The mountain maple is pinkish red. Plums and wild cherries reddish. A handsome dogwood, of the alternate-leaved variety, deep lake; it was quite a tree. The Viburnums are generally well colored at this season; the large leaves of the hobble-bush especially are quite showy now. This is the American "wayfaring tree," but on several accounts it scarcely deserves the name; though pretty in its way, it is only a shrub, and instead of giving pleasure to the wanderer, it is frequently an obstacle in his path, for the long branches will sometimes root themselves anew from the ends, thus making a tangled thicket about them; this habit, indeed, has given to the shrub the name of "hobble-bush." The blackberry-bushes are a deep brownish red; the wild raspberries purplish red. Altogether, the shrubs and bushes strike us as more vividly colored than usual. Every season has some peculiarity of its own in this way, the trees and bushes varying from year to year, which is an additional source of interest in the autumnal pageant. A particular maple, which for years has turned a deep purple crimson, is now yellow, with a flush of scarlet. Observed several ashes yellow shaded with purple, the two colors being very clearly marked on the same tree.

Monday, 16th.—Charming weather; bright and warm, with hazy Indian summer atmosphere. They are harvesting the last maize-fields; some farmers "top" the stalks, that is to say, cut off the upper half, and leave the lower ears several weeks longer to ripen. Others cut the whole crop at once, gathering the ears first, then cutting the stalks and leaving them to stand in sheaves about the fields for a few days. The maize harvest is usually several weeks going on, as some farmers are much earlier with the task than others. The red buckwheat sheaves are also left standing about some farms much longer than others; they are seen in many fields just now, in neighborhood with the maize-stalks.

The birds are quite numerous still; many robins running about the lawn. Gnats and gray flies, innumerable, are dancing in the sunshine. Saw yellow butterflies. Heard a few field-crickets chirruping cheerfully.

Tuesday, 17th.—In our walk this morning, observed a large stone farm-house, with maples grouped about in most brilliant color; a party of men were husking maize in the foreground; a group of cows grazing, in one di-rection, and a cart with a pile of noble pumpkins lying in the other. It would have made a good picture of an American autumn scene. The coloring of the trees was just what one could wish for such a purpose, and the contrast with the stone house and gray barns was all that could be desired.

It is to be regretted that we have not more superior pictures of autumnal scenes, for the subjects are so fine that they are worthy of the greatest pen-cils. It is true, Mr. Cole, and some others of our distinguished artists, have given us a few pictures of this kind; but in no instance, I believe, has a work of this nature been yet considered as a chef-d'œuvre of the painter. No doubt there must be great difficulties, as well as great beauties, connected with the subject. There is no precedent for such coloring as nature requires here among the works of old masters, and the American artist must neces-sarily become an innovator; nay, more, we are all of us so much accustomed to think of a landscape only in its spring or summer aspects, that when we see a painting where the trees are yellow and scarlet, and purple, instead of being green, we have an unpleasant suspicion that the artist may be impos-ing on us in some of his details. This is one of those instances in which it requires no little daring simply to copy nature. And then there are other difficulties in the necessary studies: three or four weeks at the utmost are all that is allowed to the painter from year to year; and from one autumn to an-other he may almost persuade himself that he was deceived in this or that tint, preserved by his sketches. In short, to become a superior and faithful painter of autumn in this country, must require a course of study quite pe-culiar, and prolonged over half a lifetime. Still, some landscape Rubens or Titian may yet, perhaps, arise among us, whose pencil shall do full justice to this beautiful and peculiar subject.

Independently of this higher branch of art, one would gladly see the beauty of our autumnal foliage turned to account in many other ways; as yet it has scarcely made an impression upon the ornamental and useful arts, for which it is admirably adapted. What beautiful arabesques might be taken from our forests, when in brilliant color, for frescoes or paper-hangings! What patterns for the dyer, and weaver, and printer; what models for the artificial-flower makers and embroiderers; what designs for the richest kind of carpeting! Before long, those beautiful models which fill the land every autumn, must assuredly attract the attention they deserve from manufacturers and mechanics; that they have not already done so, is a striking proof of our imitative habits in everything of this kind. Had the woods about Lyons been filled with American maples and creepers, we may rest assured that the shops in Broadway and Chestnut street would long since have been filled with ribbons, and silks, and brocades, copied from them.

Wednesday, 18th.–Rainy, mild. The woods, alas! are beginning to fade. Many trees are losing something of their vivid coloring, and others are rapidly dropping their leaves. People observe that the forest has not remained in full color as long as usual this fall. The last twenty-four hours of rainy weather has had a great effect. A week or two earlier, rain will often heighten the coloring, but after the leaves begin to lose their life it hastens their decay.

The larches are just touched with yellow; hitherto they have been clear green. The willows and abele-trees are unchanged. The shrubbery is getting quite gay, the rose-bushes turning scarlet and yellow. The wild roses are generally vivid yellow. The sweet-briars are already bare of leaves. The snowball is purplish; some of the lilacs are more yellow than common, while others are withering slowly, in green, as usual. Some of the scarlet honeysuckles show quite handsome branches, red, and yellow, and purple, in the same large leaf. Saw a wild gooseberry in the woods, with leaves as brilliant as those of a maple.

A number of birds about the house; passengers on their way south, or winter birds coming in from the woods. Snow-birds, chicadees, crested titmice, and sparrows. Also observed a cross-looking butcher-bird sitting by himself; this is the bird which impales grasshoppers and insects, fastening them upon the thorns and twigs about the bushes; probably he does it from that sort of instinct which makes the dog bury a bone, and the squirrel lay up nuts; having eaten enough for the present, he puts this game of his by for another occasion. We have never heard, however, whether they return to feed upon these impaled insects. The habit has a cruel look, certainly, and no wonder the bird is rather out of favor. Mr. Wilson says the German farmers in Pennsylvania call him Neuntodter, or Ninekiller, because they believe that he allows himself to impale nine grasshoppers daily; they also accuse him of devouring their *peas,* or those honey-loving insects which live in hives, called *bees* by most of us.

Thursday, 19th.—The falling leaves are still brightly colored, strewing the paths and village side-walks in many places; one is often tempted to stoop by the brilliancy of some of these fallen leaves, it seems a pity to leave them to wither in their beauty. When dried they preserve their colors a long time, especially when varnished; of course they lose a degree of brilliancy, but much less than the flowers.

The brooks and streams are often gayly strewn with the fallen foliage; the mill-dam at the Red Brook was sprinkled this afternoon with bright leaves, red and yellow, like a gay fleet from fairy-land.

Friday, 20th.—Rain. Many trees in the village losing their leaves very perceptibly; those that are yet in leaf have faded decidedly within the last thirty-six hours. The woods are still in color, however. Larches turning yellow rapidly. Willows unchanged. Evergreens in great beauty. The bare locusts brown with pods. Grass, bright green, well sprinkled with colored leaves.

Robins and a few other birds flitting about; saw sparrows, and several blue-birds, with them.

Saturday, 21st.—Mild, light rain; gnats dancing in spite of the rain-drops. Gray branches becoming more numerous every hour. Woods generally fading, though some trees brilliant still, red oaks and yellow birches; along the lake shore the trees are quite gay yet. The poplars in the village are beginning to drop their leaves. They first become bare below, while their upper branches are in full leaf, unlike most other trees, which lose their foliage from above, downward.

Monday, 23d.—Clear and cool. Light frost last night, the first we have had for a fortnight. Bright leaves here and there sailing in the light noon-day air, looking like large butterflies; some of them, after being severed from the branch, will sail about a minute or two before they touch the earth. But the woods are growing dull. Willows and abele-trees, with a few garden plants and hedges, are all that is left of green among the deciduous foliage. The apple-trees are losing their leaves; they seldom have much coloring, and often wither from green to russet without any gay tint at all.

Saw a few musquitoes in the woods. We have very few of these annoying insects in our neighborhood. In the village we seldom see one; in the woods they sometimes attack us.

The summer birds are rapidly deserting the village; the last few days have thinned their numbers very much. We have not seen one to-day.

Tuesday, 24th.—Mild rain. The chicadees are gathering about the houses again; these birds are resident with us through the year, but we seldom see them in summer; until the month of June they are often met fluttering about the groves near at hand, but from that time until the autumn is advancing, perhaps you will not see one. We have frequently watched for them in vain during the warm weather, not only near the village, but in the woods also, and we have never yet seen one at midsummer. This morning there was a large flock in the grounds, fluttering about among the half-naked branches. One is pleased to see the merry little creatures again.

The snow-birds are also resident in our hills through the year, but unlike the chicadees, they show themselves at all seasons. You can hardly go into the woods without meeting them; many are seen running in and out about the fences, and they may almost be called village birds with us; at all seasons you may find them about the gardens and lawns, and I have no doubt some of them have nests in the village. The greater number, however, retire to the fields and hill-sides. At one moment this afternoon there was a meeting in our own trees of two large flocks, chicadees and snow-birds; they were all in fine spirits at the approach of winter, restless and chirping, flitting hither and thither with rapid, eager movements. Among the throng were two little birds of another kind, much smaller in size, and of a plain plumage; they were evidently strangers, possibly on their way southward; they perched on a high twig apart from the flock, and sat there quietly together, side by side, as if weary; they remained on the same branch more than a quarter of an hour, just turning their little heads occasionally to look with amazement at the flirting frolicksome chicadees. They were about the size of wrens, but were perched too high for us to discover of what species they were.

Wednesday, 25th.—Pleasant. Long drive. Calm, sweet day. Here and there dashes of warm coloring still in the woods, although in other places they are dull, and nearly bare. The evergreens of all kinds are in triumph; their verdure is brilliantly fresh and vivid, in their untarnished summer growth, while all other foliage is fading, and falling from the naked branches. The larches look prettily; a few days since they were entirely green, but now they are wholly yellow, though in full leaf, which, from their evergreen form, attracts the more attention. The abele-trees look oddly, with their fluttering leaves, silvery on one side, and gold-color on the reverse.

A robin flew past us on the highway; how often one meets them alone at this season, as if they had been left behind by their companions.

Thursday, 26th.—Cloudy, but mild. Long drive by the lake shore. Sky, water, and fields alike gray. Woods getting bare, yet vivid touches of yellow here and there, the orange of the birch, or lighter yellow of the aspen, enlivening the deepening grays. The village still looks leafy from the distance, chiefly from its willows. We passed a group of fine native poplars, very large, and quite green still; what is singular, a very large maple near them was also in full leaf, and partially green, though very many of its brethren are quite bare. These trees stood near the lake shore. The whole bank between the road and the water was still gay, with a fringe of underwood in color. Many asters of the common sorts were growing here, with golden-rods also, and a strawberry blite in crimson flower. The asters, and golden-rods, and nabali, and hawk-worts, along this bank have been innumerable through the season, and now that they are in seed, their downy heads look prettily mingled with the plants still in blossom, and the bushes still in leaf; the weather has been quiet, and the ripening blossoms, undisturbed by the wind, preserve the form of their delicate heads perfectly, some tawny, some gray, some silvery white, powdered flowers, as it were, like the powdered beauties of by-gone fashions. The pyramid golden-rod is really very pleasing in this airy, gossamer state. A large portion of our later flowers seem to ripen their seed in this manner. The gossamer of the willow-herb and that of the silk-wort are perhaps the most beautiful kinds, so purely white, but the down lies concealed within the pods, and as soon as these are opened the seeds escape, flying off on their beautiful silvery plumes. The down of the asters and golden-rods, however, remains a long time on the plants; and so does that of the fire-weed, which is very white.

What ugly things are the shrivelled thistles at this season! They look utterly worthless, more like the refuse of a past year than plants of this summer's growth; and yet there is life in their withered stalks, for here and there a purple blossom is trying to flower among the ragged branches.

A very large flock of wild ducks, flying northward over the lake, alighted on the water within half a mile of us; there must have been a hundred of them, if not more. We seldom see so many together in our waters.

Friday, 27th.—At early dawn this morning, just as the sky was becoming flushed with sun-rise colors, we saw a large flock of wild geese flying steadily to the southward. They moved in a regular wedge-shaped phalanx, as usual, with their leader a little in advance. Perhaps they had passed the night in our lake; they are frequently seen here, though rarely shot by our "gunners." They seem often to travel by daylight. The ducks are said to migrate generally at night, especially the Mallard or common wild duck. It was a beautiful sight to see the flock, this morning; it reminded one of Mr. Bryant's noble "Water-fowl," simply, however, because one never sees the wild fowl travelling through the air, spring or autumn, without thinking of those fine verses. In the present case it was morning, and a whole flock were in movement; Mr. Bryant saw his bird in the evening, and it was alone; still the lines would recur to one:

> "Whither, 'midst falling dew,
>   While glow the heavens with the last steps of day,
> Far through their rosy depths, dost thou pursue
>   Thy solitary way."

A flock of migratory birds can never fail, indeed, to be a beautiful and striking sight. The proud ships crossing the vast ocean, with man at the helm, are not a more impressive spectacle than these lesser creatures travelling through

> "The desert and illimitable air—
> Lone, wandering, but not lost."

Doubtless the flocks which now pass over the valley are as nothing compared with the throngs that went and came when the red man hunted here; still, we never fail to see them spring and fall. Many are the different varieties which come and go, and various are their habits of travelling. Some fly by day, others at night; some are silent, others utter loud and peculiar cries; these move in a regular phalanx, those in a careless crowd; some have leaders, others need none; these move rapidly, and directly toward their goal, others linger weeks on the way. Some travel in flocks, others in pairs; with these the males fly first, with those all move together; some follow the coast, others take an inland course.

And how much pleasure the birds give and receive by their migrations! This singular instinct implanted in the breast of the fowls of the air, is indeed a very touching instance of the tenderness of Providence, who not only bestows what is necessary on His creatures, but adds to the cup of life so many innocent pleasures. Some birds are stationary, and, doubtless, it would have been easy to have ordered that all should be so; but now we find that many of the most beautiful and pleasing of the race pass and repass annually over a broad expanse of the earth, giving and receiving enjoyment as they move onward. Many of those which are the most cheering and delightful spread themselves over half the earth: among these are the delicate wrens and humming-birds, the gay swallows, those noble singers, the thrushes; while the larger and more dangerous birds of prey are few in numbers, and chiefly confined to particular regions. No doubt the change of food, of air, of climate, is a source of enjoyment to the birds; nay, the very effort of the journey itself is probably accompanied with that gratification which is usually connected with the healthful, natural exercise of the higher powers of every living being. And how much delight do they afford mankind! Their first appearance, with the hopeful hours of spring; their voices, their pleasing forms, their cheerful movements, nay, their very departure in autumn, all bring to our hearts some pleasures, and thoughts, and feelings, which we should not know without them. Wanderers though they be, yet the birds of one's native ground are a part of home to us.

Perhaps the birds generally follow the same course, year after year, in their annual journeyings. There are facts which lead one to believe so. It is already proved that the same individuals, of various tribes, will return to the same groves for many successive seasons. It has also been observed that certain birds are seen to the north and south of a particular region every year; but within certain limits they are never met with. Like the house-wren, for instance, which avoids Louisiana, and yet passes farther to the southward every autumn. Other cases of the same kind might be named. A well-authenticated story is also told by Mr. Wilson of a wild goose which had been tamed on Long Island, but the following spring flew away to join a passing flock on its way to the northward. The succeeding autumn, as the farmer was standing in his barn-yard, he observed a flock of wild geese on the wing; one of these left the flock and alighted near him, proving to be his old pet. Now, the party which the goose joined was probably the same as that with which she returned, and here they were passing directly over the same farm, going and coming.

The flocks that pass over our own little lake note it, perhaps, as the last in the long line of inland waters, the thousand lakes of all sizes passed on their way from the arctic seas. There is no sheet of fresh water of any size to the southward and eastward of our own. Possibly, the celebrated canvas-backs pass us every year on their way to the Chesapeake, for the mouth of our own river is favorite ground with those celebrated birds. Very few of the canvas-backs remain in this State; only a very small number are seen occasionally in the Hudson.

Saturday, 28th.–The woods are fading fast, losing their leaves rapidly. Here and there, however, we yet see a birch or aspen, perhaps on the lake shore, perhaps on the mountain-side, still vividly yellow. Seen thus amid the dull and dreary woods, they look like forgotten torches, burning among the wrecks of past revels.

Monday, 30th.–Mild, gray day; air soft and spring-like. Toward evening walked to the glen, along the Green Brook. Met a solitary robin. The flocks of summer birds have now entirely disappeared; only a few stragglers are seen, shy and solitary, as though they had been forgotten. We frequently throw out seeds and crumbs for the birds at this season; but it is seldom, indeed, one has the pleasure of seeing the little creatures eat them. As long as there are berries on the vines and bushes, and seeds on the flowers and weeds, they prefer to forage for themselves. They often alight near the birds-seed and bread thrown on the gravel, without touching a crumb; and the provision thrown out for them will lie unheeded until the snow falls upon it. Having made up their minds to leave us, they are not to be coaxed into staying by any friendly attentions. Perhaps our robin, in particular, may be more shy than that of Europe. We hear of the European red-breast being frequently fed upon crumbs about farm-houses in cold weather. Christiana, in the Pilgrim's Progress, thought they lived entirely on such food: "Then, as they were coming in from abroad, they espied a robin with a great spider in his mouth: so the Interpreter said, 'Look here!' So they looked, and Mercy wondered; but Christiana said, 'What a disparagement it is to such a little pretty bird as the robin red-breast is! he being also a bird above many, that loveth to maintain a kind of sociableness with men. I had thought they had lived upon crumbs of bread, or upon other such harmless matter. I like him worse than I did.'"

We have no right to complain, however, if robin prefers spiders to bread, since we in our turn are capable of making a very good meal of robin himself; and so, after abusing him for neglecting the crumbs, we give a pretty anecdote, much to his credit; it is found in the "Gleanings" of Mr. Jesse, occurred in England, and is vouched for by Mr. Jesse himself. A gentleman had directed a wagon to be packed with hampers and boxes, intending to send it some distance; its departure was delayed, however, and it was placed under a shed, packed as it was. While there, says Mr. Jesse, "a pair of robins built their nest among some straw in the wagon, and had hatched their young just before it was sent away. One of the old birds, instead of being frightened away by the motion of the wagon, only left its nest from time to time, for the purpose of flying to the nearest hedge for food, for its young; and thus alternately affording warmth and nourishment to them, it arrived at Worthing. The affection of this bird having been observed by the wagoner, he took care, in unloading, not to disturb the robin's nest; and my readers will, I am sure, be glad to hear that the robin and its young ones returned in safety to Walton Heath, being the place from whence they had set out. Whether it was the male or the female robin which kept with the wagon, I have not been able to ascertain, but most probably the latter, as what will not a mother's love and a mother's tenderness induce her to perform? The distance the wagon went in going and returning could not have been less than one hundred miles."

Tuesday, 31st.—About a mile from the village, there runs a little stream whose waters are darker in color than others in the neighborhood, and called, on that account, the Red Brook—the first humble tributary of a river which may boast many a broad and flowing branch, ere it reaches the ocean. It comes toward the highway through a narrow ravine thickly shaded by forest-trees, and then passing beneath a bridge, winds through open meadows until it joins the river. This little stream turns a saw-mill on one side of the highway, and on the other fills the vats of a tannery; several roads draw toward the point from different directions, and a little hamlet is springing up here, which has been chosen as the site of a school-house.

The building itself, standing within bow-shot of the saw-mill, is of stone, and one of the best in the neighborhood. The situation is good, and the spot might easily have been made very pleasant by merely leaving a few scattered trees here and there; but they have been all swept away to feed the saw-mill, and the banks of the ravine, beautifully shaded only a short time since, are now becoming every day more bare. A spring of water, where the children fill their pitchers, falls with a pleasant trickling sound into a rude trough hard by; a single tree, with a bench in the shade, would have given a friendly, rural look to the spot, but neither shade nor seat is there. Even a tuft of young hemlocks, which stood on the bank near the spring, have been recently cut down.

The smaller towns and villages of this country have generally a pleasing character, a cheerful, flourishing aspect, with their trees, their gardens, and neat door-yards, which give them an advantage over the more close and confined villages of the Old World. But with the hamlet, the mere cluster of a dozen buildings, the case is different. The European hamlet is often a very picturesque spot, for it frequently happens that the cottages have grown up about some half-ruined tower, or ancient bridge, or old well, or a quaint-looking mill, or perhaps some old religious stone. With us the central point of a hamlet can seldom boast of more attractions than a smithy, or a small store and post-office, or a naked school-house, while the spirit which takes pleasure in local public improvement, seems to lie dormant until aroused by the ambition of becoming a greater "settlement;" it is only then that trees which a few years before were all blindly cut away, are now carefully replaced by regular plantations, and the general aspect of things is brought under consideration. But the hamlet at the Red Brook has not yet reached this point of progress. Many trees have been cut down, scarce one set out. There is not even a classic birch within shading distance of the school-house; one looks in vain for the

> "–birchen tree
> Which learning near her little dome did stowe."

The "birchen twig," that whilome sceptre of power in the hand of dame or master, is, however, no longer an essential part of the school-house furniture; like Solomon's rod, it has well nigh become a mere tradition. The red-cherry ruler is in modern times the ensign of office.

Many, indeed, are the changes that have taken place, without and within the school-house walls, since the days of Shenstone and the dame who taught him his A B C, a hundred years ago. It is no longer a "matron old whom we school-mistress name," who is found presiding there; and all that part of the description which refers to her, has become quite obsolete:

> "Albeit ne flattery did corrupt her truth,
> Ne pompous title did debauch her ear,
> Goody – good-woman – gossip – n'aunt, forsooth,
> Or dame, the sole additions she did hear."

An elderly person acting as master or mistress of a common school, is an unheard of circumstance throughout the country; it may be doubted if such an individual could be found between the St. Croix and the Colorado. It is even rare to meet one who has decidedly reached the years of middle life; while nothing is more common than to see very young persons in this post of authority. In most situations, a young countenance is a pleasant sight; but perhaps there is scarcely another position in which it appears to so little advantage, as sole ruler in the school-house. Young people make excellent assistants, very good subordinates in a large establishment, but it is to be regretted that our common schools should so often be under their government, subject only to a supervision, which is frequently quite nominal. They may know as much of books as their elders, but it is impossible they should know as much of themselves and of the children; where other points are equal, they cannot have the same experience, the same practical wisdom. Hitherto, among us, teaching in the public schools has not been looked upon as a vocation for life; it has been almost always taken up as a *job* for a year or two, or even for a single season; the aim and ambition of those who resort to it, too often lie beyond the school-house walls. The young man of eighteen or twenty means to go into business, or to buy a farm, or to acquire a profession; he means anything, in short, but to remain a diligent, faithful, persevering schoolmaster for any length of time. The young girl of seventeen or eighteen intends, perhaps, to learn a trade next year, or to go into a factory, or to procure an outfit for her wedding; never, indeed, does the possibility of teaching after she shall have reached the years of caps and gray hairs occur to her even in a nightmare. And yet nothing can be more certain than that those young people have undertaken duties the most important man or woman can discharge; and if they persevere in the occupation, with a conscientious regard to its obligations, they will be far better qualified for the same situation twenty years hence, than they are to-day.

The metamorphosis of

<blockquote>
"books of stature small,
Which, with pellucid horn secured, are"
</blockquote>

into Dictionaries, and volumes on Science, is quite as striking as the change from old to young, in the instructors. The very name of a horn-book is never heard to-day, and perhaps there are not half a dozen persons in an American country school district who know its meaning. In this respect, our children of the present day have greatly the advantage over their predecessors; few things are cheaper and more common now than books. Possibly fingers are also more clean, and do not need the sheath of horn to protect the paper; though, upon consideration, it seems by no means certain that the hands of modern little folk are so much better washed than those of their grandparents, since it will be remembered that the dame's little troop for "unkempt hair," were "sorely shent," and where the hair was required to be nicely combed, it is but natural to suppose that faces and hands were well washed.

The flock that came tripping out of the Red Brook school-house this afternoon was composed of boys and girls, varying in ages and sizes from the little chubby thing, half boy, half baby, to the elder sister, just beginning to put on the first airs of womanhood. Different codes of manners are found to prevail in different school-houses about the country: sometimes, when the children are at play before the door, or trudging on their way to or from home, the little girls will curtsey, and the boys bow to the passing stranger, showing that they have been taught to make their manners; but–alas, that it should be so–there are other unruly flocks where the boys, ay, and even the girls, too, have been known to unite in hooting and making faces at the traveller, a disgrace to themselves and to their instructors. But the children at the Red Brook behaved very properly, albeit they were not so polished as to bow and curtsey. They told their names, showed their books, and pointed

out their different roads home in a civil, pretty way. Indeed, those instances
of unmannerly conduct alluded to above did not occur in the same neighborhood, but were observed at some little distance from this valley.

The appearance of most of the little people was creditable; they looked
cleanly and simple. Many of the children were bare-footed, as usual in warm
weather,—almost all the boys, and a number of the girls. In winter they are
all provided with shoes and stockings. Here and there among the girls there
was some show of tawdry finery: ribbons that were no longer clean, glass
jewels, and copper rings; and one of the older girls had a silk hat, which
looked both hot and heavy, beside her companions' nice sun-bonnets; it
was trimmed inside and out with shabby artificial flowers. But then, as an
offset to these, there were several among the little people whose clothes,
well washed and ironed, showed a patch here and there. Now there is nothing in the world which carries a more respectable look with it, than a clean
coat or frock which has been nicely patched; when united with cleanliness,
the patch tells of more than one virtue in the wearer: it shows prudence, simplicity, and good sense, and industry; it shows that he or she is not ashamed
of honest poverty, and does not seek to parade under false colors. There are
two situations in which patched clothing excites an especial feeling of interest and respect for the wearer; and these are, in church and at school. At a
time when a gay dress is thought as necessary at church as in a ball-room,
when constant excuses are made by women who have not much money to
spare, mothers and daughters, that they cannot go to church because they
have no "*new hat*," no "*new dress*," when husbands and sons require new
beavers and new broadcloth for the same purpose, it is honorable to that
man or woman to whom Providence has appointed the trial of poverty, that
a patched coat or a faded gown does not keep them from going to the house
of God. And when one sees a family of children going to school in clean and
well-mended clothing, it tells a great deal in favor of their mother; one might
vouch that those children learn some valuable lessons at home, whatever
they may be taught at school.

One can never look with entire indifference upon a flock of children;
those careless little ones have a claim upon us all, which makes itself felt as
we listen to their prattle and watch their busy, idle games. As much variety
of character and countenance may be found among them, as exists in their
elders, while the picture is so much the more pleasing, as the lines are always softened by something of the freshness of childhood. This sweet-faced
little girl, that bright-eyed boy, this laughing, merry young rogue, yonder
timid, gentle child, this playful, kitten-like creature, that frank and manly lad,

will each in turn attract attention; ay, even the dull, the cold, the passionate, the sullen, are not forgotten; so long as they show childish faces, we look at them with an especial interest, made up of hope as well as fear. Each has its claim. It will often happen that the most intelligent countenance is connected with ill-formed features, that the best expression of kindly feeling, or generous spirit, beams over the homely face. And then we know but too well, with the fatal knowledge of daily experience, that yonder bright-eyed boy, by abusing the talent entrusted to him, may fall with the evil-doers. We know that yonder cherub-faced girl may sink to the lowest degradation of corruption, unless she learn betimes to cherish womanly modesty, and fear of sin. And, thanks be to God, we know also, that the cold heart may learn to feel, the sullen temper may clear, the passionate may become cool, the wavering firm, by humbly taking to heart the lessons of wisdom, and earnestly, ceaselessly, seeking a blessing from their Maker and Redeemer.

Some persons, in watching a party of children, have pleased themselves by drawing an imaginary horoscope for each of the group; adding a score or two of years to each young life, they parcel out honors, and wealth, and fame, and learning to some; care, and trouble, and disappointment to others; to these they give distinction, to those obscurity; appointing the different lots, perhaps, with as much judgment and impartiality as the world will show in bestowing them at a later day. But I should care little to know which of those lads will count the highest number of thousands, I should not ask which will boast the readiest tongue, the sharpest wit, which will acquire the most learning, or which will fill the highest place. There is another question to be answered; a question of deeper import to the individual himself, and to his fellow-creatures. True, it does not involve either wealth, or honors, or fame; but it is much more closely connected than either of these with individual happiness, and with the well-being of society. I would ask, rather, which of those boys now making trial of the powers with which their Maker has endowed them, will employ those powers, both of body and mind, to the best, the most just, the most worthy purposes? That boy, though his talents may be few, his lot humble, will do more for himself, more for the real good of others, than either of his companions; his will be the healthful, quiet conscience, his that contentment which "is great gain:" his will be the example most needed in the day and society to which he belongs. The precise amount of abilities is a point of far less importance than the ends to which those abilities are devoted; wealth is daily won by evil means, honors are daily purchased at a vile price, and fame is hourly trumpeting falsehoods through this world; but neither wealth, nor honors, nor fame can ever bring true health, and peace, and contentment to the heart. He who endeavors faithfully and humbly to use his faculties for truly good ends, by plainly good means, that man alone makes a fitting use of the great gift of life; however narrow his sphere, however humble his lot, that man will taste the better blessings of this world, the best hopes for the world toward which we are all moving. That man, that lad, commands our unfeigned respect and admiration, whatever be his position in life.

To a looker-on—and one very sincerely interested in the subject—there appears a chief error in American education under most of its forms, the neglect of systematic training in childhood and youth. There are two great principles which make up the spirit of all education—*impulse,* if we may apply the word in this sense, and *restraint.* These are not equally attended to among us, though both are clearly essential to the good of the individual, and of society. There is no want of intellectual activity in our system; there is no fear that the children in the district school-house will be cramped by confining their energies within too narrow a field, no fear that their faculties will remain dull and benumbed for the want of impulse. Everything lies open before them; and motives for action are ceaselessly urged upon them by the most animating, nay, even exciting language. It is the opposite principle of restraint which seems to receive less consideration than it deserves. It is not wholly neglected, God in mercy forbid that it ever should be; but does it meet with that full, serious attention which is needed? Is it not too often rendered subservient to the former principle of impulse, and activity? And yet, let it be remembered that it is this principle of restraint which is more especially the moral point in education; where it fails, discipline and self-denial are wanting, with all the strength they give to integrity, and honor, and true self-respect, with all the decencies of good manners which they infuse into our daily habits. That must ever be the soundest education in which the proportions between the different parts are most justly preserved.

Let it be remembered, also, that the more knowledge is increased, so much the more binding becomes the obligation to keep up the just proportions between moral and intellectual instruction. We have thrown aside the primer and horn-book, let us bear in mind that every new science introduced into the school-room brings with it an additional weight of moral responsibility. And instead of the amount of intellectual culture bestowed being an excuse for the neglect of religious and moral instruction, this very amount becomes in itself an imperative demand for more earnest, energetic, hearty efforts on those vital points. In a Christian community assuming their education, the children have a clear right to plain, sound, earnest lessons of piety, truth, honesty, justice, and self-discipline. Neglect of these points becomes treachery to them, treachery to our God. And without these, though complete in every other point, what is the education of an individual? However showy in other respects, without these what is the education of a nation?

November, Wednesday, 1st.—Decided frost last night; yet very mild this morning. Bright, cloudless day. Long walk on the hills. The woods are getting bare; even the willows and abele-trees are thinning. The larches are deep orange; their evergreen forms look oddly in this bright color.

The lake ultramarine blue. Saw several butterflies and parties of gnats. A full flock of snow-birds were feeding before a cottage door; and among them was a large, handsome fox-colored sparrow, one of the handsomest birds of its tribe. It seemed quite at ease among the snow-birds.

Thursday, 2d.—Very pleasant. Delightful walk in the woods. Some of the forest-trees are budding again. Found pipsissiwa and a ground-laurel, with their flowers in bud: the first plant blooms regularly about Christmas in some parts of the country, but I have never heard of its flowering here in winter. Gathered a pretty bunch of bead-ruby; the transparent berries quite perfect, and the cluster unusually large. The mosses in flower in some spots; the handsome *Hypnum splendens,* with its red stems, and some of the other feather mosses, *Hypnum crista-castrensis,* &c., &c. Ferns, sheltered by woods, in fine preservation. The earth thickly strewed with fallen leaves, completely covering the track, and in many places burying the lesser plants—a broad, unbroken carpeting of russet. This was especially the case where chestnut-trees were numerous, for the foliage seems to fall in fuller showers in such spots. The beech-trees are dotted with nuts. The wych-hazel has opened its husks, and the yellow flowers are dropping with the ripe nuts from the branches. Acorns and chestnuts are plentifully scattered beneath the trees which bore them. How much fruit of this sort, the natural fruit of the earth— nuts and berries—is wasted every year; or, rather, how bountiful is the supply provided for the living creatures who need such food!

Friday, 3d.—Very pleasant morning; the sun shining with a mild glow, and a warm air from the south playing over the fading valley. Long walk to a neighboring hamlet.

The farmers are busy with their later autumn tasks, closing the work of the present year; while, at the same time, they are already looking forward to another summer. There is something pleasing in these mingled labors beneath the waning sun of November. It is autumn grown old, and lingering in the field with a kindly smile, while they are making ready for the young spring to come. Here a farmer was patching up barns and sheds to shield his flocks and stores against the winter storms. There ploughmen were guiding their teams over a broad field, turning up the sod for fresh seed, while other laborers were putting up new fences about a meadow which must lie for months beneath the snow, ere the young grass will need to be protected in its growth. Several wagons passed us loaded with pumpkins, and apples, and potatoes, the last crops of the farm on the way from one granary to another. Thus the good man, in the late autumn of life, gathers cheerfully the gifts which Providence bestows for that day, despising no fruit of the season; however simple or homely, he receives each with thankfulness, while, looking forward beyond the coming snows, he sees another spring, and prepares with trustful hope for that brighter season.

Half an hour's walk upon a familiar track brought us to a gate opening into an old by-road which leads over the hills to the little village where we were bound; it was formerly the highway, but a more level track has been opened, and this is now abandoned, or only used as a foot-path. These lanes are charming places for a walk; there are cross-roads enough about the country in every direction, but they are all pretty well travelled, and it is a pleasant variety, once in a while, to follow a silent by-way like this, which is never dusty, and always quiet. It carried us first over a rough, open hill-side, used as a sheep-pasture; a large flock were nibbling upon the scraps of the summer's grass among the withered mulleins; we went quietly on our way, but as usual, our approach threw the simple creatures into a panic, disturbing their noon-day meal.

Having reached the brow of a hill, we turned to enjoy the view; the gray meadows of the valley lay at our feet, and cattle were feeding in many of them. At this season the flocks and herds become a more distinct feature of the landscape than during the leafy luxuriance of summer; the thickets and groves no longer conceal them, and they turn from the sheltered spots to seek the sunshine of the open fields, where their forms rise in full and warm relief upon the fading herbage. The trees have nearly lost their leaves, now scattered in russet showers, about their roots, while the branches are drawn in shadowy lines by the autumn sun upon the bleached grass and withering foliage with which it is strewn. The woods are not absolutely bare, however, there are yet patches in the forest where the warm coloring of October has darkened into a reddish brown; and here and there a tree still throws a fuller shadow than belongs to winter. The waters of the river were gleaming through the bare thickets on its banks, and the pretty pool, on the next farm, looked like a clear, dark agate, dropped amid the gray fields. A column of smoke, rising slowly from the opposite hill, told of a wood which had fallen, of trees which had seen their last summer. The dun stubble of the old grain-fields, and the darker soil of the newly-ploughed lands, varied the grave November tints, while here and there in their midst lay a lawn of young wheat, sending up its green blades, soft and fresh as though there were no winter in the year, growing more clear and life-like as all else becomes more dreary—a ray of hope on the pale brow of resignation.

So calm and full of repose was the scene, that we turned from it unwillingly, and with as much regret as though it were still gay with the beauty of summer.

Just beyond the brow of the hill the road enters a wood; here the path was thickly strewn with fallen leaves, still crisp and fresh, rustling at every step as we moved among them, while on either side the trees threw out their branches in bare lines of gray. Old chestnuts, with blunt and rough notches; elms, with graceful waving spray; vigorous maples, with the healthful, upright growth of their tribe; the glossy beech, with friendly arms stretched out, as if to greet its neighbors, and among them all, conspicuous as ever, stood the delicate birch, with its alabaster-like bark, and branches of a porphyry color, so strangely different from the parent stem. Every year, as the foliage falls, and the trees reappear in their wintry form, the eye wonders a while at the change, just as we look twice ere we make sure of our acquaintance in the streets, when they vary their wardrobe with the season.

The very last flowers are withering. The beautiful fern of the summer lies in rusty patches on the open hill-side, though within the woods it is still fresh and green. We found only here and there a solitary aster, its head drooping, and discolored, showing but little of the grace of a flower. Even the hardy little balls of the everlasting, or moonshine, as the country people call it, are getting blighted and shapeless, while the haws on the thorn-bushes, the hips of the wild rose and sweet-briar, are already shrunken and faded. It is singular, but the native flowers seem to wither earlier than those of the garden, many of which belong to warmer climates. It is not uncommon to find German asters, flos adonis, heart's-ease, and a few sprigs of the monthly honeysuckle, here and there, in the garden even later than this; some seasons we have gathered quite a pretty bunch of these flowers in the first week of December. At that time nothing like a blossom is to be found in the forest.

There once stood a singular tree in the wood through which we were passing. Wonders are told of its growth, for it is now some years since it disappeared, and its existence is becoming a tradition of the valley. Some lovers of the marvellous have declared that upon the trunk of a hemlock rose the head of a pine; while others assert that it was two trees, whose trunks were so closely joined from the roots that there appeared but one stem, although the two different tops were distinctly divided; others, again, living near, tell us that it was only a whimsical hemlock. In short, there are already as many different variations in the story as are needed to make up a marvellous tale, while all agree at least that a remarkable tree stood for years after the settlement of the country on this hill, so tall and so conspicuous in its position as to be seen at some distance, and well known to all who passed along the road. Its fate deserves to be remembered more than its peculiarity. On inquiring what had become of it, we learned the history of its fall. It was not blasted by lightning—it was not laid low by the storm—it was not felled by the axe. One pleasant summer's night, a party of men from another valley came with pick and spade and laid bare its roots, digging for buried treasure. They threw out so much earth, that the next winter the tree died, and soon after fell to the ground. Who would have thought that this old crazy fancy of digging about remarkable trees for hidden treasure should still exist in this school-going, lecture-hearing, newspaper-reading, speech-making community?

"But it was probably some ignorant negro," was observed on hearing the story.

"Not at all. They were white men."

"Poor stupid boors from Europe, perhaps—"

"Americans, born and bred. Thorough Yankees, moreover, originally from Massachusetts."

"But by whom did they suppose the money to have been buried? They must have known that this part of the country was not peopled until after the Revolution, and consequently no fear of Cow-Boys or Skinners could have penetrated into this wilderness. Did they suppose the Indians had gold and silver coin to conceal?"

"No. They were digging for Captain Kidd's money."

"Captain Kidd! In these forests, hundreds of miles from the coast!"

Incredible as the folly may seem, such, it appears, was the notion of these men. According to the computation of the money-diggers, Captain Kidd must have been the most successful pirate that ever turned thief on the high seas, and have buried as many treasures as Crœsus displayed. It has been quite common for people to dig for the pirate's treasure along the shores of Long Island, and upon the coast to the northward and southward; but one would never have expected the trees of these inland woods to be uprooted for the same purpose. But men will seek for gold everywhere, and in any way.

This is the third instance of the kind accidentally come to our knowledge. The scene of one was in the heart of the city of New York, and the attraction a singular tree, growing in the yard of a house in Broadway, whose occupant was repeatedly disturbed by applications to dig at its roots. The other two cases occurred among these hills; and on one of these occasions the search was declared to be commenced at the instigation of a professed witch, living in a neighboring village, and regularly armed with a twig of wych-hazel!

But there is more superstition left among us than is commonly supposed. There are still signs and sayings current among the farmers, about the weather and the crops, which they by no means entirely discredit; and there are omens still repeated by nurses and gossips, and young girls, about death-beds, and cradles, and dreams, and wedding-days, which are not yet so powerless but that they make some timid heart beat with hope or fear, most days that pass over us. Most of these are connected with rural life, and have doubtless come from the other side of the ocean; one of the pleasantest, however, may possibly be traced back to the Indians—the humming-bird and its love-message.

In passing through the woods, we looked about for the ruins of the old tree, but none of our party knew exactly where it had stood. We had soon crossed the hill, and Oakdale, with its little hamlet, opened before us. Its broad shallow stream turns several mills, one of them a paper-mill, where rags from over the ocean are turned into sheets for Yankee newspapers. One of the few sycamores in the neighborhood stands by the bridge.

Saturday, 4th.—Cloudy, and toward evening rainy; I fear our pleasant weather is over.

Monday, 6th.—Mild. Heavy rain all night, and raining still this morning. About 10 o'clock some flakes of snow mingled with the rain—then sleet—then, rather to our surprise, a regular fall of snow, continuing until afternoon. The whole country white with it, to the depth of an inch or two. Yet the air is mild to-day. Thus it is: the leaves have hardly fallen before winter advances; shreds of colored foliage are still hanging on some trees and shrubs. The little weeping-willow is in full leaf, bending under the snow.

Tuesday, 7th.—Election day. The flags are flying in the snow, which still falls in showers, with intervals of sunshine. The election goes on very quietly in the village; four years ago there was rather more movement, and eight years since, there was a very great fuss with hard cider, log-cabins, and election songs to all tunes. This afternoon there are scarcely more people in the streets than usual, and very little bustle.

The shrubbery beneath the windows was enlivened to-day by a large flock of very pretty little birds, the golden-crested kinglets, with greenish-yellow and brown bodies, a brilliant carmine spot on the head, encircled with a golden border, and then a black one. They are very small, decidedly less than the common wren, and only a size or two larger than the humming-bird. In this State they are rare birds. They are hardy little creatures, raising their young in the extreme northern parts of the continent, and are chiefly seen here as birds of passage, though remaining through the winter in Pennsylvania. They are indeed great travellers, frequenting the West Indies during the winter months. It is the first time we have ever observed them here, although their kinsmen, the ruby-crowned kinglets, are very common with us, especially in the spring months, when they linger late among our maple-blossoms. The flock about the house to-day was quite large, and they showed themselves several times in the course of the morning, flickering about the lilac and syringa bushes, and hanging on the leafless branches of the creeper trained against the wall.

They have a bird in Europe all but identical with ours, the difference between the two varieties being so slight that for a long time the best ornithologists were unaware of it. The European gold-crests winter in England and Germany; in the last country they are very numerous, and although so diminutive, they are brought to market, being esteemed a great dainty; about Nuremburg, in Bavaria, they are particularly abundant, and so much prized for the table that they command a high price. When broiled their bodies can scarcely be as large as a French chestnut! What should we think of a dish of humming-birds?

It is this little bird which is alluded to in Lafontaine's charming fable of the Oak and the Reed; this is the tiny *roitelet* which the Oak pronounces a heavy burden for the Reed:

"Pour vous un roitelet est un pesant fardeau."

Wednesday, 8th.—November is considered one of the best months for fishing in our lake; all the more important fish are now taken in their best state.

We have one fish peculiar to this lake; at least, the variety found here is very clearly marked, and differs from any yet discovered elsewhere. It is a shad-salmon, but is commonly called the "Otsego Bass," and is considered one of the finest fresh-water fish in the world. In former years they were so abundant that they were caught by the thousand in seines; on one occasion five thousand are said to have been taken; the people in the village scarcely knew what to do with them; some were salted, others thrown to the hogs. They are still drawn in the seine, being seldom taken by the hook, but their numbers, as might be supposed, have very much diminished. An attempt was recently made to protect them for three years, to allow them to increase again, but after a few months the law was repealed. The best months for the bass-fishing are April, May, and June, and in autumn, November and December; they are caught more or less through the winter; but not during the heats of summer; or, if occasionally one is taken in warm weather, it is out of the usual course of things. The largest bass known here have weighed seven pounds, but they do not often exceed three or four pounds at present. They have a very sweet, fine, white meat, with a dark, gray skin.

The lake trout, or salmon-trout, taken here are also of a superior quality; the same fish, in many other lakes, is considered coarse and tasteless, but here it is frequently met with very delicate and rich, and it finds great favor with epicures. It varies very much, however, with individuals, one being very fine, another quite indifferent. The salmon-trout, in the form we know it, is said to be almost peculiar to our New York lakes; at least this same variety is not found in Canada, nor farther south than Silver Lake, just beyond the borders of Pennsylvania.[30] Our fishermen say the best time for trout fishing is during the last ten days of November; they are taken, however, at all seasons, but are more common in cool weather. The largest taken here is said to have weighed thirty pounds, and others twenty-five and twenty-seven pounds; within the last dozen years we have seen them weighing sixteen and twelve pounds, but fish of this size have now become very rare. They are caught with the seine or with baited hooks, and are sometimes speared. Some years since, seven or eight hundred were taken at one haul of the seine. In winter, the lake is well sprinkled with baited hooks, sunk through small openings in the ice, and fine salmon-trout are often taken in this way.

The pickerel fishing also becomes more active at this season; lights are seen now, every evening, passing to and fro along the shores, to attract the pickerel, and a very pretty sight they are. The pickerel is said not to extend beyond the Great Lakes. The largest caught here have weighed seven pounds.

The perch—the yellow perch—is also common in our lake; the largest are said to have weighed between three and four pounds. Besides these our fishermen take eels, dace or roach, suckers, cat-fish, and bull-pouts. Formerly, when the river was not obstructed by so many mill-dams, the herring used to visit this inland lake every year, following the stream, many a long mile from the ocean; they were a very acceptable variety to the common fare in those days, and were so numerous that they were frequently fished up in pails by the first colonists.

Thursday, 9th.—At sunrise the thermometer had fallen to 16 above zero. Snow still lying on the ground, though little of it. Gloomy, dark day. People are taking out their winter clothing, and asking each other if this can possibly last? if winter is coming in earnest, and so suddenly? Dreary walk, so different from those of last week; the road hard and rough; had the highway quite to myself; in the distance of more than a mile, did not meet a living creature.

Another visit from the little kinglets—quite a party of them in the bushes beneath the windows.

Friday, 10th.—Thermometer only 6 above zero, at seven o'clock this morning. "Don't be concerned," say the farmers, "we shall have our Indian summer yet!" One would like to feel sure of it; the very idea warms one such a day as this.

Saturday, 11th.—Very cold. The thermometer very near zero.

Monday, 13th.—Mild again. Yesterday, Sunday, there was another light fall of snow.

Tuesday, 14th.—Soft, mild day; but it has scarcely thawed out of the sunshine for the last week. Snow still lying on the ground, though very little of it; at no time has there been enough for sleighing.

Wednesday, 15th.—There is a strange story going about the village: it is said that several respectable persons have had glimpses of a panther in our hills during the last two months! Probably they have been deceived, for it seems all but incredible that one of these wild creatures should really have appeared in our woods. It is between forty and fifty years since any panther has been heard of in this neighborhood.

Thursday, 16th.—Lovely day; bright air and soft sky. Perhaps the farmers will prove right about the Indian summer, after all. The walking is very bad; the late snow and last night's rain making a sad muss. Still, those who delight in the open air, may verify the old proverb: "Where there is a will there is a way;" one may pick out spots for walking, here and there.

The new-fashioned plank-walks have not yet become general here; they are convenient in muddy weather, though very ugly at other times. The neatest side-walk for a village or rural town seems to be a strip of brick, or stone pavement, three or four feet wide, with a broad border of grass on each side, where trees are planted, such as they have them in some of the Western villages. The plank roads and walks will probably be introduced here before long; they will use up an immense amount of timber, and one would think that this must eventually put a stop to them. It is said that the hemlock timber, which is used for the purpose, never attains to any great size in its second growth; such is the opinion here; whether it be correct or not, I do not know. There seems no good reason why it should not grow out of the old forests, as well as the pine.

The roads are at their worst just now; the stage-coach was ten hours yesterday coming the twenty-two miles from the railroad. That particular route, however, crossing the hills to the railway and canal, is the worst in the county. In summer, our roads are very good; but for two or three weeks, spring and autumn, they are in a terrible state. And yet they have never been quite so bad as those in the clay soils of the western part of the State; the year before the railroad was completed between Geneva and Canandaigua, a gentleman of the first village having business of consequence at the latter town early in the spring, was anxious to keep his appointment on a particular day, but he was obliged to give it up; the road, only sixteen miles, was so bad, that no carriage would take him. He made a particular application to the stage-coach proprietors; they were very sorry, but they could not accommodate him; it was quite out of the question: "We have twelve stage-coaches, at this very moment, sir, lying in the mud on that piece of road!" Now we never heard of a coach being actually left embedded in the mud on this road of ours, bad as it is; the passengers are often obliged to get out, and walk over critical spots; the male passengers are often requested to get out "and hold up the stage for the ladies;" often the coach is upset; frequently coach, passengers, and all sink into the slough to an alarming depth, when rails are taken from the fences to "pry the stage out;" but, by dint of working with a good will, what between the efforts of coachman, horses, and passengers, the whole party generally contrives to reach its destination, in a better or worse condition, somewhere within eighteen hours. They sometimes, however, pass the night on the road.

Friday, 17th.—Although the history of this county is so short, it has yet had several architectural eras. Without including the Indian wigwam, which has become only a tradition, specimens of half a dozen different styles are seen among us to-day. First in order of time ranks, of course, the log-cabin, such as are still seen to-day in the hills, or on the skirts of the woods: low, substantial, and rustic; when well put together, and inhabited by neat and thrifty people, they look very snug and comfortable, and decidedly picturesque, also. Not long since, we passed one a few miles from the village, which had as pleasant a cottage look as possible; it was in excellent order, in a neat little yard, with flower-borders under the windows, a couple of very fine balsam-firs before the door, and a row of half a dozen luxuriant hop-vines just within the fence. Another, near the Red Brook, attracted our attention more than once, during our summer walks: everything about it was so snug; the little windows looked bright and clean, as though they belonged to a Dutch palace; the rose-bushes standing in the grassy yard were flourishing and luxuriant; a row of tin milk-pans were usually glittering in the sun, and a scythe hung for several weeks beside the door; it would have made a pretty sketch. One dark cloudy afternoon, we also passed another of these log-cottages, of the very smallest size; it was old, and much out of repair, and stood directly by the road-side, without any yard at all; but everything about it was very neat: a tub and pails were piled under a little shed at the door, the small window was bright and well washed, and a clean white curtain within was half drawn to let in the light upon a table on which lay a large open Bible, and a pair of spectacles; twice, toward evening, we chanced to see that little curtain half drawn, to let in the light upon the Holy Book; doubtless some aged Christian lived there. The building is now turned into a shed; we did not know who lived there, but we never pass it without remembering the little table and the Bible. Unhappily, all log-cabins have not such tenants; where the inmates are idle and shiftless, they are wretched holes, full of disorder and filth.

Next to the log-cabin, in our architectural history, comes its very opposite, the lank and lean style, the *shallow* order, which aimed at rising far above the lowly log-cottage; proud of a tall front and two stories, proud of twice too many windows, but quite indifferent to all rules and proportions, to all appearance of comfort and snugness; houses of this kind look as if the winter wind must blow quite through them. The roof presses directly upon the upper tier of windows, and looks as though it had been stretched to meet the walls, scarcely projecting enough, one would think, for safety, eaves being thought a useless luxury; the window-frames are as scant as possible, and set on the very surface of the building, and there is neither porch nor piazza at the door. Such is the shallow in its simplest form, but it is often seen in a very elaborate state—and to speak frankly, when this is the case, what was before ungainly and comfortless in aspect, becomes glaringly ridiculous. In instances of this kind, we find the *shallow-ornate* assuming the Grecian portico, running up sometimes one wing, sometimes two; pipe-stem columns one-fiftieth of their height in diameter, and larger, perhaps, in the centre than at either extremity, stand trembling beneath a pediment which, possibly, contains a good-sized bed-room, with a window in the apex. Such buildings are frequently surrounded with a very fanciful paling of one sort or other. One looks into the barn-yard of such a house with anxious misgivings, lest the geese should be found all neck, the cocks all tail, the pigs with longer noses, the ponies with longer ears than are usually thought becoming.

Succeeding to the common shallow, and coeval with the shallow-ornate, dating perhaps forty years back, appears the plain, straightforward style, with its square outline, its broader foundations, respectable from a pervading character of honest comfort, although capable of many improvements. Sometimes houses of this kind have a wing, sometimes two, but more frequently the addition is put up with an eye to convenience rather than symmetry, and a long, low building, containing the kitchen, wood-shed, &c., &c., projects from the rear, forming with it, at right angles with the house, two sides of a yard. These dwellings are seen in every direction, rather more common, perhaps, than any other, and where things are in good order about them, they have a pleasant, cheerful look. This plain, straightforward style has, however, received a certain development within the last ten years which, when not carried to extremes, is a progress for the better: the foundation is broader, the elevation of the building lower, the roof projects farther, the cornices and all parts of the frame-work are more substantial, the porch or verandah is in better proportions, and the whole has a look of more finished workmanship. A farm-house of this homely, substantial kind, standing beside one of the common *shallow,* or a starved Grecian edifice of the *shallow-ornate* style, appears to great advantage, and speaks encouragingly for the growth of common sense and good taste in the community.

Still more recently, however, this substantial school has been somewhat abused. You see here and there new wooden cottages, which, in the anxiety of the architect to escape the shallow, err in the opposite extreme, and look oppressively heavy, as though the roof must weigh upon the spirits of those it covers. The cornices and door-frames of these small cottages would often suit buildings of twice their size, and, altogether, they belong to the ponderous style.

It is amusing, in passing from one hamlet to the other, to observe how imitative the good people are; for there is generally some one original genius in every neighborhood who strikes out a new variation upon one of the styles alluded to, and whether the novelty be an improvement, or an unsightly oddity, he is pretty sure of being closely followed by all who build about the same time. One often sees half a dozen new houses in close neighborhood precisely on the same pattern, however grotesque it may chance to be. This imitative disposition shows itself also in the coloring of the houses;

for of course here, as elsewhere throughout the country, they change their colors every few years with the last coat of paint. Many are white; many others yellow and orange; some are red, others brown; green, blue, and pink may also be found in the county; but these last shades are more rare, not having taken generally. Two or three years since, black was the hue of the season, but at present gray is all the fashion. It is by no means uncommon to find a house under different shades, front and rear, and I have seen a small farm-house with a different color on each of its four walls; yellow, red, brown, and white. We have also seen red houses with brimstone-colored blinds. But this Harlequin fancy seems to be subsiding, and as it has already been observed, sober gray and drabs are the colors in favor to-day, as though all the houses in the land were turning Quaker.

The "rural Gothic" and "Elizabethan," which have grown rapidly into favor about the suburbs of large towns, have scarcely as yet made any impression here. There are, probably, not more than half a dozen houses of the kind in the whole county. The rounded, double-pitched roofs, so common in the older parts of the country, and the shingled walls, also, found so frequently on old farm-houses of Long Island, New Jersey, and the neighborhood of New York, are very rare here; probably there are not a dozen double-pitched roofs in the county, and we do not know of one building with shingled sides.

Certainly there is not much to boast of among us in the way of architecture as yet, either in town or country; but our rural buildings are only seen amid the orchards and fields of the farms, or surrounded by the trees and gardens of the villages, so that their defects are, perhaps, less striking, relieved, as they generally are, by an air of thrift and comfort, and softened by the pleasing features of the surrounding landscape.

Saturday, 18th.—Although the foliage has now entirely fallen, yet the different kinds of seeds and nuts still hanging on the naked branches give them a fuller character than belongs to the depths of winter. The catkins on the different birches thicken the spray of these trees very perceptibly; these are of two sorts, the fertile ones are more full than the sterile heads; both grow together on the same branch, but in different positions.

There are as many as six kinds of birches growing in this State: the *canoe birch*, the largest of all, sometimes seventy feet high, and three feet in diameter, and which grows as far south as the Catskills; the Indians make their canoes of its bark, sewing them with the fibrous roots of the white spruce. The *cherry birch*, or black birch, is also a northern variety, and very common here; it is used for cabinet work. Then there is the *yellow birch*, another northern variety, and a useful tree. The *red birch,* also a tree of the largest size, is the kind used for brooms. The *white birch,* a small tree, is of less value than any other; it is quite common in our neighborhood; we have understood, indeed, that all the birches are found in this county, except the little *dwarf birch,* an Alpine shrub, only a foot or so in height.

Monday, 20th.– The potato crop is quite a good one this year, in our neighborhood, though a portion of it will be lost. But the disease has never been as fatal here as in some other places, and the farms of the county have always yielded more than enough for the population. Some ten years since potatoes sold here for twelve and a half cents a bushel; since then they have risen at the worst season to seventy-five cents. They have been considered high at fifty cents for the last year or two, and are now selling at thirty-one cents a bushel.

Tuesday, 21st.–Again we hear of the panther story. The creature is said to have been actually seen by two respectable persons, in the Beaver Meadows; a woman who was out gathering blackberries saw a large wild animal behind a fallen tree; she was startled, and stopped; the animal, which she believed to be a catamount, got upon the log, and hissed at her like a cat, when she ran away. A man also, who was out with his gun in the woods, a few days later, near the same spot, saw a large wild creature in the distance; he fired, and the animal leaped over a great pile of brush and disappeared. It would be passing strange, indeed, if a panther were actually roving about our woods!

Wednesday, 22d.–Very pleasant day. There is still a sprinkling of snow in some woods, for the weather has been cool and dry, but the country generally is quite brown again. The western hills are entirely free from snow, while those of the eastern range are all thinly sprinkled yet. Can this difference be owing to the greater power of the morning sun?

Pleasant walk. Stopped at the mill to order samp, or cracked corn. It is always pleasant in a mill; things look busy, cheerful, and thrifty there. The miller told us that he ground more Indian corn than anything else; nearly as much buckwheat, and less wheat than either; scarcely any rye, and no oatmeal at all. The amount of wheat ground at our mills is no test, however, of the quantity eaten, for a great deal of wheat flour is brought into the county from the westward.

They grind buckwheat at the village mill all through the summer, for a great deal of this flour is eaten here. In most families of the interior buckwheat cakes are a regular breakfast dish every day through the winter. In many houses they are eaten in the evening also, and among the farmers they frequently make part of every meal. This is the only way in which the flour is used with us—it all takes the form of "buckwheat cakes." The French in the provinces eat *galettes* of the same flour; they call it there *blé de Sarazin*, as though it had been introduced by the Saracens. It came originally from Central Asia. Montesquieu speaks of these French buckwheat cakes as a very good thing: "*Nos galettes de Sarrazin, humectées toutes brûlantes de ce bon buerre du Mont d'Or étaient, pour nous, le plus frais régal.*"

It appears that the Chinese eat much buckwheat also; they make it up there in the form of dumplings, and Sir George Staunton speaks of these as a very common dish in China.

Indian corn differs from the buckwheat in being prepared in many ways by our housewives: we have *sapaen,* or hasty-pudding; griddle-cakes, made with eggs and milk; hoe-cake, or Indian bread, baked in shallow pans; samp or hominy, corn coarsely broken and boiled; Jonikin, thin, wafer-like sheets, toasted on a board; these are all eaten at breakfast, with butter. Then we have the tender young ears, boiled as a vegetable; or the young grain mixed with beans, forming the common Indian dish of *succotash;* the kernel is also dried, and then thoroughly boiled for a winter vegetable. Again, we have also Indian puddings, and dumplings, and sometimes lighter cakes for more delicate dishes. The meal is also frequently mixed with wheat in country-made bread, making it very sweet and nutritious. Besides these different ways of cooking the maize, we should not forget parched or "popped" corn, in which the children delight so much; and a very nice thing it is when the right kind of corn is used, and the glossy yellow husk cracks without burning, and the kernel bursts through pure, and white, and nicely toasted. A great deal of popped corn is now used in New York and Philadelphia by the confectioners, who make it up into sugar-plums, like *pralines.* Acres of "popping corn" are now raised near the large towns, expressly for this purpose; the varieties called rice-corn, and Egyptian corn, are used, the last kind being a native of this country, like the others.

The word *sapaen* has sometimes been supposed of Indian origin. It is not found in any dictionary that we know of, though in very common use in some parts of the country. Van der Donck speaks of the dish:[31] "Their common food, and for which their meal is generally used, is *pap,* or *mush,* which in the New Netherlands is named *sapaen.* This is so common among the Indians that they seldom pass a day without it, unless they are on a journey, or hunting. We seldom visit an Indian lodge at any time of the day without seeing their *sapaen* preparing, or seeing them eating the same. It is the common food of all; young and old eat it; and they are so well accustomed to it, and fond of it, that when they visit our people, or each other, they consider themselves neglected unless they are treated to *sapaen.*" Maize seems, indeed, to have been the chief article of food with those Indians, at least, who lived upon the banks of the Hudson, or in the New Netherlands. Van der Donck, in describing their food, does not, I believe, once mention the potato, at least not in the parts of his works which have been translated. He speaks of beans as a favorite vegetable of theirs, and one of the few they cultivated, planting them frequently with maize, that the tall stalk of the grain might serve as a support to the vine. He observes, they had several kinds of beans—probably all the native varieties, of which we have several, were cultivated by them. Squashes he mentioned as peculiar to them, and called by the Dutch *Quaasiens,* from a similar Indian word. Pumpkins were also cultivated by them, and calabashes, or gourds, which, says he, "are the common water-pails of the Indians." Tobacco is also named as cultivated by them. But, as we have already observed, in his account of their field and garden produce, he says nothing of the potato, which is quite remarkable. The maize, on the contrary, seems to have been eaten at every meal: "Without *sapaen,*" he continues, "they do not eat a satisfactory meal. And when they have an opportunity they boil fish or meat with it, but seldom when the fish or meat is fresh—but when they have the articles dried hard and pounded fine.   *   *   They also use many dry beans, which they consider dainties.   *   *   When they intend to go a great distance on a hunting expedition, or to war,   *   *   they provide themselves severally with a small bag of parched corn or meal;   *   *   a quarter of a pound is sufficient for a day's subsistence. When they are hungry they eat a small handful of the meal, after which they take a drink of water, and they are so well fed, that they can travel a day. When they can obtain fish or meat to eat, then their meal serves them as well as fine bread would, because it needs no baking." Speaking of their feasts, he says: "On extraordinary occasions, when they wish to entertain any person, then they prepare beavers' tails, bass-heads, with parched corn-meal, or very fat meat stewed, with shelled chestnuts, bruised."—Not a bad dinner, by any means. Thus we see that while they relied on the maize in times of scarcity and fatigue, it made a principal part of their every-day fare, and entered into their great feasts also; but potatoes do not appear at all.

In using the word *sapaen,* Van der Donck leads one to believe it either a provincialism of the New Netherlands, or an Indian word. Very possibly it may have been borrowed from the red man, like the *quaasiens* or *squash.* There is, however, a word which corresponds to our English *sup,* to swallow without mastication, which in Saxon is *zupan;* the Dutch are said to have a word similar to this, and *sapaen* may prove a provincialism derived from it. A regular Hollander could probably decide the question for us. *Samp* for cracked corn; *hominy* for grain more coarsely cracked; and *succotash* for beans and maize boiled together, are all considered as admitted Indian words. *Mush* is derived from the German *Musse,* for pap, and probably has reached us through the Dutch.

Thursday, 23d.—Thanksgiving-day. Lovely weather; beautiful sky for a festival. Pleasant walk. As we came back to the village the bells were ringing, and the good people, in their Sunday attire, were going in different directions to attend public worship. Many shop-windows were half open, however; one eye closed in devotion as it were, the other looking to the main chance.

This is a great day for gatherings of kith and kin, throughout the country; and many a table stands at this moment loaded with good things, for family guests and old family friends to make merry, and partake of the good cheer together. Few households where something especially nice is not provided for Thanksgiving dinner; for even the very poor, if known to be in want, generally receive something good from larders better filled than their own.

It was one of the good deeds of the old Puritans, this revival of a Thanksgiving festival; it is true, they are suspected of favoring the custom all the more from their opposition to Christmas; but we ought not to quarrel with any one Thanksgiving-day, much less with those who have been the means of adding another pleasant, pious festival to our calendar; so we will, if you please, place the pumpkin-pie at the head of the table to-day.

Surely no people have greater cause than ourselves for public thanksgivings, of the nature of that we celebrate to-day. We have literally, from generation to generation, "eaten our bread without scarceness." Famine, to us, has been an unknown evil; that fearful scourge—one of the heaviest that can fall upon a nation, accompanied, as it is, by a long train of ghastly woes—that scourge has never yet been laid upon us; the gloomy anxiety of its first approaches, the enfeebled body, the wasting energies, the bitterness of spirit, the anguish of heart which attend its course, these have caused us to weep for our fellow-beings, but never yet for ourselves; the general distress, dismay, confusion, and suffering—the excess of misery—which follow its paralyzing progress through a country, are only known to us as evils which our fellow-men have suffered, and from which we, and those we love most warmly, have ever been graciously spared. Year after year, from the early history of the country, the land has yielded her increase in cheerful abundance; the fields have been filled with the finest of wheat, and maize, and rice, and sugar; the orchards and gardens, ay, the very woods and wastes, have yielded all their harvest of grateful fruits; the herds have fed in peace within a thousand quiet valleys, the flocks have whitened ten thousand green and swelling hills; like the ancient people of God, we may say, that fountains of milk and honey have flowed in upon us; the humming of the cheerful bee is heard through the long summer day about every path, and at eventide the patient kine, yielding their nourishing treasure, stand lowing at every door.

General scarcity in anything needful has been unknown among us; now and then the failure of some particular crop has been foretold by the fearful, but even this partial evil has been averted, and the prognostic has passed away, leaving no trace, like the gray cloud overshadowing but for an instant the yellow harvest-field, and followed by the genial glow of the full summer sunshine. In this highland valley we often hear fears expressed of this or that portion of the produce being cut off by the frosts belonging to our climate; now we are concerned for the maize, now for our stock of fruits, and yet how seldom has the dreaded evil befallen us! What good thing belonging to the climate has ever wholly failed; when have we wanted for maize, when have we suffered from lack of fruit? Every summer, currants have dried on the bushes, apples have lain rotting on the grass, strawberries have filled the meadows, raspberries and blackberries have grown in every thicket, while the richer fruits of warmer climates, oranges, and peaches, and water-melons, have been selling for copper in our streets.

The only approach to anything like scarcity known here since the full settlement of the county, occurred some ten years since; but it was owing to no failure of the crops, no ungenial season, no untimely frost. During the summer of 1838, wheat-flour became scarce in the country, and all that could be procured here was of a very indifferent quality–grown wheat, such as we had never eaten before. It was during the period of infatuation of Western speculation, when many farmers had left their fields untilled, while they followed the speculating horde westward. At that moment, many houses in the county were seen deserted; some closed, others actually falling to ruin, and whole farms were lying waste, while their owners were running madly after wealth in the wilds of Michigan and Wisconsin. The same state of things was general throughout the country, and, united to speculations in wheat, was the occasion of a temporary difficulty. As yet, this has been the only occasion when anything like scarcity has been felt here.

Well, indeed, does it become us to render thanks for mercies so great, wholly unmerited as they are. As we pass from valley to valley, from one range of highlands to another, from broad and heaving plains to plains still broader, from the fresh waters of great rivers and inland seas to the salt waves of the ocean, everywhere, on either hand, the bounties of Providence fill the land; the earth is teeming with the richest of blessings. And yet, in what part of this broad land, from one utmost verge to the other, shall we find the community that may justly claim the favor of the God of truth and holiness? Which great city, which busy town, what quiet village, what secluded hamlet, has deserved the blessing of Heaven on its fields? What city, or borough, or village, or hamlet, can say: "There is no sin here, there is no fraud, no deceit, no treachery, no drunkenness; no violence, rioting, impurity; no envy, no covetousness, no injustice, no slander, no falsehood, no insubordination among us; none of those evils declared hateful in the eyes of the God we worship, are going to and fro in our streets, upon our highways, sitting down and rising up unrebuked and unrepented of—these things are unknown here—we are wholly clean!" The heart recoils from the very idea of such presumption, and we bow our heads to the dust in deep acknowledgment of our unworthiness, as individuals, as communities, as a nation. "What is man that Thou visitest him, or the son of man, that Thou so regardest him!"

Happy, indeed, is it for the children of men, that the long-suffering God sendeth his rain upon the fields of the just and the unjust, and maketh his sun to shine upon the garden of the sinner with that of the righteous. Well, indeed, does it become us to render heartfelt, humble thanks to the God "who feedeth all flesh; for his mercy endureth forever."

It may prove of some interest to pause a moment and look back at the Jewish festivals of thanksgiving for the fruits of the earth, whence our own has been derived. It is, indeed, remarkable, that while the Jewish law was, in its general character, severe and stern, as compared with the milder and more merciful nature of Christianity, its worship gave such full and frequent expression to the beautiful spirit of thankfulness. The faithful Jew, obedient to the ritual of his church, would scarcely be guilty of the sin of ingratitude; just as it is difficult that the Christian, who, at the present hour, faithfully keeps the higher festivals of the Church, should be thankless and forgetful of *all* the mercies of his Almighty Father.

In the Jewish Church there were, besides the weekly Sabbaths and other lesser festivals, three great feasts of chief importance, the Passover, Pentecost, and the Feast of Tabernacles. At each return of these, every male among the Twelve Tribes was commanded to go up to Jerusalem, and there to worship Jehovah. The women were allowed to accompany them, and were often in the habit of going, as we learn from Scripture history; but the journey was not obligatory with them. It is easy to see the many advantages that must have resulted to the different tribes from this general intercourse, hallowed by duty and religious services as it was. The Passover, as we all know, commemorated the deliverance of the Jews on that fearful night in Egypt, when "there was not a house where there was not one dead;" but like all the greater points in the Jewish ritual, it was also typical and prophetic in character, foreshadowing the salvation of the Christian Church by the death of the true Paschal Lamb, our Blessed Lord, who was sacrificed at that festival some sixteen centuries after its institution. For us, therefore, the Passover has become Easter.

The second great festival of the Jews was called by them the "Feast of Weeks," because it was kept seven weeks after the Passover; and from its following on the fiftieth day from that feast, it has received the more modern name of Pentecost. To the Jews it commemorated the proclamation of the Law on Mount Sinai, an event which took place fifty days after their departure from Egypt. To the Christian Church this has also been a high festival, for on that day took place the miraculous outpouring of the Holy Spirit upon the Church at Jerusalem, as recorded in the Acts. And this is the Whitsunday of our own Calendar.

The third great festival, the Feast of Tabernacles, was entirely Jewish, and peculiar to themselves. As the Passover occurred in spring, Pentecost in summer, so the Feast of Tabernacles was held in the autumn. On some accounts, it was the most important of all their festivals; it fell during the seventh month of their ecclesiastical year, which commenced at the Passover; but this was also the first month of their civil year, answering to our October, and a period of peculiar importance for the number of religious observances which fell during its course. The first of this month was their New-Year's day, and kept by a very singular custom, the priests blowing a solemn blast on the trumpets, whence it was called the Feast of Trumpets, and they believed, on traditional authority, that the world was created at this season. Ten days after the Feast of Trumpets followed the great national fast, or day of atonement. But it was the third week of the same month that concluded the greater festivals of the year by the Feast of Tabernacles, one of their most peculiar and most joyous celebrations. They were enjoined to live in booths for a week, to remind them of the tents of their ancestors, wanderers in the wilderness for forty years. These booths, or tents, or tabernacles—for such is the import of the latter word—were ordered to be made of branches "with boughs of goodly trees, branches of palm-trees, and boughs of thick trees, and willows of the brook." But while thus commemorating the poverty and hardships of their ancestors in the wilderness, they were also enjoined, at the same time, to "rejoice before the Lord their God," and celebrate his infinite mercies to an unworthy race by especial thanksgivings. The last, or eighth day of the celebration, "that great day of the feast," as St. John calls it, was particularly devoted to thanksgivings for the "in-gathering" of the fruits of the earth. This was, indeed, the great harvest-home of Judea.

Each of these three greater festivals to which we have particularly alluded, the Passover, Pentecost, and the Feast of Tabernacles, independently of other associations, had also a connection with the mercies of God, in bestowing upon man the fruits of the earth. Their harvest was solemnly commenced the day after the Passover by a peculiar religious observance: three sheaves of barley were gathered in three different fields of the territory of Jerusalem, and carried to the temple, where they were threshed in the court, and were then solemnly offered to the Lord by the priest, in the name of the nation. This ceremony was enjoined in Leviticus, and before it had been performed, no man was allowed to put the sickle to his barley, the first grain reaped. At Pentecost again, when the wheat harvest was over; two loaves were offered in the temple by the priest, in the name of the nation. And the Feast of Tabernacles, as we have already seen, concluded with especial offerings and sacrifices, and thanksgivings for the great national harvest, now fully completed.

But independently of these general public observances, there were others enjoined upon the Jews of a private nature. Every one was commanded to offer personally the first-fruits of his own portion to the Lord. The women, when making the bread of the family, set apart a portion for the Levite, which was considered as an offering to the Lord, the priests having no lands or harvests of their own. The fortieth or sixtieth portion of the dough kneaded at the time was reserved for this purpose. And then, again, the first-fruits of every private harvest, not only of the grain, but of the fruits also, were offered at the temple with a solemn and very touching ceremony. The time for this private observance, and the amount offered, were left to the judgment of each individual. For this purpose, the Jews, at the conclusion of their harvests, used to collect in little parties from the same neighborhood, four to twenty persons together. They were preceded by an ox appointed for sacrifice, with a crown of olives on his head, and his horns gilded, with a player on the flute before him; and thus they walked in company to Jerusalem. The offerings were carried in baskets, and consisted of wheat, barley, grapes, figs, apricots, olives, and dates. From the fortieth to the sixtieth of the crop was offered. Each one bore his own basket; those of the rich were made of gold, those of the poor of wicker-work. When they arrived at Jerusalem, their friends came out to meet them. On reaching the temple, every man, the king himself, if he were there, took his basket on his shoulder and carried it into the court, where the Levites received the party, singing the xxx. Psalm: "I will extol Thee, O Lord," &c., &c. After this, the form and ceremony enjoined in Deuteronomy were complied with:

"And it shall be, when thou art come into the land which the Lord thy God giveth thee for an inheritance, and possessest it, and dwellest therein, that thou shalt take of the first of all the fruit of the earth, which thou shalt bring of thy land that the Lord thy God giveth thee, and shalt put it in a basket, and shalt go unto the place which the Lord thy God shalt choose to place his name there.

"And thou shalt go unto the priest that shall be in those days, and say unto him: 'I profess this day unto the Lord thy God, that I am come unto the country which the Lord sware unto our fathers for to give us.'

"And the priest shall take the basket out of thine hand, and set it down before the altar of the Lord thy God.

"And thou shalt speak and say before the Lord thy God, 'A Syrian ready to perish was my father, and he went down into Egypt, and sojourned there with a few, and became there a nation, great, mighty, and populous;

"'And the Egyptians evil entreated us, and afflicted us, and laid upon us hard bondage.

"'And when we cried unto the Lord God of our fathers, the Lord heard our voice, and looked on our afflictions, and our labor, and our oppression:

"'And the Lord brought us forth out of Egypt with a mighty hand, and with an outstretched arm, and with great terribleness, and with signs, and with wonders:

"'And he hath brought us into this place, and hath given us this land, even a land that floweth with milk and honey.

"'And now, behold, I have brought the first-fruits of the land which thou, O Lord, hast given me.'

"And thou shalt set it before the Lord thy God, and worship before the Lord thy God.

"And thou shalt rejoice in every good thing which the Lord thy God hath given unto thee, and unto thine house; thou, and the Levite, and the stranger that is among you."–Deut. xxvi., 1–11.

A beautiful ceremony, indeed. Thus we see how full of this acknowledgment of the mercies of God in feeding his people, was the Jewish ritual.

The Christian, in the same spirit of constant dependence upon Almighty Providence for life of body and soul, has also been taught by Divine authority, whether rich or poor, humbly to pray for the boon of his daily bread.

Friday, 24th.—Evening; 9 o'clock. The lake has been very beautiful all day. In the morning, light gleaming blue; soft and still in the afternoon, sweetly colored by reflections of the hills and sky; and this evening it is quite illuminated by an unusual number of fishing lights, moving slowly under the shores and across the little bays.

Saturday, 25th.—Looking over the country from a height, now that the leaves have fallen, we found the fences attracting our attention. They are chiefly of wood in our neighborhood; zig-zag enclosures of rails, or worm-fences, as they are called. We have but few stone walls here; stump-fences are not uncommon. The rails used for the worm-fences are often of chestnut, which is considered the best wood for the purpose. Foreigners from the Continent of Europe usually quarrel with our fences, and perhaps they are right; they look upon this custom as a great and needless waste of wood. They say they are ugly in themselves, and that an open country, well cultivated, but free from these lines, gives the idea of a higher state of civilization, than lands where every half dozen acres are guarded by enclosures. General Lafayette, when sitting in his tower at Lagrange, in the midst of his fine farms of Brie, used to say that he could not like our fences, and thought we should yet learn to do without them; he believed the cost of the wood, and the trouble and expense of putting them up and keeping them in order, might be disposed of to greater advantage in other ways. Hedges, it is to be feared, will never suit our climate—in this State, at least—unless it be our own evergreen shrubs. The hemlock is now coming into use for this purpose, in some neighborhoods. As regards appearances, hedges, close at hand, are very pleasing; but at a little distance, they are scarcely an improvement upon the fence: they are still dark, stiff lines, crossing the country with a net-work of enclosures. Probably we might at least do with much less fencing in this country; it often strikes one that fields are unnecessarily cut up in this way.

Monday, 27th.—There is an insect very common in the lower parts of the State, which we never see here: the ball-rolling beetle, so much resembling the sacred scarabæus of the Egyptians. One observes them on all the roads about New York and on Long Island, but we have never yet seen them in this county. If they exist here at all, they must be very rare. The sacred beetle of the Egyptians is said to have been rather larger than our insect of the same kind.

Tuesday, 28th.–Very pleasant, mild weather. Charming to-day; walking excellent. The farmers were right: we have had very pleasant weather after those cold days early in the month.

Wednesday, 29th.–Very pleasant; observed gnats in some places this afternoon.

Thursday, 30th.–Pleasant. Long walk in the bare, open woods; neither heard nor saw a bird.

> "Le bocage était sans mystère
> Le rossignol était sans voix."

The long yellow petals have fallen from the wych-hazel; the nut is beginning to form, the heart slowly becoming a kernel, and the small yellow flower-cups turning gradually into the husk. On some bushes, these little cups are still yellow and flower-like; on others, they have quite a husky look. It takes these shrubs a full year to bring their fruit to maturity.

The green wheat-fields look vivid and bright lying about the gray farms. The lake is deep blue just now; it seems to be more deeply blue in the autumn than at other seasons; to-day, it is many shades darker than the sky, almost as blue as the water in Guido's Aurora.

> # *Winter*

December, Friday, 1st.–Again we hear strange rumors of the panther. The creature is now reported to have been in Oakdale, having crossed the valley from the Black Hills. We hear that a man went out of a farm-house, about dusk, to pick up chips from a pile of freshly-cut wood at no great distance, and while there, he saw among the wood a wild animal, the like of which he had never seen before, and which he believed to be a catamount; its eyes glared upon him, and it showed its teeth, with a hissing kind of noise. This man gave the alarm, and for several nights the animal was heard in that neighborhood; it was tracked to a swamp, where a party of men followed it, but although they heard its cries, and saw its tracks, the ground was so marshy, that they did not succeed in coming up with it. Such is the story from Oakdale. Strange as the tale seems, there is nothing absolutely incredible in it, for wild animals will occasionally stray to a great distance from their usual haunts. About fifteen years since, a bear was killed on the Mohawk, some thirty miles from us. And so late as five-and-forty years ago, there was an alarm about a panther in West Chester, only twenty or thirty miles from New York!

Numbers of these animals are still found in the State, particularly in the northern mountainous counties. They are also occasionally seen to the southward among the Catskills, where they were formerly so numerous as to have given a name to the stream, and the mountains whence it flows. The Dutch called this creature "Het Cat," or "Het Catlos," which, says Judge Benson, was "also their name for the domestic cat." Kater is the male; but in the Benson Memoir, the word is not spelt with the double *a*, K*aa*terskill, as we frequently see it now-a-days, when few of us speak Dutch. Catskill, or Katerskill, however, would appear to be equally correct, and the last has the merit of greater peculiarity. The old Hollanders had very formidable ideas of these animals, which they believed at first to be lions, from their skins, and

252

the representations of the Indians. Their color is tawny, or reddish gray. When young, they are spotted; but these marks are supposed to disappear when the animal sheds its hair for the first time. The tail is darker at the extremity; the ears are blackish without, light within. The largest panther preserved among us is found in the Museum of Utica, and was killed by a hunter in Herkimer county; it measured eleven feet three inches in length. Their usual length is from seven to ten feet.[32]

They are said generally to frequent ledges of rocks inaccessible to man, and called *panther ledges* by the hunters; but they will often wander far for food. They are decidedly nocturnal, and rarely move by daylight. They prey upon deer, and all the lesser quadrupeds. They seem rather shy of man in general, but are very capable of destroying him when aroused. An instance of a very fierce attack from a panther is given in the Penny Magazine; and a man was killed by a "catamount," in this county, some fifty years ago. It is now more than forty years since any animal of the kind has been heard of in our part of the country, until within these last few weeks. Probably, if this creature prove really to be a panther, it has strayed from the Catskills.

Saturday, 2d.–Very mild. Unusually dark at eight o'clock. High wind, with heavy, spring-like showers. About noon the sky cleared, and the afternoon was delightful, with a high southwest wind, and a bright sky. A high wind is very pleasant now and then, more especially where such are not common. This evening we enjoyed the breeze very much, as it flew rustling through the naked branches, tossing the evergreen limbs of old pines and hemlocks, and driving bright clouds rapidly across the heavens. Despite the colorless face of the country, everything looked cheerful, as though the earth were sailing on a prosperous voyage before a fresh, fair breeze.

The sun has nearly reached his journey's end. There is a low ridge sloping away into the valley, about half a mile to the south of us, over which he passes completely in his annual voyage. Every clear winter's evening there is a glowing sky beyond it, against which the old pines, with their dark and giant forms, look grandly, adding, as they do, perhaps, a hundred feet to the height. The sun has nearly cleared this point now, and as he turns northward immediately after passing over it, the height is called Sunset Hill in the village.

Monday, 4th.– Charming day. Light sprinkling of snow in the night; but it has already disappeared. The grass on the lawn is quite green again. A light fall of snow, without a hard frost, always brightens the grass, perhaps more even than a spring shower. It often snows here without freezing.

Tuesday, 5th.–Rainy day; but not at all cold.

[33] Among the interesting birds of this part of the world, there are a number

which, though not often seen in our State, are yet occasional visitors, or else resident here in very small numbers. The noble wild turkey, for instance, is still found in small parties in the wilds of Sullivan, Orange, and Rockland counties, and also farther westward, in Alleghany and Cattaraugus; formerly it was known in large flocks from Mexico to Canada.

The fine, peculiar, Pinnated Grouse, though rapidly disappearing, is still seen in very small parties in Orange county.

The Mocking-bird is found on Long Island and in Rockland county. This bird, indeed, is said to range from 25° south of the equator, to 44 north. They are rare in our State, however, though a few arrive in the lower counties toward the last of May.

The brilliant Cardinal Grosbeak, with his scarlet coat, breeds in our State, and is said to be found in a county adjoining our own.

The equally brilliant Scarlet Tanager, or black-winged red-bird, as it is familiarly called, is found in the lower counties, though not numerous.

The summer Red-bird, also, quite a tropical bird, is occasionally seen near New York; we once chanced to meet quite a flock of them on Long Island.

The Blue Grosbeak, and the Rose-breasted Grosbeak, both handsome birds, are also found in the State.

The Crossbills, again, are seen in our northern counties.

The Cuckoo of this part of the world is interesting from the associations connected with the cry of the same bird in Europe—and, indeed, in Asia also—it is everywhere in the Old World looked upon as a harbinger of spring. The oldest song in the English language, said to date as far back as 1250, has a *refrain* in honor of this bird:

> "Summer is ycumen in;
> Lhude sing cuccu;
> Groweth sed, and bloweth med,
> And springeth the wode nu:
>   Sing cuccu!
> Awe bleteth after lomb:
> Lhouth after calve cu;
> Merrie sing cuccu,
>   Cuccu, cuccu!
> Wel singes thou cuccu,
> Ne swik thee nauer."

The Chinese call it by much the same name as the Europeans. And so did the ancient Greeks. We have the bird, but it attracts with us comparatively little attention; the robins, and blue-birds, and song-sparrows, are much more thought of; they arrive earlier, and are more common. The American cuckoo is much better behaved than his brother of the Old World; he has no naughty habits; he builds à nest of his own, and he is very faithful to his wife and children. Our cuckoos are of two kinds, the yellow-billed and the black-billed; both differ slightly from that of Europe. They arrive in May, and pass the summer with us. Their nests are said to be rather carelessly built, as though they had not thoroughly learned the art.

It is singular, that while the cuckoo of this part of the world pairs and builds its own nest, like most of its tribe, we have another bird who has the careless, reckless habits of the European cuckoo. It is well known that our cow-pen black-bird lays her eggs in the nests of other birds; and it is re-marked that she generally chooses the nest of those much smaller than her-self, like the summer yellow-bird, the blue-bird, song-sparrow, among our nicest and best-behaved birds. One might almost fancy, that like some un-happy women who have trifled with their own characters, the cow-bird is anxious that her daughters should be better behaved than herself, for she is careful to choose them the best foster-mothers; happily, such a course has often succeeded with human mothers, but with the bird it seems to fail. There is no such thing as reformation among them.

Wednesday, 6th.—Mild rain again. We have a word or two more to say about our rare birds, or at least those which are less common than our every-day flocks. Among these are a number besides the cuckoo, in which we feel an interest, chiefly on account of their European associations.

Let us begin with the chattering Magpie—"la gazza Ladra"—whose naughty tricks, and noisy tongue, are well known to us by reputation at least. They are very rare indeed in this State, but a few are occasionally seen near Niagara; strange ground, indeed, for such vapid, thoughtless birds. There is said to be a natural antipathy between the blue-jay and the magpie, just as two great human talkers are apt to dislike each other, and keep out of each other's way; these two birds, at least, are observed rarely to frequent the same region. The American magpie is more common west of the Mis-sissippi, but even there it is much more rare than in Europe. It closely re-sembles that of Europe.

The Falcon is another bird of note, from its old feudal associations; and strange as it may appear, the Duck-hawk of this part of the world is no other than the full brother of the famous Peregrine Falcon of Europe. It is said to be only the older birds which wander about, and as they live to a great age, some of them have been noted travellers. In 1793, a hawk of this kind was caught at the Cape of Good Hope, with a collar bearing the date of 1610, and the name of King James of England; so that it must have been at least 183 years old, and have travelled thousands of miles. Another, belonging to Henri II. of France, flew away from Fontainebleau one day, and was caught at Malta, the next morning. The male bird is smaller and less powerful than the female, as frequently happens with birds of prey; it was called, on that account, a Tiercel,—a third,—and caught partridges and small birds. It was the larger female who pursued the hare, the kite, and the crane. These birds will not submit to be enslaved; they never breed in a domestic state, and the stock was replaced by taking new birds captive. Hawking is said to have been derived from Asia,—where it is still pursued, in Persia, and China.

Other kinds, besides the Peregrine Falcon, were trained for sport; the Gyrfalcon, for instance, an extreme northern bird, taken in Iceland, whence they were sent to the King of Denmark; a thousand pounds were given for a "cast" of these hawks, in the reign of James the First. Mr. Nuttall says that occasionally a pair of Gyrfalcons are seen in the Northern States, but they are very rare. The Duck-hawk, or Peregrine Falcon, is chiefly found on the coast, where it makes great havoc among the wild ducks, and even attacks the wild geese. The Gyrfalcon is two feet long; the Peregrine Falcon of this country twenty inches, which is rather larger than that of Europe. We have also the Goshawk, another esteemed bird of sport, of the same tribe; it is rare here, and is larger than that of Europe. The Gyrfalcon and the Peregrine Falcon are birds that never touch carrion, feeding only on their own prey; these belonged to Falconry proper, which was considered the nobler branch of the sport. Among the birds used for Hawking, strictly speaking, were the Goshawk, the Sparrow-hawk, the Buzzard, and the Harpy.

The Cormorant is another bird of which we have all heard a great deal, without, perhaps, having a very clear idea regarding it. They are uncouth, aquatic birds, of the largest size—about three feet in length—very expert fishers and divers, and voracious feeders. In England, they formerly used them for fishing, and the Chinese still do so. They are found on our coast, though rather rare; a few breed in Boston Bay. The double-crested Cormorant is the most common on our coast.

The Pelican, again, is allied to the Cormorant, though distinguished from most other birds by their extraordinary pouch connected with the gullet. There are two kinds: the large White, and the Brown Pelican. They are scattered all over the world. The White is the largest of all water-fowls, about six feet in length. They are common in the South of Europe, particularly on the

Danube, and also throughout Judea, Egypt, &c., &c. They frequent alike the sea-shore and rivers. These birds were formerly common on the Hudson and the inland lakes of our own State, and it is quite probable they have been seen in these very waters of ours; but they have now entirely disappeared. They are rare everywhere in the Union, except in Louisiana and Missouri. They are partial to the eddies about waterfalls. It is said that they live to a great age. They are capable of carrying twelve quarts of water in their pouch! The Brown Pelican is still an occasional visitor on the sea-shore of Long Island; farther south, it is very common. It is a smaller bird than the White, measuring four feet in length.

Wild Swans are still found in the secluded northern lakes of this State, where they remain the whole year round. Large flocks, however, come from still farther north, and winter in the Chesapeake. They have a whistle, which distinguishes them from the mute species, which is much the most graceful. The Icelanders are very partial to the whistle of the wild swan, perhaps because they associate it with the spring; and Mr. Nuttall supposes that it was this note of theirs which led to the classic fancy of the song of the dying Swan. These birds are widely spread over Europe and America, though our own variety differs slightly from that of the Old World.

The Eider-Duck is another celebrated fowl with which we have a passing acquaintance in the State. In very severe winters, a few find their way from the northward, as far as the coast of Long Island. They breed from Maine, north. They are handsome birds, with much white in their plumage, and are very gentle and familiar. Dr. De Kay thinks they might easily be domesticated in this part of the country. The female plucks the down from her own breast, for the purpose of making a soft nest for her young; but after she has laid a number of eggs, these and the down are both removed, the eggs being very palatable. The patient creature then re-lines her nest with the last down on her breast, and lays a few more eggs; again both down and eggs are taken by greedy man; the poor mother has now no more down to give, so the male bird steps forward, and the nest is lined a third time. Two or three eggs are then laid, and the poor creatures are permitted to raise these – not from any kindly feeling, but to lure them back to the same spot again the following year, for they like to haunt familiar ground. Their nests are made of sea-weed and moss; Mr. Audubon saw many of them in Labrador. When the young are hatched, the mother frequently carries them on her back to the water; and when they are once afloat, none of them return permanently to the land that season. The down is so very elastic, that a ball of it held in the hand will expand and fill a foot-covering for a large bed. It is always taken from the live birds, if possible, that from the dead bird being much less elastic; and for this reason, they are seldom killed.

There are still two or three birds of old European fame, or otherwise interesting, found occasionally in our neighborhood; to these we must give a word or two when we have leisure.

Wednesday, 6th.—Green and reddish leaves are yet hanging on the scarlet honeysuckles, the Greville and Scotch roses; and a few are also left on the little weeping-willow.

The locust-trees are, as usual, full of brown pods; one of the handsomest in the village, a fine tree in size and form, might be supposed in withered leaf at a little distance, every branch and twig being loaded with pods. A drawing, taken at this moment, would give the idea of a tree in leaf. What a luxuriant mass of flowers it must have borne last June! A good portion of these pods will remain on the tree all winter, for they fall very reluctantly; and occasionally these old rusty shreds of a past year are found among the fresh summer blossoms. They have certainly no beauty, and yet they are rather pleasing in winter, reminding one of the flowers the tree has borne. The pods of the Acacia, frequently called the Honey-locust, are handsome and very large, though the flower itself is insignificant: they are of a rich glossy brown, with a spiral, curling turn, and twelve or fifteen inches long; there are few on the tree, however, compared with the common locust, and they fall early. The birds do not seem to eat the seed in these pods, which is a pity; they would be a fine winter harvest for them about the villages.

The old brown chestnut-burs tipping the naked twigs here and there, the black shell of the hickory, also the open husk of the small beech-nut dotting the trees, the swinging balls of the sycamore, the scaly tufts on birch and alder, though dull and out of season, are also pleasing from association, and though claiming little beauty in themselves, vary the naked branches agreeably.

A flock of wild ducks flew over the village to the lake, the only birds we have seen for a fortnight.

Thursday, 7th.—Mild rain again, with dark, dull sky.

Friday, 8th.—Very mild, and cloudy, but without rain. Indeed, it is almost warm; people are complaining of lassitude, the air quite oppressive, and thermometer at 64. The grass quite green again, in patches; cows feeding in some pastures.

Saturday, 9th.—Still same mild weather, with dark skies.

A large flock of tree-sparrows about the house this morning. These birds come from the far north to winter here; they are not so common with us, however, as the snow-bird and the chicadee. The little creatures were looking for seeds and insects among the bushes and on the ground, and they seemed to pick up gleanings here and there. Though constantly fluttering about among the honeysuckles, they passed the berries without tasting them; and often, when birds have been flitting about in autumn when the fruit of the honeysuckle looked bright and tempting, I have observed that it was left untouched. The birds do not like it. The blueberries of the Virginia creeper, on the contrary, are favorite food with many birds, though poisonous to man.

The tree-sparrow is one of the largest and handsomest of its tribe, its head being marked with a brighter bay than others. Upon its breast is a dark spot, as though it bore its escutcheon there. When it first arrives in November, it has a pleasant, low warble, and it may very possibly sing well in its summer haunts. But our sparrows generally are not musical birds; the song-sparrow is the most marked exception.

This dull, cheerless winter day, while watching the sparrows searching for food among the bare and naked branches, and on the brown, cold earth, I was strongly impressed with the recollection that these little creatures were chosen by their Maker to teach us a most important lesson. The passage in the Holy Gospel in which they have a place is very remarkable, and is given to us by St. Matthew and St. Luke. The Evangelists tell us that a great multitude of people were collected, and our blessed Lord was pleased to address his disciples in their hearing. A caution against hypocrisy was given, followed by a most solemn injunction to fear God, and not man.

"But I will forewarn you whom ye shall fear: Fear him which, after he hath killed, hath power to cast into hell; yea, I say unto you, Fear him. *Are not five sparrows sold for two farthings? And not one of them is forgotten before God. But even the very hairs of your head are all numbered. Fear not, therefore, ye are of more value than many sparrows.*" Such is the passage in the Gospel of St. Luke.

In the Gospel of St. Matthew the same incident is thus related:

"And fear not them which kill the body, but are not able to kill the soul, but rather fear him which is able to destroy both soul and body in hell. *Are not two sparrows sold for one farthing? And one of them shall not fall to the ground without your Father. But the very hairs of your head are all numbered. Fear ye not, therefore, ye are of more value than many sparrows.*"

What a sublime view does it give us of the providence of God, that not one of these little birds should fall to the ground unknown to the Almighty Creator, that each one of these little creatures, the humblest and most insignificant of their race, is heeded and remembered before God! This

revelation of the direct nature of Divine Providence is, indeed, most precious and consoling; it is impossible to possess a stronger assurance of the
mercy, and wisdom, and power of God, as exercised toward us, than is given
in these words of our Redeemer; and there is no other passage on this subject in Holy Scripture so full and clear. It is one of the most extravagant follies of man that he constantly avows opinions of the attributes of his Maker
fashioned by his own miserable, puny faculties. As if it were possible that
we should know aught of the Supreme Being beyond what He is pleased to
reveal to His creatures; and as if it were not a most plain and rational duty
to believe *all* that is revealed with our whole powers of mind and soul! Even
sincere Christians, with the weakness and inconsistency of human nature,
are too often partially guilty of the same folly; we are all too often disposed
in practice, if not in theory, to measure the power, and wisdom, and justice,
and mercy, and love of our God, by our own pitiful standard; and yet, meanwhile, the blessed light of the Gospel is shining in all its fullness upon us, re-
vealing great truths connected with this most sacred subject, in the plainest
words. Happy would it be for man were he always content to know his gracious God, only as He has made himself known to us, to reject every idea
of His attributes which is not derived from Scripture, and to cling with every
energy of soul and body to the holy truths of this nature vouchsafed to us in
His word. This simple assurance of the fullness and directness of God's providence would, in that case, prove a most blessed source of comfort to every
Christian heart, amid the trials and sorrows of life; but it is with this as with
so many other instances, the boon is offered by God, but it is rejected or neglected by man. "The very hairs of your head are all numbered"–a stronger
expression of tender watchfulness could not be framed in human language;
it conveys an idea quite beyond the reach of all human power. And such
were the words of the Deity to sinful man; it was the holy voice of the Redeemer which gave them utterance. It is true, this language was addressed
to the first chosen disciples, men far holier than we; but all have been redeemed by the precious death of Christ, and every human soul, therefore,
may justly feel itself to be "of more value than many sparrows;" not one is
"forgotten before God." We all, the most humble and insignificant, may find
comfort in the passage. It is remarkable that this revelation of the directness
of the providence of God, the oversight and care bestowed by the Almighty
on the meanest of His creatures, and His tender watchfulness over His ser-
vants, should have been given when foretelling the grievous trials and per-
secutions which awaited the chosen disciples of the Lord. The same God
who feeds the young ravens that cry unto Him, sees also the falling sparrow;

He sees the evil, but permits it; when sorrows and troubles come, they must be necessary in His sight for some good and wise purpose—it may be that the evil we mourn is needed for some immediate personal end which we are too blind to perceive, or it may be required to strengthen, in the sight of men and angels, some one of those great truths by which a universe is governed. In either case, well does it become the sinful child of man to suffer meekly; alas, that it should be so difficult to "let patience have her perfect work!" Let us at least always repel the false, unfaithful notion that we are ever, under the darkest circumstances, left to the blind dealings of chance, or fate, that we are ever forgotten before our God!

It is very possible that the little sparrows of Judea were flitting about in the presence of our Lord at the moment those gracious words were spoken: "Not a sparrow falleth to the ground without your Father,—fear not, therefore, ye are of more value than many sparrows." These birds were sold for less than one cent of our money each; the Roman coin mentioned in the original being in value one cent and a half of our own copper, and two sparrows were sold for one of these, or, as St. Luke tells us, five sparrows were sold for two farthings. Sparrows are supposed to have been used in the temple for the ceremony of purifying from leprosy, and were sold for that purpose. This rite was a singular one: two birds were required; one was killed with peculiar circumstances, the living bird dipped in its blood, and the blood then sprinkled seven times on the leper, after which the priest "shall pronounce him clean, shall let the living bird loose into the open field." The flying away of the live bird, with the blood upon him, is supposed to be a type of the Atonement, like the scape-goat driven into the wilderness with the curse for sin on his head. Singular and obscure as some of these old Jewish rites appear to the happier Christian, nothing can be more clear than that each became of high import and dignity from the moment it was appointed by Divine authority; and if no common sparrow falls to the ground without our Father in heaven, ceremonies expressly ordained by Him, in which the humblest birds were employed as a means, must have been of grave importance, and blessed effect to all who faithfully kept them. It has been supposed, that after healing the leper, as recorded by St. Matthew, chapter viii., our Lord was pleased to order the man He had miraculously cured, to fulfill this same ceremony, when He bid him "Go show thyself to the priest, and offer the gift commanded by Moses."

The sparrows of this continent differ more or less from those of the Old World, although, as a common, humble bird, their character is very similar. The European sparrow is, at times, mischievous and troublesome, differing in this respect from ours, which are all very harmless little creatures. With us they have no price; they are neither bought nor sold; their plumage, voice, and flesh, having little to recommend them to the dangerous favor of man. We have many varieties belonging to different seasons and situations; all varying from the Eastern bird of the same family. The plain little chipping-sparrows are good friends with us all, found through the summer about every garden in the country, the very tamest of our birds, running in the paths we tread ourselves, and scarcely moving out of our way, as we come and go. The song-sparrow, very like the chipping-bird in size and plumage, is one of the earliest of our singing-birds. We are all familiar with its pleasing note; it is the only one of its tribe that has a fine voice. Then there is the swamp-sparrow, which passes the summer along the water-courses of the Northern States, and winters on the rice plantations of the South. The Savannah, or coast-sparrow, again, is chiefly found near the sea-shore. It is a pretty bird, but unknown among our hills. The yellow-wing is a small species, with a faint note, said to be the least numerous of its family; this autumn, however, we saw a little flock flitting about for half an hour among the shrubbery. The field-sparrow is the smallest of all its tribe, and a migratory bird here; it lives more in the open fields, and less along fences and hedges, than its brethren. The bay-wing, or grass-bird, again, is only seen in our meadows in summer, though found through the winter near New York. All these varieties either linger in small parties in the lower counties during the cold weather, or proceed to the Southern States, whence they return to us in the spring. But there are four other species which come from the northward to winter with us, and return to still cooler regions as the warm weather approaches. These are the white-throat, a pretty bird; the white-crowned sparrow, more rare; the fox-colored sparrow; and the tree-sparrow, like those we saw this morning. Thus at all seasons these little creatures are near to tell us of the direct and immediate care of Providence; they run about our doors as we come in and go out; they rise from their grassy nests in the open field; they sing to us from the thickets and bushes; we find them by the bank of the river; on the sea-shore; and as one party goes with the falling leaves of autumn, they are succeeded by others who perch among the naked branches, and remain through the cheerless winter. Each of these humble flocks as it crosses our path, whether in the storm or in the sunshine, may remind us of the same sublime truth, that they and we are ever under the care of our merciful Father in heaven, never forgotten before God.

Monday, 11th.—Very mild. A dull day closed with a cheering sunset; the clouds, in waving folds of gray, covered the whole heavens; but as the sun dropped low, he looked in upon us, and immediately the waves of vapor were all tinged with red, dark and rich beyond the pines of Sunset Hill, and paler, but still flushed, to the farthest point of the horizon.

Another little sparrow flew past us, as we were walking this afternoon.

Tuesday, 12th.—Mild, but cooler; frost last night. Long walk in the woods. Much green fern still in many places, although it is no longer erect. We have had only one fall of snow, and that a light one; but the fern is already lying on the ground, prostrate, as in spring. Adjoining these fresh leaves of the different ferns, there are large tufts of the same kind completely dry and withered, though it is not easy to see why there should be this difference. Can it be the younger fronds which are more tenacious of life? Gathered a fine bunch of the scarlet berries, of the dragon arum, as bright as in September. The ground-laurel is in flower-bud, and the buds are quite full. Many trees and plants are budding.

An old hemlock had fallen across the highway very near the same spot where another large tree fell also across the road, not long since. There are so many dead and decaying trees in our American woods, that, of a windy day, they often fall. Some persons are afraid to go in the forest when there is a high wind, but often as we walk there, we have never seen one fall.

Wednesday, 13th.—Lovely day; mild and cloudless. Walked on Mount —. The lake very beautiful as we looked down upon it; clear light blue, encircled by the brown hills.

No birds. At this season one may often pass through the woods without seeing a feathered thing; and yet woodpeckers, blue-jays, and crows are there by the score, besides snow-birds, chicadees, sparrows, and winter-wrens, perhaps; but they do not seem to cross one's path. The larger birds are never active at this season, but the snow-bird and chicadee are full of life.

Thursday, 14th.—Mild, pleasant day. Again we hear news of the panther: a very respectable man, a farmer, living a mile or two from the village, on the lake shore, tells —— that he was returning quite late at night from the village, when he was startled by hearing a wild sort of cry in the woods, above the road, sounding as though it came from Rock Hill; he thought at first it was a woman crying in a wailing kind of way, and was on the point of turning back and following the sound, but the cry was repeated several times, and he thought, after all, it was not a woman's voice. A few days later, as his little boys were crossing a piece of woods on the top of Cliff Hill, they heard a strange cry at no great distance, sounding something like a woman's voice; they answered the voice, when the sound was repeated several times in a strange way, which disturbed the little fellows so effectually, that they turned back and ran nearly a mile, until they reached the farm-house, very much frightened. Both the farmer and the boys, in this case, are a very quiet, steady set, not at all likely to invent a tale of the kind. It really looks as if the creature were in the neighborhood, strange as it may seem. It so happened, that only a day or two before the boys heard the cry in the Cliff woods, we were crossing that very ground with one of them, never dreaming of a panther being near us; if it were really there at the time, one would have liked to have caught a glimpse of it—just near enough to decide the point, and to boast for the rest of one's days of having met a real live panther in our own woods! Bad as their reputation is, they seldom, I believe, attack human beings unless exasperated; and of course we should have been satisfied with a distant and brief interview; for no doubt we should have been very heartily frightened.

Friday, l5th.—We return to the birds of more than common interest.

The bald eagle can scarcely be called a rare bird with us, for in some parts of the country it is very common; at other points, however, it is not often seen. We Americans all have a national interest in this powerful bird as the emblem of our country, and yet few among us know much about him. He is frequently supposed to be peculiar to this continent: according to ornithologists, such is not the case; he is found in the northern parts of the Old Hemisphere also. He is much more rare, however, in Europe than in the Western World, and what is singular, he is chiefly confined there to extreme northern regions, while it is rather the temperate and warmer climates of this continent which he affects. Only two instances are known where this eagle has visited Central Europe; in America, they are found from Labrador to the Gulf of Mexico, but they are most common within the milder latitudes of that space.

The Bald Eagles are more numerous along our coast than in the interior; their fondness for fish draws them to the sea-shore. Their singular habit of exacting tribute from the Osprey is well known, and is a spectacle very frequently seen along the coast, where the Fish-Hawks are most common. The Eagle sits watching upon a naked limb of some tall tree near the water, while the Fish-Hawk is soaring at the height of a hundred feet or more above the waves in quest of prey; as soon as the Hawk has dived and arisen with a fish in its talons, then the Eagle leaves his perch and pursues the luckless Osprey, with threats so well understood, that the fish is dropped, the Eagle sinks, and seizing it as it falls, carries it off to his haunts in the woods, where he makes his meal. In New York, the Bald Eagle is most common along the Sound, on Long Island, and also about Niagara; but he is no stranger to any part of the country. They are frequently seen soaring over the Highlands near West

Point. Now and then one is observed hovering over our own little lake. Their fisherman, the Osprey, also visits the interior, following our larger rivers to their head-waters; but here, one of their nests is a rarity, while on the coast, Mr. Wilson once counted twenty within a mile.

The Bald Eagles build their nest in a tall tree, perhaps a pine, or farther south, it may be a cypress. They first lay a sort of floor of large sticks several feet in length; over this are placed sods of earth, hay, moss, sedge-grass, pine-tops, &c., &c. This eyry continues to be used as long as the tree lasts, and when their old homestead has been destroyed, they will often take possession of an adjoining tree, rather than abandon the neighborhood. They resort to their nest constantly as a dwelling, at all times, repairing it when necessary, until the pile rises to the height of five or six feet, with a breadth of four or five feet. The mother-bird begins to lay in February; and it is said that while the first brood is half fledged, she lays other eggs, which the young birds help to hatch by their warmth. Whether this is really true or not, one cannot say.

Besides fish, these Eagles prey upon ducks, geese, gulls, and all kinds of water-fowls; at times, they feed upon lambs, pigs, fawns, and even deer. Mr. Audubon gives a very spirited account of their hunting the wild swan, the male and female in company. Two instances are recorded in which infants have been seized by these powerful birds, one occurring in Georgia, and given by Mr. Nuttall, the other happening in New Jersey, and related by Mr. Wilson. In the first instance, the child is said to have been carried five miles, to the eyry of the bird; it was immediately followed, but the poor creature was already dead. In the last case, the child was seized as it was playing by its mother's side, while she was weeding in her garden; a sudden rushing sound, and a scream from the child, alarmed the woman: she started up, and saw her baby thrown down and dragged several feet by a Bald Eagle, when happily the infant's dress gave way, and the bird rose, carrying off a fragment of it in his talons. The length of these birds is three feet; extent of wings, seven feet. The female, as usual with birds of prey, is the largest and most daring. They are not at all bald, as their name would imply, but, in fact, hoary-headed: the plumage of the whole head and neck being white; the tail and wing-coverts are also white; the rest of the plumage is chiefly brown; the legs and bill are of a golden yellow.

There is another gigantic fishing Eagle, called the Washington Eagle, a very rare bird, described by Mr. Audubon as decidedly larger; its length is three feet seven inches; extent of wings, ten feet two inches. They build upon the rocks along the Upper Mississippi.

Long may the Bald Eagle continue to be the national emblem of a vigorous and a united people, as long as the bird soars over the broad land! It must prove a dark hour for the country when either wing is maimed. There are always, in every community, in public as in private life, those who are not afraid to assume a character which the wise man has declared "an abomination" in the sight of their God; yes, this character "*doth the Lord hate*"—"he that soweth discord among brethren."

If, in the subject of a monarchy, loyalty to the sovereign be a just and a generous sentiment,—and most assuredly it is so,—still more noble in character is the nature of that loyalty which has for object a sacred bond, uniting in one family the beating hearts, the active spirits, the intelligent minds of millions of men; brethren in blood and in faith!

Shall such a bond be severed by distempered passions? Let us be on our guard, lest the evil be brought about by small antagonist parties whose sympathies are not loyal to the nation at large. History may teach us that small parties are often very dangerous, and nowhere more so than in republics.

* * * * * * *

It is well known that we have in the southern parts of the country a member of the Parrot tribe, the Carolina Parakeet. It is a handsome bird, and interesting from being the only one of its family met with in a temperate climate of the Northern Hemisphere. They are found in great numbers as far north as Virginia, on the Atlantic coast; beyond the Alleghanies, they spread themselves much farther to the northward, being frequent on the banks of the Ohio, and in the neighborhood of St. Louis. They are even found along the Illinois, nearly as far north as the shores of Lake Michigan. They fly in flocks, noisy and restless, like all their brethren; their coloring is green and orange, with a shade of red about the head. In the Southern States their flesh is eaten. Greatly to the astonishment of the good people of Albany, a large flock of these birds appeared in their neighborhood in the year 1795. It is a well-authenticated fact, that a flock of Parakeets were observed some twenty-five miles to the northward of Albany during that year; so that we have a right to number them among our rare visitors. They have been repeatedly seen in the valley of the Juniata, in Pennsylvania. Birds are frequently carried about against their will by gales of wind; the Stormy Petrels, for instance, thoroughly aquatic as they are, have been found, occasionally, far inland. And in the same way we must account for the visit of the Parakeets to the worthy Knickerbockers about Albany.

But among all the birds which appear from time to time within our borders, there is not one which, in its day, has attracted so much attention and curiosity as the Ibis—the sacred Ibis of Egypt. There were two birds of this family worshipped by the Egyptians—the white, the most sacred, and the black. For a long time, the learned were greatly puzzled to identify these birds; but at length the question was fully settled by MM. Cuvier and Savigny; and we now find that the Ibis of both kinds, instead of being peculiar to Egypt, extends far over the world. There are two old paintings discovered among the ruins of Herculaneum, representing Egyptian sacrifices of importance, and in each several Ibises are introduced close to the altar and the priest. The reverence in which the Ibis was held in Egypt seems, indeed, to have been carried as far as possible: it was declared pre-eminently sacred; its worship, unlike that of other divinities among them, was not local, but extended throughout Egypt; the priests declared that if the gods were to take a mortal form, it would be under that of the Ibis that they would appear; the water in the temple was only considered fit for religious purposes after an Ibis had drunk of it. These birds were nurtured in the temples, and it was death for a man to kill one. Even their dead bodies, as we all know, were embalmed by the thousand. The motive for this adoration was said to be the great service rendered to Egypt by these birds, who were supposed to devour certain winged serpents, and prevent their devastating the country. M. Charles Bonaparte supposes that this fable arose from the fact that the Ibis appeared with the favorable winds which preceded the rains and inundation of the Nile. So much for the fables which conferred such high honors upon the Ibis.

In reality, these birds, so far from being confined to Egypt, are found in various parts of the world. In the Southern States of the Union, particularly in Florida and Louisiana, they are quite numerous; and they are found occasionally as far north as the shores of Long Island. They are said to fly in large flocks, and feed upon cray-fish and small fry. Ornithologists place them between the Curlew and the Stork. It is said that sometimes, during a gale or a thunder-storm, large flocks of them are seen in movement, turning and wheeling in the air, when their brilliant white plumage produces a very fine effect amid the dark clouds. The White Ibis is twenty-three inches in length, and thirty-seven across the wings.

The Black Ibis was considered as confined to particular spots in Egypt. In reality, however, this bird is much the greater wanderer of the two; it is found in Europe, Asia, Africa, Australia, and America. It is said to be more rare on the coast of this State than the White Ibis. Their annual migration over Europe is described by the Prince of Canino as extending usually from the S. W. to the N. E.; they pass from Barbary to Corsica, and through Italy, toward the Caspian Sea, where they breed. In the north and west of Europe they are rare, though for several seasons a flock has bred in the Baltic. In Egypt it remains from October to March, and, no longer sacred, they are sold there in the markets. The Glossy, or Black Ibis, is twenty-three inches in length.

These Ibises are said to be all dull, stupid birds, quite harmless, and not timid. They live in flocks, but pair for life. They have an expert way of tossing up the shell-fish, worms, &c., &c., upon which they feed, and catching the object in their throat as it falls. Their stomachs have greater strength than their bills, for they swallow large shells which they cannot break. The nest is built on high trees; the female alone sits on her two or three eggs, but the male feeds her, and the young also, the last requiring care a long time. Their gait is said to be dignified; large parties often moving together in regular order. Their flight is heavy, but they soar high, and remain long on the wing. The first observed on our coast was shot at Great Egg Harbor, in May, 1817; since then others have been killed from time to time, as far north as Boston. So much for this noted bird, worshipped by that "wisdom of the Egyptians" in which Moses was instructed, and which he rejected for that purer faith which each of us should bless God for having preserved among men, in spite of the weak and wavering apostasy to which our fallen race is prone.

It is rather singular that we should have within the limits of this northern province three noted objects of Egyptian adoration, at least in each instance we have a closely-allied species: the Ibis, both white and black, among their sacred birds; the Nelumbo, akin to the Lotus, among their sacred plants; and the humble, ball-rolling beetle, closely allied to their Scarabæus.

Saturday, 16th.—Very mild, but half-cloudy day. We have had rather more dark skies this last week or two than is usual with us. The mornings have often been gray and lowering until eight o'clock, though we have never known candles used here after sunrise, even during the darkest days.

It is a busy time with the farmers, who are killing their pork, which makes a great deal of work within doors also; housekeepers have many things to look after just now. The position of an American housewife is rarely, indeed, a sinecure, but in the country there is always a much larger share of responsibility attached to the office than in towns. In rural life, baking and churning, the pastry and cakes, curing hams, and preparing sausages, pickling and preserving, laying down eggs and butter, and even making the coarser soaps and candles of the family, are included in her department. In towns all these things are found for cash or credit, at the grocers, or bakers, or confectioners. Of course, when the pork is brought in, there is a great deal to be done: some pork is to be corned; hams, and jowls, and bacon are to be looked after; sausage meat, head cheese, and soused pigs' feet, must be prepared.

Salt and smoked meats of all kinds are very much used in this country, more so, probably, than in any part of Europe at the present day. This sort of food made a large portion of the household stock in former ages; four or five hundred years ago fresh meat was only eaten at certain seasons. Beef, and mutton, and even geese, were regularly killed for salting in the autumn, and laid by as winter provisions. At present the amount of salted and smoked food eaten in Europe is much smaller.

With us, particularly in the country, few meals are made without some dish of this kind, either breakfast, dinner, or tea: smoked fish, or broiled or cold ham, for instance, in the morning; ham, or bacon, or tongue, or corned beef, or it may be corned pork, for dinner; and chipped smoked beef, or tongue, for tea. Towards spring, in many villages and hamlets, it is not easy to procure a supply of fresh meat; and salt provisions of all kinds become not only the *morceau de résistance,* but also the *hors d'œuvre.* It is talked of, in village parlance, as the *ham-and-egg season,* because at this time butchers are not to be depended on. A few years since such was the case here, but at present we are better supplied. As for country taverns, it may be doubted if they ever set a table without ham, broiled or fried, with eggs also, if possible. During an excursion of ten days, the summer before last, in the southern counties, we had but one meal without ham, and frequently it was the only meat on table. The Wandering Jew would have fared badly in this part of the world, especially if he moved out of sight of the railroads.

There are said to be more hogs in the United States than in all the different countries of Europe together, so that a traveller ought not to be surprised when he meets these animals in the handsomest streets of our largest towns, as he may do any day. Probably we should be a more healthy nation if we were to eat beef and mutton, where we now eat pork.

It is not improbable that this taste for salt and smoked food generally, may be owing to the early colonial habits, when the supply of fresh meats, with the exception of game, must have been small; and the habit once formed, may have become hereditary, as it were.

Monday, 18th, 7 o'clock, A.M.–Lovely, soft morning. The valley lies cool and brown in the dawning light, a beautiful sky hanging over it, with delicate, rosy, sun-rise clouds floating here and there amid the limpid blue. It will be an hour yet before the sun comes over the hill; at this season its rays scarcely touch the village roofs before eight, leaving them in shadow again a little after four.

How beautiful are the larger pines which crown the eastern hill at this moment! These noble trees always look grandly against the morning and evening sky; the hills stand so near us on either side, and the pines are of such a height and size, that we see them very clearly, their limbs and foliage drawn in dark relief against the glowing sky.

Tuesday, 19th.–Most charming day; all but too warm. Thermometer 66. Long walk over the hills. The farmers say winter never comes until the streams are full; they have been very low all through the autumn, but now they are filled to the brim. The river shows more than usual, winding through the leafless valley. This is in truth a protracted Indian summer; mild airs, with soft, hazy sunshine. Dandelions are in full flower by the road-side; cows and sheep are feeding in the pastures. They are ploughing on many farms; the young wheat-fields are beautiful in vivid verdure.

In the woods we found many green things; all the mosses and little evergreen plants are beautifully fresh; many of the feather mosses are in flower. The pipsissiwa and ground-laurel are in bud; the last has its buds full-sized, and the calyx opening to show the tips of the flowers, but these are only faintly touched with pink on the edge; unfolding them, we found the petals still green within. It is very possible that some violets may be in flower here and there, although we did not see any; but the autumn before last violets were gathered here the first days in December, though generally, this month is wholly flowerless in our neighborhood.

We passed a cart standing in the woods, well loaded with Christmas greens, for our parish church. Pine and hemlock are the branches commonly used among us for the purpose; the hemlock, with its flexible twigs, and the grayish reverse of its foliage, produces a very pretty effect. We contributed a basket-full of ground-pine, both the erect and running kinds, with some glittering club-moss, and glossy pipsissiwa, for our share; it is not every year that we can procure these more delicate plants, as the snow is often too deep to find them. Neither the holly, the cedar, the arbor vitæ, the cypress, or the laurel, grows in our immediate neighborhood, so that we are limited to the pine and hemlock. These two trees, however, when their branches are interwoven are very well adapted for Christmas wreaths.

Wednesday, 20th.–Cooler; the air more chilly. Walked in the afternoon. Gray gnats were still dancing here and there. Found a merry party of chicadees in the oak by the Mill Bridge; their cheerful note falls pleasantly on the ear at this silent season.

Thursday, 21st.–Mild, but snowing a little; we may yet have sleighing for Christmas.

It is a very busy time within doors just now; various important labors connected with Christmas cheer are going on. Cake-jars are filling up with crullers, flat, brown, and crisp; with dough-nuts, dark, full, and round; with raisined olecokes, with spicy, New-Year cookies, all cakes belonging to the season. Waffles, soft and hard, make their appearance on the tea-tables; mince-pies, with their heavy freight of rich materials, are getting under way; and cranberries are preparing for tarts. Ducks and turkeys are fattening in the poultry-yards; inquiries are heard after any grouse or woodcock that have been shot on the hills; after any salmon-trout, or bass, that may have been caught in the lake. Calves'-head soup and calves'-foot jellies are under consideration; and fresh oysters are arriving in the village from the coast by scores of kegs; in short, the activity in the rural housekeepers's department is now at its height. But at this busy season, during these Christmas preparations, the female Vatel is supported and cheered by a sort of holiday feeling which pervades the whole house; there is a dawn of the kindliness and good-will belonging to Christmas perceptible in kitchen and pantry; the eggs are beaten more briskly, the sugar and butter are stirred more readily, the mince-meat is chopped more heartily than on any other occasion during the year. A pleasant reflection this, and one upon which it is sometimes necessary to fall back for consolation when the pies are a *little* burnt in the baking, and the turkey proves *rather* tough after boiling.

But the larder, though an important item, is very far from being the only object of attention in these Christmas tasks. Greens are put up in some houses. Santa Claus must also be looked after. His pouch and pack must be well filled for the little people. Hoary heads, wise and gray, are just now considering the merits of this or that nursery-book; weighing sugar-plums and candies; examining puppets and toys. Dolls are being dressed by the score, not only your wax and paste-board beauties, such as may be seen in every toy-shop window, but also other members of the doll family which are wholly of domestic manufacture, such as those huge babies of cotton and linen, almost as large as the live baby in the cradle, with pretty painted faces, and soft, supple limbs. These "rag-babies," as they are sometimes called in the nursery—*Moppets,* as we are instructed to name them by great dictionaries— are always pets with little mammas; no other dolls are loved so dearly and so constantly as these. Look at some motherly little creature as she pets and fondles this her chief treasure; note her agony as that teasing young rogue of an elder brother threatens death and torture to her darling, and you will soon discover that, of all her numerous family, shapeless, clumsy Moppet has the largest place in that warm little heart of hers. Next to these great cloth babies, black Dinahs are the greatest pets in the nursery. It is surprising what a fancy children have for a black face; nay, it is more than a fancy, it is a very positive affection. Whether it is that the negroes, with the cheerful kindliness which usually marks their good-hearted race, have an art of their own in winning little hearts or not, one cannot say; but it is well known that a black nurse is almost always a favorite. These Dinahs of black morocco are, therefore, cherished among the doll family as representatives of the dark face children love so well; they are supposed to be taking very good care of those white linen babies in the little cradle.

But it is not only older fingers which are at work; many little slips of womankind are now busily engaged upon some nice piece of work for papas and mammas, grandfathers and grandmothers. Many are the deep mysteries concerning such matters cleverly concealed just now under an innocent expression—mysteries which Christmas-eve will unfold. And now, as the day draws on apace, all sorts of work, bags, purses, slippers, mittens, what-nots, &c., &c., are getting a more finished look every hour. The work-table is getting more and more crowded. Things wear a very different aspect from the languid, listless, make-believe appearance of summer labors of the same kind; all are in earnest now, great and small, old and young; there is not a moment to spare, Christmas is at hand! And the thought that it is so,

> ". . . . . sets a keener edge
> On female industry; the threaded steel
> Flies swiftly, and unfelt the task proceeds."

Friday, 22d.—It is snowing decidedly. We shall doubtless have sleighing for the holidays.

Saturday, 23d.—Winter in its true colors at last; a bright, fine day, with a foot of snow lying on the earth. Last night the thermometer fell to 8° above zero, and this morning a narrow border of ice appeared along the lake shore.

Sleighs are out for the first time this winter; and, as usual, the good people enjoy the first sleighing extremely. Merry bells are jingling through the village streets; cutters and sleighs with gay parties dashing rapidly about.

It is well for Santa Claus that we have snow. If we may believe Mr. Moore, who has seen him nearer than most people, he travels in a miniature sleigh "with eight tiny rein-deer:"

> "Now Dasher, now Dancer! Now Prancer, now Vixen!
> On Cupid, on Comet! On Donner and Blixen!
> Now dash away, dash away, dash away all!
> As leaves, that before the wild hurricane fly,
> When they meet with an obstacle mount to the sky;
> So up to the house-top the coursers they flew,

With the sleigh full of toys, and St. Nicholas too:
And then in a twinkling I heard on the roof,
The pawing and prancing of each little hoof."

The domain of Santa Claus has very much extended itself since his earliest visits to the island of Manhattan, when he first alighted, more than two hundred years ago, on the peaked roofs of New Amsterdam, and made his way down the ample chimneys of those days. In this part of the country he is very well known. One has regular applications on Christmas-eve for permission to hang up stockings about the chimney for Santa Claus to fill; Sunday-scholars and other little folk come stocking in hand as a matter of course, and occasionally grown persons follow their example. It seems at first rather singular that Santa Claus should especially favor stockings and chimneys; one cannot easily account for the fancy; but a notion of this sort has spread far and wide. In France the children put their *shoes* on the hearth Christmas-eve, with the hope that during the night they will be filled with sugar-plums by the "Bon-Homme Noel," who is evidently a twin brother of Santa Claus. But these are matters in which experience sets reason at defiance. The children will all tell you that Santa Claus comes down the chimney—in this part of the world he will even squeeze through a stove-pipe—and that he fills stockings with good things, always looking after that particular part of their wardrobe, though why he should do so remains a mystery yet unfathomed. It seems a silly notion, perhaps. If you belong to the wondrous-wise school, you will probably despise him for it; a sensible man, you will say, would put the sugar-plums in the child's pocket, or leave them with the parents. No doubt of it; but Santa Claus is not a sensible man; he is a funny, jolly little old Dutchman, and he and the children understand each other perfectly well. Some of us believe that he comes down the chimney expressly to make wise people open their eyes at the absurdity of the thing, and fills stockings because you would never dream of doing so yourself; and there cannot be a doubt that the little people had much rather receive their toys and sugar-plums by the way of the chimney than through the door, and that they find it far more delightful to pull treasure after treasure from the stocking than to take them in a matter-of-fact way from the hands of their respected parents.

Some people use harsh language toward our old friend; they call him an impostor, and even accuse him of being, under false colors, an enemy of the little folk; they say he misleads them. Not he, indeed; he is just as far from desiring to deceive his little friends as Mother Goose, or the historian of

Jack the Giant-killer, and little Red Riding Hood; such an idea never enters
his head. Moreover, if he tried it, he would fail. Children are not so easily
deceived as you think; for, in all simple matters, all that comes within their
own sphere of judgment, the little creatures have a remarkable instinct which
guides them with the nicest tact in deciding upon the true and the false.
They know, for instance, who loves them, and who only makes believe; they
understand fully that this friend must be respected and obeyed, while that
one can be trifled with all day long; they feel they can trust A—with the
whole confidence of their loving little hearts, and B—is an individual of
whom they have a very indifferent opinion, though they do not choose, perhaps, to express it in words. As for Santa Claus, they understand him well
enough; they feel his kindness and they respect his reproofs, for these are always made with justice; they know he is a very great friend of children, and
chief counsellor of papas and mammas; they are perfectly sure he will come
to-night, and that their stockings will be filled by him. Tom is a little afraid
he will bring a new birch twig with him, and Bessie has some fears of a great
bitter pill to cure her of crying; still, they would not have him stay away for
the world, and they go to sleep to dream of him. But at this very moment,
if you were to step into the nursery and tell Tom and Bessie that Santa Claus
is in the next room, and wishes to see them, they would not believe you. If
you were to repeat the assertion, it is probable that Bessie would reprove
you for telling a story, and Tom might go so far as to enter into a logical dis-
quisition on the subject, informing you that nobody ever sees Santa Claus,
for the reason that there is no such person; who ever heard of an old man's
driving up the side of a house, over the roof, and down the chimney! Such
things can't be done; he knows it very well. Nevertheless, next year Tom
and Bessie will be just as eager as ever for a visit from Santa Claus, and they
will continue to think his sugar-plums the sweetest, and his toys the most delightful of all that are given to them, until they have quite done with toys and
sugar-plums—with those of the nursery, at least. Happy will it be for the little
people if they never have a worse enemy, a worse friend either, among their
acquaintances, whether real or fictitious. In fact, there is no more danger that
the children should believe in the positive existence of Santa Claus, than
there is a probability of their believing the Christmas-tree to grow out of the
tea-table. We should be careful, however, to make them understand every
Christmas, that the good things they now receive as children are intended
to remind them of far better gifts bestowed on them and on us.

But most of the wisest people in the land know little more about Santa
Claus than the children. There is a sort of vague, moonlight mystery still

surrounding the real identity of the old worthy. Most of us are satisfied with the authority of pure unalloyed tradition going back to the burghers of New Amsterdam, more especially now that we have the portrait by Mr. Weir, and the verses of Professor Moore, as confirmation of nursery lore. It is only here and there that one finds a ray of light falling upon something definite. We are told, for instance, that there was many hundred years ago, in the age of Constantine, a saintly Bishop by the name of Nicholas, at Patara, in Asia Minor, renowned for his piety and charity. In the course of time, some strange legends sprang up concerning him; among other acts of mercy, he was supposed to have restored to life two lads who had been murdered by their treacherous host, and it was probably owing to this tradition that he was considered the especial friend of children. When the Dominican fraternity arose, about 1200, they selected him as their patron saint. He was also – and is, indeed, to this day – held in great honor by the Greek Church in Russia. He was considered as the especial patron of scholars, virgins, and seamen. Possibly, it was through some connection with this last class that he acquired such influence in the nurseries of Holland. Among that nautical race, the patron saint of sea-faring men must have been often invoked before the Reformation, by the wives and children of those who were far away on the stormy seas of Africa and the Indies. The festival of St. Nicholas fell on the 6th of December, but a short time before Christmas. It seems that the Dutch Reformed Church engaged in a revision of the Calendar, at the time of the Reformation, by a regular court, examining the case of each individual canonized by the Church of Rome, something in the way of the usual proceedings at a canonization by that Church. The claims of the individual to the honors of a saint were advanced on one hand, and opposed on the other. It is said that wherever they have given a decision, it has always been against the claimant. But in a number of instances they have left the case still open to investigation to the present hour, and among other cases of this kind stands that of Sanctus Klaas, or St. Nicholas. In the mean time, until the question should be finally settled, his anniversary was to be kept in Holland, and the children, in the little hymn they used to sing in his honor, were permitted to address him as *"goedt heyligh man"*–good holy man. It appears that it was not so much at Christmas, as on the eve of his own festival, that he was supposed to drive his wagon over the roofs, and down the chimneys, to fill little people's stockings. For these facts, our authority is the Benson Memoir. A number of years since, it may be thirty or forty, Judge Benson, so well known to the old New Yorkers as the highest authority upon all Dutch chapters, had a quantity of regular "cookies" made, and the little hymn said by the children in honor of St. Nicholas, printed in Dutch and sent a supply of each as a Christmas present to the children of his particular friends. But though we have heard of this hymn, we have never yet been able to meet with it. Probably it is still in existence, among old papers in some garret or store-room.

Strange indeed has been the two-fold metamorphosis undergone by the pious, ancient Bishop of Patara. We have every reason to believe that there once lived a saintly man of that name and charitable character, but, as in many other cases, the wonders told of him by the monkish legends are too incredible to be received upon the evidence which accompanies them. Then later, in a day of revolutions, we find every claim disputed, and the pious, Asiatic bishop appears before us no longer a bishop, no longer an Asiatic, no longer connected with the ancient world, but a sturdy, kindly, jolly old burgher of Amsterdam, half Dutchman, half "spook." The legend-makers of the cloister on one hand, the nurses and gossips of Dutch nurseries, black and white, on the other, have made strange work of it. It would be difficult to persuade the little people now that "Santa Claus" ever had a real existence; and yet, perhaps, we ought to tell them that there was once a saintly man of that name, who did many such good deeds as all Christians are commanded to do, works of love and mercy. At present they can only fancy Santa Claus as Mr. Moore has seen him, in those pleasant, funny verses, which are so highly relished in our nurseries:

> "His eyes, how they twinkled! His dimples, how merry!
> His cheeks were like roses—his nose like a cherry;
> His droll little mouth was drawn up like a bow,
> And the beard on his chin was as white as the snow.
> The stump of a pipe he held tight in his teeth,
> And the smoke it encircled his head like a wreath.
> He had a broad face, and a little, round belly,
> That shook, when he laughed, like a bowl full of jelly;
> He was chubby and plump, a right jolly old elf;
> And I laughed, when I saw him, in spite of myself."

Monday, 25th, Christmas-day.—There is a saying in the village that it always rains here on Christmas; and, as if to prove it true, there is a heavy mist hanging upon the hills this morning, with rain falling at intervals in the valley. But even under a cloudy sky, Christmas must always be a happy, cheerful day; the bright fires, the fresh and fragrant greens, the friendly gifts, and words of good-will, the "Merry Christmas" smiles on most faces one meets, give a warm glow to the day, in spite of a dull sky, and make up an humble accompaniment for the exalted associations of the festival, as it is celebrated in solemn, public worship, and kept by the hearts of believing Christians.

The festival is very generally remembered now in this country, though more as a social than a religious holiday, by all those who are opposed to such observances on principle. In large towns it is almost universally kept. In the villages, however, but few shops are closed, and only one or two of the half dozen places of worship are opened for service. Still, everybody recollects that it is Christmas; presents are made in all families; the children go from house to house wishing Merry Christmas; and probably few who call themselves Christians allow the day to pass without giving a thought to the sacred event it commemorates, as they wish their friends a "Merry Christmas."

Merry Christmas! Some people have found fault with the phrase, they consider the epithet of merry as ill-judged, when applied to this great holiday; but that is a notion that can only arise from a false conception of its meaning; to quarrel with it, they must suppose it to convey the idea of disorder, and riot, and folly. It is, however, in fact, a good Saxon adjective, used by some of the oldest and best writers in the language, as a synonyme for sweet, pleasant, cheerful, gladsome; Chaucer and others apply it in this sense. Hundreds of years ago our English forefathers talked affectionately of their native land as "merrie Englande," and we cannot suppose that they intended to give the idea of a country of confusion and riot, but claimed for their island-home a cheerful character. Again, the poets sung the "merrie month of May," a delightful, joyous season, assuredly; but who shall dare to see disorder and folly in the harmony and sweetness of that beautiful period of the year?

It is true that this good and hearty word of olden days has been partially abused in later times, as men have discovered

> "How *mirth* may into folly glide,
> And folly into sin."

But if we were to reject everything good and desirable in itself because it has been abused by mankind, we should soon discover that we had deprived ourselves of every blessing, not only temporal, but spiritual also. If we were to give up all terms that have been perverted from their true and natural meaning, we should soon condemn ourselves to a silence more absolute than that of the followers of Latrappe: only too many of the best words in every language have suffered grievously from bad usage. There is an old adjective of the same date as that under discussion, which comes, perhaps, nearer than any other to giving a true idea of *merry* in the sense we understand it, and that is *blithe;* and having been less tarnished by common uses, it still bears a charming meaning. But few among us, when looking at this subject, will be disposed to dispute the authority of our own translation of the Holy Bible, which is generally admitted to be a model of good, sound English; now the words *merry* and *mirth* occur quite frequently in the pages of the sacred book, and the following are some instances of the application they have received. *Merry* is applied to feasting in Genesis, when relating the joyful meeting between Joseph and his brethren in Egypt; *mirth* is applied to *laughter* in the book of Proverbs; it is opposed to *mourning* in Ecclesiastes, and it is connected with laughter and pleasure in the same book; in Isaiah it is connected with *thanksgiving,* with *joy,* with *music;* the sigh of the merry-hearted is given as a token of general affliction. In Jeremiah the term occurs repeatedly as applied to rejoicing: "the voice of *mirth,* and the voice of gladness, the voice of the bride, and the voice of the bridegroom." And again, in another chapter, in a most beautiful passage, giving a prophetic picture of a land in utter desolation: "I will take from them the voice of *mirth,* and the voice of gladness; the voice of the bridegroom, and the voice of the bride; the sound of the millstones, and the light of the candle." None but a very gloomy, or a very presumptuous mind, would take upon itself to say, that in either of these instances, anything unbecoming, or evil, is implied by the words mirth and merry; to most persons the impression would be of an opposite character; seemly gayety and cheerfulness would be the idea suggested. In the translation of the Psalms as contained in the Prayer Book, the word *merry* is used on one occasion in a very exalted connection; the 47th Psalm is held to have been written either on the removal of the ark to Mount Zion, by King David, or a few years later, on its final progress from the Tabernacle to the Temple of Solomon. The fifth verse is thus translated: "God is gone up with a merry noise, and the Lord with the sound of the trump." Here we have the word applied to religious joy upon a signal occasion. It is also remarkable that this Psalm is one of those appointed for public worship on Ascension-Day, from the application of this same verse to the Ascension of our Lord; and shall we, then, object to employing the same word in connection with the Nativity? In the translation of the Holy Bible, made a century later, the same verse is rendered as follows: "God is gone up with a shout; the Lord with the sound of a trumpet."

But as if expressly to decide the question, we find in the prophet Hosea the word *mirth* directly applied to religious festivals. When rebuking the idolatry of the Jews, and proclaiming the punishments which should in consequence fall upon them, the prophet, speaking in the name of the Almighty, declares that the land shall be deprived of her festivals:

"I will also cause all her *mirth* to cease; her feast-days, her new moons, and her Sabbaths, and all her solemn feasts."

Here we have the very word in dispute applied to the great religious festivals of the Jewish Church. The learned theologians who translated the Hebrew Scriptures, held it a fitting term in connection with festivals of divine appointment, and coming from the lips of an inspired prophet; those holy days are spoken of as a blessing, as the *mirth* of the land, which the idolatrous tribes no longer deserved, and of which they were to be temporarily deprived, as a punishment for their sins. After this passage, it were worse than idle to cherish scruples against using the word in the same sense ourselves. Let us, then, with every return of the festival, gladly and heartily wish our neighbor, all fellow-Christians, the whole broad world, a right "Merry Christmas."

It is, in good sooth, Merry Christmas! The day is bright with blessings; all its hours are beaming with good and kindly feelings, with true and holy joys. Probably a fuller, purer incense of prayer and praise ascends from earth to Heaven, upon this great festival, than at other periods of the year. Thousands and ten thousands of knees are bowed in adoration, from the remotest coasts of heathen Asia, to the farthest isles of the sea; thousands and ten thousands of voices are raised among the rejoicing nations, repeating the sublime hymn first heard upon the hallowed hills of Bethlehem, and borne onward from that hour through the lapse of ages, unbroken, unceasing, by every successive generation of the redeemed:

"Glory to God in the highest; and on earth, peace, good-will to men."

It is Merry Christmas, indeed! Every beautiful festival we hold in religious reverence, is connected with this greater festival; they all, laden with blessings and graces, follow in the train of this holy day. Ay, it is the rising of the Sun of Righteousness on Christmas morn, which has even softened the Jewish Sabbath, and given us, with every successive week, the milder, purer light of the Lord's day. What better joy have we, indeed, from the first to the last hour of every passing year of life, which does not flow from the event we this day bear in fervent, thankful remembrance? Every mercy of the past dates from the advent we joyfully celebrate to-day. Every hope for the future looks to the same great mystery. Every prayer offered to Heaven, becomes an acceptable prayer only through faith in the same ineffable Name. Every exalted anticipation of final release from sin and sorrow, of attainment to the unspeakable joys of purity and wisdom, obedience and peace, is utterly groundless, save as it is connected with the Nativity hymned this day by the Christian Church Catholic.

It is, in truth, Merry Christmas! Peace on earth, good-will to man, sang the heavenly host; and, as though even the solemn recollection of the holy words were accompanied by a blessing, we find that the sweet charities, the better feelings of the heart, become more active on this holy day. There is nothing more striking in the daily course of the world, than the recklessness with which men trifle with the precious boon of peace, the very sunshine of life; perhaps there is no one folly which so generally, so frequently, and so lamentably reminds us that we are indeed "very far gone from original righteousness." But, on this holy day, when we especially celebrate the Nativity of the Prince of Peace, the solemn import of that high event, the perfect meekness, the pure humility, the unfailing fountains of patience and charity revealed to us in His sacred character, are not so easily forgotten as at other times; our cold hearts are touched, our impatient spirits are calmed, our evil passions are lulled to pious quiet by the noble devotions of the day. Probably, of all those who on this festival gather in the places of Christian worship, there are none, unless it be the wholly blind and unbelieving, who leave the house of God without some touch of pure and healthful influences; carrying with them, for a while at least, something more than usual of the light of Truth. Upon this holy day, there is indeed an increase of "peace on earth:" those who love already, love more truly, with more of that "pure and fervent affection" enjoined by the Apostle; friends draw nearer; and even those who in the struggle of life have held themselves as enemies, look with a milder eye upon each other—they feel, perhaps, some drop of better feeling, falling like oil on the stormy waves of evil passion. In short, on this day of blessing, the Christian meets no fellow-creature with absolute indifference, he parts from none with heartless carelessness.

Merry Christmas! Throughout Christendom, wherever the festival is observed—and there are now few communities where it is entirely forgotten—alms and deeds of charity to the poor and afflicted make a regular part of its services, proclaiming "good-will to man." The poor must ever, on this day, put in a silent but eloquent appeal for succor, in their Master's name; and those who have the means of giving, open more freely a helpful hand to their afflicted brethren. The hungry are fed, the naked are clothed, the cold are cheered and warmed with fuel, the desolate and houseless are provided for, the needy debtor is forgiven, an hour of ease and relief is managed for the weary and careworn, innocent gratifications are contrived by the liberal for those whose pleasures are few and rare. Doubtless there is no one community within the broad borders of Christendom, where the poor and needy receive, even on this day, a moiety of what should be given them, if we bore more faithfully in mind the precepts of our Master; nevertheless, were the whole amount of the charities of this festival told and numbered, it would assuredly prove larger than that of any other day of the year; and the heart rejoices that it is so; we love to remember how many sad spirits have been cheered, how many cares lightened, how many fears allayed by the blessed hand of Christian Charity moving in the name of her Lord.

Merry Christmas! What a throng of happy children there are in the world, to-day! It is delightful to recollect how many little hearts are beating with pleasure, how many childish lips are prattling cheerfully, lisping their Christmas hymns in many a different dialect, according to the speech the little creatures have inherited. These ten thousand childish groups scattered over Christendom, are in themselves a right pleasant vision, and enough to make one merry in remembering them. Many are gathered in the crowded dwellings of towns, others under the rustic roof of the peasant; some in the cabins of the poor, others within royal walls; these are sitting about the hearth-stone on the shores of arctic Iceland, others are singing in the shady verandahs of Hindostan; some within the bounds of our own broad land, are playing with ever-blooming flowers of a tropical climate, and others, like the little flocks of this highland neighborhood, are looking abroad over the pure white snows. Scarce a child of them all, in every land where Christmas Hymns are sung, whose heart is not merrier than upon most days of the year. It is indeed a very beautiful part of Christmas customs that children come in for a share of our joys to-day; the blessing and approbation of our gracious Lord were so very remarkably bestowed on them, that we do well especially to remember their claims in celebrating the Nativity; at other festivals they are forgotten, but their unfeigned, unalloyed gayety help, indeed, to make Christmas merry; and their simple, true-hearted devotions, their guileless Hosannas, must assuredly form an acceptable offering to Him who Himself condescended to become a little child, and who has said, "Suffer the little children to come unto me, and forbid them not, for of such is the kingdom of heaven." Other religions have scarcely heeded children; Christianity bestows on them an especial blessing; it is well, indeed, that they rejoice with us to-day.

Merry Christmas! The words fall idly, perhaps, from too many careless lips; they are uttered by those who give them no deeper meaning than a passing friendly salutation of the moment; and yet every tongue that repeats the phrase, bears unconscious witness to the power of the Gospel—those good-tidings of great joy to all mankind. From the lips of the most indifferent, these words seem to carry at least some acknowledgment of the many temporal benefits which Christianity has shed over the earth, those cheaper gifts of hers which are yet incalculable in their value. They tell of aid to the needy, of comfort to the prisoner, of shelter to the houseless, of care for the sick and helpless; they tell of protection to the feeble, to women, to children; they tell of every natural affection purified and strengthened; they tell of kinder parents, of children more dutiful, of husbands more generous and constant, of wives more faithful and true, of the high bond of brotherhood more closely knit; they tell of milder governments, of laws more just, of moral education; they tell of a worship holy and pure. "The fear of the Lord maketh a merry heart," says the wise son of Sirach.

Tuesday, 26th.—Cold; but the lake is still open. It has often beautiful moments at this season, and we watch it with increasing interest as we count the days ere its icy mask will creep over it.

Wednesday, 27th.—This evening's papers tell us of a panther actually killed on the Mohawk, immediately to the northward of our own position, within the last week! The animal was shot near the river by the captain of a Syracuse canal boat, and there seems very good reason to believe that it is the same creature who passed some weeks among our own hills. According to the reports brought into the village, the panther, when in our neighborhood, was taking a northerly course; during the last fortnight or three weeks nothing has been heard of him; and now we hear of an animal of the same kind recently killed about twenty miles to the northward of us, upon ground where it excited as much wonder as in our own valley.

It is rather mortifying that he should not have been killed in this county, where he chose to show himself repeatedly; but in fact, our sportsmen were too much afraid of being hoaxed to go out after him; they only began to believe the truth of the story when too late.

Thursday, 28th.—Snow again. Reports from Albany say the Hudson is probably closed, and navigation broken up for the winter. The river usually freezes some time before our lake.

Friday, 29th.—Snow. A darker sky than usual.

Saturday, 30th.—Still, half-cloudy day. Snow eighteen inches deep; a fall of several inches during the night. The air is always delightfully pure after a fresh fall of snow, and to-day this sort of wintry perfume is very marked. Long drive, which we enjoyed extremely. We have put on our winter livery in earnest, and shall probably keep it, with a break here and there, perhaps, until the spring equinox. It is, indeed, a vast change from grass to snow; things wear a widely different aspect from what they do in summer. All color seems bleached out of the earth, and what was a few weeks since a glowing landscape, has now become a still bas-relief. The hills stand unveiled; the beautiful leaves are gone, and the eye seeks in vain for a trace of the brilliant drapery of autumn—even its discolored shreds lie buried beneath the snow. The fields are all alike: meadow, and corn-field, and hop-ground, lie shrouded and deserted; neither laborers not cattle are seen a-field during three months of our year. Gray lines of wooden fences, old stumps, and scattered leafless trees are all that break the broad, white waste, which a while since bore the harvests of summer.

There is, however, something very fine and imposing in a broad expanse of snow: hill and dale, farm and forest, trees and dwellings, the neglected waste, and the crowded streets of the town, are all alike under its influence; over all it throws its beautiful vesture of purer white than man can bleach; for thousands and thousands of miles, wherever the summer sunshine has fallen, there lies the snow.

The evergreens on the hills show more white than verdure to-day, their limbs are heavily laden with snow, especially those near the summits of the hills. Saw a couple of crows in a leafless elm; they looked blacker than ever.

The lake is fine this afternoon, entirely free from ice. When we first went out it was a deep, mottled, lead-color: but the sky cleared, and toward sunset the waters became burnished over, changing to a warm golden gray, and looking beautifully in their setting of snow and evergreens.

January, Monday, 1st.—New Year's. Light, half-cloudy day; very mild. The lake quite silvery with reflections of the snow; much lighter gray than the clouds. Excellent sleighing.

The usual visiting going on in the village; all gallant spirits are in motion, from very young gentlemen of five or six, to their grandpapas, wishing "Happy New Year" to the ladies.

In this part of the world we have a double share of holiday presents, generous people giving at New Year's, as well as Christmas. The village children run from house to house wishing "Happy New Year," and expecting a *cookie,* or a copper, for the compliment. This afternoon we saw them running in and out of the shops also; among them were a few grown women on the same errand. These holiday applicants at the shops often receive some trifle, a handful of raisins, or nuts; a ribbon, or a remnant of cheap calico, for a sun-bonnet. Some of them are in the habit of giving a delicate hint as to the object they wish for, especially the older girls and women: "Happy New Year— and we'll take it out in tea"—"or sugar"—"or ribbon," as the case may be.

Tuesday, 2d.—Windy, bright and cold. Thermometer fallen to 2 above zero. The blue waters of the lake are smoking, a low mist constantly rising two or three feet above them, and then disappearing in the clear atmosphere—a sign of ice. Cold within doors; the frost has found its way into the house; people's energies are all directed to keeping warm such days as this.

Wednesday, 3d.—Cold, but less severe. Half a mile of ice on the lake; the waters gray-blue beyond this point. The wind raises the fresh, dry snow from the earth in clouds, and sweeps the forest branches, bearing the flakes upward toward the sky again, ere they have touched the earth. A wintry cloud of this kind is now whirling to a great height above the hills at the head of the lake. These whirling snow-clouds, borne aloft from the earth, are what the "voyageurs" call a "*pouderie.*" Several times this morning they have been colored with a golden tint, by the sun, like sand of gold.

Excellent sleighing, but too cold to enjoy it. The driver of the stage-coach became so chilled last night, that in attempting to wrap a blanket about his body, the reins dropped from his stiffened hands, the horses ran, he was thrown from his seat, and the sleigh upset; happily no one was seriously injured, though some persons were bruised.

The mails are very irregular now; the deep snow on the railroads retards them very much. This is winter in earnest.

Thursday, 4th.—Much milder. Light showers of snow, falling from time to time through the day. We have had little bright weather for the last week or two. The lake is still more than half open. A pretty flock of sparrows came to cheer us this afternoon.

Friday, 5th.—A very stormy day; cold, high wind; snow drifting in thick clouds. Yet strange to say, though so frosty and piercing, the wind blew from the southward. Our high winds come very generally from that quarter; often they are sirocco-like, even in winter, but at times they are chilly.

All the usual signs of severe cold show themselves: the smoke rises in dense, white, broken puffs from the chimneys; the windows are glazed with frost-work, and the snow creaks as we move over it.

Saturday, 6th.—Milder and quieter. Roads much choked with snow-drifts; the mails irregular; travelling very difficult. Lake still lying open, dark, and gray, with ice in the bays. There was a pretty, fresh ripple passing over it this morning.

It is Twelfth-Night, an old holiday, much less observed with us than in

Europe; it is a great day with young people and children in France and England, the closing of the holidays. It is kept here now and then in some families. But what is better, our churches are now open for the services of the Epiphany, so peculiarly appropriate to this New World, where, Gentiles ourselves, we are bearing the light of the Gospel onward to other Gentile races still in darkness.

Monday, 8th.–Cold night. The lake is frozen. We have seen the last of its beautiful waters for three months,[34] or more. One always marks the ice gathering about them with regret. No change of wind or weather short of this can destroy their beauty. Even in December, when the woods are bare and dreary, when the snow lies upon the earth, the lake will often look lovely as in summer–now clear, gay blue; now still, deep gray; then again varied with delicate tints of rose and purple, and green, which we had believed all fled to the skies.

At 7 o'clock this morning the thermometer was three degrees above zero; this evening it has risen to twenty-six degrees.

Tuesday, 9th.–Much milder; no more frost-work on the windows. Sparrows flitting about. We have seen more of them than usual this winter.

The hens are beginning to lay; a few eggs brought in from the poultry-yard. The eggs of this county have a great reputation among the dealers who supply the large towns. They are considered superior to those of other counties, probably from their size; no other eggs but those of Canada rank as high as ours in the city markets.

Wednesday, 10th.–Bright, cold day. Thermometer 6° *below* zero this morning.

The California gold mania has broken out among us. Two months since we knew nothing of these mines. Now, many of our young men, ay, and old men, too, have their heads full of them, eager to be off. A company for emigration is forming in the county, and the notices are posted up on the village trees in every direction.

How fortunate it was, or, rather, how clearly providential, that those tempting *placers* were not found on the Atlantic coast by our ancestors! Well for them, and for us their descendants, that the rich gold mines were found in Mexico and Peru, and not in Virginia or Massachusetts, the New Netherlands, or Pennsylvania. Well for the nation that the Indians spoke the truth when they pointed farther and farther to the westward for the yellow metal. Well for the people that they had to work their way across the continent before touching that dangerous ground. Had the *placers* of California lain in the Highlands, in the White or the Blue Mountains, we should now, in all probability, have belonged to enfeebled, demoralized colonies, instead of occupying the high and hopeful ground where we now stand, and which we may, by the grace of Providence, continue to hold, if true to our God, true and united among ourselves.

Thursday, 11th.—Clear, and severely cold. Thermometer 16 *below* zero at daylight this morning. Too cold for sleighing; but we walked as usual. So cold that the children have given up sliding down hill—the winter pastime in which they most delight. The lake is a brilliant field of unsullied white; for a light fall of snow covered it as it froze, greatly to the disappointment of the skaters. The fishermen have already taken possession of the ice, with their hooks baited for pickerel, and salmon-trout.

Men are driving about in fur over-coats, looking like very good representations of the four-legged furred creatures that formerly prowled about here. Over-coats of buffalo robes are the most common; those of fox and gray rabbit, or wolf, are also frequently seen.

Friday, 12th.—Severely cold. Thermometer 17 below zero at sunrise. Clear, bright weather. White frost on the trees this morning; the sign of a thaw. Few sleighs in motion; only a wood-sled here and there, bringing fuel to the village.

Such severe weather as this the turkeys can hardly be coaxed down from their roost, even to feed; they sometimes sit thirty-six hours perched in a tree, or in the fowl-house, without touching the ground. They are silly birds, for food would warm them.

Saturday, 13th.—Quite mild; bright sky; soft air from the southwest. Pleasant walk on the lake; just enough snow on the ice first formed, for a mile or so, to make the footing sure. Beyond this the ice is clear, but unusually rough, from having frozen of a windy night when the water was disturbed.

The clear, icy field, seen in the distance, might almost cheat one into believing the lake open; it is quite blue this afternoon with reflections of the sky. But we miss the charming play of the water.

Monday, 15th.—Yesterday was a delightful day; soft and clear. To-day it rains. We always have a decided thaw this month; "the January thaw," which is quite a matter of course. The lake is watery from the rain of Saturday night, which has collected on the ice, lake above lake, as it were. The hills and sky are clearly reflected on this watery surface, but we feel rather than see, that the picture is shallow, having no depth.

Tuesday, 16th.—The days are *growing,* as the country people say, very perceptibly. It is surprising how soon one observes a difference in this respect. According to the almanac, we have only gained a few minutes morning and evening—scarcely enough, one would think, to make any impression—but one marks the lengthening afternoons at once. We seem to have gained half an hour of daylight at least. This is always the first pleasant change in the new year.

Wednesday, 17th.—Pleasant weather. Good sleighing yet. Troops of boys skating on the lake. The ice is a fine light blue to-day; toward sunset it was colored with green and yellow; those not familiar with it might have fancied it open; but there is a fixed, glassy look about the ice which betrays the deception, and reminds one what a poor simile is that of a mirror, for the mobile, graceful play of countenance of the living waters, in their natural state.

The fresh, clear ice early in the season is often tinged with bright reflections of the sky.

Thursday, 18th.—It is snowing a little. The children are enjoying their favorite amusement of sliding to their hearts' content; boys and girls, mounted on their little sleds, fly swiftly past you at every turn. Wherever there is a slight descent, there you are sure to find the children with their sleds; many of these are very neatly made and painted; some are named, also—the "Gazelle," the "Pathfinder," &c., &c. Grown people once in a while take a frolic in this way; and of a bright moonlight night, the young men sometimes drag a large wood-sled to the top of Mount ——, or rather to the highest point which the road crosses, when they come gliding swiftly down the hill to the village bridge, a distance of just one mile—a pretty slide that—a very respectable *montague russe.*

Friday, 19th.—Cold. The evergreens make less difference than one would suppose in the aspect of the country. Beautiful in summer, when all about them is green, they never strike one as gloomy; those which are natives of this climate, at least, are not of a sombre character. But as winter draws on, and the snow falls, they seem to grow darker; seen in the distance, in contrast with the white ground, their verdure becomes what the shopmen call an "invisible green," darker than their own shadows lying on the snow. They seem at this moment to have put on a sort of half-mourning for their leafless companions. But let the snow melt, let the brown earth reappear, and their beauty returns—they are green again. There are many days in our winter when the woods of pine and hemlock look all but black. The trees taken singly, however, are always beautiful.

Saturday, 20th.—A crust has formed on the snow after the late thaw, so that we were enabled to leave the track this afternoon. It is very seldom that one can do this; there is rarely any crust here strong enough to bear a grown person. We are wholly confined to the highways and village streets for winter walks. One may look up never so longingly to the hills and woods, they are tabooed ground, like those inaccessible mountains of fairy-land guarded by genii. Even the gardens and lawns are trackless wastes at such times, crossed only by the path that leads to the doorway.

Occasionally, however, a prolonged thaw carries off the snow, even from the hills, and then one enjoys a long walk with redoubled zest. Within the last few years we have been on Mount—every month in the winter; one season in December, another in January, and a third in February. But such walks are quite out of the common order of things from the first of December to the fifteenth of March. During all that time, we usually plod humbly along the highways.

*Monday, 22d.—*The Albany papers give an extract from a paper of St. Lawrence county, which mentions that an animal becoming rare in this State, has recently been killed in that part of the country. A moose of the largest size was shot in the town of Russell, near the Grass River. It is described as "standing considerably more than six feet in height, with monstrous horns to match." It was frozen in a standing position, and exhibited as a curiosity in the same part of the country where it had been shot; many people went to look at him, never having seen one before. He was supposed to have strayed out of a large tract of forest to the southward, called the "South Wood."

These large quadrupeds are still rather numerous in the northern forest counties of New York; their tracks are frequently seen by the hunters, but they are so wary, and their senses are so acute, that it requires great art to approach them. It is chiefly in the winter, when they herd together, that they are shot.

They are ungainly creatures, with long legs, and an ill-shaped head, heavy horns, and a huge nose. The other animals of their tribe are all well formed, and graceful in their movements; but the moose is awkward, also, in his gait. His long legs enable him to feed on the branches of trees, whence his name of moose, from the Indian *musee* or *musu,* wood-eater. It is well known that our striped maple is a great favorite with him. He is partial, also, to aquatic plants, the pond-lily in particular. It will also eat bark, which it peels off from old trees. In winter, these animals herd together in the hilly woods, and they are said to show great sagacity in treading down the snow to form their *moose-yards.* In summer, they visit the lakes and rivers. At this season they are light brown; in winter they become so much darker, that they have been called the Black Elk. As they grow old they generally become, indeed, almost black.

Dr. De Kay believes our moose to be identical with the elk of Northern Europe. It is from six to seven feet in length, and has a mane. Their horns

are flat, broad, and in some instances four feet from tip to tip. They have occasionally been domesticated in this State, for they are easily tamed.

The moose is decidedly a northern animal; they range on this continent
from the Arctic Sea to 43° 30′ in the State of New York.

We have in the United States six varieties of the Deer family; of these,
three are found in New York: the Moose, the American Deer, and the American Stag.

The Deer is the smallest and the most common of the three. On Long
Island, thanks to the game laws, they are thought to be increasing, and in
other southern counties they are still numerous, particularly about the
Catskills and the Highlands. They are about five or six feet in length; of a
bluish gray in autumn and winter, and reddish in the spring. They belong
rather to a warm or temperate climate, extending from the Gulf of Mexico
to Canada.

The Stag is larger than the Deer—nearly seven feet in length, and about
four feet eight inches in height to the fore-shoulders. Its color is reddish in
spring, then yellowish brown, and in winter gray. The Stag is now very rare
in this State, though still found in the northern and southwestern counties.
It is frequently called the Red Deer, and the Round-horned Elk; in fact, it
would seem often to have been called more particularly the Elk, under
which name it was described by Jefferson. There is a little stream in this
county called the Elk Creek, and it was probably named from this animal.
It differs from the Stag of Europe. Its horns are round, never palmated.

Besides these three varieties, Dr. De Kay is inclined to believe that the
Reindeer was once found in this State, and that it may even possibly still exist in very small numbers in the recesses of our northern forests. It is said to
have been known in Maine and at Quebec; and later still, in Vermont and
New Hampshire. It is about the size of the common deer, the color varying
from deep brown to light gray. Both sexes have horns, which is not the case
with other species.

Tuesday, 23d.—Pleasant, mild day. Just on the verge of a thaw, which is always the pleasantest of winter weather. Walk on the lake. Quite slippery, as
the ice is only dappled with patches of snow here and there; between these
patches it is bare, and unusually clear and transparent. Indeed, it is just now
dark almost to blackness, so free from any foreign substance—no snow being mixed with it. We never saw it more dark and pure; of course it is the
deep waters beneath, shut out from the light as they are, which give this
grave color to the ice as you look down upon it.

Troops of boys skating. There were no very scientific performers among them, nevertheless we followed them with interest, their movement was so easy and rapid. Most of them appeared to greater advantage on skates than when moving in their shoes. Some of the little rogues, with the laudable desire of showing off, whirled to and fro about us, rather nearer than was agreeable. "Where's your manners, I'd like to know!" exclaimed an older lad, in an indignant tone, for which appeal in our behalf we were much obliged to him.

Ladies and little girls were walking about, some sliding also, their sleds drawn by gallant skaters. Altogether, it was a gay, cheerful scene.

The view of the village was very pleasing, the buildings showing against a bright sunset sky. They are cutting, or rather sawing ice, to supply the village next summer; the blocks are about ten inches thick. It is said that from eighteen to twenty inches is the greatest thickness of the ice observed here.

Wednesday, 24th.—Very mild—thawing—the snow going rapidly. The hills are getting brown and bare again, and the coarse stubble of the maize-fields shows plainly through the snow. Saw a winged insect by the road-side, a very rare sight indeed in our winters. I do not know what kind it was.

Met a number of teams drawing pine logs to the saw-mill. The river runs dark and gray; it never freezes near the village; the current, though not very swift, seems sufficient to prevent the ice from covering the stream. Ice often forms along the banks, but it is soon broken and carried away, and we have never seen it stretch across the river. Very pleasant it is, in the midst of a scene so still and wintry, to watch the running, living waters gliding along with a murmur as low and gentle as in June.

Thursday, 25th.—Rainy day. High south wind. The locust pods are scattered about the lawn on the dregs of the snow, yet the number on the trees seems scarcely diminished.

They are cutting ice; the sleds and men moving about in the water which lies above the ice, look oddly enough; and, like the swan of St. Mary's, they move double also—sleds, men, and oxen reflected as clear as life.

Friday, 26th.—Beautiful morning; charming sunrise, warm clouds in a soft sky. The lake rosy with reflections.

Saw a couple of flies sailing slowly about the room; they are seldom seen here in winter. The spiders, so common in the autumn, have either been killed by the cold, or lie stowed away until spring. The whole insect world is silent and invisible, save the cricket. This is the only creature of its kind heard about the house during our long winters. We have one just now living somewhere about the chimney, which sings with a very clear, spirited note, especially of an evening when the fire burns brightly. It is said that our crickets in this country are all field crickets, which have found their way into houses by accident; they seem to like their lodgings very well, for they chirrup away gayly at all seasons, even when their companions in the fields are buried deep under the snow. They do well to haunt our houses in this way, for it makes quite different creatures of them, adding another, and apparently a merry, cheerful, half to their lives. They do not seem to require the annual sleep of their companions out of doors. The true house-cricket of Europe is not found in America. Whether the voices, or rather the chirrup, of both is precisely alike, we cannot remember; probably there is not much difference, if any. It is well known that the sounds made by these little creatures are produced by playing their wing-covers; so that, in fact, they rather fiddle than sing. It is the male only who is the musician, the females are quiet.

We owe the Mice and Rats which infest our dwellings, entirely to the Old World. The common brown rat, already so numerous here, is said to have come from Asia, and only appeared in Europe about the beginning of the seventeenth century, or some two hundred and fifty years since. The English say it came over with the Hanoverian kings. The German mercenaries, the "Hessians," of popular speech, are supposed to have brought it to this country. The Black Rat, smaller, and now very rare, is said to have also come from Europe. We have, however, one native rat in this part of the world,—the American Black Rat—differing from the other species, and very rare indeed.

The common Mouse, also, is an emigrant from Europe.

We have very many field-mice, however, belonging to the soil. Among these is the Jumping-Mouse, which builds its nest in trees, and is common through the country. The tiny tracks of the Field-Mice are occasionally seen on the snow in winter.

There is another pretty little animal, called the Deer-Mouse, which, strictly speaking, is not considered a mouse. Its body is only three inches long, while its tail is eight inches. It takes leaps of ten or twelve feet. It is a northern animal, nocturnal, and rarely seen, but not uncommon; they are frequently found in ploughed grass-lands. They feed chiefly on grass and seeds.

Saturday, 27th.—Very fine day; quite a full market-day in the village; many people coming in from the country.

The word "store" has been declared an Americanism, but it is not always easy to decide what words and terms have actually been coined on this side the Atlantic, so many of those which pass for Yankeeisms being found in the best English writers, like the *stage* of Sterne, and the *pretty considerable* of

Burke, for instance. Many other words and phrases of this disputed nature were undeniably brought over by the original colonists, and have been merely preserved by their descendants, while our English kinsmen have forgotten them. It is quite possible that the word "store" was first brought into common use when there was but one store-house in every new colony, and all the different wants of the little community were supplied from the same establishment. Although circumstances have so much changed since those days, although the catalogue of necessaries and luxuries has been so much increased, yet the country store still preserves much of this character, and would seem to deserve a name of its own. It is neither a shop devoted to one limited branch of trade, nor a warehouse implying the same branch carried out on a greater scale, nor is it a bazaar where many different owners offer goods of various kinds within the same walls. The store, in fact, has taken its peculiar character, as well as its name, from the condition of the country; and the word itself, in this application of it, might bear a much better defence than many others which have found their way into books.

Now-a-days there are always, however, more than one store in every village. Indeed, you never find one of a trade standing long alone anywhere on Yankee ground. There is no such man in the country as *the* village doctor, *the* baker, *the* lawyer, *the* tailor; they must all be marshalled in the plural number. We can understand that one doctor should need another to consult and disagree with; and that one lawyer requires another with whom he may join issue in the case of Richard Roe *vs.* John Doe, but why there should always be two barbers in an American village, does not seem so clear, since the cut of the whiskers is an arbitrary matter in our day, whatever may be the uncertainties of science and law. Many trades, however, are carried on by threes and fours; it strikes one as odd that in a little town of some 1400 souls, there should be three jewellers and watchmakers. There are also some score of *tailoresses*–and both trade and word, in their feminine application, are said to be thoroughly American. Then, again, there are seven taverns in our village, four of them on quite a large scale. As for the eating-houses– independently of the taverns–their number is quite humiliating; it looks as though we must needs be a very gormandizing people: there are some dozen of them–Lunches, Recesses, Restaurants, &c., &c., or whatever else they may be called, and yet this little place is quite out of the world, off the great routes. It is, however, the county town, and the courts bring people here every few weeks.

But to return to the "store;" there are half a dozen of these on quite a large scale. It is amusing to note the variety within their walls. Barrels, ploughs, stoves, brooms, rakes and pitchforks; muslins, flannels, laces and shawls; sometimes in winter, a dead porker is hung up by the heels at the door; frequently, frozen fowls, turkeys and geese, garnish the entrance. The shelves are filled with a thousand things required by civilized man, in the long list of his wants. Here you see a display of glass and crockery, imported, perhaps, directly by this inland firm, from the European manufacturer; there you observe a pile of silks and satins; this is a roll of carpeting, that a box of artificial flowers. At the same counter you may buy kid gloves and a spade; a lace veil and a jug of molasses; a satin dress and a broom; looking-glasses, grass-seed, fire-irons, Valenciennes lace, butter and eggs, embroidery, blankets, candles, cheese, and a fancy fan.

And yet, in addition to this medley, there are regular milliners' shops and groceries in the place, and of a superior class, too. But so long as a village retains its rural character, so long will the country "store" be found there; it is only when it has become a young city that the shop and warehouse take the place of the convenient store, where so many wants are supplied on the same spot.

It is amusing once in a while to look on as the different customers come and go. Some people like shopping in a large town, where all sorts of pretty novelties are spread out on the counters to tempt purchasers; but there is much more real interest connected with such matters in a large country store, whatever fine ladies tossing about laces and gauzes at Beck's or Stewart's may fancy. The country people come into the village not to *shop*, but to *trade;* their purchases are all a matter of positive importance to them, they are all made with due forethought and deliberation. Most Saturdays of the year one meets farm-wagons, or lumber-sleighs, according to the season, coming into the village, filled with family parties—and it may be a friend or two besides—two and three seats crowded with grown people, and often several merry-faced little ones sitting in the straw. They generally make a day of it, the men having, perhaps, some business to look after, the women some friends to hunt up, besides purchases to be made and their own produce to be disposed of, for they commonly bring with them something of this kind; eggs or butter, maple-sugar or molasses, feathers, yarn, or homespun cloths and flannels. At an early hour on pleasant Saturdays, summer or winter, the principal street shows many such customers, being lined with their wagons or sleighs; in fact, it is a sort of market-day. It is pleasing to see these family parties making their purchases. Sometimes it is a mother exchanging the fruits of her own labors for a gay print to make frocks for the eager, earnest-looking little girls by her side; often the husband stands by holding a baby—

one always likes to see a man carrying the baby—it is a kind act—while the wife makes her choice of teacups or brooms; now we have two female friends, country neighbors, putting their heads together in deep consultation over a new shawl. Occasionally a young couple appear, whom one shrewdly guesses to be betrothed lovers, from a peculiar expression of felicity, which in the countenance of the youth is dashed, perhaps, with rustic roguery, and in that of his sweetheart with a mixture of coquetry and timidity; in general, such couples are a long while making their choice, exchanging very expressive looks and whispers while the bargain is going on. It sometimes happens that a husband or father has been either charged with the purchase of a gown, or a shawl, for some of his womankind, or else, having made a particularly good sale himself, he determines to carry a present home with him; and it is really amusing to look on while he makes his selection—such close examination as he bestows on a shilling print is seldom given to a velvet or a satin; he rubs it together, he passes his hand over it with profound deliberation; he holds it off at a distance to take a view of the effect; he lays it down on the counter; he squints through it at the light; he asks if it will wash—if it will wear well—if it's the fashion? One trembles lest, requiring so much perfection, the present may after all not be made, and frequently one is obliged to leave the shop in a state of painful uncertainty as to the result, always hoping, however, that the wife or daughter at home may not be disappointed. But male and female, old and young, they are generally a long time making up their minds. A while since we found a farmer's wife, a stranger to us, looking at a piece of pink ribbon; we had several errands to attend to, left the shop, and returned there again nearly half an hour later, and still found our friend in a state of hesitation; a stream of persuasive words from the clerk showing the ribbon, seemed to have been quite thrown away. But at length, just as we were leaving the shop for the second time, we saw the ribbon cut, and heard the clerk observe—"Six months hence, ma'am, you'll come into town expressly to thank me for having sold you three yards of that ribbon!"

It frequently happens, if you are standing at the same counter with one of these hesitating purchasers, that they will appeal to you for advice as to the merit of some print, or handkerchief, &c., &c.

Monday, 29th.—Mild, with light rain. Sleighing gone, wheel-carriages out to-day.

The Crows are airing themselves this mild day; they are out in large flocks sailing slowly over the valley, and just rising above the crest of the hills as they come and go; they never seem to soar far above the woods. This afternoon a large flock alighted on the naked trees of a meadow south of the village; there were probably a hundred or two of them, for three large trees were quite black with them. The country people say it is a sign of pestilence, when the crows show themselves in large flocks in winter; but if this were so, we should have but an unhealthy climate, for they are often seen here during the winter. This year, however, they appear more numerous than common. The voice of our crow is so different from that of the European bird, that M. Charles Bonaparte was led to believe they must be another variety; upon examination, however, he decided they were the same. The habits of our crow, their collecting in large flocks, their being smaller, and living so much on grain, are said rather to resemble those of the European Rook:

> "The shortening winter's day is near a close,
> The miry beasts returning frae the plough,
> The *blackening trains o' Craws,* to their repose,
> The toil-worn Cotter frae his labor goes,"–

says Burns, in the "Cotter's Saturday Night," and he alluded to the rook, for the European crow is not gregarious. Our birds are very partial to evergreens; they generally build in these trees, and roost in them; and often at all seasons we see them perched on the higher branches of a dead hemlock or pine, looking over the country.

The Raven is rare in this State; it is found, however, in the northern counties, but is quite unknown on the coast. About Niagara they are said to be common. They do not agree with the common crow, or rather where they abound the crow seldom shows itself; at least such is observed to be the case in this country. In Sweden, also, where the raven is common, the crow is rare. The raven is much the largest bird, nearly eight inches longer, measuring twenty-six inches in length, and four feet in breadth; the crow measures eighteen and a half inches in length, and three feet two inches in breadth. Both the crow and the raven mate for life, and attain to a great age. They both have a habit of carrying up nuts and shell-fish into the air, when they drop them on rocks, for the purpose of breaking them open.

It is said that the Southern Indians invoke the Raven in behalf of their sick. And the tribes on the Missouri are very partial to Ravens' plumes when putting on their war-dress.

Tuesday, 30th.– Cooler. Wood-piles are stretching before the village doors; the fuel for one winter being drawn, sawed, and piled away the year before it is wanted. They are very busy with this task now; these piles will soon be neatly stowed away under sheds, and in wood-houses, for they are all obliged to be removed from the streets, early in the spring, by one of the village laws.

Wood is the only fuel used in this county. In such a cold climate we need a large supply of it. Five years since it sold here for seventy-five cents a half cord; it now costs a dollar the half cord. Iron stoves are very much used here; they are considered cheaper, warmer, and safer than fire-places. But how much less pleasant they are! The smell of the heated iron is always disagreeable, and the close atmosphere they give to a room must necessarily prove unhealthy. A fine, open, wood fire is undeniably the pleasantest mode of heating a room; far more desirable than the coal of England, the peat of Ireland, the delicate laurel charcoal and bronze brazier of Italy, or the unseen furnace of Russia. The very sight of a bright hickory or maple fire is almost enough to warm one; and what so cheerful as the glowing coals, the brilliant flame, and the star-like sparks which enliven the household hearth of a bracing winter's evening as twilight draws on! Such a fire helps to light as well as heat a room; the warm glow it throws upon the walls, the flickering lights and shadows which play there as the dancing flames rise and fall, express the very spirit of cheerful comfort. The crackling, and rattling, and singing, as the flame does its cheerful work, are pleasant household sounds. Alas, that our living forest wood must ere long give way to the black, dull coal; the generous, open chimney to the close and stupid stove!

Wednesday, 31st.—Cold. Walked in the afternoon. It began to snow while we were out; but one minds the falling snow very little; it is no serious obstacle like rain. The pretty, white spangles, as they fell on our muffs, in their regular but varied shapes, recalled a passage in Clarke's Travels in Russia, where he admires the same delicate frost-work as a novelty. It is common enough in this part of the world. Since Mr. Clarke's day these pretty spangles have received the compliment of a serious examination, they have actually been studied, and drawn in all their varieties. Like all natural objects, they are very admirable in their construction, and they are very beautiful also.

February, Thursday, 1st.—Stormy day. A flock of sparrows passed the night in a balsam-fir near the house, and this morning we amused ourselves with watching their *lever*. We first saw them about seven o'clock, closely huddled together under the thickest of the branches; then a movement began, some of them came to the outer branches, and shook themselves; but they soon retired again to more sheltered ground, for the tree was covered with hoar-frost, and sleet was falling at the time. One would think the little creatures must have been covered with ice themselves, and half frozen. They were a long time making up their minds to get up such a stormy morning; then they busied themselves with preening and dressing their feathers; and at length, when it was near nine o'clock, they made a general movement, and flew off together in the midst of the sleet and snow.

The Chicadees and Snow-birds scarcely mind the cold at all; on the contrary, you often see them active and merry in the midst of the whirling snow and wind. Probably all our winter birds lodge at night in the evergreens.

Friday, 2d.—Milder; a little snow. This climate of ours is a trying one for the architect. In a mechanical sense, the severe frosts, and accumulated snows, and sudden thaws of our winters, make up a season which tries men's walls, and roofs, very thoroughly. But in another way, also, our winters are a severe test of architectural merit; the buildings stand before one naked and bare, not only deprived of all the drapery of summer foliage, but rising from a ground-work of snow, they seem to stand out with peculiar boldness, and every defect challenges attention. One may feel assured that a building which bears the scrutiny of a snow climate in winter, will look like a perfect model at other seasons. There is a certain fitness in some styles of architecture which adapts them to different climates; a Grecian edifice never appears to advantage surrounded with snow; there is a sort of elegance and delicacy in its lines which seem to require softer skies, and verdure for its accessories. A Gothic pile, on the contrary, bears the snow well; it does not look chilled; it was not built of a summer's day, it was made to brave the storm and tempest of northern lands. This connection of climate and architecture would seem to have not yet received all the attention it deserves, more especially in our own country.

Saturday, 3d.—Blustering day. Among the numerous evergreens of this State are several which are interesting from European associations, and from their being rather rare in our woods, many persons believe them to be wholly wanting.

The Holly is found on Long Island, and on the island of Manhattan, and a little farther south it is very common. It grows from ten to forty feet in height, and very much resembles that of Europe, though not precisely similar.

The Yew is only seen here as a low trailing shrub, from four to six feet high. It is found in the Highlands, and is not common northward.

The Juniper, or Red Cedar, is common enough in many parts of the country. Besides this variety, which is a tree, there is another, a low shrub, trailing on the ground, found along the great lakes, and among our northern hills, and this more closely resembles the European Juniper, whose berries are used in gin.[35]

Among the trees of note in this part of the country are also several whose northern limits scarcely extend beyond this State, and which are rare with us, while we are familiar with their names through our friends farther south. The Liquid Amber, or Sweet-Gum, is rare in this State, though very common in New Jersey; and on the coast it even reaches Portsmouth, in New Hampshire.

The Persimmon grows on the Hudson as far as the Highlands, and in the extreme southern counties. It is rather a handsome tree, its leaves are large and glossy, and its fruit, as most of us are aware, is very good indeed, and figures often in fairy tales as the medlar.

The Magnolias of several kinds are occasionally met with. The small Laurel Magnolia, or Sweet Bay, is found as far north as New York, in swampy grounds. The Cucumber Magnolia grows in rich woods in the western part of our State; and there is one in this village, a good-sized tree, perhaps thirty feet high; it is doing very well here, though the Weeping Willow will not bear our climate. This tree, in favorable spots, attains a height of ninety feet. The Umbrella Magnolia, a small tree, with large, white flowers, seven or eight inches broad, and rose-colored fruit, is said also to be found in our western counties.

The Papaw, belonging to the tropical Custard-apple family, grows in rich soil, upon the banks of the western waters of New York, which is its extreme northern limit.

The Kentucky Coffee-tree, with its peculiar blunt branches, is also found in rich woods, on the banks of the rivers of our western counties. It is a rough, rude-looking tree, with rugged bark, and entirely without the lesser spray one usually finds on trees. We have one in the village, and it has attained to a good size, though scarcely forty years old.

Monday, 5th.—Fine day. Saw a Woodpecker in the village; one of the arctic woodpeckers, which pass the winter here. They are not common in our neighborhood.

Tuesday, 6th.—Rabbits brought to the house for sale. They are quite numerous still about our hills; and although they are chiefly nocturnal animals, yet one occasionally crosses our path in the woods by day. At this season our rabbits are gray, whence the name zoologists have given them, the American gray rabbit; but in summer they are yellowish, varied with brown. They differ in their habits from those of Europe, never burrowing in the earth, so that a rabbit *warren* could scarcely exist in this country, with the native species, at least. Our rabbit would probably not be content to be confined to a sort of garden in this way. Like the Hare, it makes a *form* for its nest, that is to say, a slight depression in the ground, beneath some bush, or wall, or heap of stones. It is found from New Hampshire to Florida.

The Northern Hare, the variety found here, is much larger than the rabbit. It measures from twenty to twenty-five inches in length; the Gray Rabbit measures only fifteen or eighteen inches. The last weighs three or four pounds; the first six pounds and a half. In winter our hare is white, with touches of fawn-color; in summer, reddish brown; but they differ so much in shading, that two individuals are never found exactly alike. The flesh is thought inferior to that of the gray rabbit. The hare lives exclusively in high forests of pine and fir; it is common here, and is said to extend from Hudson's Bay to Pennsylvania. There are a number of other hares in different parts of the Union, but this is the only one known in our own State. It is said to make quite a fierce resistance when seized, unlike the timid hare of Europe, although that animal is now thought to be rather less cowardly than its common reputation.

Wednesday, 7th.—Was there ever a region more deplorably afflicted with ill-judged names, than these United States? From the title of the Continent to that of the merest hamlet, we are unfortunate in this respect; our mistakes began with Americo Vespucci, and have continued to increase ever since. The Republic itself is the great unnamed; the States of which it is composed, counties, cities, boroughs, rivers, lakes, mountains, all partake in some degree of this novel form of evil. The passing traveller admires some cheerful American village, and inquires what he shall call so pretty a spot; an inhabitant of the place tells him, with a flush of mortification, that he is approaching Nebuchadnezzarville, or South-West-Cato, or Hottentopolis, or some other monstrously absurd combination of syllables and ideas. Strangely enough, this subject of names is one upon which very worthy people seem to have lost all ideas of fitness and propriety; you shall find that tender, doting parents, living in some Horridville or other, will deliberately, and without a shadow of compunction, devote their helpless offspring to lasting ridicule, by condemning the innocent child to carry through the world some pompous, heroic appellation, often misspelt and mispronounced to boot; thus rendering him for life a sort of peripatetic caricature, an ambulatory laughing-stock, rather than call him Peter or John, as becomes an honest man.

It is true we are not entirely without good names; but a dozen which are thoroughly ridiculous, would be thought too many in most countries, and unfortunately, with us such may be counted by the hundred. By a stroke of good luck, the States are, with some exceptions, well named. Of the original thirteen, two only bore Indian names: Massachusetts and Connecticut;

six, as we all remember, were taken from royal personages: Virginia, from
Queen Bess; Maryland, from Henrietta Maria, the French wife of Charles I.;
New York, from the duchy of James II.; Georgia, called by Gen. Oglethorpe
after George II., and the two Carolinas, which, although the refuge of many
Huguenot families, so strangely recall the cruel Charles IX. and the wicked
butchery of St. Bartholomew's. Of the remaining three, two were named after private individuals–New Jersey, from the birth-place of its proprietor,
Sir George Carteret, and Pennsylvania, from the celebrated Quaker, while
New Hampshire recalled an English county; Maine, the former satellite of
Massachusetts, was named by the French colonists after the fertile province
on the banks of the Loire, and Vermont, which stood in the same relation
to New York, received its French title from the fancy of Young, one of the
earliest of our American poets, who wrote "The Conquest of Quebec," and
who was also one of the fathers of the State he named. Louisiana, called after the great Louis, and Florida, of Spanish origin, are both good in their
way. Happily, the remaining names are all Indian words, admirably suited
to the purpose; for what can be better than Alabama, Iowa, Missouri, Kentucky, Tennessee, &c., &c.?

New York, at present the most populous State in the republic, is in this respect the most afflicted part of the country. The name of the State itself is
unfortunate in its association with the feeble James, while the combination
of the adjective *New,* with the brief old Saxon word York, seems particularly
ill-judged. To make the matter worse, the fault is repeated in the title of the
largest town of the Union, both State and city bearing the same name, which
is always a great mistake, for it obliges people, in writing and speaking, to
specify which of the two they mean, when either is mentioned. In fact, it destroys just half the advantage of a distinctive name. The Dutch were wiser:
they called the town New Amsterdam, and the province New Netherlands.
In old times, when the capital town ruled a whole dependent country, it
was natural that the last should be known by the name of the first; Rome
and Carthage, Tyre and Athens, could each say, "L'etat, c'est moi!" and
more recently, Venice, Genoa, Florence, Berne, and Geneva, might have
made the same boast; but we Yankees have different notions on this point:
cockneys and countrymen, we all have the same rights, and the good city of
New York has never yet claimed to eclipse the whole State. The counties
of New York are not quite so badly served: many of them do very well; but
a very large number of the towns and villages are miserably off in this respect, and as for the townships into which the counties are divided, an out-
rageously absurd jumble of words has been fastened upon too many of them.

It ought to be a crime little short of high treason, to give such names to habitable places; we have Ovids and Milos, Spartas and Hectors, mixed up with Smithvilles, and Stokesvilles, New Palmyras, New Herculaneums, Romes and Carthages, and all these by the dozen; for not content with fixing an absurd name upon one spot, it is most carefully repeated in twenty more, with the aggravating addition of all the points of the compass tacked to it.

We cannot wonder that such gratuitous good-nature in providing a subject of merriment to the Old World should not have been thrown away. The laugh was early raised at our expense. As long ago as 1825, some lines in heroic verse, as a model for the imitation of our native poets, appeared in one of the English Reviews.

"Ye plains where sweet Big-Muddy rolls along,
And Teapot, one day to be found in song,
Where Swans on Biscuit, and on Grindstone glide,
And willows wave upon Good-Woman's side!"
     *   *   *   *   *   *   *
"Blest bards who in your amorous verses call
On murmuring Pork, and gentle Cannon-Ball,
Split-Rock, and Stick-Lodge, and Two-Thousand-Mile
White-Lime, and Cupboard, and Bad-Humored Isle."
     *   *   *   *   *   *   *
"Isis with Rum and Onion must not vie,
Cam shall resign the palm to Blowing-Fly,
And Thames and Tagus yield to Great-Big-Little-Dry!"

Retaliation is but an indifferent defence, and is seldom needed, except in a bad cause. A very good reply, however, appeared in an American Review, and it is amusing, as it proves that we came very honestly by this odd fancy for ridiculous names, having inherited the taste from John Bull himself, the following being a sample of those he has bestowed upon his discoveries about the world:

"Oh, could I seize the lyre of Walter Scott,
Then might I sing the terrors of Black Pot,
   Black River, Black Tail,
   Long Nose, Never Fail,
   Black Water, Black Bay,
   Black Point, Popinjay,

Points Sally and Moggy,
Two-Headed and Foggy,
While merrily, merrily bounded Cook's bark,
By Kidnapper's Cape, and old Noah's Ark,
Round Hog Island, Hog's-Heads, and Hog-Eyes,
Hog-Bay and Hog John, Hog's Tails, and Hog-Sties."

* * * * * * *

Perhaps this taste is one of the peculiarities of the Anglo-Saxon race, about which it is the fashion to talk so much just now. The discoverers from other nations do not seem to have laid themselves open to the same reproach. The Portuguese names for the Cape of Good Hope, Labrador, Buenos Ayres, &c., are very good; both themselves and the Spaniards gave many religious names, but the navigators of these nations also left many Indian words wherever they passed. M. Von Humboldt observes that Mantanzas, *massacre*, and Vittoria, *victory*, are frequently scattered over the Spanish colonies. The Italians have made little impression in the way of names, though they have supplied noted chiefs to many a fleet of discovery; probably, however, many words of theirs would have been preserved on the hemisphere bearing an Italian name, if the language had been spoken in any part of the continent, by a colony of their own. As a people, they have produced great leaders, but no colonists. The French have generally given respectable names, either repetitions of personal titles, or of local names, or else descriptive words: la Louisiane, les Carolines, le Maine, Montreal, Quebec, Canada; for, as we have already observed, leaving a good Indian name is equal to giving one of our own. It may also be doubted if the French have placed one really ridiculous word on the map. The Dutch, also, have shown themselves trustworthy in this way; their names are rarely poetical, but they are never pompous or pretending. They are usually simple, homely, and hearty: the Schuylkill, or Hiding-Creek; Reedy Island; Boompties-Hoeck, Tree-Point; Barnegat, the Breaker-Gut; Great and Little Egg Harbors; Still-water; Midwout, or Midwood; Flachtebos, or Flatbush; Greenebos, Greenbush; Hellegat; Verdreitige Hoack, Tedious Point; Haverstroo, or Oat Straw; Yonker's Kill, the Young-Lord's-Creek; Bloemen'd Dal, Bloomingdale, are instances. Among the most peculiar of their names, are Spyt-den-duyvel Kill, a little stream, well known to those who live on the Island of Manhattan, and Pollepel Island, a familiar object to all who go up and down the Hudson; In-spite-of-the-devil-creek is a translation of the name of the stream; formerly there was a ford there, and the spot was called Fonteyn, Springs. Pollepel means a ladle, more especially the ladle with which waffles were made. So says Judge Benson.

In short, it would not be difficult to prove that, happily for the world, other nations have shown more taste and sense in giving names than the English or the Yankees. It is remarkable, that both the mother country and her daughter should be wanting in what would seem at first a necessary item in national existence, a distinctive name. The citizens of the United States are compelled to appropriate the title of the continent, and call themselves Americans, while the subjects of the British Empire spread the name of England over all their possessions; their sovereign is known as Queen of England, in spite of her heralds; their armies are the armies of England, their fleets are English fleets, and the people are considered as Englishmen, by their neighbors, whether born in the Hebrides, or at Calcutta, at Tipperary, or the Cape of Good Hope.

Fortunately for us, the important natural features of this country had already been well named by the red man. The larger rivers, for instance, and the lakes, are known by fine Indian words, uniting both sound and meaning, for the Indian, the very opposite of the Yankee in this respect, never gives an unfitting name to any object whatever. As the larger streams of this country are among the finest waters on the earth, it is indeed a happy circumstance that they should be worthily named; no words can be better for the purpose than those of Mississippi, Missouri, Ohio, Alabama, Altamaha, Monongahela, Susquehannah, Potomac, &c., &c. The lakes, almost without an exception, are well named, from the broad inland seas of Huron, Michigan, Erie, Ontario, to the lesser sheets of water which abound in the northern latitudes of the Union; it is only when they dwindle into the mere pond of a neighborhood, and the Indian word has been forgotten, that they are made over to the tender mercies of Yankee nomenclature, and show us how fortunate it is that we escaped the honor of naming Niagara and Ontario.

There are many reasons for preserving every Indian name which can be accurately placed; generally, they are recommended by their beauty; but even when harsh in sound, they have still a claim to be kept up on account of their historical interest, and their connection with the dialects of the different tribes. A name is all we leave them, let us at least preserve that monument to their memory; as we travel through the country, and pass river after river, lake after lake, we may thus learn how many were the tribes who have melted away before us, whose very existence would have been utterly forgotten but for the word which recalls the name they once bore. And possibly, when we note how many have been swept from the earth by the vices borrowed from civilized man, we may become more earnest, more zealous, in the endeavor to aid those who yet linger among us, in reaping the better fruits of Christian civilization.

It is the waters particularly which preserve the recollection of the red man. The Five Nations are each commemorated by the principal lakes and the most important stream of the country they once inhabited. Lakes Cayuga, Oneida, Onondaga, and Seneca, each recall a great tribe, as well as the river Mohawk, farther eastward. There is a sound which, under many combinations, seems to have been very frequently repeated by the Iroquois—it is the syllable Ca. This is found in Canada; it is preserved in two branches of the Mohawk, the East and the West Canada, Lake Canaderagua, to the south of the same stream; Canandaigua, and Canadaseago, and Canajoharie, names of Indian towns; Cayuga, Candaia, Cayuta, Cayudutta, Canadawa, Cassadaga, Cassassenny, Cashaguash, Canasawacta, Cashong, Cattotong, Cattaraugus, Cashagua, Caughnawaga, and Canariaugo, &c., &c., are either names still found in the Iroquois country, or which formerly existed there. This syllable *Ca,* and that of *Ot* and *Os,* were as common at the commencement of a name as *agua, aga, ogua,* were at the conclusion.

From the roving life led by the Indians, hunting and fishing in different places, according to the changes in the seasons, they have left but few names to towns and villages, and scarcely any to plains and valleys. Nor does it seem always easy to decide whether they gave their own names to the lakes and rivers, or received them from the streams; in very many cases in this part of the continent the last would seem to have been the case, especially in the subdivisions of the clans, for scarce a river but what had a tribe of its own fishing and hunting upon its banks. Their names for the mountains have only reached us in a general way, such as the Alleghany, or Endlesschain, the Kittatinny, &c., &c. Perhaps the fact that the mountains in this region lie chiefly in ridges, unbroken by striking peaks, may be one reason why single hills have not preserved Indian names; but in many instances the carelessness of the first colonists was probably the cause of their being lost, since here and there one of a bolder outline than usual must have attracted the attention of such an observant race.

Our own success in naming the hills has been indifferent; the principal chains, the Blue, the Green, the White Mountains, the Catsbergs, the Highlands, &c., &c., do well enough in the mass, but as regards the individual hills we are apt to fail sadly. A large number of them bear the patronymic of conspicuous political men, Presidents, Governors, &c., &c. That the names of men honorably distinguished should occasionally be given to towns and counties, or to any mark drawn by the hand of society upon the face of a country, would seem only right and proper; but except in extraordinary cases growing out of some peculiar connection, another class of words appears much better fitted to the natural features of the land, its rivers, lakes, and hills. There is a grandeur, a sublimity, about a mountain especially, which should ensure it, if possible, a poetical, or at least an imaginative name. Consider a mountain peak, stern and savage, veiled in mist and cloud, swept by the storm and the torrent, half-clad in the wild verdure of the evergreen forest, and say if it be not a miserable dearth of words and ideas, to call that grand pile by the name borne by some honorable gentleman just turning the corner, in "honest broadcloth, close buttoned to the chin." Indeed, if we except the man in the moon, whose face is made up of hills, and that stout Atlas of old, who bore the earth on his shoulder, no private individual would seem to make out a very clear claim to bestow his name upon a vast, rocky pile. Perhaps a certain Anthony, whose nose meets us so boldly in more than one place, might prove a third exception, provided one could clearly make out his identity. But generally it must be admitted that this connection between a mountain and a man, reminds one rather unpleasantly of that between the mountain and the mouse.

Doubtless it is no easy task to name a whole country. Those gentlemen who devote themselves to making geographical discoveries, who penetrate into unknown deserts, and cross seas where pilots have never been before them, encounter so many hardships, and have so many labors to occupy their attention, that we cannot wonder if they are generally satisfied with giving the first tolerable name which occurs to them; and it is perhaps only a just reward of their exertions that the names given by them should be preserved. But this privilege can only be claimed in the earliest stages of discovery. Those who come after and fill up the map, have not the same excuse. They have more time for reflection, and a better opportunity for learning the true character of a country in its details, and consequently should be better judges of the fitness of things.

And yet it is a mortifying fact that in this and in some other points, perhaps, public taste has deteriorated rather than improved in this country; the earlier names were better in their way than those of a later date. The first colonists showed at least common sense and simplicity on this subject; it was a natural feeling which led them to call their rude hamlets along the shores of the Chesapeake and Massachusetts Bays after their native homes in the Old World; and although these are but repetitions, one would not wish them changed, since they sprang from good feeling, and must always possess a certain historical interest. But a continued, frequent repetition not only wears away all meaning, but it also becomes very inconvenient. After the Revolution, when we set up for ourselves, then was the moment to make a change in this respect; the old colonial feeling had died away, and a good opportunity offered for giving sensible, local names to the new towns springing up throughout the country; but alas, then came the direful invasion of the ghosts of old Greeks and Romans, headed by the Yankee schoolmaster, with an Abridgment of Ancient History in his pocket. It was then your Troys and Uticas, your Tullys and Scipios, your Romes and Palmyras, your Homers and Virgils, were dropped about the country in scores. As a proof that the earlier names were far better than most of those given to-day, we add a few taken from the older counties of this State: Coldspring, the Stepping-Stones, White Stone, Riverhead, West-Farms, Grassy Point, White Plains, Canoeplace, Oakhill, Wading River, Old Man's, Fireplace, Stony Brook, Fonda's Bush, Fish-house, &c.

Long Island shows an odd medley of names; it is in itself a sort of historical epitome of our career in this way; some Dutch names, some Indian, others English, others Yankee, with a sprinkling of Hebrew and Assyrian. Long Island was the common Dutch name. The counties of Kings, Queens, and Suffolk came, of course, from England, after the conquest of the colony under Charles II.; then we have Setauket, and Patchogue, Peconic, Montauk, and Ronkonkoma, which are Indian, with many more like them; Flushing, Flatbush, Gowanus, Breuckelen or Brooklyn, and Wallabout, are Dutch; Hempstead, Oyster Bay, Near Rockaway, Shelter Island, Far Rockaway, Gravesend, Bay Side, Middle Village, and Mount Misery, are colonial; Centreville, East New York, Mechanicsville, Hicksville, with others to match, are clearly Yankee; Jerusalem, we have always believed to be Jewish; Jericho, is Canaanitish, and Babylon, we understand to be Assyrian.

There is less excuse for the pompous folly committed by giving absurd names, when we remember that we are in fact no more wanting in good leading ideas for such purposes, than other people. After the first duty of preserving as many Indian words as possible, and after allowing a portion of the counties and towns for monuments to distinguished men, either as local benefactors or deserving well of the country generally, there would no doubt still remain a large number of sites to be named. But we need not set off on a wild goose chase in quest of these. Combinations from different natural objects have been hitherto very little used in this country, and yet they are always very pleasing when applied with fitness, and form a class almost inexhaustible from their capability of variation. Broadmeadows, Brookfield,

Rivermead, Oldoaks, Nutwoods, Highborough, Hillhamlet, Shallowford, Brookdale, Clearwater, Newbridge, &c., &c., are instances of the class of names alluded to, and it would be easy to coin hundreds like them, always bearing in mind their fitness to the natural or artificial features of the spot; springs, woods, heights, dales, rocks, pastures, orchards, forges, furnaces, factories, &c., &c., are all well adapted to many different combinations in this way.

Another large and desirable class of names may be found in those old Saxon words, which have been almost entirely overlooked by us, although we have a perfectly good right to use them, by descent and speech. They will bear connection either with proper names or with common nouns. A number of these may be readily pointed out. There is *ham* or home, and *borough,* also, which have occasionally, though rarely, been used. We give others of the same kind:

Bury, means a town or a hamlet; Seabury would therefore suit a town on the sea-shore; Woodbury another near a wood.

Rise, speaks for itself, as rising ground.

Wick, has a twofold signification: either a village, or a winding shore, or bay. Sandwich would suit another village on the shore; Bushwick for a bushy spot upon some river.

Stead, and *Stowe,* and *Stock,* have all three the same general signification of a dwelling-place. Thus, Newstead means also Newtown; Woodstock means a place in the woods.

Burn and *Bourne,* signify either a stream or a boundary, and would, with other words, either proper or common, suit many villages; thus, River-bourne, where two States or counties are divided by a river. Alderburn, for a village on a brook where alders grow; Willowburn also.

Shire, means a division.

Combe, means a valley; Meadowcombe, Longcombe, Beavercombe, are instances.

Ness, is a promontory or headland; as Cliffness.

Wark, means a building; like Newark.

Worth, means a street or road, or a farm, and combined with other words, would be adapted to many a hamlet; as Longworth, Hayworth, Hopworth, &c., &c.

Werth, Wearth, and *Wyrth,* with the same sound, have the same meaning as *Worth.*

Hurst, is a thicket of young trees; Elmhurst, Hazelhurst, Maplehurst, are examples of its application.

Holt, is a wood. Grayholt would do for a hamlet near an old forest, Green-holt for a younger one; Beech-holt, Firholt, Aspenholt, are other examples.

Shaw, is also a wood, or a marked tuft of trees; Cedarshaw, Shawbeech, Oakshaw, are examples.

Weald, also signifies a wood; Broadweald, Highweald, Pineweald, would make good names.

Wold, on the contrary, is a plain or open country, little wooded.

Hithe, is a small haven or port.

Moor, is a marsh or fen.

More, on the contrary, and Moreland, signify hilly grounds.

Mere and *Pool, Water* and *Tarn,* are of course suitable for small lakes.

Thorpe, is a village; Newthorpe, Valleythorpe, Hillthorpe, are examples.

Hay, is a hedge, and would suit a small hamlet where hedges are found.

Haw and *Haugh,* mean small meadows.

Cott, or *Cote,* applies to cottages, and would suit many hamlets.

By, as a termination, means a dwelling-place; *ly* or *leigh,* a field. *Croft,* a small enclosure.

Now would not most of these, and others like them, answer much better than the constant repetition of *ville* or *town*? Let us suppose a small village to spring up in a new country; one of its most prominent inhabitants, bearing the name of Antoninus Smith, has shown much interest in the place, and contributed in various ways to its advancement. His neighbors are well aware of the fact, and wish to express their sense of his merits by naming the little place after him. Some, accordingly, propose Antoninusville, others prefer Smithville; one admires Smithopolis, another Antoninustown. They are soon agreed, however, for names are among the very few subjects which it is not thought necessary to submit to discussion in this wordy land of ours. A post is put up at the first crossing in the highway—"To Smithville, 2 miles." Now would not Smithstead, or Smithbury, have answered much better, showing that something may be done with the most unpromising name without tacking a *ville* to it?

Then, again: if there be several places of the same name in one neighborhood, as frequently happens, they are distinguished by East, West, North and South; as for example: Scienceville, East Scienceville, West Scienceville, Scienceville Centre. Now, it happens that a fine grove of oaks stands on a point quite near the principal village; let us, therefore, change the name to Oakhurst, and instead of the points of the compass, to distinguish the different hamlets, let us call them Upper and Lower, High and Nether, Far and Near Oakhurst, and would not most people declare this an improvement?

The very fact of our motley origin as colonists should provide some good materials for naming new towns and villages. Not by weak and absurd repetitions of all the European capitals in the shanties of American backwoods, but by adopting those terminations peculiar to each nation which will bear an English pronunciation. Such may easily be found. *Heim,* and *Hausen,* and *Dorf,* and *Feld,* are German words, well suited to many places in Pennsylvania. *Wyck,* and *Daal,* and *Dorp,* are Dutch words, which will bear the same connection with proper names of Dutch origin. The Huguenots from France may employ *hameau,* and *côte,* and *champ,* and *roche,* and *plaine* in the same way. Some Swedish and Norwegian words of the same kind would be well placed among the honest Scandinavian colonists who have lately gone out upon the prairies of Wisconsin and Iowa. A fit selection from Scotch, Irish, and Welsh words of the same class may well be preserved among the descendants of emigrants from those countries. Now and then it would not be amiss if some of the smaller lakes and pools, which are now worse than nameless, were to become loch Jeanie, or loch Mary, loch Davie, or loch Willie. In short, if we would but think so, we have by far too many resources in this way, to be driven perpetually to the Classical Dictionary for assistance.

Thursday, 8th. – Cool and blustering day, with sunshine in the morning. The sleighing very good, though we have but little snow on the ground. Walked near the village; a solitary bird flew past us, a sparrow, I believe; generally in winter most birds move in flocks.

Friday, 9th. – The papers this evening give an instance of a man recently killed by panthers near Umbagog Lake, a large sheet of water on the borders of New Hampshire. A hunter left home one morning to look after his traps, as usual; at night he did not return, and the next day his friends went out to look after him, when his body was found in the woods, mangled and torn, with the tracks of two panthers about the spot. So far as the marks in the snow could tell the sad history, it was believed that the hunter had come suddenly on these wild creatures; that he was afraid to fire, lest he should exasperate one animal by killing the other, and had thought it wiser to retrace his steps, walking backward, as was shown by his foot-prints; the panthers had followed as he retreated with his face toward them, but there were no signs of a struggle for some distance. He had, indeed, returned half a mile from the point where he met the animals, when he had apparently taken a misstep, and fallen backward over a dead tree; at this moment, the wild beasts would seem to have sprung upon him. And what a fearful death the poor hunter must have died! Panthers, it is said, would be very likely to have taken advantage of such an accident, when they might not have attacked the man had he continued to face them without in his turn attacking them. The body, when found, was torn and mangled; the hunter's gun, loaded and cocked, lay where it had fallen; but the creatures had left the spot when the friends of the poor man came up. They were followed some distance by their tracks, and their cries were distinctly heard in a thicket; but it seems the animals were not attacked. Perhaps the men who followed them were not armed. What a moment it must have been, when, alone in the forest, the poor hunter fell, and those fierce beasts of prey both leaped upon him!

Saturday, 10th.—Pleasant day, though coldish. We have had no very severe days, and no deep snow, since the first week in January. The season is considered a decidedly cold one; but it has been comparatively much more severe in other parts of the country than in our own neighborhood. Our deepest snow has been eighteen inches; we have known it three feet on a level.

Monday, 12th.—It is snowing this morning. Brook Trout brought to the house. They are found in many of our smaller streams. We received a very fine mess not long since; the two largest weighed very nearly a pound; there are but few of that size now left in our waters. It would seem that our Brook Trout is entirely a northern fish. Dr. De Kay observes that he has never heard of its being found north of the forty-seventh or south of the fortieth parallel of latitude. In Ohio, it is only known in two small streams. There is another variety, the Red-bellied Trout, found in our northern mountain streams, a large and beautiful fish, of a dark olive-green color, spotted with salmon color and crimson. The flesh is said to be also of a bright red, approaching carmine.

Tuesday, 13th.—Fine day. The good people are beginning to use the lake for sleighs: it is now crossed by several roads, running in different directions. In passing along this afternoon, and looking at the foot-prints of horses, oxen, and dogs, on the snow-covered ice, we were reminded what different tracks were seen here only seventy years since. Moose, stags, deer, wolves must have all passed over the lake every winter. To this day, the ice on the northern waters of our State is said to be strewed with carcasses of deer, which have been killed by the wolves. In former times, when the snow lay on these hills which we now call our own, the Indians by the lake shore must have often watched the wild creatures, not only moving over the ice, but along the hill-sides also, for at this season one can see far into the distant hanging woods, and a living animal of any size moving over the white ground, would be plainly observed. To-day the forests are quite deserted in winter, except where the wood-cutters are at work, or a few rabbits and squirrels are gliding over the snow.

It would seem that although the wild animals found in these regions by the Dutch on their arrival, have been generally driven out of the southern and eastern counties, all the different species may yet be found within the limits of the present State. Their numbers have been very much reduced, but they have not as yet been entirely exterminated. The only exceptions are the Bison, which is credibly supposed to have existed here several centuries since, and perhaps the Reindeer.

Bears were once very numerous in this part of the country, but they are now confined to the wilder districts. Occasionally, one will wander into the cultivated neighborhoods. They are still numerous in the hilly counties to the southward of our own, and they do not appear to be very soon driven away from their old grounds; within forty-five years, a bear has wintered in a cave on a petty stream a couple of miles from the village. They retire with the first fall of snow, and pass three or four months in their annual sleep, living, meanwhile, upon their own fat; for they never fail to carry a good stock to bed with them in the autumn, and they wake up very thin in the spring. Their flesh is said to taste like pork. They live on all sorts of fruits and berries, wild cherries, grapes, and even the small whortleberries. Honey is well known as one of their greatest delicacies. They also like potatoes and Indian corn. They eat insects, small quadrupeds and birds, but prefer sweet fruits to any other food. They are from four to six feet in length, and three feet in height to the fore-shoulders.

The moose, the stag, and the deer we have already noticed as still found within our borders.

The panther, also, it would seem, has made us quite a recent visit.

Next in size to these larger quadrupeds comes the Wolf. The American species measures four or five feet in length, and is rather more robust than that of Europe. Formerly it was believed to be smaller. We have two varieties in New York, the black and the gray, the first being the most rare. They are quite common in the northern counties, and are said to destroy great numbers of the deer, hunting them in packs of eight or ten. They are particularly successful in destroying their prey in winter, for in summer the deer take to the water and escape; but in winter, on the ice, the poor creatures are soon overtaken. The hunters say that the wolves destroy five deer where one is killed by man. Some years after this little village was founded, the howl of the wolf, pursuing the deer on the ice, was a common sound of a winter's night, but it is now many years, half a century, perhaps, since one has been heard of in this neighborhood.

Foxes are still to be found within the county, though not common. Two kinds belong to our quadrupeds: the Red and the Gray. The red is the largest, about three or four feet in length; there are two varieties of this fox which are less common, and highly valued for their furs. One is the Cross Fox, bearing the mark of a dark cross on its back: this sells for twelve dollars, while the common fox sells for two dollars. It is found throughout the State. The Black Fox, again, is extremely rare; it is almost entirely black, and only seen in the northern counties; the fur is considered six times more valuable than that of any other animal in America.

The common Gray Fox, again, is a different species, smaller than the red, and more daring. This is a southern animal, not seen far north of 42°, while it extends to Florida. Both the red and the gray probably exist in this county, but as this is not a sporting region, we hear little of them. Some skins of the red fox are, however, sold every year in the village.

Beavers have become extremely rare in New York. They no longer build dams, but are found only in families in the northern counties. Three hundred beaver skins were taken in 1815 by the St. Regis Indians, in St. Lawrence county; since then the animals have become very rare. They were formerly very common here, as in most parts of the State; there was a dam at the outlet of our lake, and another upon a little stream about a mile and a half from the village, at a spot still bearing the name of Beaver Meadows. These animals are two or three feet long, of a bay or brown color. They are nocturnal in their habits, and move on land in successive leaps of ten or twelve feet. They are said to eat fish as well as aquatic plants and the bark of trees. Old Van der Donck declares that 80,000 beavers were killed annually in this part of the continent during his residence here, but this seems quite incredible. Dr. De Kay has found, in a letter of the Dutch West India Company, the records of the export of 14,891 skins in the year 1635. In ten years, the amount they exported was 80,103, the same number which the old chronicler declares were killed in one year. The flesh was considered the greatest of dainties by the Indians, the tail especially; and in this opinion others agreed with them, for it is said that whenever a beaver, by rare good luck, was caught in Germany, the tail was always reserved for the table of the Emperor. The Russians, it seems, were great admirers of beaver fur, and the New Netherlanders shipped their skins to that country, where they were used as trimmings, and then returned to the Dutch, after the hair had worn away by use, to be made into hats, for which they were better adapted in this condition than at first.

Otters are now very rare indeed; they were once very common on our streams. Their habits are much like those of the beaver, but they are decidedly larger, measuring from three to five feet in length. Their fur is valued next to the beaver for hats and caps, and is in great request, selling at eight dollars a skin. These animals have one very strange habit: it is said that they actually slide down hill on the snow, merely for amusement; they come down head foremost, and then, like so many boys, climb up for the pleasure of the slide down again. They will amuse themselves for hours in this way. And even in summer, they pursue the same diversion, choosing a steep bank by the side of a stream, which gives them a dip as they come down. One would like to see them at their play. "The Otter," would be a very good name for one of the sleds used by boys for the same amusement.

Fisher is another name for the Black Cat, an animal nearly three feet in length, which was formerly very numerous. It is nocturnal, eats small quadrupeds, and climbs trees. It feeds on fish also, stealing the bait and destroying traps, whence its name.

The Sable, or Marten, is a small brown animal, about two and a half feet in length. It is nocturnal, and lives entirely in the trees of our northern forests. To procure this valuable fur, the hunters will sometimes stretch a line of traps across sixty or seventy miles of country, allowing six to ten traps for each mile! Every trap is visited about once in a fortnight. Dr. De Kay supposes that our Sable is quite distinct from the European Pine Marten, to which it is allied.

The Ermine of New York is a small creature, about one or two feet in length; in winter, it is pure white, but brown in summer. It is active and nocturnal. Our people sometimes call it the Catamingo.

Then there are two Weasels, confounded at times with the Ermine, and about twelve inches in length.

The Mink lives on fish, haunting ponds. It is about two feet in length.

The Skunk we all know only too well. There is one in the village now, which has taken possession of the cellar of one of the handsomest houses in the place, and all but driven the family out of doors. For several months it has kept possession of its quarters with impunity; our friends being actually *afraid* to kill it, lest its death should be worse even than its life.

The Wolverine is another nocturnal creature, about two feet and a half in length. It destroys numbers of small animals. Its color varies from cream to dark brown. It is very troublesome about the hunters' traps, stealing their bait, but fortunately it is rare. The Indians called it "Gwing-gwah-gay," a tough thing. It is now unknown south of 42°, though formerly extending to Carolina.

Raccoons are found all over North America; they are about the size of the

Wolverine, two or three feet in length. We saw one not long since, caught in the neighborhood, and living in a cage. Their color varies: gray, mixed with black. It has been described as having "the limbs of a bear, the body of a badger, the head of a fox, the nose of a dog, the tail of a cat, and sharp claws, by which it climbs trees like a monkey." It is very partial to swamps. The flesh, when young, is said to taste like that of a pig. He eats not only fowls, but Indian corn, so that the farmer has no great partiality for him. The fur is valuable for hats.

There is also a sort of Marmot in this State, and quite a common animal, too: the Woodchuck, or Ground-hog; it is a social creature, laying up stores of provisions in its burrow. It is about twenty inches in length. It is a great enemy to clover, upon which it feeds. They are found alike in the forest and upon the farm, making deep and long burrows.

The Muskrat, or Musquash, is an aquatic creature, about eighteen inches in length; quite common.

The Opossum is also found within our limits, in the southern counties. It lives in trees, feeding on birds' eggs and fruits. It is nocturnal, measures about two feet in length, and is of a grayish white color. East of the Hudson it is not found.

The Porcupine is about two and a half feet in length, a gentle, harmless creature, though forbidding in its aspect. It feeds on the bark and leaves of the hemlock, ash, and basswood. In our northern counties, they are still quite numerous. They leave their spines in the bodies of their enemies, but are easily killed by a blow on the nose. The Indians of many tribes seem to have had a great fancy for the porcupine quills, showing much ingenuity in using them for ornamental purposes.

Such, with the rabbit, and hare, and the squirrels, are the more important quadrupeds of this part of the country; all these were doubtless much more numerous in the time of the Red man than to-day, and probably many of the species will entirely disappear from our woods and hills, in the course of the next century. They have already become so rare in the cultivated parts of the country, that most people forget their existence, and are more familiar with the history of the half-fabulous Unicorn, than with that of the American panther or moose.

Wednesday, 14th.—Cold day. Quite a rosy flush on the lake, or rather on the ice and snow which cover it; there are at times singular effects of light and shade upon the lake at this season, when passing clouds throw a shadow upon it, and give to the broad white field very much the look of gray water.

It is St. Valentine's day, and valentines by the thousand are passing through the post-offices all over the country. Within the last few years, the number of these letters is said to have become really astonishing; we heard that 20,000 passed through the New York post-office last year, but one cannot vouch for the precise number. They are going out of favor now, however, having been much abused of late years.

The old Dutch colonists had a singular way of keeping this holiday; Judge Benson gives an account of it. It was called *Vrouwen-Dagh,* or woman's day. "Every mother's daughter," says the Judge, "was furnished with a piece of cord, the size neither too large nor too small; the twist neither too hard nor too loose; a turn round the hand, and then a due length left to serve as a lash." On the morning of this *Vrouwen-Dagh,* the little girls–and some large ones, too, probably, for the fun of the thing–sallied out, armed with just such a cord, and every luckless wight of a lad that was met received three or four strokes from this feminine lash. It was not "considered fair to have a knot, but fair to practice a few days to acquire the *sleight.*" The boys, of course, passed the day in a state of more anxiety than they now do under the auspices of St. Valentine; "never venturing to turn a corner without first listening whether no warblers were behind it." One can imagine that there must have been some fun on the occasion, to the lookers-on especially; but a strange custom it was. We have never heard of anything like it elsewhere. The boys insisted that the next day should be theirs, and be called *Mannen-Dagh,* man's day, "but my masters were told the law would thereby defeat its own purpose, which was, that they should, at an age, and in a way most likely never to forget it, receive the lesson of *Manliness, never to strike.*" As the lesson has been well learnt by the stronger sex in this part of the world, it is quite as well, perhaps, that the custom should drop, and *Vrouwen-Dagh* be forgotten. But after this, who shall say that our Dutch ancestors were not a chivalrous race?

Thursday, 15th.–Very cold. Still, bright day; thermometer 8° below zero this morning at sunrise. The evergreens feel this severe weather, especially the pines; when near them, one observes that their long slender leaves are drawn closer together, giving a pinched look to the tufts, and the young twigs betray an inclination to droop. The hemlocks also lose something of their brilliancy. The balsams do not seem to feel the cold at all.

Friday, 16th.–Very cold, clear day. Thermometer 8° below zero this morning again.

Looking abroad through the windows such weather as this, in a climate so decided as ours, one might almost be persuaded that grass, and foliage, and flowers are dreamy fancies of ours, which, like the jewel-bearing trees of fairy-land, have never had a positive, real existence. You look in vain over the gardens, and lawns, and meadows, for any traces of the roses and vio-

lets which delighted you last summer, and which you are beginning to long
for again. But turn your eyes within doors, and here you shall find the most
ample proofs that leaves and blossoms really grow upon this earth of ours;
here, within the walls of our dwellings, we need no green-house, or conser-
vatory, or flower-stand to remind us of this fact. Here, winter as well as summer, we find traces enough of the existence of that beautiful part of the creation, the vegetation; winter and summer, the most familiar objects with
which we are surrounded, which hourly contribute to our convenience and
comfort, bear the impress of the plants and flowers in their varied forms and
colors. We seldom remember, indeed, how large a portion of our ideas of
grace and beauty are derived from the plants, how constantly we turn to
them for models. It is worth while to look about the first room you enter, to
note how very many proofs of this you will find there. Scarcely an article of
furniture, from the most simple and homely to the most elegant and elaborate, but carries about it some imitation of this kind, either in its general outline, form, or color, or in some lesser details. Look at the chair on which
your friend is sitting, at the carpet beneath your feet, at the paper on the
walls, at the curtains which shut out the wintry landscape, at the table near
you, at the clock, the candlesticks, nay, the very fire-irons—or it may be the
iron mouldings upon your stove—at the picture-frames, the book-case, the
table-covers, the work-box, the inkstand, in short, at all the trifling knick-
knacks in the room, and on all these you may see, in bolder or fainter lines,
a thousand proofs of the debt we owe to the vegetable world, not only for
so many of the fabrics themselves, but also for the beautiful forms, and colors, and ornaments we seek to imitate. Branches and stems, leaves and tendrils, flowers and fruits, nuts and berries, are everywhere the models.

As for our clothing, in coloring as in its designs, it is a studied reflection
of the flowers, and fruits, and foliage; nay, even the bark, and wood, and the
decayed leaves are imitated; *feuille morte* was a very fashionable color in
Paris, once upon a time. Madame Cottin, the authoress of the Exiles of
Siberia, had a "feuille morte" dress, which figured in some book or other,
thirty or forty years ago. The patterns with which our dresses and shawls are
stamped or woven, whether from the looms of France, Italy, or Persia, are
almost wholly taken from the fields and gardens. Our embroidery, whether
on lace, or muslin, or silk, whether it be the work of a Parisian, a Swiss, a
Bengalee, or a Chinese, bears witness to the same fact. Our jewelry shows
the same impression. In short, the richest materials and the cheapest, the
lightest and the heaviest, are alike covered with blossoms, or vines, or leaves,
in ten thousand varied combinations.

And such has always been the case; the rudest savage, the semi-barbarian, and the most highly civilized races have alike turned to the vegetation for their models. Architecture, as we all know, has been borrowed almost wholly from the forest, not only in its grander forms, but also in its lesser ornamental parts; the lotus, the honeysuckle, and the acanthus, are found carved on the most ancient works of man yet standing upon the earth–the tombs and temples of Hindostan, and Egypt, and Greece. In short, from the most precious treasures of ancient art, down to the works of our own generation, we find the same designs ever recurring. The most durable and costly materials the earth holds in her bosom, stone and marble, gold, and silver, and gems, have been made to assume, in a thousand imposing or graceful forms, the lines of the living vegetation. How very many of the proudest works of art would be wanting, if there had been no grace and dignity in trees, no beauty in leaves and flowers!

Probably the first rude attempts at pottery were modelled upon the rounded forms of the Eastern gourds. The rinds of vegetables of that kind were doubtless the first vessels used by man in antediluvian times. Wherever they are found, they are employed in this way by the savage races of the present day. The Indians of this part of the world were using the rind of gourds as water-vessels in their wigwams, when the Dutch came among them; the colonists also borrowed the custom, glad to turn the "calabash" to account in this way, since crockery and other hardware were not easily procured. Before tin-ware and crockery had become so cheap, calabashes or gourds were constantly seen in American farm-houses, as water-vessels, in common use; very possibly a few may yet be found here and there, in rural, inland districts, at the present hour.

Among the remains of Aztec pottery, preserved in the Museum at Mexico, there are vessels in imitation of fruits. Others, however, are in the form of shells, a natural device for people living between two oceans.

There is a design of art very common among us to-day, which carries one far back into the forests of primeval ages, when hunters were heroes. Look at the tea-table beside you: if it be one of neat workmanship, you will probably find that the legs are carved in imitation of the claw of a lion, a device so common for such purposes, that a village workman will offer to cut it for you in the black walnut, or bird's-eye maple, or mahogany, of a continent where no lion has ever been found! When first carved, in Egypt, or Asia, or Greece, it probably recalled some signal contest within the bounds of the primeval forest, between the fiercest of savage animals and some local Hercules. From the dignity of the animal, and the renown of the hunter, the device was preserved; and it has been handed down by the most polished artists of successive ages, until it has reached our own Western World. It is very often found carved in marble, or moulded in bronze, and generally, the acanthus leaf makes part of the design.

Saturday, 17th.–Bright, clear sunshine. Thermometer 4° below zero at sunrise.

Sunday, 18th.–Cold and bright day. Thermometer 2° below zero at sunrise.

Monday, 19th.–Very cold; bright weather; thermometer 12° below zero at seven o'clock. We have had a week of severe weather; generally, the extreme cold does not last longer than three days at one time. There is a white frost, however, this morning on the trees: the forerunner of a thaw. Walked, as usual, though not far; in such weather one does not care to be out long at a time. It is something of an exertion to leave the fire-side and face such a sharp frost.

Tuesday, 20th.–Growing milder. Cloudy; thermometer above zero at sunrise; at two o'clock it had risen to twenty.

Amused ourselves this evening by looking a little into the state of things in our own neighborhood, as reported by the last general Census; comparing the condition of our own county with that of others in the same State. The growth of the inland region, to which our valley belongs, will prove, in most respects, a good example of the state of the country generally. The advance of this county has always been steady and healthful; things have never been pushed forward with the unnatural and exhausting impetus of speculation, to be followed by reaction. Neither do we possess a railroad or a canal within our limits. We have not even a navigable river within our bounds; steamboats and ships are as great strangers as the locomotive. It will be seen, therefore, that we claim no striking advantages of our own, and what prosperity we enjoy, must flow from the general condition of the country, and the industry of our population. Improvement, indeed, has here gone on steadily and gradually, from the time when the valley was shaded by the forest, some sixty-five years since, to the present hour. And now let us see what has been done in that time.

The county is one of fifty-nine in this State; its area is 892 square miles, that of the State is 45,658 miles. The population of the county in 1840, the date of the following estimates, was 49,626 souls, that of the State, 2,428,292 souls. This is the nineteenth county in the State for extent, and the thirteenth for population. The people are scattered over the hills and valleys, in farm-houses and cottages, or collected in villages and hamlets; the largest town in the county contained, at the date of these estimates, 1,300 souls.

First let us look at the state of things in agricultural matters, produce and stock, &c., &c.

	No., Value, &c., in County.	No., Value, &c., in State.		Otsego Co. ranking as—
Horses,	12,331	No.	474,543	VII.
Neat Cattle,	66,035	"	1,911,244	III.
Sheep,	235,979	"	5,118,717	I. by 20,000.
Hogs,	47,637	"	1,900,065	XII.
Poultry, value,	$825,781	Value	$1,151,418	XII.
Wheat, bushels,	148,880	Am't	12,288,418	XXIII.
Barley, "	116,715	"	2,520,068	VIII.
Oats, "	693,987	"	20,675,847	V.
Rye, "	68,236	"	2,797,320	XV.
Maize, "	122,382	"	10,973,286	XXXII.
Buckwheat, "	45,659	"	2,287,885	XVIII.
Wool, pounds,	451,064	"	9,845,295	I.
Hops, "	168,605	"	447,250	I.
Wax, "	2,941	"	52,795	II. Ulster yields more.
Potatoes, bushels,	1,239,109	"	30,123,614	IV.
Hay, tons,	106,916	"	3,127,047	III.
Hemp and Flax, tons,	33 3/4	"	1,130 3/4	V.
Tobacco, pounds,	104	"	744	II.
Silk Cocoons, "	5	"	1,735	XXIII.
Sugar, "	351,748	"	10,048,109	VIII.
Dairy Produce,	$383,123	Value	$10,496,021	VI.
Orchard "	$41,341	"	$1,701,935	X.

And now we will look at the manufactures:

Fulling-mills,	43	No.	890	I.
Woollen Factories,	4	"	323	XXVII.
Woollen Goods, value,	$11,000		$3,537,337	XXXIX.
Cotton Factories,	8	"	117	VI.

Dyeing & Printing Estb't,	1	"	12	IV.
Cotton Goods, value,	$109,817	Value	$3,640,237	IX.
Manufactories of Flax,	none	"	46,429	–
Pounds of Silk, reeled,	none	"	337	–
Tanneries,	47	No.	1,216	III.
Distilleries,	9	"	212	V.
Breweries,	1	"	83	XII.
Paper-mills,	1	"	77	XX.
Printing Offices,	5	"	321	XIII.
Musical Instm'ts made, val.	$8,500	Value	$472,900	VI.
Carriages, Wagons mnct'd,	$49,760	"	$2,364,461	XIV.
Hats and Caps, "	$18,985	"	$2,914,117	XVI.
Straw Bonnets, "	656	"	$160,248	XVI.
Grist-mills,	65	No.	1,750	I.
Saw-mills,	222	"	6,356	VI.
Oil-mills,	3	"	68	IV.
Furniture manufactured,	$1,200	Value	$1,970,779	XXIII.
Home-made Goods,	$119,507	"	$4,636,577	VII.
Wine, gallons,	90	Am't	6,799	–

We turn to the proceeds of the forest:

	No., Value, &c., in County.		No., Value, &c., in State	Otsego Co. ranking as –
Lumber, value,	$39,934	Value	$3,891,302	XXIV.
Pot and Pearl Ashes, tons,	122	"	7,613	XX.
Skins and furs,	none	Amt	15,550	–

Various other items stand as follows:

Cast-iron Furnaces,	7	No.	186	IV.
Machinery mnft'd, value,	$4,750	Value	$2,895,517	XXXVI.
Hardware " "	$660	"	$1,566,974	XXII.
Small Arms mnft'd,	565	Am't	8,308	III.
Precious Metals "	$500	Value	$1,106,208	XVI.
Granite and Marble,	$2,120	"	$966,220	XXI.
Various Metals,	$21,000	"	$2,456,792	XII.
Brick and Stone Houses,	10	No.	1,238	XIX.
Wooden "	134	"	5,198	XV.

Upon some occasion, when assailed by the statistics of his opponents, Mr. Canning is said to have quietly observed, that "few things were more false than *figures,* unless it be *facts,*" an assertion no doubt as true, as it is witty. There are probably many errors in all these tables; perhaps one might point out two items which are not strictly accurate in the statement of things in our own county. It is said, for instance, that no flax is manufactured here, while there is very frequently a little used in this way in home-made manufactures. Then, again, no furs and skins are reported: but a few fox skins are sold in the village, probably, every year. Still, the general view is sufficiently accurate to be very interesting. What a striking difference there is already, for instance, in this new county, between the produce of the forests and that of manufactures and agriculture! Furs and skins have entirely disappeared, and in the place of the beaver and deer, our valleys now feed a greater number of sheep than any other county in the State. The produce of the lumber is already less than that of the orchards. The value of the maple sugar nearly equals that of the lumber. It will be observed, that for wool, hops, fulling-mills, and grist-mills, we are the first county in the State. For wax we are the second; and doubtless for honey also, though honey is not specified in the table. For neat cattle we are the third. For wheat the twenty-third; thirty-five years ago, this was one of the greatest wheat regions in the whole country, but the weevil made its appearance, and became so mischievous that our farmers have changed their wheat-fields into hop-grounds.

Oddly enough, for tobacco we are the second county, although that does not say much, since only 744 lbs. are raised in the State, and probably most smokers would think that amount more than enough, for the quality must be very indifferent. But here and there a little is raised by the farmers for their own uses, and perhaps to fill a pipe for their wives now and then; quite a number of country women in our neighborhood are in the habit of smoking, and occasionally, young women, too. Not that the habit is a general one, though in rustic life, more women smoke than is commonly believed. Formerly, there was probably much more tobacco raised in this State than at present, for in old times, when we still had slaves among us, it was a general rule that every head of a family among the blacks had a little patch of land allotted to him expressly for the purpose of raising broom-corn and tobacco: the corn he made up into brooms and sold to the family, the tobacco he kept for himself and his wife.

Observe that the woollen and cotton goods manufactured in this State are nearly equal in value; the cotton goods amounting to $3,600,000, the woollen goods $3,500,000. The amount of home-made goods exceeds either by a million, $4,600,000. The value of the lumber, for the same year, was less than that of the home-made goods, and rather more than the value of the cotton manufactures, $3,800,000. The dairy produce is very valuable, $10,400,000.

It will be seen that there are a large number of horses in this county; and nearly a hog for every human being, babies and all. One house in fourteen, among those built that year, was of stone or brick. The proportion in the State generally, was one in six.

Wednesday, 21st.—The following are the premiums allotted by the County Agricultural Society for the best crops, at the last harvest:

Best acre of Wheat,	32 bushels,	Prize	$4 00
Second best do.	31 1/2 do.	do.	$3 00
Best acre of Rye,	33 1/2 do.	do.	$3 00
Best do. Buckwheat,	29 1/4 do.	do.	$3 00
Best do. Barley,	41 do.	do.	$3 00
Best do. Oats,	71 do.	do.	$3 00
Second best do.	61 do.	do.	$2 00
Third best do.	51 do.	do.	$1 00
Best acre of Maize,	107 do.	do.	$4 00
Second best do.	91 do	do.	$3 00
Third best do.	77 1/2 do.	do.	$2 00
Best half acre of Potatoes,	167 do.	do.	$4 00
Second best do. do.	92 do.	do.	$3 00
Best half acre Marrowfat Peas.	28 1/2 do.	do.	$3 00
Best ten rods of Carrots,	73 1/2 do.	do.	$4 00
Second best do. do.	45 do.	do.	$3 00
Best ten rods of Mangel-Wurzel,	81 do.	do.	$3 00
Best specimen of Apples,		do.	$3 00
Second best do. do.		do.	$2 00
Third best do. do.		do.	$1 00

Thursday, 22d.—Quite mild again. Cloudy. Soft, bluish haze on the hills.

Walked about the village this afternoon, looking at last summer's birds' nests. Many are still left in the trees, and just now they are capped with snow. Some birds are much more careful architects than others. The robins generally build firmly, and their nests often remain through the winter. The red-eyed vireo, or greenlet, or fly-catcher, as you please, is one of our most skillful builders; his nest is pendulous, and generally placed in a small tree— a dog-wood, where he can find one; he uses some odd materials: withered leaves, bits of hornets' nests, flax, scraps of paper, and fibres of grape-vine bark; he lines it with caterpillars' webs, hair, fine grasses, and fibres of bark. These nests are so durable, that a yellow-bird has been known to place her own over an old one of a previous year, made by this bird; and field-mice, probably the jumping-mice, are said frequently to take possession of them after the vireo and its brood are gone. But the red-eyed greenlet is rather a wood-bird, and we must not look for his nest in the village. His brother, the white-eyed greenlet, frequently builds in towns, even in the ornamental trees of our largest cities, in the fine sycamores of the older streets of Philadelphia, for instance.

The nests about our village door-yards and streets are chiefly those of the robin, goldfinch, yellow-bird, song-sparrow, chipping-bird, oriole, blue-bird, wren, Phœbe-bird, and cat-bird, with now and then a few greenlets; probably some snow-birds also, about the garden hedges or fences. This last summer it looked very much as though we had also purple-finches in the village; no nest was found, but the birds were repeatedly seen on the garden fences, near the same spot, at a time when they must have had young. Humming-birds doubtless build in the village, but their nests are rarely discovered; and they are always so small, and such cunning imitations of tufts of lichens and mosses, that they are unobserved. As for the numerous swallow tribe, their nests are never found now-a-days, in trees.

Of all these regular summer visitors, robin builds the largest and most conspicuous nest; he will often pick up long strings, and strips of cloth or paper, which he interweaves with twigs and grass, leaving the ends hanging out carelessly; I have seen half a dozen paper cuttings, eighteen inches long, drooping like streamers in this way, from a robin's nest. The pensile nest of the oriole is more striking and peculiar, as well as much more neat than any other. Specimens of all the various kinds built in trees are now plainly seen in the branches; many have no doubt fallen, but a good number have kept their place until to-day, through all the winter storms. We amused ourselves this afternoon with looking after these nests in the trees as we passed along the different streets of the village.

All these village visitors seem a very sociable race: they generally collect in little neighborhoods, half a dozen families in adjoining trees, leaving others for some distance about them untenanted. It is pleasant, also, to notice how frequently they build near houses, about the very doors and windows, as though out of friendliness to man, while other trees, quite as good as those chosen, are standing vacant a little farther off. In several instances this afternoon, we saw two, three, and even four nests in one tree, shading the windows of a house; in very many cases, the three or four trees before a house were all tenanted; we observed a cottage with three little maples recently planted in the door-yard, and so much trimmed that they could scarcely boast a dozen branches between them, yet each had its large robin's nest. The birds seem to like to return to the same trees—some of the older elms and maples are regularly occupied every summer as a matter of course.

There is another fact which strikes one in looking at these nests about the village: the birds of different feathers show a very marked preference for building in maples. It is true these trees are more numerous than others about our streets, but there are also elms, locusts, and sumachs mingled with them, enough, at least, to decide the question very clearly. This afternoon we counted the nests in the different trees as we passed them, with a view to this particular point, and the result was as follows: the first we came to were in a clump of young trees of various kinds, and here we found nine nests, one in a locust, the other eight in maples. Then following the street with trees irregularly planted on either side, a few here, a few there, we counted forty-nine nests, all of which were in maples, although several elms and lo-custs were mingled with these; frequently there were several nests in the same maple. Next we found one in an elm; then fourteen more in maples, and successively as follows: one in a yellow willow; eleven in maples; six in a row of old elms regularly inhabited every season, and as usual, an oriole nest among these; one in a lilac-bush; one in a mountain-ash; eleven in maples; one in an elm; one in a locust; six in maples; one in a balm of Gilead; two in lilac-bushes; two in elms, one of them an oriole nest, and ten in maples. Such was the state of things in the principal streets through which we passed, making in all one hundred and twenty-seven nests, and of these, eighteen were in various kinds of trees; the remaining one hundred and nine were in maples.

One can easily understand why the orioles should often choose the droop-ing spray of the elm for their pendulous nests—though they build in maples and locusts also—but it is not easy to see why so many different tribes should all show such a very decided preference for the maples. It cannot be from these trees coming into leaf earlier than others, since the willows, and poplars, and lilacs are shaded before them. Perhaps it may be the luxuriant foliage of the maple, which throws a thick canopy over its limbs. Or it may be the upward inclination of the branches, and the numerous forks in the young twigs. Whether the wood birds show the same preference, one cannot say. But along the roads, and near farm-houses, one observes the same decided partiality for these trees; the other day we observed a maple not far from a farm-house, with five nests in it, and a whole orchard close at hand, untenanted. The sumachs, on the contrary, are not in favor; one seldom sees a nest in their stag-horn branches. Neither the growth of their limbs, nor that of their foliage, seems to suit the birds.

Friday, 23d.–Very mild, sunshiny day; quite spring-like. We have just now soft, thawing days, and frosty nights, the first symptoms of spring. Cocks are crowing, and hens cackling about the barn-yards, always cheerful rustic sounds.

Saturday, 24th.–Very mild and pleasant. The chicadees are hopping about among the branches, pretty, cheerful, fearless little creatures; I stood almost within reach of a couple of them, as they were gliding about the lower limbs of a sugar-maple, but they did not mind me in the least. They are regular tree birds, one rarely sees them on the ground. The snow-birds, on the contrary, are half the time running about on the earth.

The arctic or Lapland snow-bird is not unfrequent in this State as a winter visitor, but we have never seen it, or heard of it, in this county. Probably when it comes thus far south, it seeks rather a milder climate than ours, for it has been seen even in Kentucky and Mississippi.

The white snow-bird, a pretty little creature, with much white in its plumage, is also, I believe, a stranger in our neighborhood, never having seen it or heard of it here. A few are said to breed in Massachusetts, and they are not rare in winter, in parts of this State. All these birds live much on the ground, and build their nests there, and for a very good reason, since in their proper native country, in arctic regions, trees are neither very common nor very tall. One of the north-western travellers, Capt. Lyon, once found a nest of this bird in a singular position; his party came accidentally upon several Indian graves: "Near the large grave was a third pile of stones, covering the body of a child, which was coiled up in the same manner. A snow-bunting had found its way through the loose stones which composed this little tomb, and its now forsaken, neatly-built nest, was found placed on the neck of the child."

Monday, 26th.–Pleasant day. Long drive of six miles on the lake. The snow is all but gone on shore, though it still lies on the ice to the depth of several inches; it accumulates there more than upon the land, seldom thawing much, except in rainy weather. Two very large cracks cross the lake at present, about five miles from the village; the ice is upheaved at those points, forming a decided ridge, perhaps two feet in height; it will doubtless first give way in that direction. The broad, level field of white looks beautifully just now, when the country about is dull and tarnished, only partially covered with the dregs of the winter snow. We met a number of sleighs, for the roads are in a bad condition from the thaw; indeed, wagons are out in the village. During the last week in February, and in March, the lake is generally more used for sleighing than at any other period; we have seen heavily-loaded sleds, carrying stone and iron, passing over it at such times. The stage-sleighs, with four horses and eight or ten passengers, perhaps, occasionally go and come over the ice at that season. Our people are sometimes very daring in this way; they seldom leave the lake until some horse or sled has been lost; but happily, although there have been narrow escapes of this kind, no lives have yet been lost.

Tuesday, 27th.—Lovely day. Out on the ice again. Drove under Darkwood Hill; the evergreens looked sombre, indeed, all but black. On most of the other hills, one could see the ground distinctly, with fallen timber lying like jackstraws scattered about. But the growth of evergreens on Darkwood Hill is so dense, that they completely screen the earth. Went on shore for a short distance near the Cliffs. It is pleasant driving through the woods, even in winter; once within their bounds, we feel the charm of the forest again. Though dark and sombre in the background, yet close at hand, the old pines and hemlocks are green as ever, with lights and shadows playing about them, which in the distance become imperceptible. The trunks and limbs of the leafless trees, also, never fail to be a source of much interest. The pure wintry air is still touched with the fragrance of bark and evergreens, and the woods have a winter-light of their own, filled with pale gray shadows falling on the snow. The stillness of the forest is more striking and impressive at this season than at any other; one may glide along for miles over some quiet wood-road, without seeing or hearing a living thing, not even a bird, or a chip-muck. The passing of the sleigh seems almost an intrusion on the haunts of silence.

Dead and shrivelled leaves are still hanging on some trees, here and there; not all the storms of winter have been able to loosen their hold on the lower limbs of the beeches; they cling, also, at this late day to some oaks, and hickories, and maples. The wych-hazels are oddly garnished, bearing, many of them, their old leaves, the open husks of last year's nuts, and the shrivelled yellow flowers of autumn. Within these lies the young fruit, which has made but little progress during the last three months.

Wednesday, 28th.—Delightful day. Pleasant drive on the lake. Went on shore at the Cliffs for eggs; the poultry-yard had quite a cheery, spring look.

Our winters are undoubtedly cold enough, but the weather is far from being always severe. We have many moderate days, and others, even in the heart of winter, which are soft and balmy, a warm wind blowing in your face from the south until you wonder how it could have found its way over the snow without being chilled. People always exclaim that such days are quite extraordinary, but in truth, there never passes a year without much weather that is unseasonably pleasant, if we would but remember it. And if we take the year throughout, this sort of weather, in all its varieties, will probably be found more favorably divided for us than we fancy. It is true there are frosty nights in May, sometimes in June, which are mischievous to the crops and gardens. But then it frequently happens, also, that we have charming days when we have no right whatever to expect them; delightful Novembers, soft, mild weeks in December, pleasant breaks in January and February, with early springs, when the labors of the husbandman commence much sooner than usual. We have seen the fields in this valley ploughed in February; and the cattle grazing until late in December. Every year we have some of these pleasant moments, one season more, another less; but we soon forget them. The frosts and chilly days are remembered much longer, which does not seem quite right.

It is an additional charm of these clear, mild days in winter, that they often bring very beautiful sunsets. Not those gorgeous piles of clouds which are seen, perhaps, as frequently after the summer showers, as at any other period; but the sort of sunset one would not look for in winter—some of the softest and sweetest skies of the year. This evening the heavens were very beautiful, as we drove homeward over the ice; and the same effect may frequently be seen in December, January, or February. One of the most beautiful sunsets I have ever beheld, occurred here several years since, toward the last of February. At such times, a warmer sun than usual draws from the yielding snow a mild mist, which softens the dark hills, and rising to the sky, lies there in long, light, cloudy folds. The choicest tints of the heavens are seen at such moments; tender shades of rose, lilac, and warm gold, opening to show beyond a sky filled with delicate green light.

These calm sunsets are much less fleeting than others: from the moment when the clouds flush into color at the approach of the sun, one may watch them, perhaps, for more than an hour, growing brighter and warmer, as he passes slowly on his way through their midst; still varying in ever-changing beauty, while he sinks slowly to rest; and at last, long after he has dropped beyond the farther hills, fading sweetly and imperceptibly, as the shadows of night gather upon the snow.

THE END.

Notes

1. Three other varieties have been observed in North America, but they are all rare. The beautiful violet-green swallow of the Rocky Mountains, Vaux Chimney Swift, on the Columbia, and the rough-winged swallow of Louisiana.

2. Sometimes twenty feet high, in this county.

3. The sugar maple does not thrive in England, seldom growing there to more than fifteen feet in height. The silver maple, on the contrary, succeeds very well in Europe.

4. *Tiarella Cordifolia.*

5. *Trientalis Americana.*

6. *Polygalia Pancifolia.*

7. This field yielded ninety-three bushels of maize to the acre the following autumn.

8. Gay-wings, *Poly-gala paucifolia;* Cool-wort, *Tiarella cordofolia;* Fairy-cup, *Mitella dyphylla;* May-star, *Trientalis Americana;* Bead-ruby, *Convallaria bifolia;* Squaw-vine, *Mitchella repens;* Partridge plant, *Gualtheria;* Dew-drop, *Dalibaraa.*

9. Dr. Torrey.

10. These *borers* are the young of different beetles, some of which live several years in the wood before their transformation.

11. The trees destroyed on the Mississippi by the earthquake of 1811 are standing to-day, when nearly forty years have elapsed (Dec. 1849). And many similar instances might, no doubt, be found, if people had watched these dead inhabitants of our forests.

12. Dr. Torrey's State Botany.

13. See State Reports for 1835.

14. *Asagard,* the country of the gods.

15. *Mimer,* the god of eloquence and wisdom.

16. *Urda,* the Norna, or destiny of the past.

17. *Hrimthusser,* frost-demons; *hrim,* or frost, is the origin of our English word *rime,* for hoar frost; and *thuss,* or demon, is supposed by Major Frye to be the origin of the English word *deuce,* though the dictionaries give another derivation.

18. *Utgard,* land of giants.

19. *Niffelheim,* land of fog.

20. *Nidhòg,* a monster dragon.–(*See Major Frye's Translations of the "Gods of the North."*)

21. The Cicada, or great harvest-fly.

22. We have known it 97 in the village; 103 is said to be the highest it has ever reached in the State, and that was in Orange County.

23. See Letters of the Jews to Voltaire.

24. It is said that Linnæus firmly believed that the swallows went under water during the winter; and even M. Cuvier declared that the bank swallows had this habit. At present the idea is quite abandoned for want of proof.

25. We have recently heard of a white lily gathered from the lake about two years since, but have never seen one ourselves. Formerly, they are said to have been more common here.

26. The deer are also very fond of the water-lilies.

27. These were the last swallows seen that season in our neighborhood.

28. In West Chester County, they have recently had the good sense to extend the protection of the game laws to many birds of the smaller kinds, useful to the gardener and farmer, such as the robins, which destroy many troublesome insects.

29. NOTE.–This onward course in truthful description should not stop short at inanimate nature. There is a still further progress which remains to be effected; the same care, the same attention, the same scruples should, most assuredly, be shown by the conscientious mind, in writing of our fellow-creatures. If we seek to give a correct picture of a landscape, a tree, a building, how much more anxious should we be never willingly to give a distorted or perverted view of any fellow-man, or class of men; of any fact bearing upon the welfare of our fellow-creatures, or of any class of facts with the same bearing! We claim, in this age, to be more especially in quest of truths–how, then, shall we ever find them, if we are all busy in throwing obstacles in each other's way? Even in fiction, nay, in satire, in caricature, there are just proportions which it is criminal wholly to pervert. In such cases, political writers are often avowedly without shame; and, alas! how often do Christian writers conform, in this way, to the world about them! Perhaps

there is no other commandment of Holy Scripture more boldly trampled on, in spirit at least, at the present day, than the ninth, "Thou shalt not bear false witness against thy neighbor." It is to be feared that the present age is more especially a slanderous one; slanderous not only upon individuals, but upon classes. Where shall we find the political party, the school of philosophy, the religious sect or party, wholly pure from this poison? These are among the facts which teach our race a lesson of perpetual humility.

30. Dr. De Kay's Report on the Fishes of New York.

31. In 1653.

32. Dr. De Kay's Zoology of New York.

33. We are none of us very knowing about the birds in this country, unless it be those scientific gentlemen who have devoted their attention especially to such subjects. The same remark applies in some measure to our native trees and plants; to our butterflies and insects. But little attention has yet been given by our people generally, to these subjects. In Europe such is not the case; many persons there, among the different classes of society, are familiar with these simple matters. Had works of this kind been as common in America as they are in England, the volume now in the reader's hands would not have been printed, and many observations found in its pages would have been unnecessary. But such as it is, written by a learner only, the book is offered to those whose interest in rural subjects has been awakened, a sort of rustic primer, which may lead them, if they choose, to something higher.

If it will not be considered an assumption of importance, in a volume of the chit-chat, common-place character of that now before the reader, the writer will venture to express her thanks to Dr. De Kay and Mr. Downing, not only for their published works, but also for their kindness in directing her course on several occasions.

34. The lake opened the following spring just three months from the day it closed—on the 8th of April.

35. Sir Charles Lyell supposes the American white Cedar, or Cypress, so common on the Mohawk, to have been the food of the Mastodon, from an examination of the contents of the stomach of one of these animals.

Emendations

Following the page and line number (e.g., 123.28) is the emended reading that appears in this edition; in the third column is the corresponding 1850 text.

2.6	Inscribed	Iuscribed
3.6	fireside	fire-side
5.4	Bonaparte	Buonaparte
5.26	blue-jay	bluejay
8.3	year,	year
8.4	the return	is the return
8.4	robins;	robins,
8.25	Phœbe-birds	Phœbe birds
11.15	blue-birds	bluebirds
18.15	blue-birds	bluebirds
18.22	7*th*.	6*th*.
23.22	livelong	live long
24.27	*hepaticus*	*hepaticas*
26.12	Old World	old world
27.14	barn-swallows	barn swallows
27.16	currants	currents
36.36	Susquehannah	Susquehanna
37.12	Old World	old world
45.32	become	became
49.5	Juneberry	June-berry
52.13	dollars	dollars'
54.6	months	month
56.35	thirsty	thristy
60.35	pewee	pewce
61.23	by-the-by	by-the-bye
64.8	Michaelmas daisies	Michaelmas-daisies
64.35	out-building	outbuilding
64.35	plantains	plaintains
64.38	pimpernel	prinpernel

75.38	19th.	9th.
85.13	martyre!"	martyre!
80.32	flounces	flowers
92.12	are	is
96.32	catnip	catnep
97.25	water colors	water-colors
98.34	days'	day's
104.14	mussels	muscles
113.19	pipsissiwa	pipsissima
129.13	tamarack	tamarach
132.1	but one	but if one
132.39	8,170,000 dollars'	$8,170,000 dollars
137.23	"Les	'Les
143.21	Gospel	Gosple
144.9	sickly,	sickly;
144.9	flowers;	flowers,
145.7	night-hawks	night hawks
147.2	death wound	death-wound
147.31	the	he
168.4	name before	namebefore
168.10	chimney-swallows	chimney swallows
168.20	chimney-swallows	chimney swallows
171.19	belongs	belong
175.3	as	and
174.14	wych-hazel	wych-havel
175.2	insignificant	insignficant
184.3	bur-marigolds	burr-marigolds
192.8	road, a	road, called near a
196.7	Tuesday	Wednesday
206.6	. . .	. .
207.23	*pâle*	*pale*
208.13	period.	period
219.12	They	they
220.1	alone;	alone,
226.19	excites	excite
229.22	&c., &c.	*&c., &c.*
231.15–16	notches; elms,	notches elms;
231.23	their wardrobe with the season	theirason.awrob with rdwite h tes he
241.22	woods!	woods.!
242.1	cakes."	cakes.'
242.26	*pralines.*	*pralines*

243.3–4	Van der Donck	Vanderdonck
243.8	might	migt
243.35	Van der Donck	Vanderdonck
249.20	populous;	populous;'
254.29	wode	wde
260.18	He	he
260.36	His	his
260.36	and His	and his
260.36	over His	over his
260.39	unto Him	unto him
261.1	He	he
261.2	His	his
261.34	He	he
261.35	He	he
263.12	dragon arum	dragon-arum
267.11	gods	Gods
270.33	Mill Bridge	mill bridge
272.33	Comet	Cornet
273.24	sugar-plums	sugar plums
274.3	think; for,	think for;
280.3	Christian	Christain
291.36	"store"	store
295.8	Bonaparte	Buonaparte
296.32	Thursday	Friday
300.32	Berne	Bern
302.22	words:	words
302.23	Canada;	Canada
304.19	led	lead
307.8	found	fonud
312.24	Van der Donck	Vanderdonck
319.18	XXXII.	XXXII
320.17	Value	Am't
320.19	Am't	[blank]
320.29	Value	Am't
320.31	Am't	[blank]
320.32	Value	"
329.8	Nidhòg	Nidhog

Glossary

Babes in the Woods: a tale from a sixteenth-century ballad in which an infant son and daughter are abandoned in a forest by a relative who plans to inherit their property. When they die, Robin-redbreast covers them with leaves.

Bess of Shrewsbury: Elizabeth Talbot, countess of Shrewsbury (1518–1608). She acquired a great fortune through four marriages and built both Chatsworth and Hardwick Hall.

black-cat: the fisher, a member of the weasel family.

clape, or golden-winged woodpecker: the flicker.

grass-bird: the bay-wing sparrow.

greenlet: a vireo.

grown wheat: wheat that has sprouted in the ear after reaching maturity.

lake: a reddish pigment made from lac or cochineal, or by combining animal, vegetable, or coal-tar coloring matter with a metallic oxide.

Moore, Benjamin (1748–1816): second Protestant Episcopal bishop of New York and president of Columbia College.

Moore, Clement Clarke (1779–1863): His "A Visit from St. Nicholas" was published anonymously in the December 23, 1823, *Troy Sentinel,* and in Moore's *Poems* (1844).

olecakes: possibly a local dialect word, of Dutch or German origin, for "oilcake," a cake that involved linseed oil; compare the German *Ölkuchen.*

Palemon: In "Autumn," the fourth book of James Thomson's *The Seasons* (1726–30), the story of the gleaner Lavinia and the landowner Palemon parallels the story of Ruth and Boaz, told in the book of Ruth.

snow-bird: The Lapland snow-bird is the Lapland longspur; the white snow-bird is the snow bunting; by a general reference to a snow-bird, Cooper intends the slate-colored junco.

Tartar, caught a: to catch someone or something too powerful to control or release.

tripe de roche: Literally "guts of the rock"–Canadian name given to edible lichens of the genera *Gyrophora* and *Umbilicaria.* Slightly nutritious, but bitter and purgative.

Vatel: François Vatel was steward to the Prince de Condé when he committed suicide because he feared the fish would not arrive in time for a meal being prepared for Louis XIV.

Weir, Robert Walter (1803–89): American painter and educator.
yellow-bird: yellow warbler.
Zip Coon: a minstrel song and dance whose tune was borrowed for the later "Turkey in the Straw."

Authors and Works Cited

THE FOLLOWING LIST is intended as a contribution to the study of Susan Cooper's reading, exclusive of poetry. In some cases, a work listed may not be the precise work, or the same edition, referred to in *Rural Hours*.

Addison, Joseph (1672–1719). *Remarks on Several Parts of Italy, &c., in the Years 1701, 1702, 1703*. London: Tonson, 1705.

Audubon, John James (1785–1851). *Orinthological Biography, or An Account of the Habits of the Birds of the United States of America*. 5 vols. Philadelphia: J. Dobson, 1831 (vol. 1); Boston: Hilliard, Gray & Co., 1835 (vol. 2); Edinburgh: A. & C. Black, 1835–39 (vols. 3–5).

Barthelemy, Jean-Jacques (l'Abbé) (1716–95). His *Voyage de jeune Anacharsis en Grèce* (Paris, 1788) was translated and published in several editions, including *Travels of Anacharsis the younger in Greece*. 6 vols. London: C. and J. Rivington, 1825.

Benson, Egbert (1746–1833). *Memoir, Read before the Historical Society of the State of New-York*. New York: Mercein, 1817.

Canning, George (1770–1827). His numerous publications include *Select Speeches of the Right Honourable George Canning*. Philadelphia: Key and Biddle, 1835.

Chateaubriand, Francois Auguste Rene, vicomte de (1768–1848). Among his volumes of travel and memoirs the reference in the Cooper text is likely the following translation: *Travels in Greece, Palestine, Egypt, and Barbary, During the Years 1806 and 1807*. Philadelphia, 1813.

Clarke, Edward Daniel (1769–1822). *Travels in Various Countries of Europe, Asia, and Africa*. Philadelphia, 1811.

Clinton, DeWitt (1769–1828). *A Memoir on the Antiquities of the Western Parts of the State of New-York Read before the Literary and Philosophical Society of New-York*. Albany, 1818.

Condolle, Alphonse de (1806–93). Among his various botanical works is *Theorie elementaire de la botanique, ou, Exposition des principes de la classification*. 3d. ed. Paris: Roret, 1844.

Cottin, Madame [Sophie] (1770–1807). *Elisabeth; ou, Les Exiles de Siberie*. Limoges: Barbou freres, 1844.

Cuvier, Georges, baron (1769–1832). *The Animal Kingdom Arranged in Conformity with Its Organization.* Trans. Henry M'Murtrie. New York: Carvill, 1831.

DeKay, James Ellsworth (1792–1851). *Zoology of New-York, or the New-York Fauna; Comprising Detailed Descriptions of All the Animals Hitherto Observed Within the State of New-York, with Brief Notices of Those Occasionally Found Near its Borders, and Accompanied by Appropriate Illustrations.* Albany: Carroll and Cook, printers to the Assembly, 1842–44.

Donck, Adriaen van der (1620–55). His *Beschryvinge van Nieuw-Nederlant* (Amsterdam, 1656) was available in the translation by Henry C. Murphy, *The Representation of New Netherland* (New York: Bartlett and Welford, 1849).

Downing, Andrew Jackson (1815–52). Among several works of landscape and garden design that Cooper probably knew are *Cottage Residences; or, A Series of Designs for Rural Cottages and Cottage-Villas, and Their Gardens and Grounds* (New York: Wiley and Putnam, 1842); and *A Treatise on the Theory and Practice of Landscape Gardening, Adapted to North America; with a View to the Improvement of Country Residences* (New York: Wiley and Putnam, 1841).

Humboldt, Alexander von (1769–1859). Humboldt wrote several works about his South American travels, among them *Reise in die æquinoctial-gegenden des neuen continents in den jahren 1799, 1800, 1801, 1803, and 1804* (Stuttgart: Cotta, 1815). His works were widely translated.

Jefferson, Thomas (1743–1826). *Notes on the State of Virginia.* Paris 1784–85.

Jesse, Edward (1780–1868). *Gleanings in Natural History.* London: Murray, 1838.

Long, Stephen Harriman (1784–1864). *Account of an Expedition from Pittsburgh to the Rocky Mountains: Performed in the Years 1819 and '20.* Philadelphia: Carey and Lea, 1822–23.

Lyell, Charles, Sir (1797–1875). Among his numerous publications that Cooper may have consulted are *Principles of Geology; being an attempt to explain the former changes of the earth's surface, by reference to causes now in operation* (3 vols; London: Murray, 1830–33) and *Elements of Geology* (London: Murray, 1838).

Lyon, George Francis (1795–1832). *The Private Journal of Captain G. F. Lyon, of H.M.S. Hecla, During the Recent Voyage of Discovery Under Captain Parry.* London: Murray, 1824.

Nuttall, Thomas (1786–1859). *A Manual of the Ornithology of the United States and of Canada.* Cambridge: Hillard and Brown, 1827.

Œhlenschlager, Adam Gottlob (1779–1850). *The Gods of the North, an Epic Poem.* Trans. William Edward Frye. London: Pickering, 1845.

Porter, Robert Ker, Sir (1777–1842). *Travels in Georgia, Persia, Armenia, Ancient Babylonia, &c., &c. During the Years 1817, 1818, 1819, and 1820.* London, 1821.

Rich, Claudius James (1787–1820). Rich published three works on Babylon: *Memoir on the Ruins of Babylon* (London, 1818); *Second Memoir on Babylon* (London, 1818); and *Narrative of a Journey to the Site of Babylon in 1811* (London, 1839).

Savigny, Marie Jules-César Lelorgne de (1777–1851). *Systeme des annelides, principalement de celles des cotes de l'Egypte et de la Syrie, offrant les caracteres tant distinctifs que naturels des ordres, familles et genres, avec la description des especes* (Paris, 1820).

Segur, Louis Phillippe, comte de (1753–1830). Segur's several works of European history, ancient and modern, and his memoirs were available in *Œuvres completes* (Paris, 1824–27), and they were translated into English.

Staunton, George, Sir (1781–1859). Among his numerous volumes on Chinese culture that Cooper may have consulted are *Miscellaneous Notices relating to China, and our Commercial Intercourse with that Country, including a few translations from the Chinese Language* (London: Murray, 1822) and *Notes of Proceedings and Occurrences during the British Embassy to Pekin* (London: Murray, 1824).

Torrey, John (1796–1873). *A Flora of the State of New-York: Comprising Full Descriptions of All the Indigenous and Naturalized Plants Hitherto Discovered.* Albany: Carroll and Cook, printers to the Assembly, 1843.

Tupper, Martin Farquhar (1810–89). *Proverbial Philosophy.* London: Rickerby, 1838.

Weems, Mason Locke (1759–1825). *The Life of General Francis Marion, a Celebrated Partisan Officer.* This work, first published in 1809, appeared in several editions.

Wilson, Alexander (1766–1813). *American Ornithology; or, The Natural History of the Birds of the United States.* Philadelphia: Bradford and Inskeep, 1808–14.

Index